NT/hc

o/p.

£22

TRADITIONAL DOMESTIC ARCHITECTURE
OF THE BANBURY REGION

TRADITIONAL
DOMESTIC ARCHITECTURE
OF THE BANBURY REGION

by

RAYMOND B. WOOD-JONES
M.A., B.ARCH., PH.D., A.R.I.B.A., F.S.A.

Senior Lecturer in Architecture in the
University of Manchester

MANCHESTER UNIVERSITY PRESS

Published by the University of Manchester at
THE UNIVERSITY PRESS
316–324, Oxford Road, Manchester 13
1963

Printed in Great Britain by Butler & Tanner Ltd, Frome and London

To
MY MOTHER AND FATHER

Author and publishers are indebted to the Trustees of the Marc Fitch Fund, and to the British Academy, for generous contributions towards the cost of publication

CONTENTS

PREFACE

WITHIN recent years, much new light has been thrown on the living conditions of the agrarian community in England from the end of the Middle Ages as a result of two parallel developments in research. The first has been the opening up of vast accumulations of documentary material in the archives of public and private bodies, enabling the historian to delve more deeply into the regional aspects of social history. Secondly, this research has illuminated and given new impetus to the intensive architectural and archaeological examination and recording of surviving vernacular buildings within particular regions, the two approaches combining to provide a comprehensive picture of the functional, traditional architecture of the countryside. Since 1946, a series of regional surveys of minor domestic architecture has been carried out by members of the Manchester University School of Architecture, under the inspiration and direction of the late Professor R. A. Cordingley, who himself pioneered the study of regional architecture, and devised and perfected the system of recording. The primary aim within each region has been the recording and examination on comparative grounds of all buildings dating from before *c*. 1840, this comprehensive, statistical survey providing the basis for the assessment of regional development in terms of planning, structure and architectural character, from medieval times to the early 19th century. In the course of the present study, carried out between 1952 and 1961, over 1100 buildings have been recorded in the villages around Banbury. The rapid encroachment of the Welfare State on even the most remote and undisturbed village communities has rendered this aspect of study a matter of considerable urgency, in order that the evidence of vernacular buildings should be assessed and permanently recorded before it disappears in the spate of demolitions and alterations with which field-work could hardly keep pace. It is in the minor domestic architecture of the countryside that the tradition of fine, functional buildings and design, for which at least until the present century this country has been unrivalled, can be studied at its highest level.

RAYMOND B. WOOD-JONES

Manchester University
  April 1963

ix

ACKNOWLEDGEMENTS

Above all, I am indebted to Professor Cordingley, both for introducing me to this field of study, and for first suggesting to me the unspoilt potential of the Banbury Region; his advice, guidance and deep interest at all times helped me to bring this work to completion, and I cannot too fully express my indebtedness to him. Professor Cordingley's final contribution was to read and correct the proofs of this book, and it is deeply to be regretted that he did not live to see the publication of the first volume in the series of regional studies which he had envisaged.

The proposal for a series of regional studies of domestic architecture, of which it is hoped that this will be the first volume, emanated from the combined interest of Professor Cordingley and Mr. W. A. Pantin. It has been largely as a result of Mr. Pantin's energetic intervention that this book is now being published with the aid of grants from the Marc Fitch Fund and the British Academy. His generous assistance in this way, and his advice on many aspects of the study, are alike gratefully acknowledged.

In the course of this work, many people have generously provided me with information, or otherwise assisted me in obtaining material, and I would particularly acknowledge the contribution of the following: Sir Cyril Fox and Lord Raglan, for their continued advice and encouragement, and for permitting me to quote certain comparative material from their monumental study, *Monmouthshire Houses*; Mr. Howard Colvin, for information on historical sources, particularly relating to Deddington; Dr. Eric Gee, for information on Oxfordshire masons, and for advice and guidance in reading the original typescript; Mr. John H. Harvey, for advice on historical sources; Mr. Peter S. Spokes, for assisting me from his own wide knowledge of the region, and for permitting me to use certain of his photographs; Dr. W. G. Hoskins, for permitting me to make use of his plans of Leicestershire houses; Mr. G. Forsyth Lawson, for information drawn from his vast practical knowledge of building in this region; Dr. T. L. Marsden, Mr. R. W. Brunskill, and Mr. G. L. Worsley, for permitting me to quote comparative material from their own unpublished researches at Manchester; Mr. M. W. Barley, and other members of the Vernacular Architecture Group, together with earlier researchers at Manchester, who have permitted me to draw on their experience in order to place my own studies in a wider perspective.

I would also acknowledge the kindness of all those residents of the Banbury Region who so readily invited my wife and myself into their homes, freely to study and examine every corner of these houses in which they themselves take such pride. In particular, I am grateful for the warm hospitality of the Rev. and Mrs. C. E. Glynne Jones, of Middleton Cheney, who throughout the greater part of my study of the region offered me the freedom of their Rectory as a base for my field investigations. The kindness and interest of all those I have met in the course of this study have done much to increase the pleasure of the work. My final acknowledgement must be to my wife, for the long hours she has shared with me in surveying both fine houses and decaying cottages, and for her help at all times.

NOTE ON THE ILLUSTRATIONS

WITH the exception of Broughton Castle (Fig. 5), all the buildings of the region illustrated in line drawings have been measured and drawn by the author. All measured surveys are reproduced to a series of common scales, in order that direct comparisons may be made between the houses. Hatching is employed only to distinguish major building periods, the original building of whatever date, in all cases, being solidly filled in on plan and later work obliquely hatched, with modern work shown in outline: no attempt has been made to distinguish such minor amendments as altered windows. Reference to buildings in both text and illustration is complicated by the lack of houses or street names, many of the smaller dwellings being known simply by the name of the present occupant. In such cases it has been considered sufficient to refer to houses by the names of the villages, with a reference to the illustration, the context in all cases adequately differentiating between dwellings in the same village.

Plates 2a, 6c, 17a and 22c are reproduced by permission of Mr. Peter S. Spokes, and Plate 1b by courtesy of Mr. and Mrs. C. J. Buchanan-Dunlop.

LIST OF FIGURES IN THE TEXT

LIST OF PLATES
(*End of Book*)

B

CHAPTER I

THE BANBURY REGION

THE strongly marked regional characteristic of English architecture finds particular expression in the field of the minor domestic architecture of the countryside, and few areas should be more profitable for architectural research than that which has been defined as the Banbury Region. Within this small but quite populous agrarian area there has evolved a distinctive regional style of domestic building of remarkable homogeneity in material and character, all too often overlooked in the general and incorrect classification of 'Cotswold Architecture', to which it is nevertheless closely related. Building within the region is moreover largely confined to a single century; although the 17th century is a period of major building activity in many parts of the country, in few areas is the limitation of time so marked as in the villages around Banbury. There is, however, sufficient evidence of both the antecedents of this period and of subsequent developments within the region to trace the evolution of the small house from medieval times, through the regional building period to its decline in the 18th century, and to examine the progressive rise of dwellings of different social status above the datum line of architectural permanence. Banbury lies near the border which has been successively defined by Innocent,[1] Walton[2] and J. T. Smith[3] as separating south-eastern and north-western building practices, and its village buildings reveal the effect of influences from north and south, from Highland and Lowland practices, to which the region, by its position, prosperity and trade, would be susceptible throughout its history. The decline in prosperity and importance, which commences as early as the end of the 17th century, has left the region undisturbed to a singular degree, with a rich survival of vernacular architecture and customs which are only now being swept away under the influence of post-war planning development.

The title of the Banbury Region has been given to an area primarily to be determined by geology, for this has occasioned, both

[1] Innocent, *The Development of English Building Construction*, 1916.

[2] James Walton, 'Hog-back Tombstones and the Anglo-Danish House', *Antiquity*, No. 110, June 1954, p. 68.

[3] J. T. Smith, 'Medieval Roofs: A Classification', *Archaeological Journal*, Vol. CXV, p. 139.

directly and indirectly, the distinctive character of the regional architecture. Centrally placed on the Jurassic ridge, traversed by several ancient highways and with evidence of continuous occupation since early British times, the region has played an important part in national history and has witnessed many great battles from pre-historic times to the 17th century.[1] Within the Jurassic system the outcropping of the marlstone beds of the Middle Lias has defined an irregular upland area averaging fifteen miles around Banbury, the only large town and the social and economic centre of the region.[2] Banbury itself lies on the west bank of the Cherwell at the meeting place of three counties, and the region includes the northern part of Oxfordshire and portions of Warwickshire and Northamptonshire. The greater part of the zone constitutes the Banbury and Bloxham hundreds, for the rest being made up of portions of the hundreds of Chadlington, Wootton, Kineton and Sutton; altogether there are over seventy villages and hamlets, all expressing an architecture of a common, regional type.

The uplands of north Oxfordshire beyond Deddington, and the parts of the adjoining counties, are an undulating region lying generally between the 400- and 500-foot contours, divided by tributaries which flow down between a series of rounded spurs to the Cherwell valley on the east. To the west there is some increase in elevation to the Edge Hill escarpment, 710 feet above sea level, marking an abrupt change from these uplands to the lowland plain of the Vale of Warwick, whilst south and west of Deddington the land rises again to the oolitic outcrops which form the continuation of the Cotswolds.[3] Only in the north-east is this geological boundary less clearly defined, with some extension throughout Northamptonshire to Rutland, the regional style of architecture—sharply defined on all other sides —here also extending north-eastwards.

Within this region, the oolitic limestone—the building stone of the Cotswolds—has been weathered down to the underlying beds of the Middle Lias, which occurs as a sandy ferruginous limestone—

---

[1] The name of Banbury (in Saxon times Banesbyrig or Baranbyrig) appears to have derived from a place of battle—Saxon 'Bana' = manslaughter.

[2] The social and economic significance of Banbury as the centre of this region is illustrated in the population returns of 1841. The district comprised within the Banbury 'Poor-Law Union' coincides with remarkable exactitude to the Banbury Region as here defined on geological and architectural grounds, and is the only political determination of the region which has been noted. This schedule is given in Appendix II, including the population figures.

[3] The Cotswolds end three miles within Oxfordshire at Burford, but the architecture of the whole of north Oxfordshire is frequently included in the general classification of 'Cotswold'.

the marlstone—with sandy clays below, providing good building stone and some ironstone. The beds of stone increase in thickness in the Edge Hill area where they have been extensively quarried from medieval times, particularly at Hornton and Burton Dassett. The rock can, however, be found at a moderate depth in most places, and weathers with exposure, loosing lime and carbon dioxide to become a soft, rusty-looking stone, which varies in colour from a grey brown to a rich rust.[1] Apart from those quarries which have exported their stone outside the region, the marlstone has been quarried where required, and its ready occurrence has given architectural definition to an area which closely corresponds to the geological zone, wherein the brownstone has been the almost exclusive walling material up to the present century. The churches alone appear to have introduced to any major extent the freestone of the oolite beds—itself varying in colour from a creamy yellow to a blue grey—for use in dressings, spires and moulded work, for which the coarser ironstone is less well suited. On the fringes of the region, apart from the west, there is some admixture of the materials in domestic work, both stones being obtainable from the same local quarry. This is usually for decorative effect —the use of alternating courses of oolitic stone and marlstone, the distinction of the principal elevation in a different material to the rest, or the use of a contrasting stone for window dressings, the scarcer material providing the embellishment. A somewhat poorer stone than the oolitic limestone, the marlstone has resulted in simpler, coarser detail than that which distinguishes the Cotswolds, whilst the primary roofing material is straw thatch, with only a very limited distribution of stone slates, which can be traced to the quarries of Stonesfield to the south, and possibly Collyweston in Northamptonshire.

The incidence of the lias beds is of considerable economic importance to the region, and in influencing the economy contributes further to the creation of an individual architectural expression. The marlstone has produced the rich, red, corn soil long noted as being among the best in Oxfordshire, the lias clays of the valleys being more suitable for grass, whilst to the south the Cotswold soil is paler in colour and more stoney, the land more completely given over to sheep farming. In the Middle Ages the greater part of Oxfordshire was still densely wooded, the principal areas of forestation being the thick oak forests of the central lowlands, including the Forest of Wychwood, together with the dense beech woods of the Chilterns. The Cotswolds were barer uplands with patches of woodland where the clay outcropped, and in the extreme north of the county it is

[1] *British Regional Geology*, London and Thames Valley.

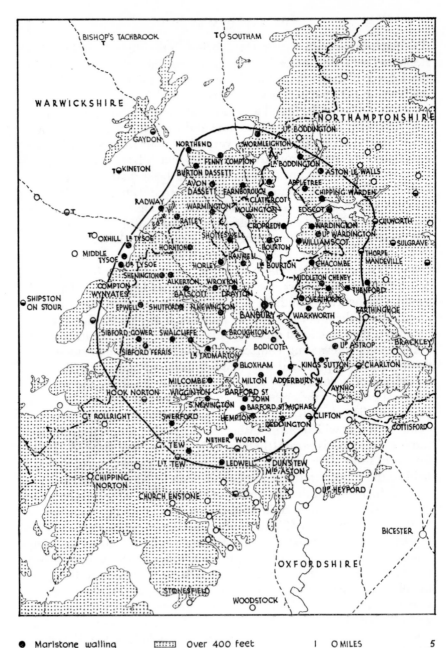

BISHOP'S TACHBROOK   T SOUTHAM

WARWICKSHIRE   NORTHAMPTONSHIRE

          GAYDON   NORTHEND   UP. BODDINGTON
                                    WORMLEIGHTON
       T KINETON   FENNY COMPTON   L. BODDINGTON
                    BURTON DASSETT   ASTON LE WALLS
                    AVON   APPLETREE
                    DASSETT FARNBOROUGH   CHIPPING WARDEN
          RADWAY   WARMINGTON CLATERCOT
                      MOLLINGTON   EDGCOT
              RATLEY   WARDINGTON   CILWORTH
                    SHOTESWELL CROPREDY UP WARDINGTON
       T OXHILL L. TYSOE   GT WILLIAMSCOT   SULGRAVE
          O MIDDLE HORNTON   BOURTON
          T TYSOE UP TYSOE HORLEY BANBURY LT BOURTON   CHACOMBE THORPE
                    SHENINGTON   MIDDLETON CHENEY MANDEVILLE
                  ALKERTON WROXTON   THENFORD
       SHIPSTON COMPTON BALSCOT DRAYTON   OVERTHORPE
       ON STOUR WYNYATES   FARTHINGHOE
              EPWELL SHUTFORD N. NEWINGTON BANBURY T
                                    WARKWORTH
          SIBFORD GOWER SWALCLIFFE BROUGHTON
              SIBFORD FERRIS   UP ASTROP BRACKLEY
                    LT TADMARTON BODICOTE
                        BLOXHAM   KINGS SUTTON CHARLTON
              MILCOMBE   MILTON ADDERBURY W.
       HOOK NORTON WIGGINTON BARFORD ST   AYNHO
                    S. NEWINGTON JOHN
              SWERFORD   BARFORD ST MICHAEL
       GT ROLLRIGHT   LEMPTON CLIFTON
                            DEDDINGTON   COTTISFORD
              GT TEW   NETHER WORTON
          LIT. TEW LEDWELL DUNS TEW
       CHIPPING   MID ASTON
       NORTON   UP HEYFORD
          CHURCH ENSTONE

                                    BICESTER

                            OXFORDSHIRE

          STONESFIELD
              WOODSTOCK

● Marlstone walling   ⬚ Over 400 feet   I O MILES   5
○ Grey limestone walling   — Boundary of Region
◖ Admixture of stone   —·— County boundaries
T Timber frames   ----- Principal roads

                    THE BANBURY REGION
          DISTRIBUTION OF WALLING MATERIALS
                    FIG. I.

probable that timber survived mainly in the clays of the river valleys, with ash and elm as the principal timbers. The early settlement of north Oxfordshire and of the adjoining Felden district of Warwickshire appears to have been responsible for the early clearance of the ancient woodland of this region.[1]

Throughout its history the region has been one of mixed farming, in contrast to the predominantly pastoral character of the Cotswolds, the 'two-field' system of the Midlands persisting until the 18th century, with a number of four-field parishes in the neighbourhood of Banbury, as at Adderbury West, Hanwell, Swerford and Tadmarton.[2] Sheep-raising was nevertheless of considerable importance, and the region has generally shared the fortunes of the west country wool trade. The early enclosures of the 15th and 16th centuries which derived from the growth of the wool trade appear, however, to have had little effect in the region, as indeed in the Cotswolds.[3]

Shortly after 1538, Leland includes the following notes of the Banbury region:[4]

From Sutton to Banbury is 3 miles, all by champain barren of wood. . . .

I roade from Banbury to Warwick 12 miles by champain grounds, fruitfull of corn and grasse, barren of wood, and 2 miles by some enclosed and woody groundes. . . .

From Southam to Banbury 10 miles all be champaine, noe wood, but exceeding good pasture and corne. . . .

From Banbury to a small through-fare Towne . . . a 3 or 4 miles by champaine grounds. Thence by like grounde a 7 miles to Bercester. . . .

The most part of the whole Towne of Banbury standeth in a valley, and is enclosed by north and east with lowe groundes, partly medowes, partly marishes; by south and southwest the ground somewhat hilly in respect of the site of the town.

By the time of the abortive Oxfordshire uprising of 1597, to obtain 'Relief for corne and putting downe of inclosures', it was declared

[1] As far back as early British times this region, which formed the north-eastern part of the territory of the Dobuni, appears to have been noted for its fertility, being called Dobuni Dofn, from the rich and fertile soil. The early history of the region is considered by E. T. Leeds in 'Early Settlement in the Upper Thames Basin', *Geography*, Vol. 14, 1927–8.

[2] A. Ballard, 'Notes on the Open Fields of Oxfordshire', *Oxfordshire Archaeological Society Report*, 1908.

[3] The Commission of 1517 record only two cases of enclosure at Adderbury, involving 40 and 30 acres respectively, and show that north Oxfordshire was virtually untouched. In the adjoining parts of Warwickshire, Burton Dassett, now a deserted village with a fine church, is the only significant example of depopulation, being enclosed in 1508 by Sir Edwin Belknap (Beresford, *The Lost Villages of England*, 1954, p. 131).

[4] L. C. Smith, Ed., Leland, *Itinerary*, 1538, part V, 1908, pp. 38 and 109.

that around Banbury 'verie manie have inclosed, in everie place somewhat',[1] but the evidence suggests that such enclosures were still very limited in extent. Still later, the enclosure of the waste for arable or pasture in neighbouring Northamptonshire and parts of Oxford-shire led to the Midland Riots of 1607, which do not appear to have affected the region. An account published in the *Gentleman's Maga-zine*[2] in 1772 of a journey through Northamptonshire contrasts the condition of the north of the county, where there was enclosure for pasture, with resultant depopulation and bad farming, with the un-enclosed arable in the Brackley to Oxford area, where the country-side was well-populated, since it had not been affected by 'this evil genius of field inclosing'.

The richness of the Banbury Region, and of Oxfordshire in general, is borne out by many subsequent topographers. Camden[3] described the county as 'a rich and fertile county, the lower parts are inclosed into pleasant fields and meadows; the hills are covered with great stores of wood'. In 1636, Taylor[4] declared that 'Oxford-shire is scarce second to any county in England for plenty of corne and pasturage, woods and fruits of all sorts, that this Kingdome yields'. Later in the 17th century, Dr. Robert Plot[5] noted that agri-cultural practices followed similar lines throughout Oxfordshire, and described the northern region as follows: 'Though most parts of it bear corn very well, yet the greatest glory is the abundance of meadows and pastures, to which the rivers add pleasure and con-venience.' The agricultural reformers of the late 18th century spoke in equally favourable terms of the richness of the area, the Banbury Region being described as 'chiefly strong, deep land, partly arable and partly in a pastoral state, appropriated principally to the dairy'.[6] A little later, in 1807, Arthur Young classified Oxfordshire into four regions, the Banbury Region being described as 'The Red Land District', and noted:

> The soil in the northern part of the county is the rich red loam and sandy on a red gritstone rock . . . the soil uncommonly good; . . . There are some exceptions; but a finer district of soil is not often to be met with, whether in grass or arable. . . . This red district, in respect of soil, may be considered as the glory of the county.[7]

---

[1] Quoted in *Victoria County History of Oxfordshire*, Vol. 2, p. 195.
[2] *Gentleman's Magazine*, Vol. XLIV, 1774, p. 411.
[3] Camden, *Brittania*, 1586.   [4] William Taylor, *Collected Works*.
[5] Robert Plot, *Natural History of Oxfordshire*, 1676.
[6] Richard Lewis, *General View of the Agriculture of the County of Oxford with observations on the manner of its improvement*, 1794.
[7] Arthur Young, *View of the Agriculture of Oxfordshire*, 1813.

The villages developed in the nucleated form characteristic of the Midlands, and it is rare to find a dwelling in isolation from the villages of earlier date than the parliamentary enclosures of the 18th century, when the Banbury Region was one of the first areas to become enclosed, although some parishes, including Deddington, retained their open fields until the early years of the 19th century. The settlements have been established where springs combined with a dry situation, circumstances generally to be found in the small lateral valleys excavated in the lias, and in these most of the villages are grouped.

Banbury was at all times the economic centre of this rich agricultural zone, and the principal market for its agricultural produce and the wool for which Oxfordshire was famous.[1] Leland in the 16th century spoke of its market as 'very celebrate', and in 1608, James I granted a wool market to the town, which became as renowned in the next two centuries for its woollen industry as for its puritanism. From the 15th century much of the activity of the village communities was transferred to the town, which developed rapidly with the increasing importance of manufactures, all of which depended on local agriculture for their raw materials. Camden described Banbury as 'at present most famous for making good cheese', but textiles remained the principal activity, and by the beginning of the 18th century a number of industries had developed, including the manufacture of worsted plush and of webbing, together with the dyeing of fabrics.[2] Home industries extended to the neighbouring villages, Middleton Cheney[3] and Chacombe producing stockings, whilst the manufacture of plush and of gloves extended to Bloxham, Bourton, Wardington and Adderbury,[4] with spinning a common occupation of most households in the neighbourhood.

The geology and agriculture of the Banbury Region, as so far defined, have established the background for a vernacular architecture of homogeneous material, providing the homes of a prosperous farming community, with the later development of a semi-

[1] Brackley gained some significance as a market town and centre of the wool trade in the late 13th and early 14th centuries, but by 1540 Leland declared that 'Brakeley market . . . is now desolatyd', the centre of wool production having moved to the Cotswolds.

[2] References to jersey combers, jersey weavers, worsted, silk, linen and yarn spinners are noted in the parish registers of the early 18th century. Beesley, *History of Banbury*, 1841, pp. 566-7.

[3] 'Silk-stocking making used to be largely carried on at Middleton Cheney by the Hortons. Since I can remember there was a loom in most of the cottages for the purpose.' George Herbert, *Shoemaker's Window*, 1814–1902, p. 106.

[4] *Gent. Mag.*, 1820, pt. ii, p. 396.

industrial peasantry in the villages around Banbury, and in the town itself. Equally significant with the exclusiveness of the primary building materials is the limit in time of domestic building in the region, the preponderance of activity being between the end of the 16th century and the beginning of the 18th, with comparatively little subsequent building apart from the cottage developments of the late 18th and 19th centuries. In few areas of England has vernacular building activity of the 17th century retained such slight traces of its antecedents, or been followed by so marked a decline. This limitation of the regional building period can only be explained by further reference to the social evolution of the village community within the region, whose dwellings are to be examined in this work.

The predominating regional house type, with which this study is primarily concerned, is that of the yeoman farmer, a social class which gained prominence throughout England in the 15th to 17th centuries. The desire for personal freedom, which had evolved steadily from the time of the Conquest, gained final impetus in the social revolution which marked the reign of the first Elizabeth. From the almost general status of serfs, bound to the soil, the peasantry gained freedom and security by the commutation of their servile rents for cash payments, a process which started as early as the 11th century. Domesday gives the householders of Oxfordshire, excluding Oxford itself, as 6775 persons, of whom 334 may be classed as free and 6441 as servile. By 1279, the Hundred Rolls show the householders to have risen in number to 9287 with an impressive increase in the proportion of 3461 freemen to some 5826 unfree tenants, and it is noteworthy that the free element predominates in Banbury hundred as the forerunners of the later rich yeoman class.[1] In 1341, Oxfordshire had become one of the wealthiest of all counties, largely due to the development of the woollen industry, and in this prosperity the Banbury Region took full share.[2] In 1343 the county was placed among the first five counties for cost of wool, and by 1503 it ranked as the second richest county in England.[3] This early prosperity is reflected in the extensive church building which took place in the region in the latter half of the 14th century, producing, among many others, the magnificent churches of Bloxham, Adderbury, Kings Sutton and Middleton Cheney, as well as that which was

[1] *V.C.H., Oxon.* Vol. 2, pp. 166–7.
[2] The early development of the woollen industry in the county is shown by the fact that the City of Oxford was one of the earliest towns to have a weavers' guild, existing as early as 1130 (Barnard, *Companion to English History*, 1902, p. 269).
[3] Thorold Rogers, *History of Agriculture and Prices*, i, 110; iii, 704; iv, 89.

destroyed in Banbury in 1790.[1] Despite legislation to solve the labour problems which followed the Black Death, favourable towards the landlords, the emancipation of the peasantry continued throughout the 15th century, whilst the rapid development of industry and the growth in importance of such towns as Banbury provided employment for the labour set free from the land. The breakdown of manorial authority and organization is clearly reflected in the Oxfordshire court rolls of this time, and it appears that a prosperous tenantry had almost entirely commuted labour service for rent by the end of the 15th century.

The villein serf, who had already gained freedom by 1400, in the keenly competitive struggle for land which characterized the 15th and 16th centuries, rose to call himself 'yeoman', or if unfortunate fell to the rank of labourer, almost without land and working for a wage. In contemporary writing the chief basis for yeoman status was frequently noted as the holding of free land to an annual value of 40 shillings,[2] but it is clear that the term was more widely applied than this and that many yeoman held land copyhold and not freehold, whilst others with this title in the 17th century simply farmed land which they leased from larger landowners. The term yeoman in Elizabethan times is, however, essentially related to the land and is a description of occupation as well as of status, and it is in this context that the word is used throughout this work. Two other groups are similarly identified in descending social scale—the husbandman, who appears to have ranked below the yeoman as a small farmer of less substance and standing, and the labourer or cottager. It is important to note that in the 16th century there was no strict division between these classes or between the gentry and yeomanry, the yeomanry often including the 'younger brothers of gentile families living in lowe wages clouded often amongst the yeomanry'.[3] There was much inter-marriage between the classes, and the rise of yeomen to the ranks of the gentry was a commonplace in Elizabethan and Stuart times. This circumstance is reflected in the similarity in character and even in size between the smaller manor houses of the region and those dwellings of the more substantial yeomen, who by

[1] Speaking of the 14th-century architecture in the region, J. H. Parker states that almost all the churches of the Banbury district are of this period, and notes: 'I do not remember in your neighbourhood an instance of a church of the 15th century, which is singular, since in many districts almost all churches are of that date, and in most they are very common' (Beesley, *History of Banbury*, 1841, p. 108).

[2] The origins of the name yeoman, and the evolution of the social classes of the agrarian community, are fully discussed in Campbell, *The English Yeoman*, 1942.

[3] Thomas Fuller, *The Holy State*, p. 133.

William Harrison's description 'commonly live wealthily, keep good houses and travailleth to get rich'.[1]

Due to the general prosperity of the region in the 16th and early 17th centuries, it would appear that the lower class of labourers knew better conditions than their fellows in other areas, being usually possessed of some land of their own; it might be expected from this that their dwellings would be of more permanent form than in less prosperous regions.

The 16th century brought further revolutionary changes in the agrarian field, with the virtual ending of subsistence farming to fulfil the increased demands for produce and land which accompanied the rise of prices in the early-16th to mid-17th centuries. The growing need of Elizabethan landlords for larger money incomes accelerated the distribution of manorial estates and the formation of more small holdings, whilst after the Dissolution large quantities of monastic land—of which there were considerable areas in the region—came early on to the market and within reach of the smaller yeoman land-owner. In Warwickshire, land that brought £8 in 1556 had increased in price to £66 13s. 4d. in 1648.[2]

Prices of farm produce increased steadily, wheat selling in 1650 for more than three times the price it brought in 1570.[3] Bringing hardship to many, it was to the advantage of the farmer, and in 1618, Robert Royce spoke of the yeoman as the only class which was increasing in prosperity, being free from 'the costly charges of these unfaithfull times'.[4] There was, however, less prosperity in wool than in grain in the 17th century, due to protection in foreign markets, over-production and other causes, and the Banbury Region shared with the Cotswolds the depression in the cloth trade which coincided with the disturbances of the Civil Wars in which the neighbourhood of Banbury was seriously engaged. By 1636, Oxfordshire had declined from second to 17th place amongst English counties in order of wealth,[5] and the region never recovered its former affluence. Thereafter the economy pursued a more stable and lower course, only occasionally disturbed by further economic depressions, as in 1693, when it is recorded that the mob rose at Banbury and 'took away the corne by force out of the wagons'.[6]

At the end of the 18th century the whole aspect of the Banbury Region was changed by the parliamentary enclosures, which led in-

[1] William Harrison, *Description of England*, Bk. II, p. 133.
[2] S. Copland, *Agriculture Ancient and Modern*, 1866, p. 27.
[3] Campbell, p. 185.   [4] *Breviary of Suffolk*, 1618, p. 58.
[5] Thorold Rogers, *Agriculture and Prices*, Vol. 69, pp. 104 ff.
[6] Wood, *Life and Times*, iii, p. 422.

directly, with the decline in prices which followed the Napoleonic wars, to further depression in the area, in which even the textile industries of Banbury were seriously affected. Astrop and Kings Sutton attained some local popularity for their medicinal wells, but this was short-lived and has left no mark on building in the area. The region has from that time sunk into obscurity, out of touch with the industrial developments of our time.

These changes in the fortunes of the peasant community are reflected in the regional periods of building activity, although a marked time lag is notable between cause and effect. In the 16th century, it is known that masons were being impressed from local regions to work on the major building projects at Oxford, and this may have contributed to a scarcity of masons within the region which would in some degree account for this time lag. The yeoman or husbandman of the 16th century consolidated his new wealth and position by building a new house, this phase of building starting in the latter years of the 16th century and continuing almost to the end of the 17th century, although overlapping the period which is statistically shown to be one of comparative depression. The almost total disappearance of the peasant dwellings which existed before these new stone houses indicates their less permanent construction, and they would presumably be of timber, as would be general throughout the country for all but the more important dwellings. By mid-16th century, shortage of timber was a matter of general concern in the country, and was to become more acute in Stuart times. The readily available building stone provided an outlet and an improvement. Dr. Plot[1] in 1676 reflects on this shortage and other changes that took place following the civil wars, declaring that

the hills, 'tis true, before the late unhappy wars, were well enough beset with woods, where now 'tis so scarce, that 'tis a common thing to sell it by weight, and not only at Oxford but at many other places in the northern part of the shire; where if brought to mercat, it is ordinarily sold for about one shilling the hundred, but if remote from a great towne, it may be had for seven pence; and this is everywhere but in the Chiltern country.

Banbury itself suffered considerably from the wars—in 1646 a petition at the House of Lords notes that 'one halfe of the Towne is burned down'[2]—and parliamentary grants of materials from the demolished castle contributed to the rebuilding.[3] There was a general

[1] Robert Plot, *Natural History of Oxfordshire*, 1676.
[2] Quoted in Beesley, op. cit., p. 424.
[3] The vicarage, dated 1649, is one of many houses erected in Banbury at this time. No dated buildings in the region have been recorded between 1640 and 1645.

increase in building activity throughout the region from this time which continued to the latter years of the century, with locally quarried stone as the exclusive building material. The deplorable state of the roads described in contemporary reports[1] prevented the movement of other building materials, although bricks were being made as near as Woodstock in 1604, and were being used extensively in Warwickshire. It was only for the more important dwellings and barns that stone slate could be imported from north or south. Even after the Oxford canal was built in 1769, affording the region communication by water with all parts of the country, stone continued to be the prime material for what little building was being carried on, except in Banbury itself, although there appears to have been a considerable importation of blue slates into the area.

In the last decade of the 17th century the number of dated examples show that there was still considerable building activity, but after this there is a decline continuing through the next century. Apart from the dwellings of merchants and tradesmen in Banbury and other large villages, and some few new dwellings for the larger farmers and landowners, building is largely devoted to additions and extensions to earlier houses, and the erection of small farm-houses and cottages which in this century assume permanent form in the tradition of the yeoman houses of the preceding century. Many of these later cottages were tied to the lands of larger landowners who had grown wealthy with the enclosures at the expense of the cottagers; by mid-19th century the latter had lost all their little plots and were completely reduced to the status of wage-earning labourers.

The character of the regional architecture retains its medieval associations even in the 18th century, and as late as 1700 it is often only in details of mouldings that any Renaissance influence can be detected. This may be attributed to a deep-rooted tradition within the building crafts, but also to the conservative character of the yeomen which was a subject for contemporary comment. Norden, at the end of the 16th century, declared: 'They only shape their courses as their fathers did; never putting in practice any new device.' [2] Two hundred years later, James Donaldson, an 18th-century agricultural improver, recorded that farmers met him with the reply: 'We will satisfy ourselves with such measures as our Fathers

---

[1] Arthur Young says in 1813: 'I remember the roads of Oxfordshire forty years ago, when they were in a condition dangerous to the bones of all who travelled on wheels. . . . At that period the cross roads were impassable but with real danger' (*View of the Agriculture of Oxon,* 1813).

[2] John Norden, quoted in Campbell, op. cit., p. 169.

have followed hitherto.' [1] The delay in the introduction of new forms of building is no doubt attributable to this attitude. Fashionable architecture, with the first manifestations of 'Gothic' cottage building, appeared in the region whilst the native tradition was still strong. Sanderson Millar, in 1744–50 at Radway and Edge Hill, and John Claudius Loudon, early in the 19th century at Great Tew, interposed new elements into the pattern of regional development, but their works stand out in isolation against the continuing flow of regional tradition.

Tradition therefore remained the root of regional domestic architecture, and nowhere is this more clearly seen than around Banbury in the perpetuation of forms of structure, plan and detail. Within this basic tradition, which has much in common with that of England in general, detailed study has revealed a pattern of consecutive development of plan and structure which evolved to serve the needs of the yeomen farmers of the 17th and 18th centuries, whilst still preserving so much of the ancient character and association.

It is with the lesser domestic architecture of the region that this study is concerned, the homes of the yeomen and husbandmen in which traditional and regional factors played so important a part.

These developments will be considered chronologically from early medieval times to the beginning of the 19th century—when transport and industrialization finally began to undermine the regional character of village society—the final chapters being devoted to the summary of regional characteristics which go to make the particular character of the traditional domestic architecture of the Banbury Region.

[1] James Donaldson, quoted in Campbell, op. cit., p. 169.

CHAPTER II

THE ANTECEDENTS OF THE YEOMAN HOUSE
1300–1550

LITTLE has survived of lesser domestic architecture within the region prior to the end of the 16th century, when stone building began to replace the earlier timber structures, and what little architectural evidence remains is largely confined to the greater houses and manors. These more important buildings attained permanent form in stone principally in the 14th century, a period which produced so many fine churches, great houses and barns in this area, but left the homes of the peasantry to continue as frail timber structures, inviting renewal in the prosperity of the Elizabethan period. The only timber-framed buildings which now survive are in the Cherwell valley; in Banbury itself a few houses remain in much altered condition, but they are of urban character, unrelated to the regional tradition. In addition to these dwellings, two fragments of walling have been recorded in Kings Sutton, dating from the 16th century. It is probable that the medieval peasant homes were of simple and poor character in timber, for there is in the 17th century—the period of major regional building activity—little to suggest the existence of a preceding timber tradition of any quality, unless the known shortage of timber in these times may be held responsible for the poverty of timber construction in the stone dwellings. Roofs, beams and partitions—which might be expected to reflect earlier building practices —are invariably of poor scale and craftsmanship, and almost entirely lack enrichment. The earliest surviving buildings within the region are built in stone, and the form of the early roof structures suggests an early recourse to the abundant native building stone for all buildings of any social importance.

The most significant regional characteristic which emerges from the study of medieval building around Banbury is the evidence of a localized form of roof structure, apparently derived from the orthodox cruck building principle in its application to stone-walled structures, which was to influence the construction of the small house in the 16th and 17th centuries. Lying on the eastern fringe of the zone,

which as already noted[1] has been defined as the cruck-building area,
it might be expected that features of the south-eastern box-frame
tradition would exert some influence, but there appears to be little
evidence of this, the regional cruck form depending entirely on its
early adaptation to stone-walled structures. This interesting form of
structure is seen at its best in a number of fine surviving tithe barns in
north Oxfordshire, dating from the late 14th and early 15th centuries, notably those at Church Enstone, Adderbury, Swalcliffe and
Upper Heyford, all being attributable to important monastic or
collegiate rectors.

The evidence which barns and other agricultural buildings may
provide in a consideration of traditional domestic architecture is
difficult to assess. As with domestic buildings, there is considerable
variation in social significance, the rectorial and manorial barns
ranking high in the scale. The replacement of agricultural buildings
is generally much delayed in relation to houses, barns tending to
continue in service longer than domestic buildings. Building techniques appear to undergo a commensurate time-lag, barns revealing
the use of structures and materials which may have been progressively
superseded in the various social levels of domestic architecture.
These great tithe barns would, however, rank little below the status of
the manor houses, being considerably in advance technically of the
minor domestic architecture. Their forms, on the other hand, are
rudimentary in comparison with the 14th-century roofs surviving in
a number of churches in the region. This time-scale is evidenced by
the comparison of the structure of these barns first in relation to an
earlier house, Leadenporch House, Deddington, at the upper end of
the domestic scale, and at the other extreme, the small yeoman
houses of the late 16th century to be described later, all of which
reproduce on different scales the structural forms so clearly exem-
plified in the barns.

The rectorial barn at *Church Enstone, Oxfordshire* (Fig. 2) is of particular significance and interest because of the fine 14th-century
date-stone built into the structure, making the building an invaluable
if controversial dating point in regional building. The manor and
parish of Enstone belonged to the Benedictine Abbey of Winchcombe
in Gloucestershire since the ninth century,[2] and in 1307 the living
was appropriated to the abbey by Pope Clement V.[3] In 1382, the
Abbot of Winchcombe, Walter de Wynforton, erected a barn at the

[1] Chap. I, p. I.
[2] J. Jordan, *Parochial History of Enstone*, 1857, chap. 3.
[3] *Calendar of Papal Letters*, ii, p. 27.

c

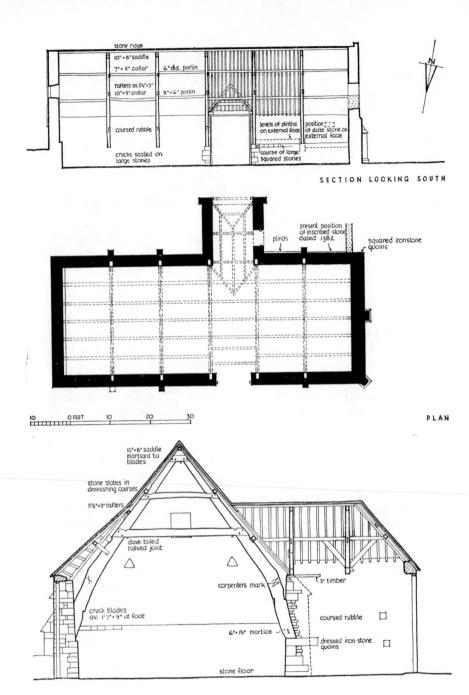

SECTION LOOKING SOUTH

stone ridge
10" × 8" saddle
7" × 5" collar
6" dia. purlin
rafters av. 5½" × 3"
10" × 9" collar
9" × 6" purlin
coursed rubble
levels of plinths
on external face
position of date stone on
external face
crucks seated on
large stones
course of large
squared stones

present position
of inscribed stone
dated 1382
plinth
squared ironstone
quoins

PLAN

10   0 FEET   10   20   30

10" × 8" saddle
morticed to
blades
stone slates in
diminishing courses
5½" × 3" rafters
dove-tailed
halved joint
carpenters mark
3" timber
cruck blades
av. 1'1" × 9" at foot
coursed rubble
6" × 1½" mortice
dressed iron-stone
quoins
stone floor

CROSS SECTION LOOKING EAST

5   0 FEET   5   10   15

THE RECTORIAL BARN   CHURCH ENSTONE   OXFORDSHIRE

FIG. 2.

request of the bailiff of the monastic grange at Enstone, this fact being recorded in a Latin inscription, now to be found on the external face of the south wall of the barn, which reads:

Ista Grangia facta et fundata fuit
A.D. M CCC LXXXII per Walterum de
Wynforton abbatem de Wynchecumbe ad
exorationem Robertii Mason ballivi loci istius.

This may be translated as:

'This barn [or grange] was founded and built in the year 1382 by Walter de Wynforton, Abbot of Wynchcombe, at the petition of Robert Mason, bailiff of this place.' The inscribed stone, which reveals fine craftsmanship, is somewhat arbitrarily placed in the rubble masonry of the south wall, protected by what appears to be a much weathered horizontal drip-mould with sculptured stops. There is no reason to doubt the authenticity of the stone, but it has certainly been reset in its present position, having been removed from another part of the present barn, or possibly from an earlier structure. The building measures internally 72 feet by 26 feet, with a through cartway, and is divided into six bays, averaging 12 feet wide. The cruck blades, averaging 1 foot 6 inches deep by 9 inches wide at the bottom, rest in the wall at a height of 5 feet above ground, seated on a course of large squared stones, the wall rising to a total height of about 12 feet. The crucks are of oak, roughly squared, but showing the outer bark in places, and appear to be paired from the same tree-trunks. The blades are shaped, curving from the feet to a slight knee, then rising almost straight to the ridge, with an even taper, the apex being formed by a saddle 10 inches high, mortised and pegged to the tops of the blades. On top of this is a further triangular block, pegged through the saddle, raising the 4-inch square ridge pole clear of the crucks. Two collars are provided, the lower at a height of 17 feet from the floor, secured to the crucks by dove-tailed halved joints, but there are no cruck spurs extending to the top of the wall. Two purlins on each side are housed into the upper edges of the blades, there being no wind-braces, nor does there appear to be a wall-plate, the rafters—roughly squared and averaging $5\frac{1}{2}$ inches by 3 inches laid flat—being built into the stonework at the top of the wall. The pitch of the roof is about 50 degrees, the present roof covering being of Stonesfield slates.[1]

---

[1] Until the beginning of the 19th century roofing slates were quarried one mile south of Enstone at Fulwell Field. These were not split by frost action, like the Stonesfield slates, but were a naturally fissile development of the Taynton

The outward thrust of the trusses is resisted by small buttresses in the lateral walls, but the absence of any tie until more than half-way up the cruck has created a tendency for spreading at the foot, which has almost certainly resulted in extensive rebuilding of the masonry. Enstone lies on the southern fringe of the Banbury region and the walls, averaging 2 feet 10 inches in thickness, are of coursed rubble, consisting of grey oolitic limestone with dressings of the dark brown lias limestone, the regional material. The use of the two stones together, for decorative effect, is characteristic of this border area, where the two materials can be obtained from the same local quarry.

Architecturally, the barn is not pretentious, lacking the finish and craftsmanship of many of the great 14th-century barns. It is not comparable in quality of detailing, whether of timber or masonry, with the barns at Swalcliffe or Adderbury, appearing to have more of the character of vernacular building, despite its monastic foundation. The dating of the structure is therefore of particular interest, and a number of points invite consideration. There is evidence of considerable rebuilding, and it is conceivable that the absence of an adequate tie to the principals may have caused the original structure to become unsafe soon after it was built. The north wall appears to have been completely reconstructed, at which time the buttresses, if original, were reset, but not bonded to the masonry; alternatively, they may have been introduced for the first time. The crucks here are seated on large stones, or on oak beams built into the walls. The west gable bears evidence of a change of building in its upper stages, and the east wall appears to have been considerably renewed. It is therefore probable that the gable walls, part of the south wall, the buttresses and the crucks, alone represent the dated structure of the late 14th century. The two existing entrances are of considerable size, but in their present form lack any architectural pretension, and are largely the result of rebuilding and alteration in the 17th century and later. A comparison with the Swalcliffe barn and other late 14th-century barns in Oxfordshire and the Cotswolds would suggest that the entrance or entrances in their original form would have been finished with stone gables and archways, and the date-stone may well have been removed from such a gable.

By comparison with orthodox cruck forms recorded elsewhere in this country, the raised cruck form of construction at Enstone would

---

Stone. W. J. Arkell suggests that Fulwell Slates were used from Roman times, and it is probable that much of the stone slating in Enstone derives from this source rather than from Stonesfield itself (W. J. Arkell, *Oxford Stone*, p. 149).

at first suggest a somewhat later date. The practice of placing the foot of the cruck upon a stone stylobate or plinth to provide a secure and dry foundation, free from damp and decay, is common in this country, but the elevation of the complete cruck structure half-way up the wall is less commonly encountered and can be regarded as a distinguishing regional characteristic. This structure does not fall within the category of the upper cruck as defined by the authors of 'Monmouthshire Houses'[1] where the curved foot of the cruck blade springs from the tie-beam at first-floor-level spanning between stone walls, above which cruck spurs continue to support the wall-plate, so maintaining the relationship of cruck and wall. The Enstone crucks appear to represent an interim stage between the full cruck and the later derivative truss forms, which simply rest upon the top of the wall. In stone barns of 15th-century date recorded in Monmouth-shire, Yorkshire and Cumberland, the crucks normally spring from a stone base near the ground level, but a stay or cruck spur normally projects from the knee of the cruck to the wall top to relate the wall-plate to the cruck. In the Oxfordshire form, the omission of the wall-plate has been noted in a number of cases, and where provided it is quite independent of the cruck frame.

The method of erecting the crucks in their elevated position is also of interest. In the cruck to the east of the principal entrance, there is a 6-inch by $1\frac{1}{2}$-inch mortise near the foot, which may correspond to the lifting or levering hole commonly found in Yorkshire and northern crucks. A wooden lever, or it may be a tenon, has been sawn off in the mortice. This feature does not occur on the only other exposed foot on the west side of this entrance, and all other blades are built into the stone walling. There is also to be noted a housing in the lower edge of several crucks, particularly those related to rebuilt walling, at a height of approximately 8 feet above floor level. There are no indications of the fixing of a permanent post or partition, and it is conjectured that these recesses may be related to the rebuilding, forming seatings for temporary props to take the weight of the cruck whilst its seating was being rebuilt. A similarly shaped notch is noted in one blade of a cruck at Grayrigg Hall barn in Westmorland, where the cruck has obviously been temporarily supported in this way to allow a decayed foot to be cut off, and a new stone plinth built up in support.

The rectorial barns at Swalcliffe, Upper Heyford and Adderbury also date from the end of the 14th century or early 15th century, all having been erected at the instance of William of Wykeham, Bishop

[1] Sir Cyril Fox and Lord Raglan, *Monmouthshire Houses*, I, p. 67.

of Winchester, the founder and builder of the New College of St. Mary at Oxford, which he endowed with these livings.

The *Swalcliffe barn* (Fig. 3), over 130 feet long, is architecturally the finest of the Oxfordshire barns and its structural form is closely related to that at Enstone. The building measures 128 feet by 22 feet 9 inches internally and is of 10 bays, averaging 12 feet 9 inches. The feet of the cruck trusses are here still further elevated as compared with Enstone, 11 feet 6 inches above ground level, seated on large stones within the walls, which are 3 feet thick, in finely-worked coursed brownstone rubble, with a fine series of buttresses on the side walls. The crucks are also paired members, averaging 15 inches by 9 inches at the feet, where they are similarly curved, but the upper and lower collars are here mortised and pegged to the principals, with finely shaped arched braces. In a number of instances, where blades sufficiently curved at the foot could not be obtained, additional firring pieces have been pegged to the members to make up the profile of the foot. Triangular blocking pieces are provided on the backs of each blade, below the lower purlins, and from these spring curved wind-braces. Recent restoration of the roof has removed most of the wind-bracing, but a description of the barn in 1887 notes that wind-braces were then applied to both upper and lower purlins.[1] As at Enstone, the ridge is supported on a saddle linking the blades. The roof structure more nearly approaches the conventional arched-braced roof truss form—in scale and finish approaching church architecture—but its close relationship to the raised crucks of Enstone is obvious. The character of the masonry is also of a higher order, the two entrance porches, at each end of the east wall—the barn lies north and south with its south gable to the road—retaining their stone gables and archways. On the west wall were two small doorways with pointed arches, one of which has been lost in the formation of a more recent, larger opening. The roof, which has been recently renewed, is of Stonesfield slates, probably replacing earlier stone slates.

The barn at *Upper Heyford*, beyond the southern limit of the region, was also built for New College, early in the 15th century. It measures 120 feet by 24 feet internally and is of basically similar structure. Of this fine group of barns, *Adderbury* alone has been seriously altered, when Lord Halden leased the Rectory for hunting from 1877 to 1878, and turned the barn into stables. Its dimensions were more comparable with those of Enstone, but architecturally the

[1] Sir Henry E. L. Dryden, 'Notes on Swalcliffe Parish Church, etc.', *Oxfordshire Archaeological Society Report*, Vol. XXIII, 1887, pp. 7, 8.

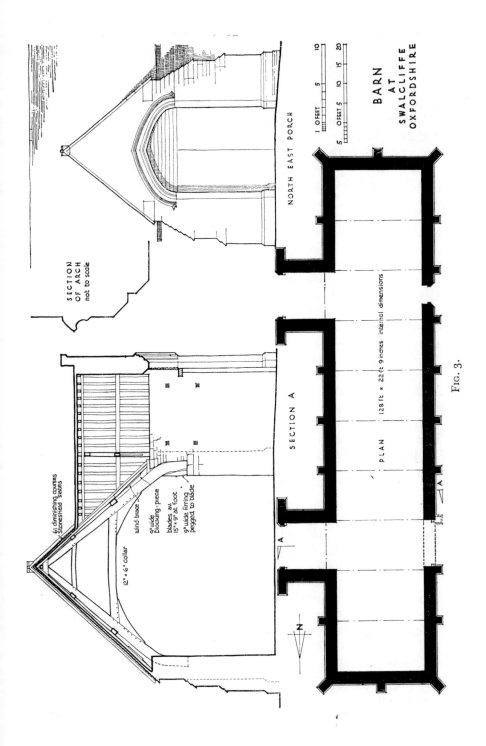

SECTION OF ARCH
not to scale

NORTH EAST PORCH

61 diminishing courses
Stonesfield Slates

wind-brace

9" wide blocking-piece

blades av.
15" × 9" at foot

9" wide firring
pegged to blade

12" × 6" collar

SECTION A

PLAN   128 ft × 22 ft 9 inches internal dimensions

A

A

N

BARN
AT
SWALCLIFFE
OXFORDSHIRE

1 0FEET   5   10

0FEET 5   10   15   20

5   10

FIG. 3.

character of the work is more closely related to that of Swalcliffe. The structure is now only of five bays, measuring 65 feet by 27 feet internally, but has almost certainly been reduced in length. The barn was probably built between 1421–3, when a kitchen, bakehouse, pigstye and sheep-hovel were also erected by one Simon Vesey, all for £86.[1] It is also known that William Mason was paid £20 5s. 4d. for building walls of the tithe barn at this time, with seven buttresses.

A further barn of similar type survives at Tadmarton, but its character and workmanship are less pretentious, and it is probably of later date.

The common influence of craftsmen, both masons and carpenters, working under the patronage of William of Wykeham, can be seen in this series of New College barns. Richard de Winchcombe,[2] who is known to have worked between 1398 and 1440, was employed as master mason in the rebuilding of Adderbury chancel for New College between 1408–18, but there is no evidence to connect him with the building of the barn, completed probably three years after this date. He was, however, employed at Swalcliffe manor from 1405 to 1406 and may well have been responsible for the masonry of the barn there. A somewhat tenuous link is provided also with the Enstone barn in the fact that Richard was probably master mason for Winchcombe Abbey, to which Enstone was appropriated, it being just possible that the barn built in 1382 might have been one of his earliest works. Richard probably worked at Enstone in 1420 on the reredos of the parish church.

John Jylkes,[3] carpenter employed by New College, provides a further common link, being employed at Swalcliffe on the hall and stable in 1397–8, on farm buildings in 1408–9 and 1412–13, and on chambers and chapel in 1423–33. Jylkes also worked at Upper Heyford between 1423–4, at Adderbury, and between 1411–12, at Drayton in south Oxfordshire, where a cruck barn similar to those described, provides a contrast with the aisled barn of later date illustrated in Fig. 66.

One other barn deserves notice, as exhibiting a variation of this raised cruck form, which appears to bring it nearer to the orthodox cruck principle. The form of the truss would appear earlier, as an interim stage between the full cruck and the raised cruck, but the poor quality of the material and finish places the building considerably lower in the social scale than those already described, and the

---

[1] *Country Life*, 1949, pp. 30 and 86.
[2] John Harvey, *English Medieval Architects*, p. 296. E. A. Gee, 'Oxford Masons', *Archaeological Journal*, Vol. CIX, 1952, p. 69.   [3] John Harvey, op. cit., p. 152.

construction is probably another evidence of the time-lag already noted. The crucks survive in an almost derelict barn of otherwise later build at *Warmington, Warwickshire* (Fig. 16), on the north-western fringe of the region, adjacent to the lowland plain where timber-framed structures continued to be built well into the 17th century. Although the building has obviously undergone consider-able rebuilding, it is unlikely, because of the crudeness of the finish and craftsmanship, that the structure was ever other than a barn. Two pairs of crucks remain, 12 feet 9 inches apart, framing a through cartway, the bay being arbitrarily placed in a later stone-walled structure which measures 19 feet 6 inches wide by 25 feet long internally, the crucks not being quite square to the outside walls. It is probable that there was at least one further frame to the south beyond the present stone partition, but this portion of the building has been further altered and raised in height, adjoining a house of 17th-cen-tury build. The cruck blades are seated on stone walls at a height of approximately 2 feet 3 inches from the ground, and can therefore be classed as 'full' crucks; they reach a height of approximately 27 feet to the apex, which is formed in the usual way with a saddle sup-porting the ridge. There are two collars, the lower 13 feet above floor level, halved and pegged to the blades and projecting past them to support the lower purlin. The crucks themselves are cruder than any others recorded, measuring 11 inches by 5 inches at the knee, only slightly shaped, and paired from the same trees of such mean dimensions that the blade section is almost semi-circular, with the bark still showing on the outer face. Rafters are similarly crude, being rough poles, dressed on two sides, and the roof covering is now of thatch, as no doubt it always has been. The foot of one cruck has been cut off and supported by props, and the structure is generally in poor condition.

The lack of squareness in the placing of the frames suggests a re-building of the walls, which may originally have been of timber, although the absence of cruck spurs renders this unlikely. The exist-ing coursed rubble walls are 26 inches thick at the base, reducing to the wall top, which bears a wall-plate. It is possible that the lower collar represents the orthodox tie-beam supporting an original wall-plate on its extremities in conjunction with timber wall-framing, but the beam is really too high for this to be an acceptable solution, 11 feet above the seating of the crucks. The elucidation of this building must remain in some doubt, but it probably dates from the first half of the 16th century, and is of value in its relationship to both the raised and the orthodox cruck forms.

As has been already stated, evidence of medieval domestic structure is limited to the more important stone-walled dwellings, including such great houses as Broughton Castle and other large manor-houses, all of which have undergone extensive rebuilding at later periods. Such larger houses do not come within the scope of this study, possessing little regional character, the manor-houses in particular having developed in virtual independence of local influences. In the 13th century, the manor-house was in the final process of settling into a type to be fairly uniformly followed throughout the country.[1] The chief and dominating element was the common hall, divided by a screens passage from service rooms, such as buttery and pantry, which might have a private solar above them: sometimes the solar was a separate chamber, detached from the hall. Beyond or near the service rooms was the kitchen, set apart from the main building as a precaution against fire, but usually linked by a covered passage. From about 1300, the solar appeared with increasing frequency at the 'upper' end of the hall, away from the service rooms, raised over a ground-floor cellar (later, parlour) in the grander manor-houses, whilst the kitchen came into definite association with the hall, reached by a passage between the buttery and pantry. The lesser medieval manor-houses often were wholly ground-floor structures, especially if in timber, but with these it was an appreciably longer time before the full sequence of solar, hall, screens passage, service room and kitchen was attained.

The scarcity of medieval houses in the region below manorial rank and the obvious influence of the manor-house on the subsequent development of the yeoman house, calls for consideration of such instances within the region which preserve sufficient evidence of the original arrangements. *Manor Farm, Cottisford,* in Oxfordshire (Fig. 4), lying beyond the north-east boundary of the Banbury Region, in the area of grey limestone south of Brackley, is of particular interest as representing the manorial plan with the hall at first-floor level. This is an established plan type of the 12th and 13th centuries, a development from 'Norman' instances, such as Boothby Pagnell in Lincolnshire, and ultimately related to the stone defensive keeps or donjon towers of the Norman castle. The building, which may have been the former manor-house,[2] dates from the late

[1] The manorial plan in the 13th century is considered in some detail by Margaret Wood in *Thirteenth Century Houses,* with some note of Oxfordshire examples.

[2] It would appear that from 1100 there was no resident lord of the manor at Cottisford, the estate being in monastic and subsequently collegiate hands, the administration of the lands being left to a bailiff or steward. An indenture of

13th or early 14th century—the evidence of architectural detail suggests the later date, although there is a window in the north gable dating from *c.* 1200 which has presumably been re-used—and there have been extensive alterations in the 16th century and more recently. A plan of the house was recorded by Turner and Parker in 1851,[1] and since this date there has been further addition and modernization.

The manor-house, a rectangular structure with stone walls averaging 2 feet 6 inches in thickness, was originally of two storeys, although the existing first floor and its beams are 16th-century renewals. The plan comprises two 'units',[2] with the principal rooms formerly on the first floor and open to the roof. These would be the hall and solar, the former measuring 27 feet by 15 feet wide. There are, in addition, two small projecting wings on the west wall, the more northerly opening from the solar and measuring 5 feet 6 inches by 9 feet internally, providing a small closet on the first floor. Within this small apartment is an original stone trough and drain on the north wall, together with two contemporary windows of rectangular form with simply splayed jambs. The fine 14th-century stack which surmounts this projecting wing, octagonal in plan, with battlemented cresting, does not connect with a fireplace and is presumably a vent to the closet. The central projection may be of later date, and its purpose is not clear, although opening from the hall it could be a small service room or store. The principal stair is contained in this projection, but there is no trace of the original stair, that in the southeast corner being of recent date. In its original state the ground floor presumably provided storage and service accommodation. It has, however, been extensively altered in the 16th century when the floor was converted to provide the principal living apartments; these subsequent developments are considered in a later chapter. Few of the original details have survived these alterations, apart from two trefoil-headed lancet windows in the north wall of the solar.

The Rectorial Manor House at Swalcliffe (Fig. 4) is of particular

---

1325 records details of the manor-house of that date, including a hall and chamber, with kitchen and servery, and a close and garden complete with fishery and dovecote. The present manor-house is of 18th-century date and is known to have replaced an earlier structure built in the 16th century. It is possible that the description of the 14th-century house could refer to the present manor-farm, then held by a tenant of the monastic owner (*V.C.H. of Oxfordshire*, Vol. 6, p. 104).

[1] Turner and Parker, *Some Account of Domestic Architecture in England, 1851* Vol. 1, 12th–13th centuries, pp. 161–3.

[2] The term 'unit' has been used throughout to denote a room or compartment occupying the full width of the dwelling, hence 'single-unit', 'two-unit', and 'three-unit' plans, comprising respectively one, two and three principal rooms.

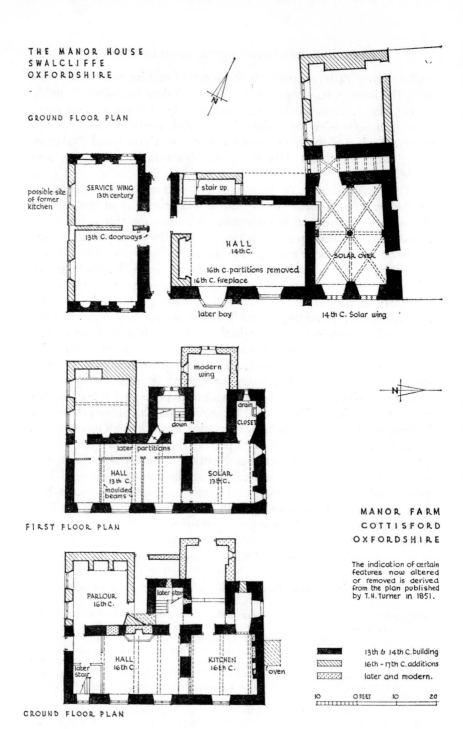

THE MANOR HOUSE
SWALCLIFFE
OXFORDSHIRE

GROUND FLOOR PLAN

N

possible site
of former
kitchen

SERVICE WING
13th century

stair up

13th C. doorways

HALL
14th C.

16th C. partitions removed

16th C. fireplace

SOLAR OVER

later bay

14th C. Solar wing

modern
wing

down

drain

CLOSET

later partitions

HALL
13th C.
moulded
beams

SOLAR
13th C.

FIRST FLOOR PLAN

N

MANOR FARM
COTTISFORD
OXFORDSHIRE

The indication of certain
features now altered
or removed is derived
from the plan published
by T.H.Turner in 1851.

PARLOUR
16th C.

later stair

later
stair

HALL
16th C.

KITCHEN
16th C.

oven

13th & 14th C. building

16th - 17th C. additions

later and modern.

10   0 FEET   10   20

GROUND FLOOR PLAN

MANORIAL PLANS OF THE THIRTEENTH & FOURTEENTH CENTURIES
Fig. 4.

interest as a smaller example of the manorial class, comparable in scale with later yeoman dwellings; although considerably altered and modernized, the original 13th-century plan can still be recognized. The service wing, of two-storey height, is the earliest part of the building, and although extensively rebuilt, the nature of the architectural details shows it to be of mid-13th-century date. The north-west wall adjoining the lower end of the hall is part of the original build, being 3 feet thick and retaining the original dual service doorways in the middle of the wall. The doorways, one foot apart and presumably opening to pantry and buttery, have two-centred arches with hood moulds with moulded stops, and rebates for doors on the screens side (Pl. 2a). The opposite wall on the south-west has been rebuilt, leaving no trace of the access to the kitchen, which it is assumed would be a detached building outside the screens passage.[1] Both front and rear walls of the wing average 2 feet in thickness, but that facing south-east is of more finely dressed stonework than the other wall. The interior arrangements of the wing are largely the result of alterations from the 16th to the 19th centuries, the ground floor being divided into two parlours and panelled, and the first floor also being rebuilt, whilst the kitchen has been removed to the north-west end of the later solar wing.

This 13th-century part of Swalcliffe belongs to the same class as the previous house, but with the important qualification that it seems never to have served in isolation as the whole house, as did Cottisford, but was apparently connected with a ground-floor timber-aisled hall (the second main type of manor-house—perhaps of Saxon derivation or earlier—just as the first-floor hall belongs to the Norman castellated or defensive class) as may be judged from the position of the original service doors on the ground floor. The solar at this time would be over the service rooms, approached by a stair from the timber hall—perhaps in the same position as the 16th-century stair shown on the plan.

The existing hall and solar are of 14th-century date.[2] By the time the timber hall was converted into stone in the 14th century, it had become customary to place the solar at the upper end, and the old

---

[1] The great kitchen which survives at Stanton Harcourt in south Oxfordshire is a fine and unusual example of this feature, being quite detached and built on a scale befitting a great house of the 14th century. That this is, however, not a typical example, even in its day, is shown by a reference made by Robert Plot at the end of the 17th century, in which he speaks of this kitchen as being 'so strangely unusual'.

[2] As already noted, work on the manor-house was in progress between 1397 and 1423.

solar over the service wing would be relegated to secondary chambers. Successive alterations have left little even of the later hall, apart from the original entrance doorways at either end of the screens passage, the openings having pointed arches of two hollow splayed orders which die into flat-splayed jambs. The jambs and part of the rear arch of one of the hall windows have also survived the later rebuilding. The hall itself measured approximately 19 feet by 38 feet, and was probably of three bays, the walls again being 2 feet 6 inches in thickness. In the 16th century a first floor and new roof were introduced, the latter at a higher level than the original, of which no evidence has survived.

The 14th-century solar wing is architecturally of some pretension, consisting originally of two storeys, the lower being vaulted in four quadripartite bays with a central column; a vaulted passage leads along the north-west wall of this undercroft presumably to a stair in the north corner. The wing may have combined a chapel with a solar, but extensive rebuilding has removed all evidence; an original 14th-century window, with pointed arch and hollow-splay jambs has, however, survived on the north-east wall.

The vaulted undercroft with its connecting passage finds a close counterpart in the great house at Broughton, which contains work of the 14th, 15th and 16th centuries, and exhibits the typical hall plan of the 14th century on an altogether grander scale. The plan has been illustrated (Fig. 5) as an indication of the comparative scale of a great house of the Middle Ages in the Banbury Region, and because it reveals the great house as the antecedent of the later yeoman plan. *Broughton Castle, Oxfordshire*, standing in a walled and moated enclosure, was built by the de Broughton family early in the 14th century and was formerly known as Broughton House. Under successive owners—the Wickhams, who obtained licence to crenellate in 1467, and the Fiennes—the building has been considerably altered, particularly in the second half of the 16th century, but the original arrangements can readily be determined. The hall, although subsequently subdivided to its present three-storey height, retains its original plan, whilst 14th-century buttresses and window details survive on the south wall. It was formerly of four bays, as indicated by the buttresses, the roof having been rebuilt, and measures 54 feet 6 inches by 28 feet 9 inches wide, with the entrance and screens passage at the west end. The north door has been blocked by an Elizabethan bay window, but one jamb of the south doorway has survived. The western service wing was largely rebuilt in the 16th century, in accordance with the contemporary practice of adding dining-rooms at the

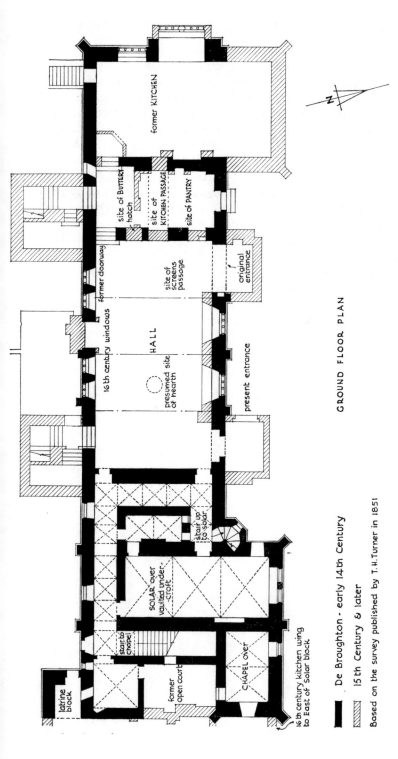

former KITCHEN

site of BUTTERY hatch

site of KITCHEN PASSAGE

site of PANTRY

former doorway

16th century windows

site of screens passage

original entrance

HALL

presumed site of hearth

present entrance

SOLAR over vaulted under-croft

stair up to solar

stair to chapel

former open court

CHAPEL over

latrine block

16th century kitchen wing to East of Solar block

■ De Broughton - early 14th Century

▨ 15th Century & later

Based on the survey published by T.H.Turner in 1851

GROUND FLOOR PLAN

10 0 FEET 10 20 30

BROUGHTON CASTLE OXFORDSHIRE

Fig. 5.

lower end of the hall, to rob that apartment of one more of its original functions. The wing formerly comprised a kitchen separated by buttery and pantry from the screens passage, which was presumably defined by a wooden screen across the hall. The solar wing in general retains its original form, although the solar itself has been modernized and re-roofed. On the ground floor a series of passages with groined vaulted roofs lead from the south-east corner of the hall to a broad stone stair which communicates with the chapel on the first floor, and also to a smaller newel stair giving access to the solar. Chapel and solar are planned over an elaborate system of vaulted undercrofts, used as cellars. The roof of this wing has also been raised in the 16th century, to provide a third floor.

Fuller consideration of these socially more important dwellings is inappropriate to a study of minor domestic architecture, but in the absence of surviving examples of smaller houses of the Middle Ages, these hall plans well illustrate the pattern of domestic building within the region, if on a more elaborate scale, providing the antecedents of the later yeoman plans, as the great barns give evidence of the antecedents of structure.

CHAPTER III

LESSER HALL HOUSES OF THE MIDDLE AGES
1300–1550

THE particular function and character of the Manor House presents factors of plan which can not be properly related to the smaller homes, and the buildings already considered are of interest primarily as illustrating features of structure and plan which, in accordance with the scale already noted, linking time and social status, ultimately descend to the lower levels of minor domestic architecture. Five houses of particular interest have been recorded in the region, dating from before 1550, which are not manorial buildings, and although certainly of some social significance as the homes of men of substance can be more directly related to the succeeding pattern of vernacular building. Two of these dwellings illustrate the use of cruck forms in medieval hall-houses, and all retain medieval features, despite extensive alteration in later centuries. The process of modernization throughout the ages in all these earlier dwellings has been such that the elucidation of original plans must remain a matter of reasoned conjecture based on the analysis of surviving evidence.

The Leadenporch House, Deddington (Fig. 6) is probably the most interesting house recorded within the region, and although successive alterations from the 17th century onwards have obscured the original form, it is clear that the building was originally a single-storey hall-house of considerable architectural significance.

The present parlour end is a complete addition of the 17th century, and the trusses divide the original extent of the building into five bays, three of which average 8 feet wide, with a wider bay of 10 feet 3 inches over the entrance, which exists as a through passage, probably on the original lines, and a further bay of the same dimension beyond this. The principals are of the raised cruck form, with curving feet seated in the stone walls approximately 10 feet above the floor level, and five feet below the top of the wall as now existing, the blades tapering evenly to the apex which is formed by a saddle, mortised and pegged. A single collar is provided with arched braces below, and on it stands a king-post, strutted on either side to the principals, with curving braces each side to support the

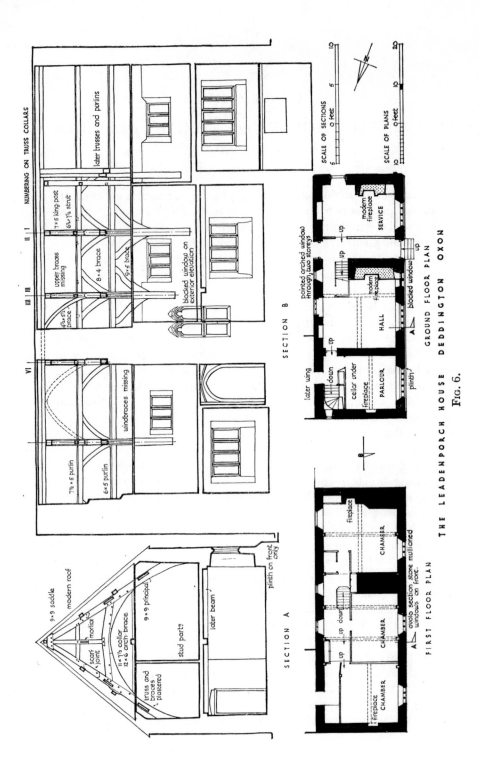

NUMBERING ON TRUSS COLLARS

later trusses and purlins

7 × 5 king post
6½ × 7½ strut

upper braces
missing

8 × 4 brace

9 × 5 brace

4¼ × 5½
brace

blocked window on
exterior elevation

SECTION B

7½ × 5 purlin

6 × 5 purlin

windbraces missing

9 × 9 saddle

modern roof

mortice?

scarf
joint

11 × 7½ collar
12 × 6 arch brace

9 × 9 principal

truss and
braces
plastered

stud part?

later beam

plinth on front only

SECTION A

pointed arched window
through, two storeys

modern
fireplace

SERVICE

up

up

modern
fireplace

up

HALL

blocked window

later wing

down

cellar under

fireplace

PARLOUR

plinth

A— ovolo section, stone mullioned
windows on front.

GROUND FLOOR PLAN

Fireplace

CHAMBER

up
up down

CHAMBER

up

CHAMBER

fireplace

FIRST FLOOR PLAN

SCALE OF SECTIONS

0 feet

SCALE OF PLANS

0 feet

N

THE LEADENPORCH HOUSE DEDDINGTON OXON

FIG. 6.

ridge-beam between trusses—a feature not elsewhere recorded within the region in domestic work.[1] Although basically similar to those already described, there is a significant variation in the form of the principal rafters, which are here of square section, approximately 9 inches square at the foot, each being in two pieces, scarved and pegged above the collar. The trusses show a system of numbering, indicating a degree of prefabrication—the only occasion this has been noted in the area, although carpenter's work marks can be seen on the Enstone blades. Each truss is numbered consecutively on either side of the collar with a different Roman numeral, from I and II on the most northerly frame, to a VI on the exposed southern face of the truss which is embedded in the later stack. The most southerly truss was presumably numbered VII and VIII, but its surface has been so badly attacked by beetle that this cannot be verified. It would appear from all these early buildings that there were no end frames, but that the gable wall was always built up in stone to support the ends of purlins and ridge. Three tiers of wind-braces were provided, rising from the principals and housed into the backs of the purlins, the upper braces springing from the purlins themselves. The roof timbers are finely finished and chamfered, and are heavily encrusted with soot, particularly between frames numbered I, II and III, IIII, indicating an original open central hearth with smoke probably discharging through a louvre in the roof, of which there is, however, no further evidence. The two southern bays appear to be less blackened, and the decay which has attacked the end truss alone may be due to its lacking the protection afforded by the soot, and it seems probable that the roof was partitioned at frame V, VI. The original rafters and roof covering have been largely replaced by a recent roof of Stonesfield slates, and the narrower spacing of the trusses suggests that the original roofing material was stone slates.

On the south-west elevation to the road, there survives the pointed arched doorway and one of the great windows to the former hall, the window now blocked by the later fireplace. Both are fine details and there is every reason to believe that they are the undisturbed features of the original hall-house. Of the original 'leaden porch' there is no trace, if indeed this ever related to the entrance door.

[1] The nave roof of Adderbury Church is of 14th-century date and is also of king-post form, the simple squared post rising from a cambered tie-beam spanning 23 feet, with large arch-braces below to wall-posts. The king-post is similarly strutted to the principals on either side, both struts and principals being cusped, and there are also curving lateral braces on either face of the post extending to the ridge. The roof pitch is however only 31°, as compared with 57° at Leadenporch House, and was presumably designed for a lead covering.

There is also a pointed arched window through two storeys on the east front, but this is modern work, presumably replacing an original opening.

The dating of this house is of considerable importance in relationship to subsequent developments in the region. There is no known record of the house or its ownership before the 15th century when the building was acquired by the Dean and Canon of Windsor. It was then noted by its present name as the capipe messuage of a freehold estate consisting of four yardlands in the common fields of Deddington, and had obviously been erected by a person of substance. It is further recorded that in the 16th century, the house was leased by its owners to the Pope family, and the house is traditionally declared to have been the birthplace of Sir Thomas Pope. Sir Thomas, who was born about the year 1508 and died in 1559, was certainly a native of Deddington, educated at Banbury Grammar School, and is noted as the founder of Trinity College, Oxford.

The architectural evidence would support a date considerably earlier than any recorded, from consideration of the nature of the surviving architectural details, the structure and plan. The hall window is of two lights with pointed heads cut out of the same stone, with heavy flat-splay mullion and transom, and cusps set in the chamfers of the heads. There is no enclosing hood-mould and the tympanum above the lights is not pierced but sunk to follow the line of the arch. The 17th-century fireplace obscures the interior form of the window—but accounts for its sole survival—but there is a window seat in the cupboard occupying part of the embrasure. The details here described invite comparison with windows at Stokesay and other houses dating from the end of the 13th century.

The entrance doorway (Fig. 77, Pl. 2b) has a two-centred arch with a roll-section hood-mould terminating in carved stops. The mouldings are simple and without enrichment, whilst the inner archway is segmental and chamfered, the whole agreeing with a date at the beginning of the 14th century. The only other worked stone is the plinth on the road front, which is simply weathered.

The raised cruck roof structure is obviously related to the barns previously considered, but is more finely executed and more sophisticated in form, with the addition of the braced king-post and windbraces. A form of king-post (crown-post) is recorded in many 13th century houses in the south-eastern part of the country in association with the support of collar purlins in the characteristic eastern counties type of roof. The solar at Charney Bassett Manor, Berkshire, dating from c. 1280, is a noted example of this type, which is seen in

Oxfordshire in the hall of the Warden's Lodging at Merton College, Oxford, dating from 1200 to 1300 (Fig. 66-2). The king-post does not appear to be a structural necessity at Deddington, and its inclusion may result from this neighbouring lowland tradition, the method of strutting of the post being typical of these southern roofs. In the tithe barns, the king-post is not included, and as these structures would occur lower in the time scale than a house of this importance, it seems probable that they are of later build, putting the date of the house at latest in the early 14th century.

The evidence of date given by the nature of the detail and structure can be supported by consideration of the hall-plan. Although all existing partitions are later, and the rear wall largely rebuilt, the variation of bay sizes clearly indicates the existence of an original screens passage on the present lines, dividing the building into a three-bay hall with central hearth, and a service room below the entrance, the building being partitioned throughout its height on the line of truss V, VI. The building of this frame into the later stack unfortunately prevents verification of this point, but there is no evidence of partitioning at any other point. The screens passage would therefore be outside the hall, in the manner associated with the spere-truss, a form that may have originated in the lowlands, but which has developed in upland areas in the north and west of the country. Sir Cyril Fox, also writing of an upland zone in Monmouthshire,[1] suggests that 'the service ends of our little halls, each with a framed truss . . . on the line of the former screens reflect, in our rural tradition, the spere-truss framework . . .' The size of the service end, encompassed by the two wider bays—20 feet in length as compared with the 25 feet length of the hall—is unusual and can not be explained. The kitchen would presumably be a detached building near the lower end, perhaps linked by a covered way. There is no evidence of an original solar beyond the upper end of the hall, however, and the possibility of the private apartments being situated over the service end must also be considered here—as at Swalcliffe in the 13th century—although there is nothing to support this in the form of the trusses at this end. A solar above the lower end is not unusual in the 13th century, there being a good example in Northamptonshire in the Prebendal House at Nassington, where the screens end of the single-storey hall is flanked by a two-storey wing which combines the private and service rooms, the solar being on the first floor. The absence of a solar would however again endorse a date around 1325 for Leadenporch House.

[1] Op. cit., Vol. I, p. 88.

The subsequent history of the Leadenporch House may be noted here to further explain the plan shown in Fig. 6.[1] In the second half of the 17th century—on the evidence of the window mullions, cellar, etc.—the building was 'modernized' and converted into a typical 'three-unit' regional house of two storeys, retaining the through passage entrance, and adding a parlour at the north-west end with a cellar under. This gable was presumably taken down to facilitate the construction of the basement, as it would otherwise have required under-pinning; the ends of the purlins were then supported on a truss which subsequently has been reinforced to leave no less than three frames now existing at this point. Fireplaces were introduced in hall and kitchen, and new windows inserted, those on the road front at least having stone mullions of ovolo section and flat label moulds, with dressings of light grey limestone—an admixture found in other yeoman houses in Deddington. A wing of stables and barns of later date adjoins the north-west corner of the house. The original stair position cannot be positively determined, but it was probably placed on the rear wall adjacent to the stack, where the modern stair is situated.

After the enclosure of Deddington early in the 19th century, the house was abandoned by the tenant for a new farmhouse, and Leadenporch became a 'Beer-shop.' By the 1830's it was described as being in a 'complete state of delapidation', the north wall being 'actually falling down'. Yet the terriers note that by 1843 the house had been 'neatly repaired', to which date certain Gothic Revival details at the lower end can be attributed; the house has been sub-sequently maintained in good repair as a private residence. The fundamental weakness of the roof trusses, lacking a suitable tie to restrain the heavy principals, has here, as at Enstone, resulted in some spreading of the feet and deformation of the truss frames, and would account for the earlier collapse of the north wall.

Deddington retains other evidence of medieval domestic build-ing, including the 13th-century nucleus of Deddington Castle House, noted in Chapter VII, and a groin-vaulted cellar under the former Plough-Inn in New Street. Medieval work of more significance in the history of vernacular building also survives in the house now called *Castle End* (Fig. 65). Although extensive alteration and rebuilding in the 17th and 18th centuries has largely obscured the original plan form, the building provides further evidence of domestic construc-tion of the medieval period. Externally, the house suggests two prin-cipal building periods, a 17th-century wing containing hall and

---

[1] The hatching of this plan does not discriminate between work carried out in different periods before 1800, only modern work being differentiated.

parlour with a porch dated 1646, and to the west of this an extended service wing of 18th-century character. Closer examination, particularly of the roof structure, reveals that the latter portion is of considerably earlier date and represents an earlier house built not later than *c*. 1525, retaining its original entrance doorway with four-centred arch and two surviving bays of the fine medieval roof.

The wing has walls of small rubble, 2 feet 7 inches thick, and now measures internally 48 feet by 17 feet 9 inches. Two trusses survive unaltered, that over the east side of the screens passage being originally a closed truss, with a fine arch-braced truss with straight principals at a bay spacing of approximately 8 feet 6 inches, curved wind-braces being provided. The original roof continues westwards for a further bay, but the third truss has been lost in the building of the 18th-century chimney-breast; and beyond this point the roof has been completely renewed during the modernization of the wing to provide service accommodation up to 18th-century requirements. As the west wall has been considerably rebuilt, it is possible that the wing is not of its original length, the present extent allowing for six bays in all, of which the eastern bay forms the through passage with possibly three bays for the hall and two for a western parlour. It is not clear whether the structure represents a single-storey hall of unusual height—29 feet to the ridge—or whether there was originally a first floor, possibly containing the hall itself. Indications of blocked windows on the north front at two levels are inconclusive, as these may well represent 17th-century insertions, themselves replaced by the later sash windows. The original service end would presumably be to the east of the entrance, the position of which has not altered through successive rebuildings, this end having been swept away in the rebuilding of 1646 when the former upper end was relegated to the position of service wing to a new and finer hall and parlour—a not uncommon inversion of status.

The third house which appears to have particular significance in relation to subsequent planning and structural evolution is *Chinners Farm, Chacombe* (Fig. 7), lying near the north-eastern limit of the region in Northamptonshire. Here again there survives what is believed to have been a late medieval hall-house, enlarged and modernized in the 17th century, exhibiting the only use of the orthodox cruck form recorded in the region. It is particularly unfortunate that, even more than at Deddington, the architectural history of this most important structure remains obscure and a matter for conjecture as a result of later rebuilding.

The earliest part of the house comprises a three-bay thatched

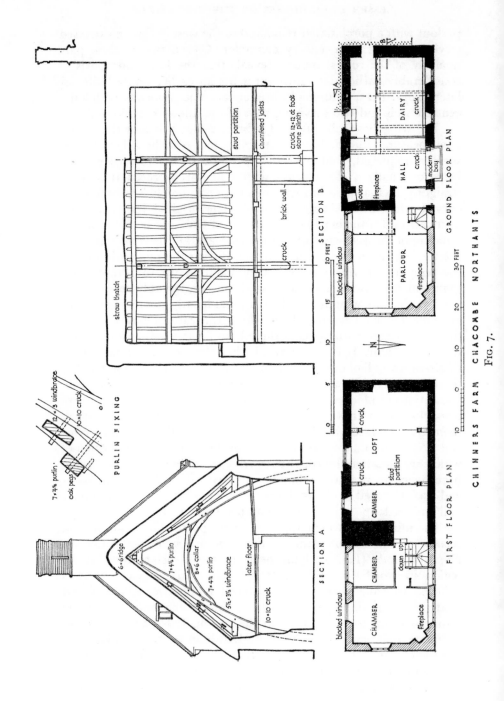

PURLIN FIXING

7×4½ purlin
oak peg
12×4⅜ windbrace
10×10 cruck

SECTION A

6×6 ridge
7×4½ purlin
8×6 collar
7×4½ purlin
5⅜×3½ windbrace
later floor
10×10 cruck

SECTION B

straw thatch
stud partition
chamfered joists
cruck 12×12 at foot
stone plinth
brick wall
cruck
blocked window

20 FEET

FIRST FLOOR PLAN

blocked window
CHAMBER
CHAMBER
CHAMBER
fireplace
down up
cruck
LOFT
cruck
stud partition
cruck

GROUND FLOOR PLAN

oven
fireplace
HALL
cruck
modern bay
DAIRY
cruck
PARLOUR
fireplace
blocked window

A
B

N

0   5   10   15   20 FEET
0   10   20   30 FEET
0   10

CHINNERS FARM CHACOMBE NORTHANTS
FIG. 7.

hall, measuring internally 35 feet by 18 feet, and containing two pairs of crucks, at 14-foot centres, the blades averaging 11 inches square at the base, and springing from a low stone stylobat 18 inches above the present floor level. The crucks are built into rubble walls averaging 2 feet 6 inches in thickness near the base, and only the insertion of a modern bay window has revealed the foot of one blade. At the apex, a yoke secures the crucks, and there is one collar with arch braces, the timbers being well shaped and chamfered, and all joints being tenoned and pegged. There is no tie-beam, but cruck spurs are provided at eaves level, mortised to the crucks and built into the walls, there being presumably a wall-plate resting on these spurs at the top of the wall. Sprockets on the backs of the crucks reduce the pitch to 52½ degrees and carry the purlins and wind-braces. The cruck frame is gracefully proportioned, with a slight ogee curve, a late form in comparison with examples recorded elsewhere in the country, and suggests a date early in the 16th century. Whether the crucks were originally free standing, with timber-framed walls, or whether they were built, archaistically, in conjunction with the heavy stonework is a matter for conjecture, but it may be significant that one of the cruck spurs appears to have been cut off against the stone wall, instead of being built in, as if the wall had been taken up later.

There is at present a first floor in the bay at the east end of the hall, the cruck frame being filled in its upper stage with stud partitioning. A number of solutions offer themselves as to the original form of this building, the first being that it was a timber-framed structure of three equal bays, with framed gables, the floor and partition at the east end being original, with the partition extending the full height of the frame, separating a two-bay hall of single storey with open hearth from a two-storey solar bay, access to the upper floor being by a ladder. Three factors however principally oppose this solution; firstly the absence of any soot blackening on the timbers, which would prove the existence of an open fire, and secondly the improbable form of the eastern crucks—essentially of open form with cruck spurs instead of tie-beam—as an original partition frame. The lack of any trace of end frames is the third objection to this having been originally of timber-frame construction. It is of course possible to explain away these points, as the roof timbers may have been cleaned when the gable fireplace was introduced, the partition may have been introduced later to sub-divide an originally open hall, and end frames may have existed but, being exposed, may have decayed and involved replacement by stone gables.

A further and more tenable solution presents itself, however, if it

is assumed that the present hall fireplace, on the east gable, is contemporary with the crucks, although obviously altered in the 17th
century when the oven was added.[1] In Monmouthshire, Sir Cyril
Fox proves that 'among the lesser gentry and yeomen . . . the
change-over from the smoke-filled interior of the Middle Ages to the
comparative comfort of a smokeless room . . . took place while a
significant medieval social custom, that of living in a hall open to
the roof, was still current'. The plan of Chinners Farm is directly
comparable in form and dimensions of bay and span with the Monmouthshire house of Pool Farm, Llangattock-vibon-avel, which is
dated between 1500 and 1550, although there the house is of two bays,
divided into hall and 'cellar'. Fox and Raglan record this transfer
from central hearth to gable fireplace in the first half of the 16th
century in a number of stages—first the addition of a stone stack
beyond the cruck gable, then within the gable, thirdly with the gable
cruck incorporated in the stack, and finally the association of gable
stack with stairs and an upper floor.

In accordance with this assumption, Chinners Farm may be
considered as a single-storey hall-house of three bays without
original partitions, the walls being probably of stone from the first
and with an original gable fireplace on the east wall. The entrance
would be adjacent to the fireplace, possibly by a through passage
behind the chimney breast, and below this a service end may well
have existed on the site of the later parlour. There is however a
difference in the character of the stonework between the two portions, and it is clear that the 17th-century parlour wing was either an
altogether new structure or involved complete rebuilding of the
former service wing. The absence of partitioning in a hall of this size
and type—its dimensions of 35 feet by 18 feet are larger than many
manorial halls, that at Swalcliffe measuring 38 feet by 19 feet but
including the through passage—cannot however be adequately
explained, although a parallel can again be sought in Monmouthshire. The Old Forge, Llangattock Lingoed, is the only three-bay
medieval cruck hall recorded in the Monmouthshire survey. This is a
stone-walled structure of three bays with a gable fireplace, the trusses
similarly being of open form with spurs instead of tie-beams, the
open hall measuring 33 feet 2 inches by 16 feet 8 inches. The building
is presumed to have been originally a timber-framed structure, with
other crucks at the present stone gables, and the members are
described as being 'rough and comparatively slight'.

---

[1] The introduction of ovens at the side of earlier fireplaces in the later 17th
and 18th centuries has been recorded in a number of cases. See Chapter XII, p. 272.

A third possibility, that the original use of the building was other than domestic has also been considered, but there is little to support such a theory which would oppose the more normal order of descent which has frequently turned abandoned hall-houses into barns in other areas. The elaboration of the arch-braced crucks is also incompatible with this theory.

In 1657 the house was brought up to date by the provision of a two-and-a-half-storey parlour wing, with chamber and attic above, separated by a narrow bay, containing stairs and possibly a small pantry, from the east wall of the hall. As already noted, this was either an altogether new wing, or the rebuilding of the earlier service end. The additions are dated by a crudely-inscribed stone introduced into the earlier stone walling over the entrance. The new wing is of characteristic 17th-century form, with angle fireplace in the parlour and mullioned oak windows, of ovolo section on the front elevation and gable, and flat splay on the rear face—an economy which, together with the retention of part of the old structure, indicates a considerably lower social status of the owner as compared with his wealthy neighbour who three years earlier had erected the completely new house, now called Poplars Farm (Fig. 30), a short distance away, with fine stone mullions on the front, oak mullions being altogether relegated to the rear elevation. The old hall now became the lower end of Chinners Farm, and was not turned to very effective account. A portion was cut off to make a kitchen with a bedroom over, and the rest used as a service room or dairy, later being roughly ceiled over, the loft above being disused and accessible even now only by a ladder. More recently the ground-floor partition in the old hall has been removed further west and renewed in brick.

A number of other houses have been recorded which have early features of structure and which may be interpreted as having been single-storey halls. The majority of these buildings are more closely related in their architectural details to the regional character of the 17th century and will be considered in the following chapter. There are however two further houses which merit inclusion with these earlier hall-houses primarily on account of their unusually fine medieval details, which relate them more closely to these earlier antecedents.

In the south-west corner of the hamlet of Balscott[1] are two houses

[1] 'Balscot, a hamlet to Wroxton. . . . It was not until the 28th April 1821 that the burial ground of Balscot was consecrated; previously to which they were interred at Wroxton. There are in this place some interesting specimens of domestic architecture' (Joseph Skelton, *The Antiquities of Oxfordshire*, 1823).

which provide evidence of medieval work in doors and windows of considerable architectural distinction. The names of both houses— Priory Farm and Grange Farm—suggest an early ecclesiastical association, which may either account for this quality of their details, or may more recently have derived from these features. The Priory of Wroxton, a house of Canons Regular of St. Augustine, was founded early in the 13th century by Michael Belet, of a family connected with Beletscot or Balscot, a chapelry relating to Wroxton. When the monastery was dissolved under an act of 1535, its possessions included:

Balnescot. Tenement, lands, cottage and mill £6 18s. 4d.[1] Subsequently the buildings of the monastery were sold by the king's officers, and such specific items as 'Item, The ffrater howse on both sides . . . Item, The dorter, with the roffe thereof',[2] are listed in a subsequent sale to Thomas Pope, Esq. The possibility of items from this source featuring in buildings at Balscott must be considered in the examination of these two dwellings. Throughout the region many medieval features, particularly doors and windows, have been recorded as fragments incorporated usefully or purely decoratively in later houses. A fine 13th-century doorway of ecclesiastical character forms the entrance to a 17th-century house standing behind the Joiner's Arms in Bloxham, and a 13th-century window can be seen in the gable of another house in Balscott, near the church, almost certainly re-used. The dissolution of such monasteries as Wroxton, Chacombe and Clattercote, all within the Banbury Region, must have provided in the 16th century abundant material of this nature, providing it could be transported, and this fact renders more difficult the dating and elucidation of houses containing such features.

The two farms at Balscott both exhibit features, apart from the doors and windows already noted, which indicate an origin in the 16th century or earlier, clearly existing before the main period of regional building in stone, and as each includes a medieval window to light a hall of more than single-storey height, they are included for consideration in this chapter.

Priory Farm (Figs. 8, 9) is a large two-unit house with through-passage, set back from the road, from which it is almost screened by farm buildings. It now comprises a hall, subdivided to provide a small service room at the west end, and a parlour, the latter having been formerly the service end, raised and improved in the 18th

---

[1] Caley and Ellis's *Dugdale*, quoted in Beesley, *History of Banbury*, p. 84.
[2] Warton, *Life of Sir Thomas Pope*, pp. 368–73. The present mansion of Wroxton Abbey, built on the site of the priory, was completed in 1618, and incorporates part of the original monastic structure.

century. The broad through-passage is flanked on either side by stone walls, and the door to the service room is almost centrally placed, both these features being noted in other houses of 16th-century date. The hall, now subdivided by a stud partition, was formerly of unusually large size, measuring 17 feet wide by 19 feet long to the breast of the fireplace which backs on to the passage. On the rear wall of the house, near the centre of the south wall of the hall, is a window of four lights, over 6 feet in height, with square head and label mould with dropped ends, the mullions, now missing, having been of hollow-moulded section. The heads of the lights are filled with fine curvilinear tracery of ecclesiastical character, which can not be later in date than the 14th or early 15th century. The window, which has a cambered rear-arch, is now blocked, apart from a small opening to the end room, but the infilling indicates that the window was at one time open, and has not been planted on the surface of the wall as a decorative feature. In the north wall of the hall, the entrance front, are two flat-splay stone-mullioned windows of 17th-century date, the wall above having been raised and two wood-framed windows inserted, probably in the 18th century, with smaller openings above.

The main entrance to the through-passage on the north eleva-tion is by a fine doorway, almost 4 feet wide, with four-centred arched head contained within a square label of medieval section with dropped ends and enriched lozenge-shaped stops. The spandrels are filled with quatrefoil enrichments, with a central vine-leaf decoration, and the deeply recessed profile of the jambs would agree with a date in the late 15th or early 16th centuries. The doorway retains an early, heavy-planked door, secured internally by an oak drawbar sliding in the wall. This doorway is of particular interest as affording a medieval precedent for forms which appear within the region in the late 16th- and 17th-century building period, the arch mouldings gradually developing into more classical profiles. The lozenge-shaped stops become very characteristic of 17th-century work in this area and throughout the adjacent areas of the limestone belt.

There is another medieval window of two lights and smaller dimensions in the front wall of the parlour, the jamb mouldings resembling those of the adjacent doorway. The small window has been altered and may originally have contained arched heads to the two lights. The south wall of the parlour has been completely re-built in mid-18th century, with sliding-sash windows of early Georgian proportions and character on two storeys, the rear entrance

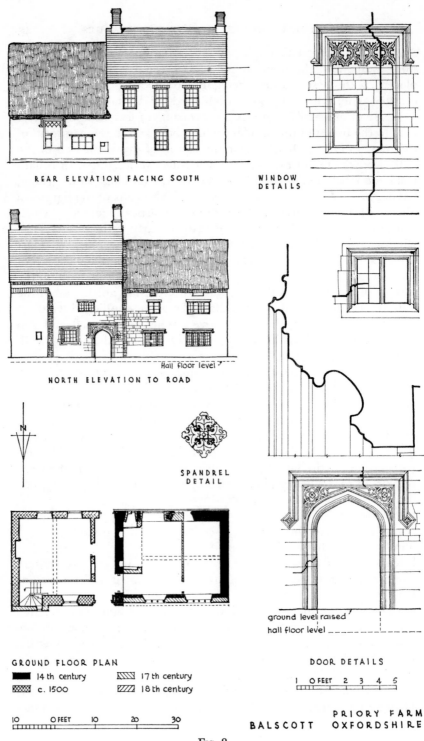

REAR ELEVATION FACING SOUTH

WINDOW
DETAILS

NORTH ELEVATION TO ROAD

Hall floor level

SPANDREL
DETAIL

N

ground level raised
hall floor level

GROUND FLOOR PLAN

■ 14th century   ▨ 17th century
▧ c. 1500   ▨ 18th century

10 O FEET 10   20   30

DOOR DETAILS

1 O FEET 2 3 4 5

PRIORY FARM
BALSCOTT OXFORDSHIRE

FIG. 8.

18th century roof

internal profiles of late 15th century window and door on North front shown by broken lines

former ground-floor

later floor and truss

floor inserted in 17th century

SECTION LOOKING SOUTH

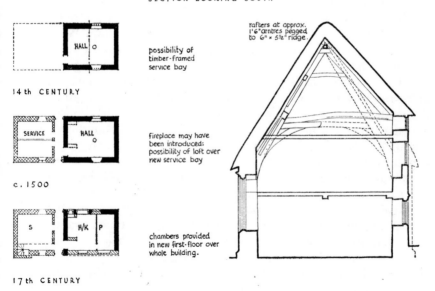

HALL o

14th CENTURY

SERVICE   HALL o

c. 1500

S   H/K │ P

17th CENTURY

possibility of timber-framed service bay

fireplace may have been introduced: possibility of loft over new service bay

chambers provided in new first-floor over whole building.

rafters at approx. 1'6" centres pegged to 6" × 5½" ridge.

HISTORICAL DEVELOPMENT

10   0 FEET 10   20   30   40   50

5   0 FEET   5   10   15

SECTION THROUGH HALL

PRIORY FARM
BALSCOTT   OXFORDSHIRE

FIG. 9.

to the through-passage also having been modified at this time. At this period, also, fine bolection-moulded fireplaces were added in the newly formed parlour, and in the chamber over. The stair, contained in a rectangular projection on the north front, is probably part of the 17th-century improvements. The first floors of the two portions of the house appear to be of different dates, that over the hall being supported on a spine-beam in the earlier manner, the floor over the parlour being of 18th-century date with joists spanning from a transverse beam. Until reconstructed in 1959, the roof over the hall retained its thatch, its structure being basically medieval although extensively altered in the 17th century. The roof over the parlour block was raised and renewed in the 18th century, being finished with blue slates. It is apparent that it was then intended to reroof the whole of the house at this level, and to extend the Georgian fenestration across the complete south elevation.

In attempting to determine the original form of this house, a number of factors invite particular consideration. The structure represents not less than four well-defined building periods, it being possible to attribute work to the 14th, late 15th or early 16th, 17th and 18th centuries. The unusually fine quality of the architectural detail inevitably invites consideration of the theory of the re-use of architectural details from an ecclesiastical source, perhaps Wroxton Priory. Some support for this view is found in the obvious re-use in a first-floor chamber of a fragment of a finely-carved cresting mould, clearly of ecclesiastical origin; this has, however, evidently been more recently introduced as an improvised prop to a beam. The Perpendicular doorway, unusually fine for this class of work, appears truncated and there are signs of adjacent rebuilding, suggesting that this detail may have been reset; this can be equally well-explained by the alteration in levels, the ground level at the north front now being as much as 16 inches above the hall floor, whilst there has clearly been considerable rebuilding of the north wall.

Against such an explanation is the very homogeneous character of the hall, with its surviving great window, walls of medieval thickness, and its roof also of medieval character. This most clearly refutes the suggestion of earlier details being re-used in a later structure, and it must be accepted that the present hall represents an original structure of the 14th century. The fireplace is clearly later than this date and the hall probably measured 23 feet 4 inches long by 17 feet wide by 25 feet high to the ridge, with walls averaging 2 feet 6 inches in thickness, battered on the inner face and having an external plinth, still to be seen on the south front. The structure was of two unequal bays, the single truss being placed off-centre presumably to avoid the great window, which is placed nearer to the west end of the hall; there may well have been a similar window on the north wall, which has however been completely rebuilt, to a reduced thickness, in the 17th century.

There is no clear evidence for the position of the original doorway, presumably placed at the lower end, on the east or north walls.

It remains to consider the original function fulfilled by this 14th-century structure, which may possibly have extended eastwards on the site of the present parlour. In the absence of documentary evidence, it was first suggested that the building was originally a chapel, with priest's house adjoining, to explain the fine character of door and window. Windows of almost identical character are to be seen in the parish church of St. Mary Magdalene at the other end of the village, on the north side of the nave, and it seems probable that Priory Farm was erected at the same time as the 14th-century rebuilding of the church. In considering this possibility, a close parallel within the region is provided in the 13th-century chapel at Little Dassett in Burton Dassett parish, Warwickshire; this comprises a chapel of similar width but greater length, 17 feet by 36 feet, to which a two-storeyed single-cell priest's dwelling was added in the 17th century.[1] Notwithstanding this general similarity of form, there is architecturally no other evidence of ecclesiastical use beyond the quality of the window, nor is there any documentary evidence for a chapel at Balscott. Windows of similar type are not exceptional in important domestic work of the period, good examples being found in Northamptonshire at Norborough Manor, and also in the priest's house at Muchelney in Somerset. The architectural evidence therefore indicates that Priory Farm was built in the 14th century as a domestic structure, erected by the monastery of Wroxton in connection with its possessions at Balscott, possibly as a dwelling for a priest or other agent of the Priory. Beyond the form, structure and detail of the 14th-century hall, as already described, the plan of the original house cannot be determined, there being no evidence of an original service wing to the east of the hall. The extensive soot blackening of the hall roof timbers, however, gives unmistakable evidence of an open fire within the hall before the present hearth was introduced.

Within the period under consideration, the house went through a second important phase of building in c. 1500, when it was enlarged and modernized by the addition (or improvement) of an eastern extension to provide service rooms separated from the hall by a

---

[1] These buildings are described in Chapter VIII.

E

through passage to which the fine Perpendicular style doorway gave entrance. The original north and east walls of this block are again of 2 feet 6 inches in thickness, and include the two-light medieval window already noted. A stone wall divided the passage from the service end, and there are indications of two doorways from the passage, giving access to separate buttery and pantry. It is probable that a chamber was provided within the roof space over the service-rooms.

It is not clear whether at this period the fireplace was added within the hall, in the manner already proposed for this interim period of development at Chinners Farm, or whether this represents part of the extensive 17th-century rebuilding to be described later.[1] The extent of this rebuilding suggests that the structure had by then deteriorated seriously, requiring the complete rebuilding of the north wall of the hall together with the north side of the roof. It seems probable that with the dissolution of the monastery in 1537, Priory Farm fell into disuse and disrepair for approximately one hundred years.

The structure of the hall roof has unusual features (Pl. 7a), un-fortunately obscured by succeeding alterations; the raising of the north wall in the 17th century involved the reconstruction of the roof on that side at a lower pitch. The principal of the almost centrally-placed truss survives on the south wall, and is basically of raised cruck form, the flat blade with curving foot, similar to other examples described earlier, being seated within the wall 9 feet 6 inches above ground level. There is a lower collar with arched braces, and wind-braces from the foot of the blade to the underside of the lower purlin. At this point, similarity to other examples ceases, the cruck blade terminating 6 inches above the collar, and the heavy purlin resting directly on the end of the blade, being scarf-jointed over this point of support. It is possible that the blade is tenoned into the purlin, although this could not be determined. Above this purlin level, the pattern of the roof is altered, secondary principals springing from the purlin itself at two interim points, to divide the length of the hall from west wall to chimney breast into two approximately equal bays. These principals have upper collars, and support upper purlins with curved wind-braces, and a ridge seated on a saddle. This quite unique form of construction, together

---

[1] The subsequent history of Priory Farm is further reviewed in Chapter X in relation to the general process of alteration and improvement in the region. A number of other buildings are there noted which have assumed classical façades whilst retaining earlier features on the rear elevation.

with the very arbitrary spacing of the bays both above and below purlin level, make it difficult to accept this as a homogeneous construction. It is nevertheless possible that the unusual form of the roof was dictated by the placing of the large traceried windows, raised 'base-crucks' being placed off-centre to avoid these openings, and the bay-spacing being amended above purlin level by the use of secondary principals. The Tithe Barn at Frocester in Gloucestershire, built by Abbot John de Carnage (1284–1306) affords some precedent for such a structure, having raised base-crucks of this type finishing at the level of a collar, with secondary principals between the base-crucks rising from the lower purlin, the wind-braces being similarly arranged. If, however, the roof at Priory Farm does represent two periods of building, the alteration to the original raised-cruck structure must itself have been carried out before 1550, and may possibly relate to the second building period already described. All timbers of the roof, before the 17th-century work, appear to be equally soot-blackened. The extensive rebuilding of the roof, and a lack of complete accessibility to the structure unfortunately precluded a more positive elucidation before it was modernized in 1959.

Some support for this solution to the problems of Priory Farm can be found in the study of *Grange Farm, Balscott* (Fig. 10; Pl. 2*c*, *d*) which lies almost opposite to the building already described. The house presents very similar problems in that it also possesses a fine and unusually large four-centred arched entrance on the south elevation, and on the same front a large hall window of two lights with stone mullion and transom and Perpendicular tracery contained within a square head (Pl. 2*c–d*). Part of the head and jamb of a similar window, widened at a later date, survives on the same front, with a four-centred arched doorway of simpler design on the north front. The details on the south front are of late 15th- or early 16th-century date, while the north doorway and parlour fireplace would also agree with a date in the 16th century.[1] The difference between the details of the north and south fronts is accentuated by an apparent difference in stone, the south door and hall-window being in a very dark brown stone which has weathered badly, whilst the north door has been unaffected. This may, however, be explained by difference in exposure. The unusual proportion of the transomed window, in which, moreover, the external jamb moulding is not developed in the sill, again introduces the possibility of the re-use of details, although here their character is essentially domestic.

[1] Doors and fireplaces of this simple, sub-medieval type are also common in 17th-century work.

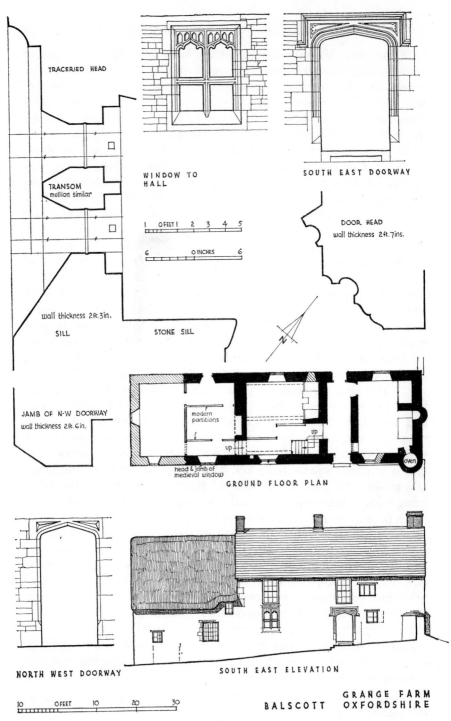

TRACERIED HEAD

WINDOW TO HALL

SOUTH EAST DOORWAY

TRANSOM mullion similar

DOOR HEAD wall thickness 2 ft. 7 ins.

1 O FEET 1 2 3 4 5

6 O INCHES 6

wall thickness 2 ft. 3 in.
SILL

STONE SILL

N

JAMB OF N-W DOORWAY
wall thickness 2 ft. 6 in.

modern partitions

up

up

head & jamb of medieval window

GROUND FLOOR PLAN

oven

NORTH WEST DOORWAY

SOUTH EAST ELEVATION

10 O FEET 10 20 30

GRANGE FARM
BALSCOTT OXFORDSHIRE

FIG. 10.

It seems probable, however, that Grange Farm was a dwelling of some social significance erected in the first half of the 16th century. Its plan provides a link with the yeoman houses to be considered in the next chapter, introducing the three-unit plan of hall, service and parlour. The disposition of the house reverses the more normal arrangement of placing the service rooms at the lower end of the site—here the parlour being at the lowest point, its floor level being below that of the hall from which it is approached by a flight of steps. The broad entrance passage is flanked on either side by stone walls, and there are indications of two openings into the service bay suggesting that here, as at Priory Farm, there were separate rooms for pantry and buttery. These were later formed into a kitchen, probably late in the 17th century, when a fireplace and oven were added. The hall fireplace, backing onto the passage, may also be an addition. The transomed window already noted lights the hall, the first floor cutting across its head. Internally this window reveals no evidence of re-use or alteration, being rebated for shutters with sockets for shutter drawbars. A similar window also lit the parlour, which is provided with a fireplace with arched stone head of similar detail to the north door. Walls throughout average 2 feet 5 inches in thickness, with the internal batter associated with early masonry in this region. The joists of the first floor over the hall span from spine-beam to lateral wall-beams, instead of being built into the side walls, the significance of which in relation to early or inserted floors is discussed in the next chapter. It may be noted, however, that this method of construction is adopted for the floor later introduced into the hall at Leadenporch House. It is clear that in this building, the hall was originally open to the roof, possibly with chambers over the parlour and service rooms. Successive rebuildings make it difficult to determine whether the house as described was of one build, or whether the difference in character of the architectural details justifies the theory that the parlour was added to an original two-unit house, the first floor, and hall and kitchen fireplaces, together with the north door being introduced at the same time. It is possible that the fragment of medieval window in the south wall of the parlour may have come from the north wall of the hall, which has been largely rebuilt and re-fenestrated. There is, however, no clear indication in the masonry of such an addition.

Built probably at about the same time as the second stage of building was taking place at Priory Farm, the name of the house suggests a similar explanation for the unusual quality of its architecture—a dwelling erected by Wroxton Priory to farm lands in

Balscott. The subsequent history of the two houses is also very similar. There was further rebuilding in the 17th century, as already suggested, with a final modernization in the 18th century. At that time the walls of hall and kitchen were raised in height to provide more lofty chambers with sliding-sash windows on the first floor under a slated roof, and the present stair was introduced, probably replacing a 17th-century stair in the same position. At the same time, the building was extended beyond the parlour to provide an extra service room at the lowest end of the site.

The plan, structure and architectural detail of these buildings present certain precedents which can be clearly related to subsequent regional developments. The planning of these earlier houses, from *c.* 1300 to mid-16th century, follows the basic later medieval hall-house pattern with screens passage and open hearth, lacking a separate solar unless one is provided over the lower end. The screens passage, outside the hall from Leadenporch House onwards, becomes a stone-walled unit at the end of the 15th century with the introduction of a fireplace on the gable of the lower end of the hall, before the provision of upper floors over the hall was contemplated. The pattern is that which has been established in Monmouthshire and elsewhere as the accepted domestic plan in upland regions. It is probable that the manor houses, in which the hall had special functions, would always have solars, until 1300 either completely separate or over the service wing, and later at first-floor level at the upper end of the hall. Manor Farm at Cottisford, six miles beyond the eastern boundary of the region, presents an early stage in this pattern, with its suggestion of vertical development in the tradition of the military keep, the hall and solar being at first-floor level. The possible relationship of this plan-type to a number of houses limited to single unit plan, although otherwise of some architectural quality, is considered in Chapter VIII.

It is in the structure of walls and roof that the most interesting regional characteristics are to be noted, particularly in the evolution of the raised cruck trusses, in association with stone walling. The early forms noted at Leadenporch House and Chinners Farm, as well as those of the tithe barns described in Chapter II, find counterparts in houses built in the transitional period in the second half of the 16th century—to be considered in the following chapter—and provide a link with forms of roofing adopted in the regional building period of the 17th century.

Although little survives of domestic craftsmanship in stone or wood of the medieval period, there is evidence of considerably greater richness than is found in the 17th century in this neighbour-hood. The houses so far considered are, however, almost all of greater social significance than the yeoman dwellings of the regional period and their character and detailing is naturally more elaborate than in later dwellings of the vernacular tradition.

CHAPTER IV

THE YEOMAN HOUSE IN THE 16TH CENTURY

THE houses considered in Chapter III are the most important precursors of the later yeoman house which can be related by aspects of plan, structure or detail (at Leadenporch House, all three) to the medieval period. Apart from these houses, a small number of dwellings have been found which, whilst more closely related to the 17th-century regional style, nevertheless reveal common characteristics, particularly of structure, which place them earlier than the main period of regional building activity in stone. Such examples are again few, and their examination is of particular interest in further establishing the immediate antecedents of the 17th-century house, as a link between the medieval hall and the later developments of the yeoman plan.

The style of minor domestic architecture which now appears as characteristic of the region emerged towards the end of the 16th century, and by 1600 had reached an established regional form which was to evolve on a more obvious pattern throughout the 17th century under the increasing influence of Renaissance culture and improved social conditions. The rise of the yeoman farmer to wealth and social importance has already been noted; and his earliest stone dwellings of which remains survive fall within the period of the single-storey hall, which appears to have persisted until the middle of the 16th century. The dissolution of the monasteries, the decline in the manorial estates, together with the demand for more food to feed growing urban populations, with consequent increase in the price of corn as well as of wool, promoted the wealth and status of the farming community in the 16th century. It is not however until the 17th century that this enhanced status finds full architectural expression. The Renaissance practice of dating buildings reflects the increasing importance of the yeoman and husbandman, and his pride in his new permanent house caused him to inscribe his initials, frequently coupled with those of his wife, on a stone with the date of the erection of the building. The earliest date recorded in the region is 1579, at Northend, but the beginnings of the new stone style can be dated from at latest the middle of the 16th century.

The next group of buildings to be considered comprises houses of yeomen or husbandmen erected in the transitional period at the middle of the 16th century. All have undergone modification in later periods, and in many cases this has so obscured the original form of the house that the plan cannot be determined with confidence. Dating presents further problems in that the earliest structural forms, which are the principal distinguishing characteristic of this interim phase, may in certain cases merely represent archaistic practices associated with buildings of somewhat lower social class.

By 1550 the single-storey hall generally had been superseded in most parts of the country in the upper classes of building, and the yeoman dwellings quickly followed this improvement.[1] The introduction of the wall fireplace in place of the open hearth or brazier—not an innovation, for it was known from the 11th century in castles and first-floor halls—removed the major obstacle to the introduction of upper floors which soon became general, except in the poorer dwellings. The upper floor was at first built partly within the roof space as a loft or attic, lit by dormer windows or windows in the gables, and in many cases the floor was over part of the building only. The 'one-and-a-half' storey height, when associated with early forms of roof structure, is further evidence of early date, although this height is found in buildings of lower social scale—the later cottages—to the present century. The windows to the first floor were simply projected half their height above the eaves level, and the thatch swept over them. Gabled dormers, with mullioned windows in stone, to light the first floor are unknown in the region, although a common feature of the Cotswolds. Full dormers are at all times infrequent, and, where they appear, relate to the attics above the two principal floors in larger 17th-century houses of two-and-a-half-storey height.

The plan form already noted as developing in the first part of the 16th century from the hall-house, is further developed towards the full 17th-century plan; the through entrance passage with service-room and hall becomes general, whilst a third apartment, the ground-floor parlour, serving both as bedroom and withdrawing room, is added in the larger houses.

Two houses which conform to this early type of yeoman house were demolished in *Kings Sutton, Northamptonshire* (Fig. 11) in 1956, being recorded in detail whilst being dismantled. The evidence of early date in both buildings is structural, and it is interesting to note

---

[1] Great halls continued to be built until the end of the century, that at Kirby Hall, Northants, dating from 1570–5, having ovolo mullions to the tall windows. This is one of the first great houses to incorporate Renaissance details in a formal elevation.

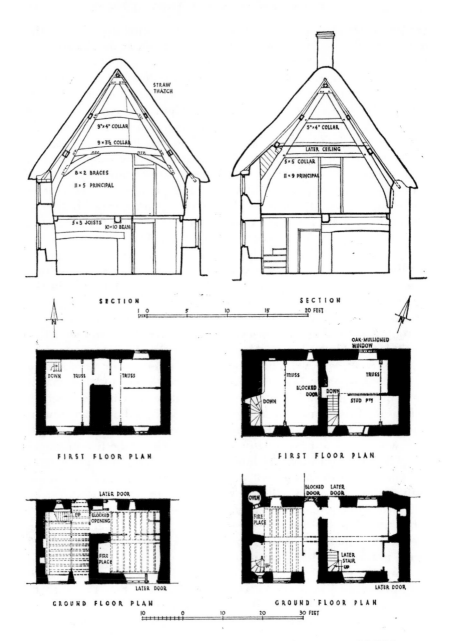

STRAW THATCH

9" × 4" COLLAR

9 × 3½ COLLAR

8 × 2 BRACES

11 × 5 PRINCIPAL

5 × 3 JOISTS

10 × 10 BEAM

5" × 4" COLLAR

LATER CEILING

5 × 5 COLLAR

11 × 9 PRINCIPAL

OAK MULLIONED WINDOW

SECTION   SECTION

1 0   5   10   15   20 FEET

N

DOWN   TRUSS   TRUSS

TRUSS   TRUSS

BLOCKED DOOR

DOWN   DOWN

STUD PTN

FIRST FLOOR PLAN   FIRST FLOOR PLAN

LATER DOOR

UP

BLOCKED OPENING

FIRE PLACE

LATER DOOR

BLOCKED DOOR   LATER DOOR

OVEN

FIRE PLACE

LATER STAIR UP

UP

LATER DOOR

GROUND FLOOR PLAN   GROUND FLOOR PLAN

10   0   10   20   30 FEET

TWO HOUSES AT KINGS SUTTON NORTHANTS

FIG. 11.

the parallel between the truss forms of these houses and those of the barns already described, which ante-date the domestic buildings by not less than 150 years.

The first of these dwellings was a small, thatched structure measuring 29 feet by 16 feet internally, with through-passage separating hall from a narrow service-room, the hall fireplace backing onto the passage. The rubble walls averaged 2 feet 8 inches in thickness, reducing irregularly at first-floor level, and the roof was supported on two trusses which divided the house into three almost equal bays averaging 9 feet 6 inches, the central stack not affecting the spacing. The form of the truss closely resembled that at the Swalcliffe barn, on a much reduced scale, the principals measuring 11 by 5 inches, well finished, matched and chamfered, with curving feet shallowly seated in the stone wall just above the present floor level. The ridge was supported on a saddle joining the blades, and there were two collars, the lower being arch-braced, all joints being mortised-and-tenoned and pegged (Pl. 6b). The stair was in the corner of the service room, but was clearly of more recent date, and it is probable that an earlier stair was built against the centre of the west wall where there survived the lower chamfered jambs of an opening or recess 6 feet wide. The screen partition had disappeared, but the narrow 4-inch wide head-beam remained in situ, its chamfer being stopped against the original door posts, centrally placed in the screen. The central position of the service door here, as at Priory Farm, Balscott, was itself an early feature, the door being at one side of the building in later houses. A difference was noted in the first-floor construction, that over the service-room appearing to be of earlier date, with heavy and closely spaced rafters, averaging 7 inches by 3½ inches laid flat, spanning longitudinally from fireplace wall over the screen to a wall-beam adjacent to the west gable. The floor over the hall also had characteristics which place it before the general practice of the 17th century. It was more finely constructed, with a heavy spine-beam splayed and moulded, with decorative stops to the chamfer, and 5-inch by 3-inch joists of similar section spanning from spine-beam to beams set against the lateral walls. The purlins appeared to have been renewed, and the rafters were rough poles, with no trace of a wall-plate, the rafter feet being built into the stonework. Courses of stone slate survived at the eaves, underneath the later thatch, and the close spacing of the trusses indicated that the roof was originally slated.

On the upper floor, the house was divided by what was probably an original partition flanking the stack, in the form of a half truss infilled with mud plastered on wattles. The other first-floor walls were plastered stud partitions and probably were later, although still of some antiquity. The windows of the house had been completely renewed and additional doors added to convert the dwelling into two cottages, linked in a later terrace of similar buildings.

The structure of this house gave evidence of 16th-century date, and the plan form had not been materially altered. The difference between the first floors of the two apartments, together with the well-finished arched-braced trusses, showed that the hall was originally of one storey only, open to the roof, with a loft over the service room, perhaps to provide a solar or bedroom, terminating at the original partition noted against the stack. A ladder presumably would give access to this upper chamber. At the end of the 16th century a floor was inserted over the hall, the use of wall beams to receive the ends of the joists simplifying the construction. At this time, or later in the 17th century, a stair would be added on the rear wall adjacent to the chimney stack.

The resemblance between truss forms of this house and the Swalcliffe barn finds a counterpart in a similarity between those of the second house to be noted at Kings Sutton and the Enstone crucks. This house was larger than the first, but also comprised two rooms with through-passage, the rubble walls again averaging 2 feet 8 inches in thickness and the roof being thatched. The truss spacing was very arbitrary, unless a central truss or chimney stack is assumed to have been removed either during the 17th-century alterations or when the house was converted into two cottages in the 19th century. The trusses spanned 16 feet and were similar to those already described, but without arch-braces. There were curved windbraces springing from behind the foot of the principal in the southeast corner of the house, which appeared to be simply embedded in the wall and not secured to the roof structure. These certainly were not original, but probably inserted to stiffen the weakness in the roof caused by the removal of the central truss or support. Here again there was no wall-plate for securing the ends of the rafters.

The evidence of roof and wall structure places the building within the second half of the 16th century, but the plan as existing in 1956, with fireplaces incorporating ovens on the gable walls, was that of the late 17th century, and it would seem that the house was drastically modernized at that time when both fireplaces were introduced. There were further alterations at the end of the 18th century when this house, originally no doubt a dwelling of importance, sank still further in social grade by being converted into two cottages, a second stair being added in the hall. Subsequently the building was linked in a terrace of cottages, the adjoining cottage being dated 1833.

These alterations had so altered the plan of the building that it is not possible now to restore its original form with any certainty. The first floors cannot be distinguished in date, apart from there being a wall-beam in the service-room, receiving the ends of the joists. The incongruity of the late form and position of the two hearths, in conjunction with the obviously early structure, and the unlikely possibility of a central masonry stack having been altogether removed, supports the theory that this may have been originally a single-storeyed dwelling of two units, with screens passage in its present position and an open fireplace in the hall. Truss spacing, allowing for a missing central frame removed at a later date, is 12 feet, with reduced bays at either end. The western truss is infilled with mud plastered on heavy, chamfered studs, and this partition may have defined the original solar occupying part of the floor over the service. Unfortunately the evidence is inadequate to substantiate this theory, the trusses having been whitened, and any signs of smoke blackening thereby obscured. The alternative suggestion of a hall fireplace backing on the present cross passage, as in the first house in Kings Sutton, would imply the later removal of this feature, and the re-building of a new stack on each gable—a less probable sequence. The house cannot therefore be securely fitted into the sequence of plan development, but remains an important example of 16th-century structure.

Near the original centre of *Bloxham*, in the neighbourhood of *Tank Lane*, a number of houses survive which present features prior to the 17th century, and may again represent a subsequent stage in this sequence of plan and structural development before the emergence of the full regional style. The most important of these is the house called *Blue Gates* in King Street (Fig. 12; Pl. 5a), where the original form of a substantial 16th-century house has survived with very little alteration. The plan introduces the full three-unit yeoman arrangement, with through entrance onto which the hall fireplace backs, flanked by a service-room at the lower end and a parlour at the upper, which has a second fireplace also with a four-centred stone head. The original entrance was from King Street, along which the house lies, by a fine four-centred arched doorway with medieval jamb mouldings and spandrel decoration, closely allied to that described at Priory Farm, Balscott. This entrance was closed in the 18th century, and the doorway rebuilt in the middle of the east wall.

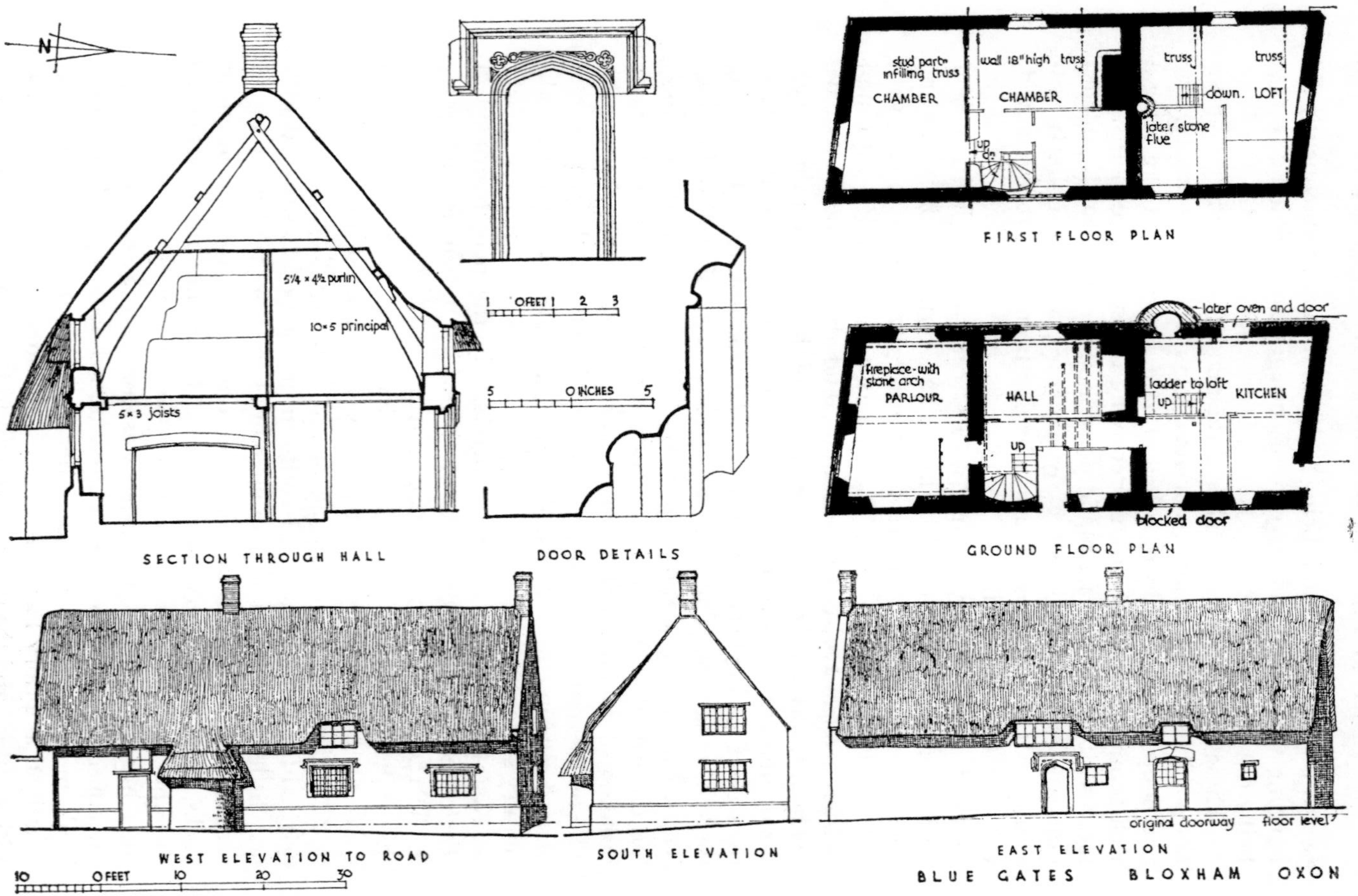

FIRST FLOOR PLAN

truss   truss
down. LOFT

truss   later stone flue

wall 18" high truss

stud parttn
infilling truss

CHAMBER   CHAMBER

up

GROUND FLOOR PLAN

later oven and door

ladder to loft
KITCHEN

up

blocked door

HALL

up

fireplace with stone arch

PARLOUR

SECTION THROUGH HALL

5¼ × 4½ purlin

10 × 5 principal

5 × 3 joists

DOOR DETAILS

OFEET 1   2   3

5   0 INCHES   5

SOUTH ELEVATION

EAST ELEVATION

original doorway   floor level?

BLUE GATES   BLOXHAM   OXON

WEST ELEVATION TO ROAD

OFEET 10   20   30

FIG. 12.

The rear entrance doorway, now blocked, also has some architectural pretension, with a stone-arched head, simply chamfered. The walls of the house are again thicker than the 17th-century average, measuring 30 inches and reducing to the eaves, with a plinth on the road front only. Ground-floor windows, now altered, were provided with flat-splay stone mullions; this is a form that cannot be dated with any accuracy for its use appears to extend from the end of the medieval period to the 19th century within the region, almost without intermission, and contemporary with more distinctive profiles. The label mould to windows and doorway is, however, clearly related to medieval precedent. The dormers to the first floor, partly contained in the roof space, are comparatively modern.

The roof principals once more are of the raised cruck derivation, of flat squared section, 10 by 5 inches at the foot, with a single collar, and are regularly spaced at 14-foot centres, ignoring the intrusion of the chimney breast. The apex of the blades, as revealed in the service-room, presents a departure from the method previously noted, the blades being crossed and pegged to receive the ridge-pole in the intersection, corresponding to the general practice of the 17th century in the region. The purlins, moreover, are not housed into the blades but are pegged or supported by cleats.

The service-room is still open to the roof, but there are chambers over hall and parlour. The floor joists, chamfered, with moulded stops, span from spine-beam to longitudinal wall-beams in the manner already noted. Between hall and parlour is a stone cross-wall, which does not rise above first-floor level, being continued as a stud partition in the truss frame. The present staircase is of later date, being partly set into the thickness of the wall at the upper end of the hall, adjoining the parlour. This position for the stair is more widely adopted in the second half of the 17th century, probably because of its relationship to the cellar introduced below the parlour. The first-floor construction, together with the later windows to the first floor, suggests that the house may originally have been open to the roof, with the possible exception of a floor over the parlour, but it is more probable that Blue Gates represents an early stage in the introduction of an upper floor over the hall itself at a time in mid-16th century—when the earlier traditional features were still strong. The closing of the street door by the building of a large bread oven, at the same time bringing the main entrance onto the back of the house, are 18th-century features which will be considered later.

The *Joiner's Arms* (Fig. 82) provides a second example in Bloxham of a mid-16th-century yeoman's dwelling, offering an interesting comparison with Blue Gates, which it closely resembles in size, structure, plan and detail. It has, however, been more extensively modernized and the roof almost wholly renewed following a fire which destroyed the original thatched structure. The house is again of three ground-floor rooms, with a through-passage 5 feet 4 inches wide entered from the road front by a fine doorway with four-centred arch contained within a flat label with dropped ends, the spandrels having quatrefoil enrichments and the mouldings being of simple Perpendicular character. The detail of this doorway is very close to that at Blue Gates, but the much greater scale of the opening —4 feet 7 inches wide—finds a closer counterpart in the two houses at Balscott. The rear entrance, of equal width, has a heavy timber frame and lintel, much renewed. Walls are of unusually heavy construction, the front wall of 2 feet 6 inches thickness, whilst the rear wall averages 3 feet, reducing towards the top by an internal batter; and as further evidence of early date, the broad through-passage is flanked on either side by stone walls. Only two early windows survive, both at first-floor level, that on the entrance front over the hall being of three lights with flat-splay stone mullions and label, the rear window, now blocked, over the service end having three lights with oak mullions and lintel. Despite the complete renewal of the roof structure, now slated, the feet of the original raised crucks in certain cases remain in position built into the wall, as in the stair well, although cut off at eaves level. Here, as at Blue Gates, the first floor over the hall is supported on spine-beams and longitudinal wall beams, and the house presents similar problems. The hall fireplace, the first floor over the hall and the stair appear to be of one build, and it remains to determine whether these features belong to the original house, or whether they represent improvements to an original single-storey hall-house. It seems probable that the Joiner's Arms and Blue Gates both fall into this intermediate period of development already noted at mid-16th century, and that it was originally of 'one-and-a-half storey' height, with the possible exception of the service bay. There are fireplaces in the service room and parlour, completely modernized, but these presumably are later additions.

A counterpart to this dwelling is to be found nearby in *Sycamore Terrace, Tank Lane* (Fig. 80), which includes a number of houses of varying dates. The earliest dwellings in the terrace are two adjoining houses, one-and-a-half storeys high, with flat-splay stone mullions. The end house, of 17th-century date, will be considered in the following chapter, but the second building contains similar early structural features to those already noted, and can be safely placed in the 16th century if not earlier on the evidence of its structure alone. Here once again the terrace has undergone extensive alteration at several periods, finally being converted into cottages for weavers in the 19th century and broken up into smaller compartments, whilst in 1956 the whole group was completely modernized. The buildings were recorded whilst this last remodelling was in progress.

The medieval house appears to have been of three bays, the trusses at 9-foot centres spanning 17 feet 6 inches. One truss alone survives, its timbers well shaped and finished, with flat section principals curving at the feet, which spring from first-floor level. There is one chamfered collar, with small arch braces below, and two inclined queen-post struts above to the upper purlins, which in this case have been tenoned to the blades, possibly employing loose tenons, taken right through the principal. The apex had been altered but it seems probable that there was no ridge-beam. Windows with flat-splay stone mullions light the ground floor on both elevations, and on the street front there are also mullioned windows to the upper floor, which may be later. One of these is of more complex section, with ovolo-moulded reveals and a double splay to the mullion. The side walls of the house average 2 feet in thickness; the gable walls are almost 3 feet. There is no evidence of the original entrance, which may have been from the west gable, but there was clearly no entrance from the street front. The two stairs and the brick-built fireplaces date from the division of the house into cottages in the 19th century. No distinguishing features are recognizable in the first-floor construction, and all internal stud partitions are of 19th-century date. A sculptured stone slab, re-used in the flagged ground floor, has now been set into the road elevation.

The evidence is here too insubstantial to allow recovery of the original plan and this building is included mainly to provide further important evidence of early roof structure. The fine roof truss, with its arch-braces, is certainly of 16th-century date or earlier, and the presence of the braces makes it seem likely that it was built to be seen from an open hall. The absence of any sign of an original fireplace suggests that the hall may have been heated by an open hearth, but the truss has been plastered and any supporting evidence of soot incrustation thus removed or obscured. The adjoining two-unit house to the west is of one-and-a-half storeys, built early in the 17th century, and is considered in the next chapter. Whether the earlier building continued as an independent dwelling in the 17th century is not known, but it seems probable, from the absence of the fireplace,

F

that it served the later house as an upper end, or even as a farm build-ing. The extent of subsequent amendment, however, makes this largely a matter of conjecture.

Other evidence of this transitional period which preceded the building activity of the 17th century is even more fragmentary. Two further roof structures may be noted as providing an additional link between the raised crucks described earlier and the standard forms of roof truss employed in the 17th century. The roof of *Manor Farm, Cottisford, Oxfordshire* (Fig. 67-12; Pl. 6c), rebuilt in the late 16th century, is of interest in this context. The principals are here quite straight, rising from a tie-beam, but preserving the earlier treatment of the apex with a saddle mortised to the tops of the blades, with the squared ridge resting on edge in a notch cut to receive it. There is one collar at intermediate level, with inclined struts between tie and collar, and curved wind-braces are provided between the purlins. The trusses span 14 feet 6 inches, and the bay spacing averages 8 feet. The deeply moulded transverse beams of the first floor are also part of the late 16th-century rebuilding.

The roof of the older portion of the *Old Malthouse Cottage, Tad-marton* (Fig. 61) represents a similar development more clearly related to the raised crucks. Two periods of building are here indi-cated, the original nucleus being a single-room building of one-and-a-half-storey height, with walls of 2 feet 6 inches thickness in which survives one stone-mullioned window, the flat-splay mullions and label being of unusually heavy section. There is also an early oak-mullioned window in the chamber above. This room is divided into two bays by a central truss spanning 15 feet 6 inches, the blades being rather roughly shaped and chamfered, following an ogee curve and seated in the wall at eaves level. Two collars are provided, the lower at the level of the modern ceiling, whilst the apex is of the saddle type, raised by a triangular block to receive the squared ridge. The truss is therefore similar to those described at Kings Sutton and elsewhere, lacking only the curving feet to the blades.

The original plan again cannot be determined, assuming that this portion of the building originally stood alone, for there is no fireplace or stair within the room, and no evidence to indicate an open fire. In the 17th century the house was developed as a three-unit plan of one-and-a-half storeys, but there was still no communica-tion at attic level between the two parts of the house. The later development of this building is considered in Chapter X, p. 209.

Also in Tadmarton, in *Cotswold Cottage*, there is a single truss with the curving principals in a small single-unit house, now of one-and-a-half storeys, and distinguished by the addition of a particularly large bread-oven of circular form, projecting into the roadway and thatched. The house has been much altered and details of the roof obscured by a later ceiling.

Parish's Farmhouse, Hempton (Fig. 59) illustrates yet another example of raised cruck structure in a small thatched house of the same height, the extensive improvements of 17th-century date making it impossible to determine the original plan. The truss here is closed, with rough vertical studding, and spans 16 feet, the bay spacing apparently being 12 feet. There are no braces and the work is poor in character, the later ceiling at collar level obscuring details of the apex. It is probable that many such fragments of early structure may survive undetected in houses outwardly of later character.

The buildings described in this and the two previous chapters represent the most important surviving evidence which has been uncovered of the antecedents of the main 17th-century phase of the regional architecture, and are therefore of considerable importance, despite their all too fragmentary and rebuilt condition. The pattern of evolution of plan and structure alike moves clearly and logically from the period when dates first appear on buildings, and these buildings show the earlier stages of this pattern. It is therefore appropriate to summarize the evidence provided by these earlier structures before proceeding to the principal stage of regional building. The roof structure, the construction of first floors, and wall thicknesses, rather than evidence of plan or architectural detailing, have been the principal indications of mid-16th century or earlier build in all these dwellings.

The principle of the raised cruck has been established in Chapter II in relation to its first manifestations in the 14th century. In the 16th-century examples now considered, the applications and derivations of this form present an interim stage of development between the full cruck and the 17th-century roof truss. The roofs of the buildings described in this chapter can be considered in three groups in order of development, the two houses at Kings Sutton affording examples of the earliest type, very closely related to the 14th-century antecedents; whilst the houses at Bloxham and at Hempton in the second group, and thirdly the Cottisford and Tadmarton roofs, each represent succeeding steps in the progression towards the 17th-century trusses. All these roofs are shown in Figs. 66–7 in relation to later developments within the region.

The Kings Sutton houses retain the principals of curving shape, springing from first-floor level in the stone walls with the ridge seated

on a saddle. In the second group at Bloxham, both houses have similarly shaped trusses, but there is no saddle, the ridge at Blue Gates
being seated in the crossing of the principals in the manner adopted in
the 17th century. The third group has straight principals but retains
the earlier treatment of the apex, a difference noted at Cottisford being
the diagonal seating of the ridge. At Tadmarton the principals spring
from the walls themselves, but those at Cottisford—a full two-storey
building—spring from a tie-beam at the level of the first-floor ceiling,
and the roof trusses of the 17th century are related to both these
types, the height of the building being the determining factor.

Further variation in detail is also noted, as in the arrangement
and support of purlins, which are with only one exception continuous
over the trusses, being either housed into the backs of the blades or,
as at Blue Gates, supported by wooden cleats on the backs of the
principals to which they are also pegged.

The house in Sycamore Terrace provides a rare example of
practice associated with the Lowland Zone of England, the purlins—
now removed—being butted against the principal rafters and supported by tenons. The principals here cross at the apex, but there is
no evidence of a ridge, and it seems probable that there was no
such member, a further indication of south-eastern practice. The
truss also appears to be of rather better finish than the others
described, of which the workmanship is generally rather rough,
members being approximately squared and roughly chamfered,
with pegs projecting unevenly.

Spans vary considerably, from 19 feet at Blue Gates, 17 feet 6
inches in Sycamore Terrace, 16 feet in both houses at Kings Sutton
and in that at Hempton, to 15 feet 6 inches at the Old Malthouse,
Tadmarton, the Cottisford roof being of course limited to the 14
feet 6 inches span of the earlier building. This factor appears to be
without chronological significance, the variation in size being at all
times primarily related to the social status of the house. The variations in bay size are, however, more informative. The Blue Gates
trusses are at 14-feet centres, supporting a thatched roof. At Kings
Sutton, the bay is reduced to 10-feet and 12-feet centres, Hempton
also being 12-feet, and at Cottisford—as in the earlier roof at Leadenporch House—it is only 8-feet, the roof now being finished with
modern slates. It is probable that these smaller bays were designed
for stone slates,[1] which as already noted have been discovered below

---

[1] These examples all occur in the fringe areas of the region, and were presumably originally roofed with the limestone 'presents' deriving from the oolitic
beds. Prior to the introduction of the Stonesfield slates, probably at the end of the

the thatch in the first dwelling at Kings Sutton. Apart from the later brace introduced at Kings Sutton, Cottisford Manor alone has wind-braces, of curved form.

The unusual treatment of the first-floor joists, spanning from a spine-beam to narrow beams set against the external wall, or as noted at Kings Sutton, spanning between cross walls, is peculiar to the earlier houses, and the use of wall-beams in many cases may be regarded as an indication of inserted floors. In these later buildings, however, it is more likely that this represents an early stage in floor building practice, and overcomes the problem of building small joist ends into the rubble masonry. It is also possible to see in this practice an extension of the preceding timber-framed tradition, framing the floor up as a complete unit in itself with the minimum number of supports from the crude and heavily built rubble walling. The heavy, flat, floor joists at Kings Sutton are probably of early date, and there is little evidence of enrichment. Beams at Cottisford are more heavily moulded on the splays, with good stops, than is elsewhere found in the region, which in the 17th century at least is not distinguished by good wood-work. Original partitions are few, and also give little indication of any sound timber tradition. The infilling of the half-truss noted at Kings Sutton is of heavy mud plaster on wattles and appears to be original work. Other partitions, as at Blue Gates and Hempton, are of light stud construction, the studs averaging 3 inches square, roughly chamfered and tenoned to light sill and head beams, and the whole continuously plastered over one side on split laths. The thickness of masonry walling is one of the surest indications of early date; the majority of these examples have rubble walls of 2 feet 6 inches in thickness or over, reducing to the eaves by an internal batter, comparing with the 22-inch thickness so constantly maintained from the end of the 16th century. Plinths have been noted at Priory Farm, Balscott and at Blue Gates, in both cases restricted to the main elevations.

The accurate determination of the original plan has generally presented difficulty because of later alterations, but there is sufficient evidence to trace the evolution from the previous sources. No further examples of the first-floor hall have been noted in this period; the Old Malthouse, Tadmarton, appears to have been originally a single room on plan, but there is no suggestion of vertical development. The through-passage plan is common to all houses of the period,

---

16th century, it is probable that thatch was the exclusive roofing material within the greater part of the region. (See also note 1, p. 232).

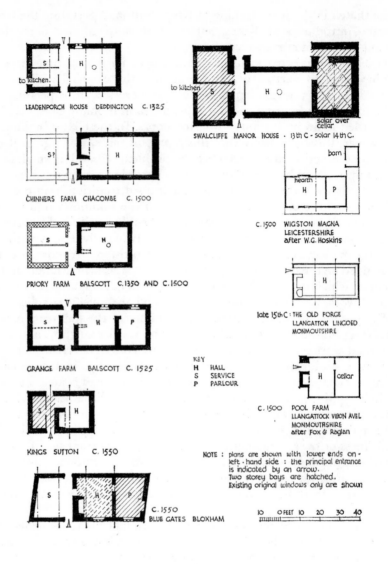

LEADENPORCH HOUSE DEDDINGTON C. 1325

SWALCLIFFE MANOR HOUSE · 13th C - Solar 14th C.

CHINNERS FARM CHACOMBE C. 1500

C. 1500 WIGSTON MAGNA
LEICESTERSHIRE
after W.G. Hoskins

PRIORY FARM BALSCOTT C. 1350 AND C. 1500

late 15th C : THE OLD FORGE
LLANGATTOK LINGOED
MONMOUTSHIRE

GRANGE FARM BALSCOTT C. 1525

KEY
H   HALL
S   SERVICE
P   PARLOUR

C. 1500 POOL FARM
LLANGATTOCK VIBON AVEL
MONMOUTSHIRE
after Fox & Raglan

KINGS SUTTON C. 1550

NOTE : plans are shown with lower ends on-
left - hand side : the principal entrance
is indicated by an arrow.
Two storey bays are hatched.
Existing original windows only are shown

C. 1550
BLUE GATES BLOXHAM

10 0 FEET 10   20   30   40

COMPARATIVE HALL PLANS
13th TO 16th CENTURIES

FIG. 13.

with a stone fireplace backing onto the passage—corresponding to the 'screens passage' of the manor-house—and with the addition at Blue Gates of a ground-floor parlour with its own fireplace. First floors are also being introduced, in all cases partly contained in the roof space, and lit presumably by small gable windows, although no original first-floor windows survive, with the possible exception of the Joiner's Arms, Bloxham. The original extent of upper floors is not clear—in the first house at Kings Sutton the hall was probably of one storey with a solar over the service end, as deduced in the previous chapter, whilst at Blue Gates the upper floor may have been limited to the parlour end. All dwellings lie along the road frontage, appear to have no common orientation and, except at Sycamore Terrace, were entered from the side towards the road.

There are few remains of stone mouldings, but sufficient to indicate an increasingly close relationship to 17th-century regional practice. Blue Gates and Grange Farm, Balscott, are among the very few dwellings in the region below manorial scale which have stone-headed doorways on both elevations. The details at Blue Gates and the Joiner's Arms are closely related to the more elaborate Perpendicular details at Balscott, somewhat reduced and simplified to the scale of minor domestic architecture. Window details at Bloxham and Tadmarton include flat-splay stone mullions, the most common regional type during the 17th century, but the label-moulds are nearer to the medieval prototype.

CHAPTER V

THE REGIONAL HOUSE
1550–1640

THE first house of vernacular character in the region may be dated as early as *c.* 1325. This is, however, an isolated example, and no others of note may be firmly ascribed to dates earlier than the first half of the 16th century. There are some dwellings which on the evidence of date-panels were clearly founded in the last quarter of that century, but almost without exception these buildings have been so altered that their original arrangements cannot be determined. Among the authentically dated houses, that built in 1607 is the first to give indisputable evidence of the character of the regional style. After this there is some increase in the number of dated buildings, but they remain few until 1646, and so provide rather uncertain evidence of the chronological advance of the style in the first half of the 17th century. As is to be expected, date-stones first occur on manors and large houses, such as at Williamscot, Farthinghoe and Hornton; only from 1620 are they to be found on houses truly of the yeoman class.

The regular practice of employing date-stones on houses begins in the Banbury Region within the period formally allotted to the Renaissance (i.e. from 1558), as is usual elsewhere in the country, although the houses themselves remain for some time firmly medieval in character. The practice could hardly begin earlier in this area, for apart from those few dwellings already described, the dwellings of the yeoman class do not emerge in permanent form before the later 16th century, as has been shown. In the neighbouring Cotswold zone, which socially and architecturally is linked to the Banbury Region, consolidation in stone seems to take place about twenty-five years earlier. Whilst the first dated building there is a large house built in 1577, much the same time as for the earliest dated structure of a comparable class in the Banbury area, many more dated yeoman houses are found in the Cotswolds in the period prior to 1620.[1] All these Cotswold dwellings similarly retain a medieval character, but very much more often exhibit that particularly significant medieval

[1] Information derived from G. L. Worsley, 'Traditional Domestic Architecture in the Cotswold Region', Manchester University Thesis, 1956.

characteristic, the hollow-section mullion. Moreover, these early yeoman houses of the Cotswolds are of notably rich character; they are of one-and-a-half-storey height, the upper floor almost wholly contained within the roof and lit by elaborate gable dormers,[1] a type which in more impoverished style infrequently occurs in the Banbury Region at so early a date; for the most part, the one-and-a-half-storey houses in this area are altogether a poorer class of dwelling which persisted throughout the 18th century, and represent an inferior social grade. The only houses which are truly comparable with the Cotswold examples referred to are those mentioned in the previous chapter, of which solely that at Sycamore Terrace, Bloxham, exhibits stone-mullioned semi-dormers, and these are not now gabled. Of those rare examples thereafter in the region showing mullioned dormer windows to a first floor, in no case is the dormer finished by a gable, the thatch being simply elevated over the flat top of the window. It is possible to argue that this particular form of upper-floor window, as compared with the characteristic Cotswold dormer, derives from the use of thatch roofing instead of stone slates, in conjunction with a poorer building stone; the more elaborate gabled dormer does, however, appear in the region on thatched houses, but only in connection with structures of two-and-a-half-storey height, from early in the 17th century.

It is clear that the earliest stone houses in the Cotswolds rarely find a counterpart around Banbury, although after *c.* 1620 development in the two regions is remarkably parallel.

The 16th-century houses already described all exhibited the through-passage plan, with the hall separated by an entrance passage from a service-room, the hall fireplace being placed on the end wall against the passage. This plan-type is dominant in the Banbury Region and indeed appears to be characteristic throughout the Highland Zone of Great Britain from the later 16th century onwards. It is the almost exclusive type in such regions as the Eden Valley of Westmorland,[2] and in Monmouthshire,[3] and in other upland areas of the north and west. The two-unit version appears in the region before that with three ground-floor apartments; the first

[1] A typical Cotswold elevation—Laverton, near Broadway, dated 1582—is illustrated in Davie and Dawber, *Old Cottages, Farmhouses etc., in the Cotswold District*, Plate XXXIV.

[2] R. W. Brunskill, 'Traditional Domestic Architecture in the Eden Valley', Manchester University Thesis, 1952.

[3] In Monmouthshire, the authors note that 'both the spere truss and the axial fireplace are more common in, if not peculiar to, the Highland Zone. One construction, the truss, suggests that the cross-passage is outside the hall; the other, the fireplace, eliminates the cross-passage from the hall' (op. cit., Vol. I, p. 87).

appearance of the parlour is noted at Grange Farm, Balscott, and thereafter it becomes an increasingly important part of the house. The earliest vernacular dwellings that have been described were 'hall-houses', that is to say, the hall and subsidiary apartments were open to the roof in single-storey structure. An upper floor came to be provided—and was occasionally introduced in existing dwellings by reducing the ground-floor height—from *c.* 1550 in houses of superior social status and *c.* 1600 in those of yeoman class, although in the latter, lofts over subsidiary rooms occur from mid-16th century.[1] At the end of the century, the larger houses advanced to the two-and-a-half-storey height (having the second floor partly contained within the roof), which was progressively attained by the yeoman houses during the 17th century. Not only in matters of accommodation but in all respects, the superior houses of the lesser gentry anticipated the yeoman class by some fifty years. The earlier forms of the regional house in the period under consideration can therefore be seen initially in instances of superior house-types, dating from the end of the 16th century or beginning of the 17th, including two which although rating as manors are modest buildings of their class and approximate to the vernacular.

Shutford Manor, Oxfordshire (Figs. 14, 15; Pl. 7a) is a large three-storeyed house of some architectural significance. A manor of the Fiennes (Fenys or Ferris) family, who in the 15th century had acquired by marriage the manor and castle of Broughton, there appears to be no evidence of building on the site earlier than the last quarter of the 16th century. The family declined in importance after the death in battle of William de Fenys, the last for the time of the Barons Saye and Sele, who, having been twice imprisoned, had been obliged to mortgage the greater part of his lands to pay his ransoms.

At the end of the 16th century, his descendant Richard Fenys,

---

[1] Interesting information derived from documentary sources is available concerning the introduction of upper floors in Wigston Magna, but it is clear that this area of Leicestershire, where timber construction was widely employed in the 17th century, was considerably behind the Banbury Region in aspects of plan and structure. W. G. Hoskins notes that 'the peasant house with two upper rooms was still uncommon in Wigston before the 1620's. Timber was scarcer in the East Midlands than almost anywhere in England. In better-wooded regions it is probable that complete boarding-over was more common and earlier in date.' (This certainly appears to be the case in the Banbury Region.) In Wiltshire also, evidence is available about the extent to which upper floors had been introduced by 1631-2. 'Out of 355 houses, just over one half (188) had been completely lofted over, although many of these only had one ground-floor room. One house in three (116) was still only partly lofted; and one in every seven (51) was not lofted at all, but consisted only of ground-floor rooms' (W. G. Hoskins, *The Midland Peasant*, pp. 288-9).

Esq., succeeded in restoring the family fortunes. A Member of Parliament for Banbury in 1585, in 1595 he is styled Sir Richard Fenys, Knight, and in 1603 James I revived in his person the barony of Saye and Sele. He died in 1612, and his son William Fenys, who was born at Broughton in 1582, was raised to the dignity of Viscount Saye and Sele by James I in 1624.

Sir Richard is reputed to have resided at one time at his manor-house at Shutford[1] and may well have been the builder of the present house between 1580–1600.

The building has been extensively modernized in this century and restored to its former dignity following a long period of use as a farm-house, but in the course of these improvements the original arrangement of the ground-floor plan has been unfortunately obscured. There are now three rooms on the ground floor, from west to east, a small room now serving as a dining-room; the great hall, which now measures 20 feet by 38 feet but was probably shorter in length as the ground floor partitions have been renewed; and beyond this an equally spacious parlour. Both hall and parlour have large fireplaces on the rear long wall of the house, the hall fireplace being elaborately moulded. There are two early entrances with arched stone heads on the south front, both coinciding with entrances on the north elevation. The western doorway has a four-centred arched head with mouldings of simple, classical character, the corresponding door on the north front unfortunately having been modernized. The entrance at the east end of the south front is protected by a porch of unusually elaborate detail, having a Tudor arch with similar mouldings to the western door, framed by attached columns and entablature of well-developed classical character. The corresponding north door has a similar Tudor arch, with simple splayed jambs. The porch, with its interesting combination of medieval and classical detail, is clearly an addition, probably of mid-17th-century date.

A small projecting block, providing a closet on three floors, has been added on the west gable, and adjoining this, of still later date within the 17th century, is an almost square kitchen of two storeys with attic which can only have communicated directly with the main building through the closet itself.[2]

Within the spacious hall, a fine square-headed doorway with

[1] Beesley, op. cit., p. 238.

[2] The modernization of the present dining-room and kitchen, together with the addition of a modern lean-to annexe on the north front, has obscured the original arrangements, and unfortunately access was not obtained to investigate fully the kitchen block.

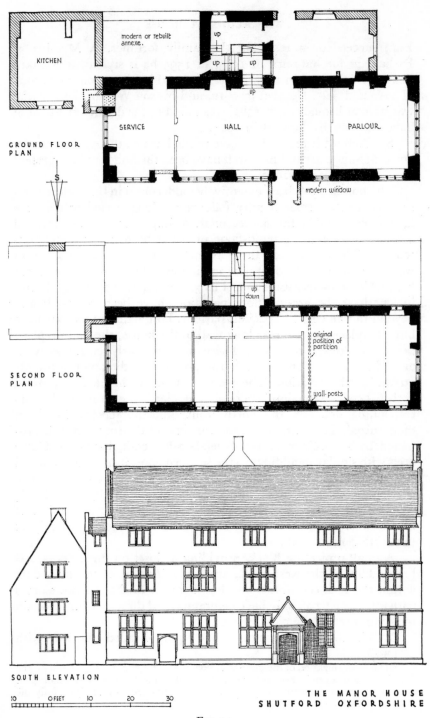

KITCHEN

modern or rebuilt
annexe.

up

up   up

up

SERVICE   HALL   PARLOUR

GROUND FLOOR
PLAN

S

modern window

SECOND FLOOR
PLAN

up
down

original
position of
partition

wall-posts

SOUTH ELEVATION

10   0 FEET   10   20   30

THE MANOR HOUSE
SHUTFORD OXFORDSHIRE

FIG. 14.

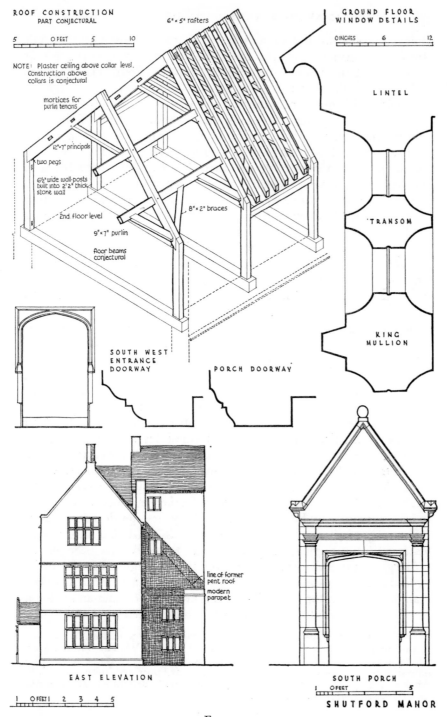

ROOF CONSTRUCTION
PART CONJECTURAL

6" × 5" rafters

5   0 FEET   5   10

NOTE: Plaster ceiling above collar level.
Construction above
collars is conjectural

mortices for
purlin tenons

12"×7" principals

two pegs

6½" wide wall-posts
built into 2'2" thick
stone wall

2nd floor level

9"×7" purlin

floor beams
conjectural

8"×2" braces

GROUND FLOOR
WINDOW DETAILS

0 INCHES   6   12

LINTEL

TRANSOM

KING
MULLION

SOUTH WEST
ENTRANCE
DOORWAY

PORCH DOORWAY

line of former
pent roof

modern
parapet

EAST ELEVATION

1 0 FEET 1 2 3 4 5

SOUTH PORCH

1   0 FEET   5

SHUTFORD MANOR

FIG. 15.

splayed jambs and lintel opens by the side of the fireplace to a stair tower of unusual scale, projecting boldly from the north or rear elevation of the house—the present entrance front. The stair has solid oak baulk steps around a built-up central newel, the flights 5 feet wide with quarter landings, and gives access to the two upper floors, then continues to a small chamber at the top of the stair tower, the highest part of the building. To the east of this, a two-storey annexe has been added at the end of the 17th century, originally with a pent roof, and there is a similar annexe between kitchen and stair tower which, however, appears to be quite modern, reproducing the 17th-century character. Stair and annexe, together with the added closets and kitchen, have flat-splay stone mullions and jambs to their windows, unlike those of the main building.

The presence of two entrances, both of which appear to have provided 'screens passages', renders more difficult the elucidation of the ground-floor plan. The duplication of doorways at upper and lower ends is a development to be found in large three-unit yeoman plans at the end of the 17th century,[1] but is less common at this date. The large six-light window on the east gable clearly indicates that this apartment was the parlour, whilst the siting of the later kitchen adjoining the north-west angle gives further conclusive evidence of the west being the 'lower end'; the present dining-room being the former buttery and pantry, perhaps originally subdivided. The western doorway on the south front would communicate with the original screens passage, defined by timber partitions from hall and service rooms. The somewhat earlier form of this doorway, with four-centred arch as compared with the Tudor arches of the eastern doors, suggests that the latter openings may have been introduced at the same time as the porch. This is by no means certain, however, and the arrangements at Shutford may be a further instance of a manor house anticipating by more than fifty years developments later appearing in yeoman dwellings. If it is assumed that this second entrance is not original, the parlour must formerly have been almost as large as the hall—this is the case at Warmington Manor, to be considered later—unless a small chamber was introduced between hall and parlour, for which Warmington again provides an analogy.

First and second floors are similarly sub-divided by timber parti-

---

[1] The Mansion House Farm, Mollington, and The Mount, Hornton, are late 17th-century examples of this plan described in Chapter VI. The 'Priory', Marcham, Berkshire, not far from the Banbury Region, provides one example of a late 16th-century house having original entrances at upper and lower ends (P. S. Spokes and E. M. Jope, 'The "Priory", Marcham, Berkshire', *The Berkshire Archaeological Journal*, Vol. LVII, 1959).

tions with broad panels to provide three spacious chambers on each floor, the top floor perhaps further sub-divided over the hall, fireplaces being provided in most upper rooms. The difference in window mullion details between stair tower and main building, together with some superficial difference in the appearance of the masonry of the second floor, raises speculation as to whether both stair-tower and second floor may also be of later date, but this seems improbable. There is no change in the character of the masonry, the slight change in appearance resulting from differential weathering and repointing, whilst the upper floor has hollow-moulded mullions, with transomed gable windows, similar to those on lower floors. The ubiquitous flat-splay mullion occurs in the region in building from the 16th to the 18th centuries, often in company with windows having mullions of more elaborate section. The character of the baulk stairs and the roof structure would agree with a date of approximately 1600 rather than later in the 17th century.

Structurally, Shutford Manor is also significant, introducing alien elements in the form of its roof, of collar-rafter construction unmistakably belonging to the south-eastern tradition of building (Pl. 7a). Each pair of rafters is tied by a collar, with principal rafters, also with collars, dividing the extent of the roof into eight bays, averaging 9 feet 6 inches, the top floor spanning 20 feet 7 inches. The 12-inch by 7-inch straight principal rafters are mortised and tenoned to 6½-inch wide wall-posts built into the stone wall, which here averages 2 feet 2 inches in thickness, the posts apparently rising from tie-beams at second-floor level. Bays which do not have windows are stiffened by horizontal wall-timbers between the posts to which they are tenoned, whilst the original transverse partitions were also tenoned to the posts. Purlins, averaging 9 inches by 7 inches, are butted against the principal rafters in true south-eastern fashion, supported on long tenons taken through the principal. Some variation in fixing is noted, in some cases the tenons being cut on the end of one purlin, in others an independent 'floating tenon' being used. The roof, which is exposed in the eastern chamber up to collar level, was not accessible above this point, but it seems improbable that there should be a ridge beam. Straight wind-braces spring from the feet of the principal rafters to the undersides of the lower purlins, to which each 6-inch by 5-inch rafter is pegged. As the rafters are built into the wall, it could not be ascertained whether there was a wall-plate, possibly jointed to the wall-posts, or whether the rafters themselves were supported on the wall. The most easterly truss shows signs of alteration, being mortised and pegged for arched braces to a collar originally at higher level, but it seems reasonable to assume that these timbers are re-used, probably deriving from an earlier manor-house.

This remarkable roof provides a completely framed top-floor structure, supporting the roof almost independently of the heavy stone walls, and despite the generally lowland style of building, there is a clear reflection of upper cruck construction in the jointed wall-posts and principal rafters. The earliest complete second floor in a house of this size recorded in the region, it reveals an experimental approach to the problems of building at this level, still treating the floor as a raised attic.

The walls of the manor-house are 2 feet 10 inches thick at ground-floor level, reducing to 2 feet 7 inches at first-floor and 2 feet 2 inches at second-floor by external set-backs defined by string courses which act as continuous label-moulds to the windows. On ground and first floors the windows are of three or four lights with transoms, with six-light windows, having transoms and king-mullions on the east gable, all mullions being of the sub-medieval hollow section. The irregular disposition of doors and windows on the south front is completely medieval in character.

Despite the queries which must remain as to the dating of the eastern entrances, the stair tower and upper floor, Shutford Manor is an important example, providing a direct antecedent for the yeoman house of the regional period. In particular, the almost detached kitchen block is of great interest: although of later date than the house, it must surely have replaced a similar detached structure, and is the only proven instance in the region of this medieval arrangement. The placing of the hall fireplace on the long wall instead of on a cross wall is generally regarded as 'lowland' practice, but is common to the larger halls of manorial class throughout the country.[1] Apart from this, the disposition of the different elements anticipates the form of the yeoman house throughout the regional period.

A further development from the three-room plan with separate kitchen is to be seen in a second manor-house of similar date, *Warmington Manor, Warwickshire* (Figs. 16, 75; Pl. 20a), comparable in size and character, and again clearly related to the 17th-century regional tradition. The manor of Warmington, formerly in the possession of the Carthusian monastery of Witham in Somerset, changed hands a

---

[1] Tretower Court, Brecon, combines an upland type hall plan with passage outside the hall, with the lateral fireplace, and similar examples are common in large houses in other upland regions, including Westmorland. In the Banbury Region, Broughton Castle has already been noted as having had a lateral fire-place added in the 16th century.

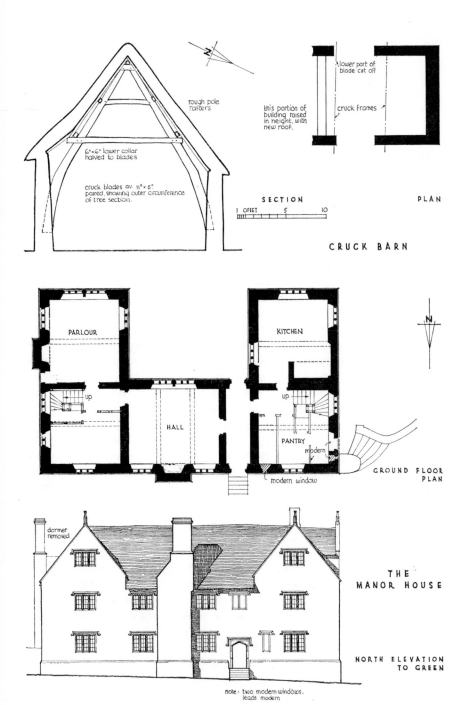

N

rough pole
rafters

this portion of
building raised
in height, with
new roof.

lower part of
blade cut off

cruck frames

6"×6" lower collar
halved to blades

cruck blades av. 11"× 6"
paired, showing outer circumference
of tree section.

L

SECTION

PLAN

1 OFEET   5   10

CRUCK BARN

PARLOUR

KITCHEN

up

up

HALL

PANTRY

modern

N

GROUND FLOOR
PLAN

modern window

dormer
removed

THE
MANOR HOUSE

NORTH ELEVATION
TO GREEN

note: two modern windows.
leads modern

10   OFEET   10   20   30

WARMINGTON   WARWICKSHIRE

G

FIG. 16.

number of times after the dissolution before being purchased in
1572 by Richard and Thomas Cupper or Cooper, the former being
described in the deeds as 'yeoman of Warmington'. Richard died in
c. 1605 and was succeeded by his son Henry Cooper, and it is significant that in the deeds Henry has risen to the status of 'Gentleman'.

The manor-house faces north across the village green, and is
entered from this front. It is basically of three-unit cross-passage
plan, with additional accommodation in equal wings projecting
from each end of the southward facing rear elevation, giving a
'U'-shaped plan. Apart from the wings, the scale and accommodation is similar to that of later yeoman dwellings, the hall spanning
only 18 feet by 22 feet 9 inches in length, but the building is distinguished by the quality and range of its timber and stone tech-
nique, notably in such features as the early use of the ovolo mould,
the arched internal doorways, twin stairs and moulded beams.
There are fine entrance doorways at each end of a through-passage,
having four-centred arches enclosed in rectangular labels with blank
shields carved in the spandrels. The principal entrance on the north
front retains its original iron-studded oak door. From the screens
passage, which is outside the hall in the 'upland' style, flanked on
either side by heavy stone walls, a doorway with arched stone head
opens into the stone-flagged hall.

A similar doorway at the upper end of the hall leads to the
eastern bay, containing a fine stair separated by original timber-
framed partitions from a small private apartment, the function of
which is not known, and thence to the main parlour. The hall fireplace, with moulded jambs and four-centred head, is placed on the
long side wall, as at Shutford, projecting from the external face of the
north front. Opposite to it, on the south wall, is a great window of
six lights with central 'king' mullion. A similar window occurs in the
south wall of the parlour, contained in the projecting south-east
wing. West of the screens passage is a service bay containing the
second and similar stair, the original arrangements of this room
altered by modern partitions and the provision of a new entrance on
the west front. The kitchen occupies the projecting south-west wing,
having a large fireplace arranged axially to the wing; like the parlour, it is almost equal in area to the hall.

The two staircases, one at each end of the house, are of a scale
superior to those found during the 17th century in dwellings of
yeoman class; they wind around framed newels, large enough to
contain cupboards, with some parts remaining of the original flat,

shaped balusters of Elizabethan character. There is a gabled dormer window on the west wall over the staircase, a corresponding dormer over the eastern stair having been removed when it became ruinous, in improvements of this century.

Floor-beams over the hall span transversely, seated on modern stone corbels, and are moulded, somewhat after the style of those already noted at Cottisford, whilst the floors over kitchen and parlour are also supported on transverse beams. The first floor provides a series of fine, well-lit chambers divided by heavy, timber-framed partitions. Openings in the partitions have Tudor-arched heads cut in timber, and retain several original three-plank doors with wrought-iron strap hinges and wood latches. The area over hall and screens passage was originally a single great chamber, but has now been subdivided. Small chambers are provided within the roof, which has tie-beam trusses with queen-struts. The roof is finished with stone slates with swept valleys and raking parapets to the gables, but lacking the decorative kneelers which become characteristic of later 17th-century work; each gable has a tall finial on its apex.

The character of the masonry is unusually elaborate for a house of this size in the Banbury Region. All windows have stone mullions of ovolo section, and label moulds are unusual in that they also incorporate ovolo mouldings. The king mullions on the south front are particularly elaborate, forming a small column internally. Mason's marks of three types (Fig. 75) occur extensively and prominently on windows and other dressed stonework, the only instance of such markings noted in domestic work in the region. This suggests that the work may be that of other than local craftsmen, which would account for the unusual sophistication of detail and also the unusually early use of the ovolo mullions. Although this form appears in Elizabethan great houses in the last quarter of the 16th century, the first firmly dated example within the region is at Wroxton Abbey, a great house built in 1615, whilst no examples have been recorded in a dated yeoman house until 1647. It seems improbable that these classical details would appear in a small manor-house before 1600.

In plan, also, the house presents a later development of the sub-medieval arrangements of Shutford Manor, the more symmetrical and formal disposition of the rooms, with twin staircases and ordered fenestration revealing increasing classical influence. There is improvement also in the inclusion of the kitchen under the same roof as the hall, whilst the importance given to both parlour and kitchen represents a step towards the gradual reduction in importance of the hall itself. Although built as a large farm-house rather than a manor-house, Warmington Manor is clearly of a class of building superior to that of a yeoman dwelling, and this further suggests the work of Henry Cooper, Gentleman, in *c*. 1603, rather than his predecessor, Richard Cooper, Yeoman of Warmington.

A third large house, *Abbey Lodge, Farthinghoe, Northamptonshire* (Pl. 8*a*), in the fringe area of admixed building stone, bears a Victorian date-stone over the entrance doorway. The date of 1581 is believed to be authentic, and is not contradicted by the architectural evidence. The plan, of through-passage type with extended parlour wing, has obvious affinities with Warmington Manor, although the architectural character is less rich. Although very much altered, the original arrangements can be deduced. To the left of the entrance is the kitchen, possibly the former service-room with a gable fireplace added in the 17th century. Both front and rear entrances to the through-passage have four-centred arches, as also does that leading into the hall. The fireplace in the hall backs onto the passage, having lozenge decorations similar to those of the hall fireplace at Shutford Manor. The upper end of the hall communicates with the large parlour in the forward projecting wing, the stair again being placed in the angle between hall and parlour. Upper-floor windows having ovolo mullions in brown stone, which contrasts with the grey limestone walling, occur on the lower end gable, and there is one first-floor window with oak mullions of the same section, but these may well result from later building. The house is distinguished by the archway of Jacobean character which presumably stood at the entrance to the front garden of the house.

Other dated houses before 1600 are of little interest because of subsequent rebuilding, and the next significant dated building to be noted is another of high rank, *Hornton Manor, Oxfordshire* (Fig. 17), but again sufficiently modest in its character to be considered in relation to the type of building with which this study is primarily concerned. It bears a date-stone of 1607, with the initials CE. Alterations and renovations of the 19th century have done much to obscure the original character of the house, the entrances having been rebuilt with Gothic arches and the fireplaces completely altered. The plan is of the through-passage type, with large hall and kitchen, the hall fireplace—now rebuilt in brick—being in the appropriate position against the passage, with a second large hearth in the kitchen, also altered. The original position of the stair can only be conjectured, but was probably on the rear wall of the house, perhaps adjacent to the hall fireplace. An early newel stair, which may be original, exists in the north-east corner, providing access from

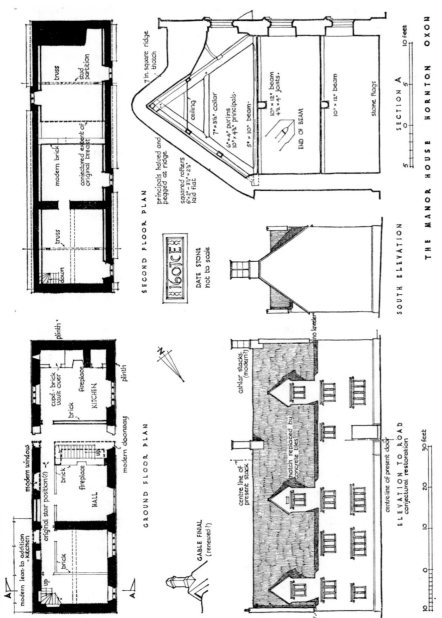

SECOND FLOOR PLAN

principals halved and
pegged at ridge

7 In. square ridge

thatch

squared rafters
6" x 2" - 3½" x 2½"
laid flat

ceiling

7" x 3½" collar

6" x 4" purlins
10" x 4½" principals

5" x 10" beam

10" x 12" beam
4½ x 4" joists.

END OF BEAM

10" x 12" beam

stone flags

SECTION A

5   0   5   10 feet

DATE STONE
not to scale

160CE

SOUTH ELEVATION

GROUND FLOOR PLAN

modern window

A

original stair position(?)

up

brick

HALL

fireplace

brick

modern doorway

cupd.- brick
vault over

fireplace

brick

KITCHEN

plinth

plinth

plinth

modern lean-to addition
KITCHEN

N

GABLE FINIAL
(renewed?)

modern brick

conjectural extent of
original breast

truss

stud
partition

truss

down

ashlar stacks
(modern)

centre line of
present stack

hatch replaced by
concrete lids

no kneeler

centre line of present door

kneeler

ELEVATION TO ROAD
conjectural restoration

10   0   10   20   30 feet

THE MANOR HOUSE   HORNTON   OXON

FIG. 17.

ground floor to roof. The upper end of the house is the least altered portion of the building. A modern brick wall now divides the parlour into two rooms, used as pantry and dairy, but there is some evidence in the arrangement of the windows that there always has been such a sub-division, formerly demarcating the parlour from an inner room, with possibly a larger stair in the north-east corner. If such a division is not assumed, the parlour, lit by two windows on each wall, would have been of considerable size, larger than hall or kitchen, for this date an unprecedented relationship to which the previous plans are, nevertheless, leading. All original windows have the flat-splay stone mullions with label moulds, with flush dormers to the second floor, projecting into the roof. The roof finish was thatch—used even on large houses in this central part of the region—with parapet gables, again without kneelers. The present stone stacks are entirely modern replacements.

Two original roof trusses survive, which—together with the cross-walls—divide the roof into bays averaging 10 feet; they are of the tie-beam type already noted, but with a single collar and with the principals crossed at the apex to receive the ridge, set diagonally in the fork. The most northerly truss retains part of the original partitioning, with light chamfered studs tenoned to the collar and plastered over one side on split laths. The first floor is almost entirely modern work, the floor and ceiling levels having been raised except over the parlour end where the original levels and structure are undisturbed.

For the next chronological step, it is necessary to descend from these larger houses to those of yeoman class. These present humbler techniques, and at the beginning of the 17th century are at the one-and-a-half-storey stage, carrying on the developments already noted at Blue Gates, Bloxham. All of the houses belonging to this phase and class are undated, but it is doubtful whether any are earlier than 1615, their archaistic character being attributable to the operation of the time-scale already considered. The most important dwelling among them to merit consideration is *Cromwell Cottage, Hornton* (Fig. 18; Pl. 5*b*), a building of good architectural quality, with an elaboration of masonry enrichment equalling that of the lesser manor-houses described above, although the building is of considerably smaller scale. The house gains its name from its reputation of having once lodged Cromwell during the Civil Wars, a distinction claimed by other houses in this part of the region in respect of the Royalist and Parliamentarian leaders. The legend may in this case have some justification, for the house stands high in its class and does ante-date

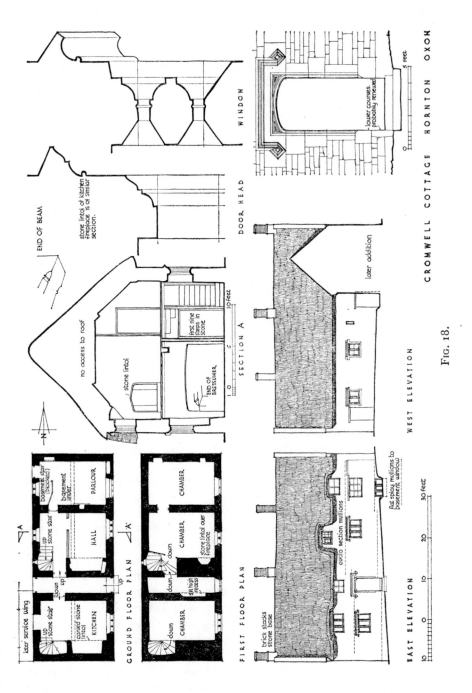

END OF BEAM

stone lintel of kitchen fireplace is of similar section.

WINDOW

DOOR HEAD

lower courses probably renewed

5 feet

CROMWELL COTTAGE HORNTON OXON

no access to roof

stone lintel

END OF BRESSUMER

first nine steps in stone

SECTION A

0   5   10 feet

later addition

WEST ELEVATION

Fig. 18.

later service wing

basement stair (blocked)

basement stair under

PARLOUR

up stone stair

HALL

down

up

down

up stone stair

canted stone lintel

KITCHEN

GROUND FLOOR PLAN

CHAMBER

CHAMBER

down

stone lintel over fireplace

sill high recess

down

down

CHAMBER

FIRST FLOOR PLAN

brick stacks
stone base

ovolo section mullions

flat splay mullions to basement window

EAST ELEVATION

10   0   10   20   30 feet

the Civil Wars—a matter of some doubt in the case of many other such claimants. This dwelling is of particular interest for its combination of early 17th-century characteristics with features which are innovations for its day and class.

The plan is again of the through-passage type with three units, the height being still one-and-a-half storeys, except that over the kitchen bay a full two-storey height is obtained due to changes in floor levels contrived on the falling site. The through-passage is here flanked on either side by stone walls of 2-feet thickness, an arrangement already noted in houses of the previous century but which becomes progressively more rare after 1600. There is a fireplace in the hall, backing onto the passage, and another in the kitchen. The parlour is separated from the hall by a further stone wall, but the fireplace built against this partition is of modern introduction. The hall fireplace is of conventional 17th-century form, spanned by a bressumer of which the edge chamfer finishes in moulded stops; the kitchen fireplace is of more elaborate design, with a moulded stone arch of 7-feet span, framed with a moulded label or mantel, with ornamental spandrels, the whole being similar in detail to the entrance doorway. At the side of both kitchen and hall fireplaces, the door intervening in the latter room, are winding stairs, taken partly into the thickness of the rear wall, and having the lower nine steps in stone, a very unusual feature in the region. The ground floor is flagged and the upper floors boarded, the latter supported on joists spanning from a central spine beam, chamfered with moulded stops. All three stone dividing-walls are taken up to the roof, eliminating the need for principal rafters, but producing a narrow 4-feet-wide chamber on the first floor over the passage. A recess 6 feet long by 5 feet high has been made in one wall of this chamber with an oak bressumer above built into the masonry, presumably to allow a bed to be accommodated. Originally it may not have been lit, the present opening being of later date, although possibly it represents an enlargement of a smaller window. There is no doorway to provide communication between the rest of the first floor and the principal bedroom above the kitchen, which therefore attains complete privacy. Fireplaces with four-centred arched heads in stone are provided in the chambers over kitchen and hall, there being now only one brick chimney, 1 foot 10$\frac{1}{2}$ inches square on each stack, which suggests that ground- and first-floor fireplaces share a common flue, a feature not elsewhere encountered.

Original windows have stone dressings with an early form of label mould, similar to that over the sub-medieval door at Blue

Gates, in conjunction with stone mullions of ovolo section externally, splayed on the inner face. The first-floor windows rise above eaves level, that over the hall being a full, flat-topped dormer, with the thatch interrupted to pass over its head. The entrance door has elaborately moulded stone dressings with cambered arch and sunk spandrels contained within a flat label with dropped ends, having lozenge-shaped stops of the kind noted in the medieval door at Balscott (Fig. 8). In this case, however, moulding profiles of jamb and label are classical, as becomes increasingly the case with examples throughout the 17th century. Under the parlour is a basement cellar, originally approached by a stair (now blocked) in one corner of the parlour, and lit by a flat-splay stone-mullioned window on the entrance front. New windows have been subsequently provided in the parlour, but despite the superficial difference which this imparts to the elevation, there is no suggestion that this part has been added.

Innovations to the class to which this building belongs include the form of the door moulding, the ovolo mullions, the camber arch to door and fireplace, the fully developed kitchen replacing the service room, the basement cellar and the provision of bedroom fireplaces.[1] These are all features which by reference to dated structures within the region would suggest a later period than is in fact clearly indicated by such early 17th-century characteristics as the one-and-a-half-storey height in combination with the stone partitions, the positions of the stairs, and the early detailing of the window label-moulds. As already noted, ovolo-moulded mullions cannot be firmly dated in a yeoman dwelling before 1647, whilst the first dated cellar in houses of this class within the region occurs in a small house in Charlton in 1637, a dwelling of lowland plan-type to be considered in a later chapter. It thus seems probable that Cromwell Cottage, despite its unassuming name, was of some social importance as the home of a wealthy 'considerable yeoman', to use an 18th-century term, dating from the first quarter of the 17th century. The classical profile of the moulding would hardly agree with a date before 1615 in work of this social class, although they need not be much later as the mullions are clearly an early example of the ovolo form and are associated with the sub-medieval label-mould. The introduction of the camber arch,[2] in preference to the flat or four-centred head

[1] Fireplaces with stone arched heads are provided to the principal first-floor chambers at Warmington Manor, as also at Shutford Manor.

[2] The earliest use of the camber-arch which can be dated is at Alkerton Rectory, a two-unit house of lowland plan dated 1625, having mouldings of similar character (Fig. 78).

appears to be a later characteristic, and in all, a date *c.* 1615 is indicated for this house. The house is anomalous in many respects, but the proximity of the Hornton stone quarries, providing stone at this time for more important architectural works both within and beyond this region, could account for some advance in the character of the masonry dressings.

A similar disposition of entrance passage, hall fireplace and principal stair is to be found in a number of other three-unit houses which are estimated to date from before 1640. This regional plan-type was passed down progressively to the smaller dwellings as the century advanced, whilst the larger yeoman-houses proceeded to develop fresh traits. As there is no strong indication of social grade among these houses, it is often difficult to estimate dates of the lower grades with certainty. Frequently lacking any evidence from mouldings or other architectural features, dating must depend largely on the stage of development of plan and general form.

Beech Tree House, Lower Middleton Cheney, Northamptonshire (Fig. 19), possesses the planning characteristics of a small, early, yeoman dwelling, lying parallel to the road, with its yard and farm buildings at the rear. The internal span is only 15 feet, and the building originally had no more than a single fireplace in its three-room plan, a fact which might appear to indicate an early 17th-century date. There are, however, other characteristics to be noted which place the date of building nearer to 1640 if not later. Entry is by a through-passage, against which the hall fireplace is situated, the door to the hall being once more off the rear of the passage, between the fireplace and the stair. The latter is narrow, but of unusual convenience compared with the more common newel-stair, planned in an elongated projection from the rear wall of the house; its form is one of the principal arguments for a date at the end of this phase in *c.* 1640. The contemporary bread-oven which projects slightly from the front wall of the house, at the side of the fire, again is a feature not found in dated houses until mid-17th century, although ovens contained completely within the limits of the house certainly appear earlier than this. A stud partition, now plastered over, divides the hall from a large inner room or parlour, in which a lateral fireplace has been subsequently introduced, whilst the service-room was also subdivided by a stud partition into pantry and buttery. The building is of full two-storey height, except for the service bay, of which both the roof and floors are at a slightly lower level. As at Cromwell Cottage, the combination of seemingly early characteristics with features which become more common in the second half of the century adds

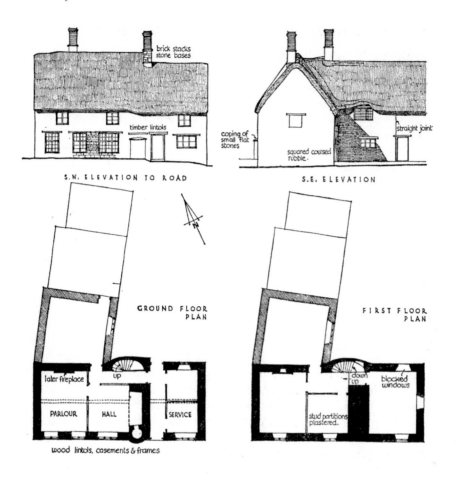

brick stacks
stone bases

timber lintols

coping of
small flat
stones

squared coursed
rubble.

straight joint

S.W. ELEVATION TO ROAD

S.E. ELEVATION

N

GROUND FLOOR
PLAN

FIRST FLOOR
PLAN

later fireplace

up

down
up

blocked
windows

PARLOUR

HALL

SERVICE

stud partitions
plastered.

wood lintols, casements & frames

BEECH TREE HOUSE
LOWER MIDDLETON CHENEY   NORTHAMPTONSHIRE

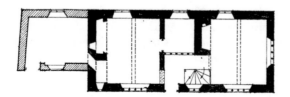

GROUND FLOOR PLAN

SPRINGFIELD HOUSE
MIDDLETON CHENEY
NORTHAMPTONSHIRE

10   0   10   20   30 FEET

FIG. 19.

to the problem of dating. In this case the smaller scale and poorer architectural character in conjunction with other criteria referred to indicate that this was a small house of moderate social status built in *c*. 1630–40. All windows were renewed in the 18th century, when the house was extended at the rear to provide additional service accommodation.

The third house selected to represent the present group is *Sunnyside Cottage, Swerford* (Fig. 20; Pl. 15*c*), the structure of which underwent extensive re-modelling in the following century. Comparable with the previous example in scale and architectural quality, the house is again of three units, with through-passage flanked by the hall fireplace, originally the only hearth in the house. The fireplace is here nearer to the rear wall of the house, the entrance to the hall from the passage being immediately adjacent to the street entrance, so avoiding the necessity of walking round the back of the fire to enter the hall, as in the plans previously noted. The stair has been added later in the 17th or 18th century in a broad rectangular projection on the back of the house, opening from the hall. A trimming in the joists of the first floor, near the stair, suggests that access to the chambers above may originally have been by a steep ladder-like stair.[1] The stud partition between hall and parlour has been renewed and the inner room sub-divided to provide a pantry at the side of the parlour; these improvements also date from the 18th century, when, too, fireplaces were added in the service-room, the parlour and the bedroom over the upper end of the house. At that time the upper floor, originally an attic contained completely within the roof space, was improved by raising the height of the lateral walls (the change of build is discernible), inserting tall, transomed wood frames, and providing a new slate roof of lower pitch than the thatched structure it presumably replaced. The earlier windows, as at Beech Tree House, Lower Middleton Cheney, would originally have had either stone or wood mullions. In this class of house, either type of window might have been provided, both stone-mullioned windows (for superior types of building) and wood-mullioned forms being in general use at this time. The parlour or inner room was small, and the first floor

---

[1] Speaking of this same period in Wiston Magna, Leicestershire, W. G. Hoskins notes that 'where a house was completely lofted over, an opening was left (perhaps against the back wall, out of the way) through which a ladder, fixed or moveable, could be inserted. Only one Wigston inventory specifically mentions this mode of access. Robert Smith's house in 1637 had "a little ladder to go up by into the chamber"; but the arrangement was so commonplace that there was generally no need to mention it.' He adds that 'it is evident that stairs were rare in rural houses, even of yeoman class, before 1650' (op. cit., pp. 290–1).

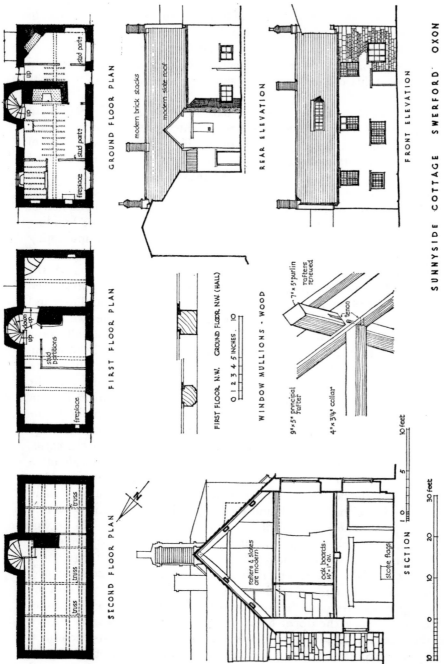

SECOND FLOOR PLAN

FIRST FLOOR PLAN

GROUND FLOOR PLAN

REAR ELEVATION

FRONT ELEVATION

stud parts

truss

truss

truss

stud partitions

fireplace

fireplace

stud parts

up

up

up down

up

modern brick stacks

modern slate roof

rafters & slates are modern

oak boards. 14" × 1" av.

stone flags

N

FIRST FLOOR. N.W.   GROUND FLOOR. N.W. (HALL)

0 1 2 3 4 5 INCHES.   10

WINDOW MULLIONS - WOOD

7" × 5" purlin

rafters renewed

9" × 5" principal rafter

tenon

4" × 3¼" collar"

SECTION

10   0   5   10 feet

10   0   10   20   30 feet

SUNNYSIDE COTTAGE   SWERFORD   OXON

FIG. 20.

spine-beam spanned from the gable at the upper end of the house to
the hall fireplace, with a similar beam over the service bay. The
simple character of Sunnyside Cottage, lacking any evidence of
dressed stonework externally, together with the single fireplace and
the possibility of a ladder stair, again suggest a building of moderate
social level of about 1630.

In addition to the three-unit plans so far considered, there are a
number of early 17th-century houses which are only of two units,
which allow alternate combinations. The earliest plan-types, of
which few instances occur, follow the two-unit arrangement of the
16th-century houses described in the previous chapter, omitting the
inner room or parlour; later, the two-unit house, with combined
kitchen-hall and parlour, becomes general, and in the second half of
the 17th century this will be seen to develop as the major building
type for important yeoman houses. The earliest and most interesting
of these two-unit plans is in *Sycamore Terrace, Bloxham* (Fig. 80), adjoining the house described in the previous chapter. It follows the
earlier form of two-unit plan, the service now becoming a full kitchen
by the addition of a fireplace and bread-oven. In architectural
quality this building returns to the fine standards of the two houses
previously noted in Hornton. The house, of one-and-a-half-storey
height, comprises hall and kitchen with chambers over. The principal
entrance, having a flat, stone shouldered lintel, simply chamfered
(Pl. 23*a*), is on the rear elevation facing south, opening into the
kitchen with an internal projecting stone 'spere' to shield the entrance. There is also a doorway on the street front, opposite to the
other entrance and forming a virtual through-passage in the appropriate position for this plan type. No partition, however, exists,
and it cannot indeed be determined whether there was originally a
door to the street; the present opening, with wood lintel, appears to
date from the later alteration of the house in the 19th century. There
are fireplaces in both hall and kitchen, each having a small oven in
the reveal. The provision of a second fireplace, making the service
bay into a kitchen, together with the provision of ovens, again suggests a date nearer the end of this period, *c.* 1625, despite the presence
also of early features. The stair is in timber, of some convenience,
winding round a newel, and is built partly within the thickness of the
wall, projected shallowly from the rear of the house. A central spine-
beam supports the upper floor over the hall, but above the kitchen
the joists run longitudinally, as in the 16th-century house described
at Kings Sutton. There is a small but well-formed fireplace in the
bedroom over the kitchen, with a cambered and chamfered lintel

(Pl. 17c); the use of this chamber as the principal bedroom is further indicated by the interesting 19th-century decorative plaster frieze over the fire, assuming that this feature ante-dates the division of the house into two cottages. All internal roof structure is concealed by plastered ceilings, but there are no roof principals, the stone fire-place wall providing intermediate support for purlins and ridge. The roofing is of thatch. Stone-mullioned windows, with flat-splay sections, occur on both sides of the house; the upper windows are taken into the roof as flat-topped dormers, not needing label-moulds as they are tucked under the thatched eaves. Both this house and the adjoining 16th-century structure were each sub-divided into two single-cell cottages in the 19th century when the rest of the terrace was either built, or else adapted from farm-buildings, to provide cottages for weavers, the doors and windows being suitably amended. Such examples as this, representing the earlier stages of the regional two-unit house are, as stressed earlier, rarely encountered around Banbury.

One further two-unit plan is of relevance in this study of the earlier expressions of the regional plan, although once more it must be dated near to 1640. *McGreal's Farm-house, Milton, Nr. Bloxham* (Fig. 21), follows what in this region is the later and more usual form of two-unit plan, combining hall and parlour. The entrance now appears on the end wall of the house, although in its customary position in relation to the hall, between fireplace and stair. The stair is, as usual, on the rear wall of the house, in the south-east corner of the building, and, as at Sycamore Terrace, Bloxham, is contained in a shallow projection of the wall. The hall fireplace is of the usual form with timber bressumer and ingle seats, without any oven, and there is also a small fireplace in the parlour and in the bedroom over the hall. The parlour floor is raised by three steps above the level of the hall to accommodate a cellar below, the floor being supported on a transverse beam, whilst a separate stair descends between hall and parlour into the basement cellar. Windows to the cellar have flat-splay stone mullions, and the cellar stair is lit by a small lancet window with chamfered jambs. A small window of similar detail, but with squared head, lights the principal stair; such decorative windows to stairs have been recorded in many 17th-century houses. In the far corner of the cellar the floor is dropped by a further two steps, and signs of rebuilding in the gable at this point suggest that there may have been an original external entrance here. A small, shaped sinking in the floor near these steps has been noted but cannot be satisfactorily explained; it may possibly have formed a

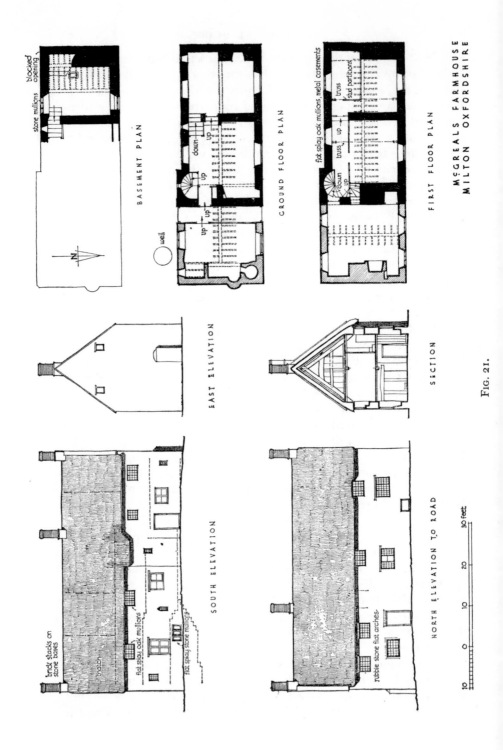

blocked opening

stone mullions

BASEMENT PLAN

N

GROUND FLOOR PLAN

well

up

down

up

up

flat splay oak mullions, metal casements

truss

stud partitions

truss

up

down

up

FIRST FLOOR PLAN

McGREALS FARMHOUSE
MILTON OXFORDSHIRE

EAST ELEVATION

SECTION

FIG. 21.

brick stacks on stone bases

thatch

flat splay oak mullions

flat splay stone mullions

SOUTH ELEVATION

rubble stone flat arches.

NORTH ELEVATION TO ROAD

10   0   10   20   30 feet

lodgement for a barrel which would project over the steps, allowing a vessel to be filled in this way. The house is of full two storeys, with attics over, the first yeoman house of this height to be noted, it having been hitherto restricted to dwellings of manorial scale. The upper floors are supported on central spine-beams, simply chamfered, the bedroom over the parlour being elevated by two steps to allow for the change of levels on the ground floor. Both bedrooms are now sub-divided by stud partitions of 18th-century date. At first-floor level the stair leaves the external wall of the house and ascends against the side of the hall fireplace. The stone partition wall between hall and par-lour terminates at first-floor level, and the roof space is equally divided into three bays of 10 feet by framed trusses, the principals seated in the walls just below second-floor level, and the one collar only 3 feet above the attic floor. The principals cross at the apex and a squared seating is cut in the fork to receive the ridge; this is the form of roof general to the smaller yeoman houses of the 17th century, in contrast to the tie-beam roof already noted at Hornton Manor, which is used in more important houses. Apart from the cellar windows, all openings, including the entrance door, have timber lintels, with wood window-frames probably introduced in the 18th century and later. It is possible, to judge from the large size of the present openings, that the original windows had stone dressings, as in the cellar.

In the 18th century the house was extended by the addition of a through-passage and kitchen, and its plan as it now stands con-forms to the full three-unit regional plan.[1] It is possible that such a development was always envisaged when further resources permitted, or even that a kitchen or service bay of earlier timber construction adjoined the stone building, perhaps part of an earlier house on the site. The well is to be seen at the side of the added bay, on the back of the house, in what appears to be a planned relationship to the building, suggesting that the addition of a further bay was at least considered before the well was made. It is clear, however, that the introduction of the cellar into the regional house provided a sub-stitute for the service room, which increasingly tends to be omitted later in the century, and it is possible that no third unit was en-visaged. By the 18th century the need for a separate kitchen had returned, as is shown by additions to this and many other two-unit dwellings.

The roof of this house is still thatched, without gable parapets in the original build, the smoke vents, as usual, rising about 6 inches

[1] The further development of this house is described in Chapter X, p. 212.

above the ridge, later being surmounted by brick chimneys. The building is set back from the roadway with a garden in front and the wide farm-yard behind, at the back of which is a large 18th-century barn, lying parallel to the house, with other farm-buildings flanking the yard.

In addition to dwellings of three and two units of the regional type, one example has been identified of an early single-cell house belonging to the present phase, which provides the same relationship of entrance, stair and fireplace in a two-storey structure with a single room on each floor. This house, *the Old Turnstiles, Barford* (*c.* 1600), has the early hollow-moulded stone mullions associated with work of the immediately post-medieval period (Fig. 47). The building is, however, to be considered separately in Chapter VIII, in relation to the particular problems associated with single-cell houses, together with a number of other dwellings which show the alternative relationship of stair and entrance described above at Swerford.

To pause briefly to consider general matters; the introduction of the basement cellar necessitated the provision of an additional flight of steps at the parlour end, and by 1640 it had become common practice to have one principal stairway from basement to attics in a position dictated by the presence of the cellar, i.e. between hall and parlour. This system is in marked contrast to the inconvenience of three separate stairs at different levels, as is the case at McGreal's Farm, Milton. The new position for the stair had also the advantage of giving a more private approach to the bedroom over the parlour, which was to become the principal chamber, in which the more elaborate fireplaces are later found. In later 17th-century two-unit plans, to be described in the following chapter, the stair arranged centrally between hall and parlour also gave more private access to the three bedrooms then usually arranged on the first floor, and this factor may have influenced the general adoption of this new stair position in both two- and three-unit plans. In the latter, a second stair was often provided in the service bay, which became a full kitchen with the addition of a fireplace and oven.

The first instances of this plan occur before 1640, and closely successive developments are illustrated in two large three-unit farmhouses in Bloxham, both having cellars. The earlier is a house called 'Bennetts', dating from *c.* 1630–40, which was investigated shortly after the roof was destroyed by fire in 1954. The plan was of the 'upland' through-passage type, with kitchen, hall and parlour, all having wide fireplaces with timber bressumers (Fig. 22). The entrance from the street was blocked and there was no trace of a parti-

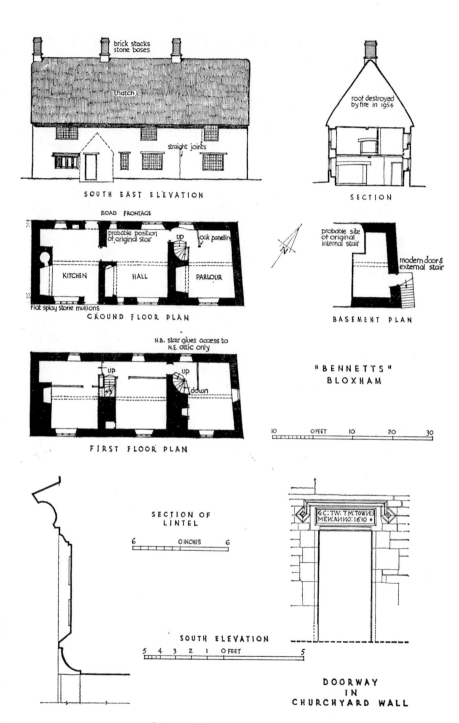

brick stacks
stone bases

thatch

straight joints

SOUTH EAST ELEVATION

roof destroyed
by fire in 1954

SECTION

ROAD FRONTAGE

probable position
of original stair

oak panelling

up

KITCHEN   HALL   PARLOUR

flat splay stone mullions

GROUND FLOOR PLAN

probable site
of original
internal stair

modern door &
external stair

BASEMENT PLAN

N.B. stair gives access to
N.E. attic only

up   up   down

FIRST FLOOR PLAN

"BENNETTS"
BLOXHAM

10   0 FEET   10   20   30

SECTION OF
LINTEL

6   0 INCHES   6

G C: TW: T M: TOWLES
MEN:ANNO: 1610

SOUTH ELEVATION

5 4 3 2 1 0 FEET   5

DOORWAY
IN
CHURCHYARD WALL

BLOXHAM OXFORDSHIRE

FIG. 22.

tion on the kitchen side of the through-passage. All three fireplaces, axially disposed as usual, here lie near to the back wall of the house, bringing the hall doorways closer to the street entrance, and so providing a more direct entry to the hall without the necessity of going around the back of the fireplace.[1] This represents a departure from the more general earlier form of through-passage plan already described, and approximates more nearly to the arrangement at Sunnyside Cottage, Swerford. Unlike this earlier dwelling, however, the stair at 'Bennetts' is also brought nearer to the front wall of the house. The parlour fireplace is sited on the wall dividing the room from the hall, instead of on the gable wall, as is more usual. It is against the side of this stack that the stair is placed, rising from the cellar below the parlour to the cock-loft over this bay. The other two attic chambers, over hall and kitchen, are separately approached by a second stair which commences at first-floor level against the side of the hall chimney-stack, dividing to approach the two chambers separately. The possibility of this second stair having been originally continued to the ground floor has been considered, but there appears to be no way in which this could have been planned, unless the present door into the hall from the passage has been removed from a position immediately adjoining the north wall of the house. Fireplaces are provided in both end bedrooms, that in the room over the parlour possibly being of later introduction.

The windows of the house have been largely renewed, with the exception of one four-light window with flat-splay stone mullions and label in the south wall of the kitchen. The whole house has undergone considerable modernization at various periods, and there are indications of rebuilding or change of build on the south wall which at first suggested that the parlour bay had been added with its independent stair, but it has been concluded that the work is of one build.

The final house to be considered in this chapter is also in *Bloxham* (Fig. 23), a large farm-house lying along the main road immediately south of the church. Similar in size to 'Bennetts,' the house is a little later in date, as indicated by its more advanced plan type and in particular the position and form of the stair. It was probably built at the end of this period, in *c.* 1640. Both hall and kitchen, divided by the through-passage, have large fireplaces with ovens, and the parlour, separated from the hall by a stone wall, has a smaller hearth

---

[1] Plans in this volume are normally drawn with their principal entrance at the bottom of the page. In the drawing of 'Bennetts', it is however the present entrance on the rear front which is so arranged, as the street doorway has been blocked (Fig. 22).

on the gable. The timber newel-stair is contained in a large semi-circular turret projecting from the rear wall of the house midway between hall and parlour, and leads by a flight of stone steps to the cellar under the parlour, and by wooden steps to the first floor and attics. There is a small fireplace in the bedroom over the parlour, which presumably is the principal chamber, having the maximum privacy. A second stair has subsequently been introduced into the corner by the fireplace in the kitchen, the large apartment over this bay probably having been sub-divided into two rooms. As in the case of 'Bennetts', this house was also examined when in a ruinous condition, after the collapse of the thatched roof; the structure of the roof truss was similar to that at Milton, cross-walls, here, being taken up to provide additional support for purlins and ridge.

The house had been modernized in the 18th century, when the front elevation was provided with new fenestration to accord with contemporary taste. The windows were completely altered, with stone three-piece lintels to hall and parlour, having stressed keystones and tall casement windows, whilst internally the reveals were taken down to floor level, with shutters and architraves. One original window survives on the rear elevation to the parlour, having a chamfered wood lintel, with flat-splay oak mullions, rectangular glazing lattices and iron casements. In addition, there is in the stair turret (Pl. 18c) an interesting small window with a cusped triangular head, a characteristic vernacular detail, whilst the cellar window has a stone surround with two flat-splay stone mullions, probably re-used, placed together in the middle. It is likely that in a house of this scale the original windows on the front wall would have stone mullions and dressings, with wood frames on the rear elevation, a common combination in the 17th century. Like the two preceding houses, this was a large and important farm-house, and the limits of the yard are defined with later farm-buildings at the back of the house. The house recently has been rebuilt in such a way as to destroy all evidence of its original layout.

These twelve houses bring the study of the yeoman house-type within the region to the point when building was interrupted by the Civil Wars in 1640, new developments being noted in dated structures after the resumption of building activity in 1646. The buildings so far described represent the characteristic forms of the regional yeoman house from the commencement of the general rebuilding period in stone in the 16th century up to this intermission. There are many other dwellings where it is even more difficult to state with certainty that the structure was built before 1640, as similar plans to

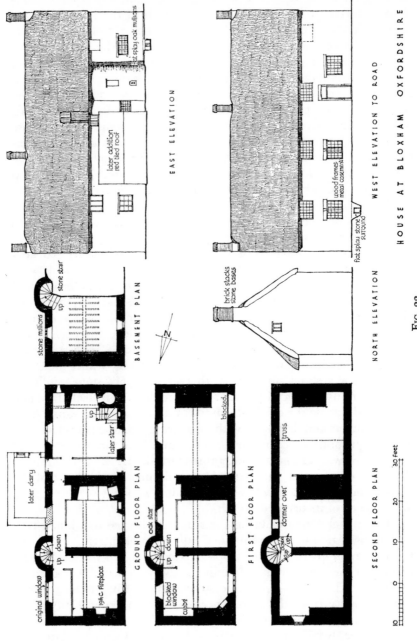

EAST ELEVATION

stone mullions

stone stair

BASEMENT PLAN

N

later addition
red tiled roof

later dairy

up down

19th.c. fireplace

original window

later stair

up

GROUND FLOOR PLAN

oak stair

up down

blocked window

cubbd

blockd.

FIRST FLOOR PLAN

truss

dormer over

up down

SECOND FLOOR PLAN

st. splay oak mullions

WEST ELEVATION TO ROAD

wood frames
metal casement

flat splay stone
surround

NORTH ELEVATION

brick stacks
stone bases

HOUSE AT BLOXHAM OXFORDSHIRE

10   0   10   20   30 feet

FIG. 23.

these earlier houses continue to appear throughout the century at the same time as more advanced layouts were being introduced for the more sophisticated class of dwellings.

Structurally, the first 17th-century buildings reveal some advance on those few earlier yeoman dwellings of the 16th century described in Chapter IV. Stone is the exclusive walling material for this class of house, although it is probable that the humbler cottages of the period, of which no examples survive, continued to be built of light timber-framing with wattle infilling. Apart from the larger manor-houses, walls have assumed a uniform and consistent thickness of approximately 1 foot 10 inches, with an internal batter, and contrast with the heavier masonry of the previous century, while internal partitions are still largely of stone; at Cromwell Cottage and Warmington Manor stone walls separate the entrance passage from the service, as in earlier 16th-century dwellings. Internal cross-walls are normally taken up to the roof to support purlins and ridge, McGreal's Farm being an exceptional case with the walling finishing at eaves level. Shortage of suitable timber for trusses may have necessitated the use of such stone supports. Original internal partitions other than those of stone are rarely found, the passage partition usually having been renewed or refaced; the plastered stud partition described at Hornton Manor affords one indication of the type of internal stud walling used at this time.

Buildings progressively increase in height from one-and-a-half to two-and-a-half storeys, but the attics in the early yeoman houses have little value as living rooms, being obstructed by collars at knee-height and lit only by small openings in the gable walls. Floors of random-width boards are supported by joists chamfered on the underside, spanning from the central longitudinal beams in all cases with no enrichment of the timber other than an occasional simple stop to the plain chamfer. The arrangement of the floor beams in the hall at Warmington Manor in c. 1603, where they span across the building, receiving some enrichment, is not repeated in the lesser houses, the length of the hall at Warmington probably accounting for the adoption of this system there.

Two truss forms can now be distinguished, the most usual being closely related to the raised cruck derivatives described in the last chapter. The principals are straight, built into the walls just below eaves level, tied by one collar and crossed at the apex to receive the ridge, usually a squared beam set in a shaped seating in the fork. The tie-beam roof, in which the principals are tenoned to a transverse beam at eaves level, occurs in the two manor-houses at Warmington

and Hornton, elevating the roof timbers out of the first floor altogether while providing a loftier second floor, in both cases lit by large
gabled dormers. The spacing of the roof supports is somewhat
irregular, due to the practice of using cross-walls, amplified by
occasional trusses to reduce bays to a maximum of 12 feet. At Hornton Manor and Milton, the bay averages 10 feet, whilst in the last
two houses described in Bloxham the average is 12 feet, the large
kitchen unit at the second house being sub-divided by a truss into
two 8-feet bays. Spans show similar variation, varying from 15 feet
at Beech Tree House, Lower Middleton Cheney, to almost 18 feet at
Sycamore Terrace—the latter clearly a house of some importance—
but the remaining dwellings and other examples of this period average 16 feet wide internally.

Shutford and Warmington Manors provide the only exceptions
to the general use of thatch in these houses, and gable parapets also
are only provided in the more significant architectural structures at
Shutford, Warmington and Hornton. Those at Swerford belong to
the rebuilding of the roof in the 18th century. Apart from those at
Shutford, decorative kneelers are not found, these features appearing
to be a characteristic of the second half of the 17th century. Stone
chimneys are generally taken up to the ridge level, with a stone capping a few inches above the thatch; in all cases brick stacks have
been added in later times.

The yeoman plan of the early 17th century is directly related to
the development of the hall-house outlined in the previous chapter.
The larger houses, built just before or after 1600, are of particular
interest in providing a link between the medieval manorial plan and
the smaller sub-medieval three-unit yeoman houses of the first half
of the 17th century, at the same time illustrating the working of the
time-scale already noted. Shutford Manor retains the later medieval
four-unit arrangement of detached kitchen, service-room, screens
passage, hall and private room—the parlour of the 17th century—
the stair being in a projecting tower at the upper end of the hall. At
Warmington Manor this plan is basically repeated in more formal
manner, the kitchen now closely adjoining the service room, whilst a
second stair is added at the lower end in addition to one between hall
and parlour. In both cases, the principal chambers are over hall
and parlour.

Turning to the lesser 17th-century dwellings, it can be seen that
there is some compression of function to suit the smaller scale of these
buildings, the hall combining the function of kitchen, with separate
service and parlour at lower and upper ends respectively. This

arrangement is seen in the houses at Swerford and Lower Middleton Cheney. An alternative arrangement of the three-unit plan soon becomes general whereby the service-room receives the addition of a large fireplace, so becoming a kitchen, the hall and parlour retaining their identities. At Cromwell Cottage, this early dispensation with the service-rooms coincides with the introduction of a basement cellar for storage. In all these early examples having kitchen, hall and parlour, the hall shows evidence of losing its former significance, becoming progressively smaller, until in the last house to be described, by the church at Bloxham, dating from c. 1640, it becomes the smallest of the three rooms, although still having a large fireplace. The parlour or inner room beyond the hall greatly increases in importance through the first half of the 17th century, frequently being provided with a fireplace, usually on the gable but sometimes on the hall side.[1]

In all but the two larger manor-houses, the hall fireplace is planned against the screens passage to produce the characteristic 'upland' plan already seen at Blue Gates, Bloxham, and other 16th-century houses. To enter the hall from the street usually involves walking along the passage behind the fireplace and entering between the side of the breast and the stairs. Swerford reveals what is probably an alternative arrangement which gains popularity after 1646, whereby the hall entrance is brought to the front of the passage while keeping the stair on the back of the house, the position it occupies in all these early small houses. At 'Bennetts', a further alternative is found, the fireplaces being placed adjoining the rear wall, which similarly brings the hall entrance nearer to the doorway from the village street. This improved plan is also more widely adopted in the second half of the century.

All dwellings described have complete first floors, partly contained within the roof space in the earlier small houses. In a number of cases, including Cromwell Cottage, the chamber over the lower end appears from its extra privacy and the provision of a fireplace, sometimes the only first-floor hearth, to be the principal bedroom following the tradition of the solar over the service already noted in medieval dwellings. In certain of these houses there is a second stair at the lower end, giving private access to this bedroom which, at Cromwell Cottage, does not communicate at first-floor level with the rest of the house. By 1640, however, the distinction of best bedroom is more commonly given to the room over the parlour, the change

[1] Early instances of fireplaces in the parlour have been noted in Chapter IV, including Blue Gates, Bloxham, and Grange Farm, Balscott.

perhaps being associated with the change in staircase position or deriving from the influence of two-room plans after mid-century which omitted the lower end. McGreal's Farm is an early instance of this arrangement.

The provision of a cellar under the parlour is an important development which was to have several effects on the yeoman plan. The introduction of this feature into the region cannot be dated with certainty; as already noted, the first dated house with a cellar was built at Charlton in 1637, but this is an isolated example and it is not until 1654 that cellars start to appear regularly in dated structures. In Monmouthshire, the authors attribute the introduction of cellars in approximately 1590 to the need for storage for cider, basements being generally planned to take advantage of sloping sites and having external accesses.[1] Fynes Morison notes in his itinerary of 1617 that 'most of the house in cities and towns have cellars under them, where for coolness they lay beer and wine'.[2] It is probable that the basement within the Banbury Region developed a little later, but certainly before mid-17th century. From the time of its introduction the cellar is invariably placed under the parlour, only twelve examples having been noted of basements under kitchens or halls. A number of reasons can be proposed for this arrangement. The siting of all these houses follows the general practice of laying the kitchen at the lower end of the site, where there is any fall in the level of the ground, the parlour being at the higher point. Even on quite level sites, there are normally changes of level throughout the house, with a step up from kitchen to passage, again up to the hall and a further step to the parlour. The elevation of the parlour was utilized in placing the cellar underneath, the arrangement incidentally providing this important apartment with the comfort of a boarded floor as compared with the earth or flagged floors used elsewhere in the house.

The purpose of the basement appears to have been entirely that of a storage cellar, and its introduction has two possible effects on planning. One is that the addition of this storage space obviated the need for a separate service, the hall fulfilling the duties of kitchen also, and the service-room is progressively omitted when cellars are introduced, particularly after 1640. Secondly, the introduction of the cellar at the upper end of the hall may account for the removal of the stair from its position by the hall fireplace to a new site between hall and parlour where it could serve from cellar to attics. This new position, which has been anticipated in the larger houses at Shutford, Warmington and Farthinghoe, becomes general from c. 1635 in three- and

[1] Op. cit., Vol. III, p. 19.   [2] *Itinerary*, 1617.

two-unit plans, providing a more private approach to bedrooms over hall and parlour, corridors being unknown in these smaller homes. It is also possible that the new stair position may have originated for this reason in the two-room plans which were to predominate in the second half of the 17th century.[1] It is evident that the new position of the stair is associated with the change in the position of the 'best bedroom' from over the service to the room over the parlour, which becomes most marked after 1640, the best or the only first-floor hearth then being at this end of the house.

The four-unit plan of Shutford Manor, comprising kitchen, service, hall and parlour, having been reduced in yeoman dwellings at the beginning of the 17th century to service or kitchen, hall and parlour, the next stage in development is the elimination of the now redundant hall, producing a two-unit plan once more. A survival of the medieval two-room arrangement noted in Chapter IV, having no inner room, occurs in Sycamore Terrace, the service here having developed into a full kitchen, still with the principal bedroom over. McGreal's Farm is an early instance of the hall and parlour arrangement, a development which is, however, really associated with the second half of the century, when two-unit plans of this type become the accepted form for even large and important yeoman dwellings.

In architectural detailing these houses illustrate the regional character of the period. Due principally to later alterations, stone dressings are infrequently found in the houses of yeoman class before 1640, save in the larger and socially more significant dwellings. Stone-mullioned windows are invariably of the ubiquitous flat-splay section, the hollow-moulded form being rarely recorded in the region, whilst the classical ovolo section is also rare before 1646. Oak mullions certainly were used on the rear elevation of one of the Bloxham houses, and, originally, may have been provided in several of the smaller buildings. The use of stone dressings is derived from practice in the larger houses and manors, while oak-mullioned windows are related to the earlier timber-framed tradition, continued at the same time—and often in the same house—particularly in the poorer class of dwelling.

Fenestration in all the early yeoman houses is confined to the long walls; Shutford Manor and Warmington Manor have large windows on their gables, but this practice is not adopted in the lesser homes until mid-17th century when gable fenestration is developed within

[1] It is noteworthy that with the introduction of corridor partitions in the 18th century, the staircase is again frequently placed by the side of a gable fireplace, particularly in smaller dwellings.

the region with unusual elaboration for a comparatively short period. Apart from the flat-topped semi-dormers at Sycamore Terrace and Cromwell Cottage, the full dormer with gable is the prerogative of the manor-house, lighting a more spacious second floor. Stairs reveal little architectural character, invariably being in timber—Cromwell Cottage provides a rare exception in stone—of newel form, contained behind a door. Later stairs attain greater convenience by being placed in turrets projecting from the rear of the house, following the precedent set in greater houses such as Shutford. More elaborate stairs are only found in the greater houses, such as that at Warmington, and there is also a good stair with turned balusters in a large house at Fenny Compton, dated 1593.

All the houses so far described, and others to which a date before 1640 can be attributed, invariably lie with their main frontage parallel to the road, with a yard at the rear, flanked by farm-buildings and barns. No evidence has been found of outside kitchens, which have been proposed in Monmouthshire, although there are later outbuildings with kitchens and ovens—a good example is to be seen at Hornton Manor—which were probably provided for farm labourers, all being of 18th-century date or later. The through-passage gives access through the dwelling from the road to the yard, while a cartway is usually arranged at one end of the house, the corners of the gable frequently being rounded off to facilitate the turning of passing wagons. The well is invariably found near the rear doorway, sometimes contained in the later extension of dairies, brewhouses and other structures of the farm.

CHAPTER VI

LATER DEVELOPMENTS OF THE REGIONAL HOUSE
1646–1700

THE Banbury Region was seriously engaged in the Civil War between 1640 and 1646, and the peaceful existence of the area was interrupted by the passage of armies and the outbreak of warfare. Middleton Cheney, Cropredy, Deddington and other villages were the scene of bitter conflict; Banbury was besieged, plundered and burnt; many great houses were destroyed; and a major battle was fought at Edgehill.[1] Apart from the association of a number of dwellings with the names of the opposing Royalist and Parliamentarian leaders, reputed to have lodged therein,[2] the principal effect of the wars on the region is seen in the total absence of dated buildings between 1640 and 1645, and it would seem that building activity virtually ceased for this period. Immediately the disturbances had ceased, building was renewed on an increasing scale, and the period between 1650 and 1660 provides more dated structures than any other decade—over 17 per cent of all dated houses before 1800 recorded within the region.

The evidence of dating suggests that the third quarter of the 17th century saw the peak of regional building for the more important yeoman dwellings, and with this renewal of activity in 1646, a number of further developments of the regional house plan become apparent. These changes, which result from the increasing desire for privacy and convenience on the one hand, and the influence of national Renaissance building on the other, result primarily in a

---

[1] A full account of the Civil Wars in relation to the region is given in Alfred Beesley's *History of Banbury*, 1841, pp. 291–437.

[2] The king is reputed to have breakfasted on the morning of the battle of Edgehill in a cottage at Radway. The two nights following the battle of Cropredy Bridge, the king slept at 'a very poor man's house' at Williamscot. 'An old and humble dwelling in this place is pointed out as the habitation in which, within a night or two of the Battle of Cropredy bridge King Charles slept' (Joseph Skelton, *The Antiquities of Oxfordshire*, 1823). Beesley mentions that this dwelling 'has been but lately removed' (1841). The manor-house at Culworth (27th June 1644) and a 'Yeoman's House' at Grimsbury (28th June 1644) also provided shelter for the king (Beesley, op. cit., pp. 358–9).

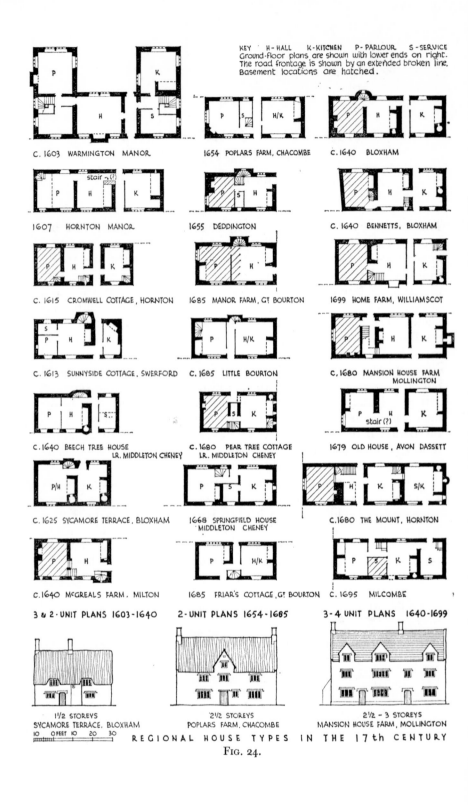

KEY : H - HALL   K - KITCHEN   P - PARLOUR   S - SERVICE
Ground-floor plans are shown with lower ends on right.
The road frontage is shown by an extended broken line.
Basement locations are hatched.

C. 1603   WARMINGTON   MANOR   1654   POPLARS FARM, CHACOMBE   C. 1640   BLOXHAM

1607   HORNTON   MANOR   1655   DEDDINGTON   C. 1640   BENNETTS, BLOXHAM

C. 1615   CROMWELL COTTAGE, HORNTON   1685   MANOR FARM, GT. BOURTON   1699   HOME FARM, WILLIAMSCOT

C. 1613   SUNNYSIDE COTTAGE, SWERFORD   C. 1685   LITTLE BOURTON   C. 1680   MANSION HOUSE FARM
                                                                                        MOLLINGTON

C. 1640   BEECH TREE HOUSE
          LR. MIDDLETON CHENEY   C. 1680   PEAR TREE COTTAGE
                                               LR. MIDDLETON CHENEY   1679   OLD HOUSE, AVON DASSETT

C. 1625   SYCAMORE TERRACE, BLOXHAM   1668   SPRINGFIELD HOUSE
                                                  MIDDLETON CHENEY   C. 1680   THE MOUNT, HORNTON

C. 1640   McGREALS FARM, MILTON   1685   FRIAR'S COTTAGE, GT. BOURTON   C. 1695   MILCOMBE

3 & 2 - UNIT PLANS   1603 - 1640   2 - UNIT PLANS   1654 - 1685   3 - 4 UNIT PLANS   1640 - 1699

1½ STOREYS
SYCAMORE TERRACE, BLOXHAM   2½ STOREYS
                                POPLARS FARM, CHACOMBE   2½ - 3 STOREYS
                                                             MANSION HOUSE FARM, MOLLINGTON

10   0 FEET   10   20   30

REGIONAL   HOUSE   TYPES   IN   THE   17th   CENTURY
FIG. 24.

change of emphasis in the use of rooms, with a reduction in the importance of the hall. The hall—from medieval times the major element of domestic living, meriting the title of the house or house-place in many regions—is progressively reduced in size and significance until by the 18th century it has generally become the entrance hall which it remains today. Plans already described have seen an increase in the size and importance of the parlour and kitchen, both being provided with hearths in addition to that in the hall. This trend is further developed in the second half of the century, in particular in the greater number of important two-unit houses of fine architectural quality which simply combine a large parlour with a second room serving primarily as a kitchen. In 1674, Warden Woodward of New College, Oxford, notes with approval the house of Abraham ffinch at Shutford, in the south-west of the region, 'where there is a Kitchen & Hall, or Parlour, very handsome'.[1]

Fewer houses of the three-unit plan are recorded after 1646, these also showing the reduced status of the hall, which by 1700 is frequently deprived of a fireplace, and simply contains the entrance and the principal stair, the latter now being occasionally more conveniently planned. In height, the yeoman house is invariably of two full storeys, with attics above, or cock-lofts as they are described in contemporary writing; these upper rooms within the roof continue to be badly lit from the gables only, dormer windows being at all times rare features within the region, associated with the most prosperous yeoman dwellings and manor-houses. Structural forms described in the previous chapter show little alteration throughout the century, the two types of truss already noted being used, with walls of the standard 22-inch thickness. The reduction in the number of stone internal walls is noticeable, the fireplaces being placed on the gable walls, and light stud-partitions used to divide rooms and to frame the through-passage on either side. The inadequacy of many of these partitions to support heavy spine-beams results in the arrangement of principal floor-beams spanning across the house, while on upper floors, spine-beams are occasionally tenoned to the tie-beams of roof-trusses.

Bedroom fireplaces continue to be something of a luxury, usually provided in the larger houses only, and often in the principal bedroom alone, normally over the parlour. The hearth-tax returns of 1665[2]

[1] *Progress Notes of Warden Woodward round the Oxfordshire Estates of New College, 1659–1675.* Oxford Record Society, 1945.
[2] M. B. Weinstock, Ed., *Hearth Tax Returns, Oxfordshire.* Oxford Record Society, 1940.

show that two hearths to a house was the most common number at
the time throughout the region, presumably in the two principal
rooms, kitchen and hall or parlour.

The architectural character of the yeoman house in the second
half of the 17th century reveals the increasing influence of the Renaissance on minor domestic building. The first dated use of ovolo-
section mullions (apart from the great house at Wroxton) has been
recorded in one of the largest and first yeoman houses to be erected
after the Civil Wars, Castle End, Deddington, built in 1647 (Pl. 9b).
The use of this detail is found in many dwellings built in the next
twenty-five years, generally in the larger and more prosperous
houses: the flat-splay mullions, however, continue to predominate
now as before 1640. Windows show some increase in size and number,
four- and five-light openings being more often employed, even in
quite small houses, whilst gable windows are frequently adopted, and
become a regional characteristic. The end walls are given considerable prominence, with tiers of windows symmetrically disposed, the
gables finished by parapets with decorative kneelers. Classical influence is seen also in the increased formality and symmetry of the
principal elevation. The placing of houses at right angles to the road
is more frequently noted than in the earlier part of the century, frequently to gain a southern aspect for the principal apartments. The
majority of such dwellings are not, however, of through-passage
plan.[1]

Towards the end of the century, windows tend to become larger.
The increase is achieved in one of three ways; by a wider spacing of
the mullions; increasing the length of the mullions, the window tending to assume a vertical form; or by providing transomed windows
of increased height. This phase, in the last decade of the century,
also sees the reappearance of the early hollow-splay mullion section,
which is so rarely encountered within the region in its earlier sub-
medieval association. The transomed window in stone is rarely
found in minor domestic work, but from the end of the century the
mullioned window begins to give way to the transomed wood-frame,
lighting loftier rooms, the first dated example recorded being in a
large house—Cropredy Old Manor House—in 1694.

These characteristics of the regional house in the latter half of the
17th century may first be studied in a number of large three-unit
houses, and, secondly, in many more buildings with only two principal rooms. The small house at *Culworth* (Fig. 25), in the fringe area

[1] The relation of the regional house to its site is separately considered in
Chapter XIII.

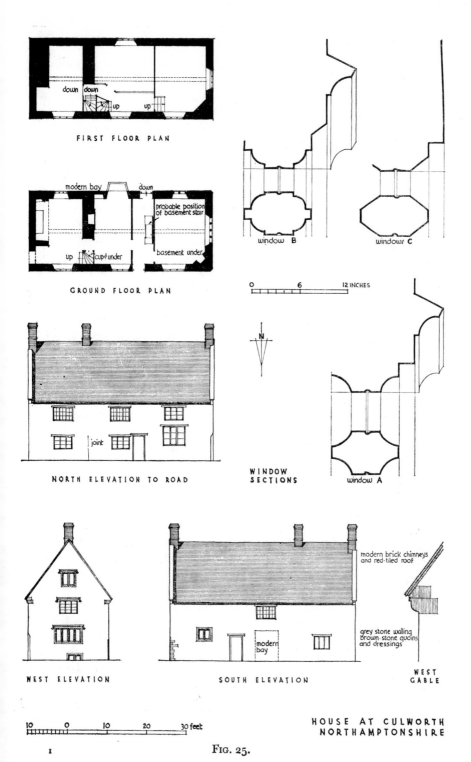

FIRST FLOOR PLAN

down down
up up

GROUND FLOOR PLAN

modern bay down
probable position of basement stair
up cupd under
basement under

window B

windows C

0   6   12 INCHES

N

WINDOW SECTIONS

window A

NORTH ELEVATION TO ROAD

joint

WEST ELEVATION

SOUTH ELEVATION

modern bay

modern brick chimneys and red-tiled roof

grey stone walling brown-stone quoins and dressings

WEST GABLE

10   0   10   20   30 feet

I

HOUSE AT CULWORTH
NORTHAMPTONSHIRE

FIG. 25.

of mixed building stone in the north-east, shows signs of a change in build in the 17th century which has resulted in a later version of the three-unit through-passage plan, in which the hall fireplace no longer backs onto the passage but is placed at the upper end of the hall, with stud partitions flanking either side of the passage. There is a second large hearth in the parlour, but the room at the lower end, presumably a service-room, does not appear originally to have had a hearth, although a later corner-fireplace has been introduced. The cellar is here placed under the service-room, an arrangement less frequently recorded than under the parlour, but which does become more popular in the latter part of the century—possibly in a desire to relate more conveniently the storage and kitchen accommodation. The stair is in the later position between hall and parlour against the front wall of the house, and the cellar position necessitates a separate stairway from the service-room. This house is of interest in combining the three common varieties of mullion section, including the later, more slender, concave-section mullions, all on the same elevation, with dressings of the marlstone to contrast with the grey limestone walling.

Lexton House, Lower Middleton Cheney, dated 1691 (Pl. 18*b*), is an important yeoman house which also illustrates the placing of the cellar under the kitchen in an almost identical plan to the last. The building has, however, been modernized and extended, its façade rebuilt, with large sash-windows, in the 18th century.[1]

Home Farm, Williamscot (Fig. 26), bearing the date of 1699 and the initials R^{B}M, provides a still later instance of this final stage of the full three-unit plan, the sophisticated and classical detailing of the entrance front contrasting sharply with the sub-medieval form of the building. This is a large farm-house of the usual two-and-a-half storeys, modern dormer windows having been added on the back to complement the original gable lighting of the attics. Here the hall is still an important room, having a bay window, and with the fireplace again placed at the upper end of the room, leaving only stud partitions to frame the through-passage, a second hearth and oven being provided in the kitchen. The cellar is here more conventionally placed under the parlour, which has no fireplace, a stack having been added at this end in recent years. A broad, framed stair, probably of contemporary date, with a 'dog-gate', is situated on the front wall opposite to the hall fireplace, where it relates to the cellar steps, and also to the attic stairs. A second staircase of more traditional

---

[1] The subsequent improvement and extension of many houses built at this time is described in Chapter X.

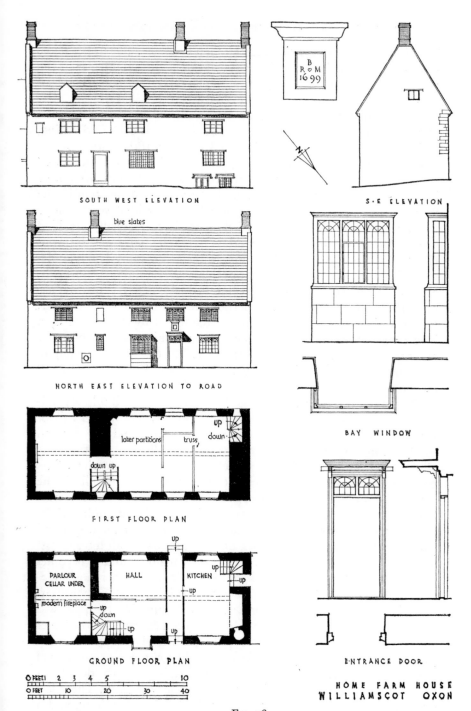

SOUTH WEST ELEVATION

B
R ♥ M
16 99

S·E ELEVATION

blue slates

NORTH EAST ELEVATION TO ROAD

BAY WINDOW

up
down

later partitions   truss

down up

FIRST FLOOR PLAN

PARLOUR
CELLAR UNDER

HALL

KITCHEN

up

up

modern fireplace

up
down

up

up

up

GROUND FLOOR PLAN

ENTRANCE DOOR

0 FEET 1 2 3 4 5   10
0 FEET   10   20   30   40

HOME FARM HOUSE
WILLIAMSCOT   OXON

FIG. 26.

form is provided at the side of the kitchen fireplace. The upper floors have been modernized, but it seems that only the chamber over the hall has an original fireplace, set in one angle of the room. The roof also is much renewed and now finished with blue slates.

The architectural detail of the north-west elevation to the road shows an unusual architectural refinement for this class of dwelling, and relates to the more sophisticated class of 18th-century house described in Chapter IX. Windows have moulded wood lintels and frames, being of three lights with iron casements and decorative leads, and are grouped in a balanced disposition in relation to the front entrance door. This is distinguished by a moulded wood canopy and fanlight over the six-panelled door set in a classically-moulded frame. A fine rectangular bay window lights the hall from this front (Pl. 22d), with a 'bull's-eye' window to the cellar stair. The rear elevation is markedly less elaborate or advanced, retaining a sub-medieval character with simpler wood-lintelled casements, whilst the use of stone-mullioned windows is perpetuated in the basement cellar. In the 18th century, the house was extended at the lower end by a long range containing an outer kitchen and dairy, with stables and other farm buildings in a wing at the rear. The circular patterning in the cobbled paving outside the entrance to the dairy show the 'tread' for a donkey or other small animal operating the churns.

The full development of the cock-loft as a habitable second-floor is seen only in the largest yeoman houses. *The Mansion House Farm, at Mollington* (Fig. 64), is an unusually large and fine yeoman dwelling, now somewhat decayed, standing a little apart from the village and approached through elaborate stone gate-piers. The house has been extensively altered, its interior virtually rebuilt, in the 18th century and later, and there are now two entrances on the principal elevation, with stone camber arches and splayed jambs, whilst a porch with elaborate doorway has been added over the upper end entrance. Much of the stonework has been renewed, all too successfully reproducing regional detail in the local stone, and it becomes difficult to identify original work, or to determine whether new stonework represents the direct reproduction of original features, or alternatively disguises modern improvements. Presumably the plan was similar to those already noted, with an original entrance at the lower end, perhaps by a through-passage, although the lower partition has gone and the rear doorway blocked by the introduction of a medieval two-light window, with squared cusped head—an early detail, re-used—this also being blocked by an added dairy outshut. There is a stone head to the kitchen fireplace, of doubtful authenticity, and a large rectangular oven projecting from the back of the fire, probably of 18th-century date. The hall fireplace, again quite modern, is at the upper end of the hall, with the parlour beyond, under which is a cellar. The principal stair lies between hall and parlour, and has also been much altered. It is lit from the rear wall by a tall stair-window under a stone label-mould, with wood mullion and transom and small squared leads, which probably represents an early 18th-century improvement,[1] presumably replacing separate mullioned windows. Within the parlour, the fireplace is on the rear wall of the house, having a gabled chimney stack, this arrangement of the fireplace occurring, in small houses, only in this part of the region.

The second entrance from the south front, protected by the porch, opens into the stair bay between hall and parlour, and despite the renewal of the stonework, the arrangement may well be as originally built. It is probable that the house dates from the last quarter of the 17th century, when the provision of upper and lower entrances is sometimes noted. This feature has been described at Shutford Manor, where it may be an improvement of late 17th-century date. A further parallel with Shutford is seen in the development of the attic space as a full second floor. Here, as in other large houses at the end of the 17th century, the eaves level, instead of occurring immediately over the first-floor windows, is raised 4 to 5 feet above this level to provide more headroom near the outer walls, which are taken up further as a series of gabled dormer windows on the face of the building. This arrangement is a final step towards the full third floor already seen at Shutford, and to be noted in larger 18th-century dwellings. The roof of the Mansion House Farm is now finished with red tiles, the use of which is limited to the north-west of the region, where they presumably replaced thatch in the 18th century.

There is at Mollington a small fireplace in the hall, but in a number of three-unit houses dating from the end of the 17th century, the hearth is omitted from this room. A fine and unusual example of such an omission is seen in the *Old House, Avon Dassett*, dated 1679 (Figs. 27, 28, 76), where the entrance from the front elevation is into the hall—the smallest of the three rooms—separated by a 2-feet-thick stone wall from the kitchen. There is now a through-passage, but the partition wall and the rear doorway are not original work, and the house may have had only one door, anticipating developments of the

---

[1] As already noted, transomed windows of this type can be firmly dated from 1694. In plan and form this house would agree with such a date, but the completely sub-medieval character of the front elevation would be somewhat archaistic for this late date. It is nevertheless possible that this window is part of the original building of *c.* 1690.

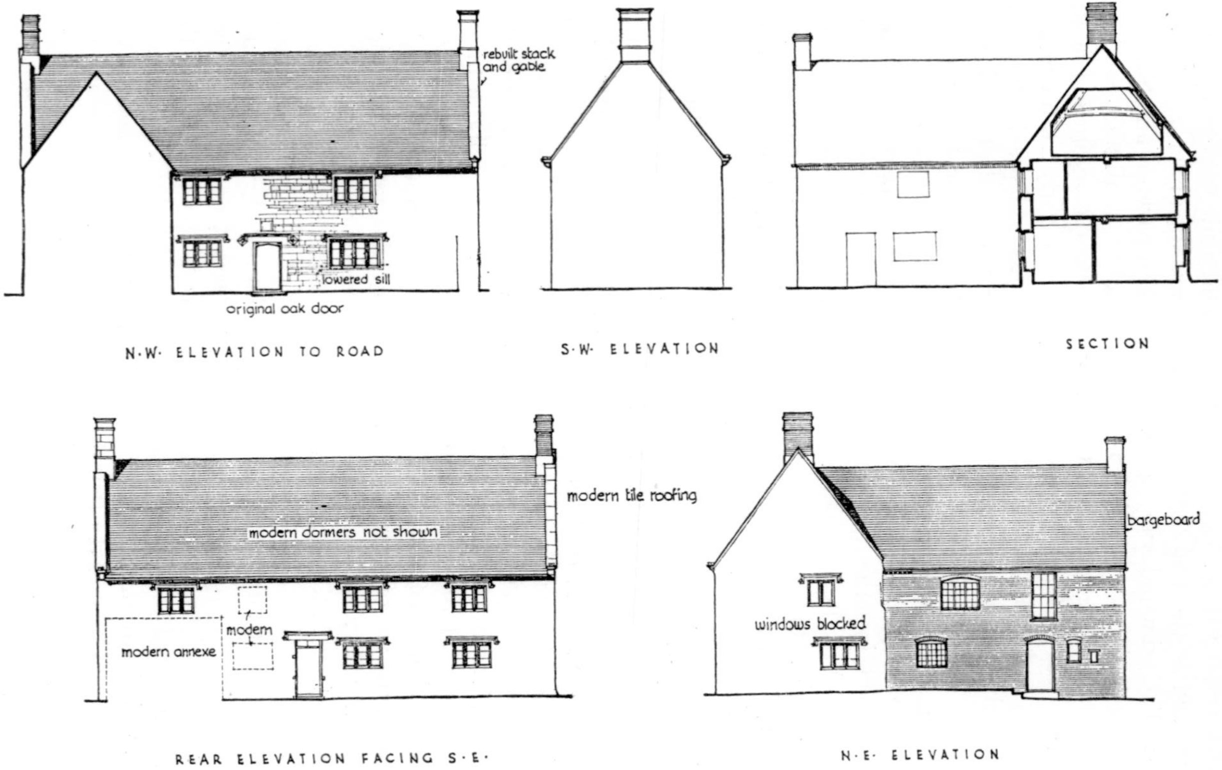

SECTION

S·W· ELEVATION

rebuilt stack
and gable

lowered sill

original oak door

N·W· ELEVATION TO ROAD

bargeboard

windows blocked

N·E· ELEVATION

modern tile roofing

modern dormers not shown

modern

modern annexe

REAR ELEVATION FACING S·E·

FIG. 27.

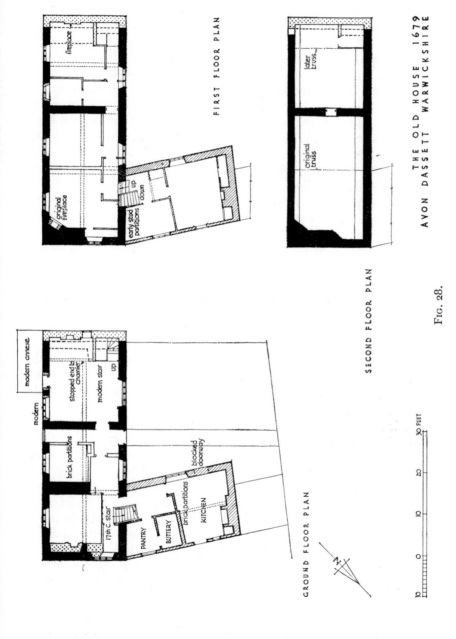

FIRST FLOOR PLAN

fireplace

original fireplace

early stud partitions

up down

SECOND FLOOR PLAN

later truss

original truss

modern annexe

modern

stopped end to chamber

brick partitions

modern stair

up

17th C. stair

PANTRY

BUTTERY

brick partitions

KITCHEN

blocked doorway

GROUND FLOOR PLAN

N

10   0   10   20   30 FEET

THE OLD HOUSE 1679
AVON DASSETT WARWICKSHIRE

FIG. 28.

following century in houses similarly planned. The stone wall between hall and kitchen is taken up to support roof timbers, but that between hall and parlour terminates at first-floor level, with a truss over. The arrangement of cross-walls in relation to the entrance seen here is unusual, bringing the through entrance into the hall for the first time. The kitchen on the right of the entrance has lost its original fireplace on the north-west gable, which has been rebuilt in recent times. The principal stair was probably on the front wall between hall and parlour, with a second stair by the side of the kitchen fireplace, now renewed. Within the principal bedroom, over the parlour, is a fine angle-fireplace with stone surround, its detail corresponding to the stone dressings of the entrance door, with four-centred arch and moulded jambs under a flat label (Fig. 76). The door-head has lozenge-shaped stops, already noted as being characteristic of the region. Early in the 19th century, the house was extended by a two-storey wing projecting forward from the parlour, to provide a new kitchen, attended by pantry and buttery, and the present stairway is contained in this extension. This stair, with flat, shaped balusters, is probably of earlier date than the house, and this fact, together with its larger scale, suggests that it has been introduced from another building.

A more orthodox version of this plan is to be seen at Dixon's Farm, Horley, where the through-passage is again formed by light partitions, with the main stair between hall and parlour, a second stair in the kitchen, and hearths in kitchen and parlour only. The windows are of the late hollow-splay section, which assists in dating the building to c. 1690.

The Mount, Hornton, Oxfordshire (Fig. 29; Pl. 10a), is a large house of particular interest, presenting the final stage in the evolution of the three-unit 'upland' plan; it provides a clear link with the four-unit sub-medieval arrangement described at Shutford Manor, whilst also relating directly to the development of the two-unit plan after 1646. The plan provides a parallel to that of the Old House, Avon Dassett, comprising a parlour, with moulded spine-beam, fireplace on the inner cross-wall, and basement under; and a small hall, now reduced to the function of an entrance and containing a broad straight-flight stair against the rear wall, together with front and rear entrance doorways. The through-passage may have been originally defined by a stud partition, but this is improbable—there are indications of a corner of the hall having been later screened off to form a pantry—and as at Avon Dassett the through entrance is within the hall, in contrast to the upland arrangement already defined. A heavy stone wall

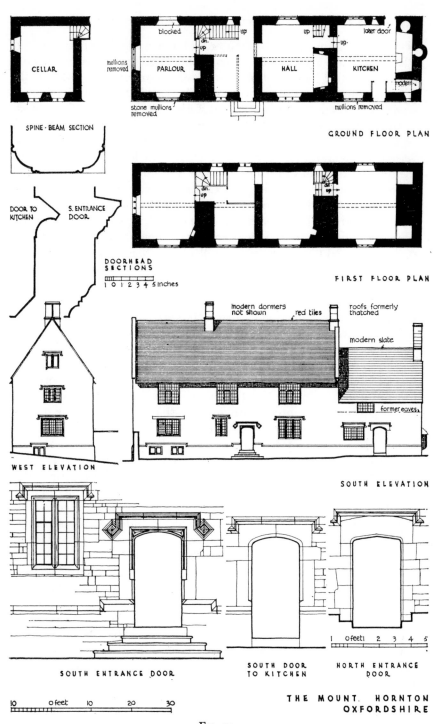

CELLAR

blocked   later door

mullions
removed   PARLOUR   HALL   KITCHEN

                                                                   modern

stone mullions
removed   mullions removed

GROUND FLOOR PLAN

SPINE·BEAM SECTION

DOOR TO   S. ENTRANCE
KITCHEN   DOOR

DOORHEAD
SECTIONS
1 0 1 2 3 4 5 inches

FIRST FLOOR PLAN

modern dormers   red tiles   roofs formerly
not shown   thatched

                                        modern slate

                                        former eaves

WEST ELEVATION

SOUTH ELEVATION

SOUTH ENTRANCE DOOR   SOUTH DOOR   NORTH ENTRANCE
                             TO KITCHEN   DOOR

1 0 feet 2 3 4 5

10   0 feet   10   20   30

THE MOUNT. HORNTON
OXFORDSHIRE

FIG. 29.

below the entrance separates hall from kitchen, the latter containing a large fireplace and a smaller second stair, also on the rear wall. The plan is extended by the return of the service-room at the lower end, of single-storey height, connecting with the kitchen and having a separate entrance on the south front. Originally this room, the largest in the house, had windows on the west gable, later blocked by the addition in the 18th century of a large fireplace with ovens, which converted the room into a full kitchen. There may have been a loft over the service, lit from the gable, but more recently the walls and roof have been raised to provide a bedroom. Corner fireplaces are provided only in the chambers over the parlour and the original kitchen. Modern dormers light the attics, formerly having windows only in the gables, and the roofs have been much renewed, the former thatch replaced by red tiles over the main block and blue slates over the service. The disposition of the building on its site reverses the traditional arrangement, the house being end-on to the roadway, with the parlour at the point of lowest level, adjoining the road. Internally, however, the normal 'upper' and 'lower' ends are maintained, the parlour being elevated over the basement, and the floor levels descending to the service-room by steps between each room.

The architectural enrichment is of some quality, as befits what was obviously an important yeoman dwelling, all three doorways having arched stone heads: the main south doorway has moulded jambs and camber arch, with lozenge-shaped stops to the label-mould. All ground-floor windows are stone-mullioned, having the late, tall mullions of flat-splay section. First-floor windows have timber frames and iron casements, of three lights with transoms and small squared leads, which may be contemporary with the date of the house, again within the last quarter of the century. A simple splayed plinth is limited to the entrance front and west gable to the road. On the rear elevation, formerly lighting the cellar stair, is a blocked two-light window of rather crude, early medieval character, having round-headed lights cut in a semi-circular head-stone (Pl. 21c). It is possible that this is a re-used medieval fragment, or alternatively—as suggested in Chaper XII—simply a decorative feature of 17th-century vernacular craftsmanship.

From these examples, it will be seen that the three-unit house is following a consistent pattern of development at the end of the 17th century, although at the same time, the less sophisticated dwellings continue to reflect the earlier versions of the regional plan, which thus continue to appear throughout the 18th century also. The reduction in the significance of the hall which has been noted, probably accounts for the adoption of a two-cell plan by the majority of dwellings after 1646, many of which both in size and architectural character are superior to the three-unit houses already described. The two rooms are presumably the kitchen, and a combined hall and parlour, the stair being placed between the two apartments, often with the addition of a pantry in this central position. Cellars continue to be used in many houses, site conditions no doubt influencing their inclusion.

The Poplars Farm, Chacombe (Figs. 30, 31), is one of the largest and finest two-unit houses within the region, bearing the date of 1654. It takes the last two plans to a further stage by eliminating the hall, leaving only a central through-passage entrance, adjoined by the stair and a small service-room between two large ground-floor rooms, the hall or kitchen being over 16 feet square and the parlour only one foot less in length. The through-passage is defined by original stud partitions surviving on either side, while the stair is placed at the upper side of the passage, at the back of the house, with a small pantry (approximately 9 feet by 6 feet) adjacent to it, lit by a two-light opening on the entrance front. This is again separated from the parlour by a further stud partition, there being no solid cross-walls in the clear 43 feet internal length of the building. Both fire-places are on the gables, that in the parlour placed across one corner of the room. First-floor joists are supported by a spine-beam which spans across the stud partitions, being scarfed to provide a continuous length. The roof is divided into bays averaging 12 feet, by roof trusses of tie-beam type, the principals curving at the foot where they are tenoned to the tie, in a manner which probably relates to the preceding cruck tradition; the second-floor spine-beams are supported from the tie-beams, to which they are tenoned. Renaissance influence reveals itself on the elevations, the principal front and the upper end gable being given more emphasis than the back, with a central dormer-window (Pl. 24a) and fine grey limestone dressings to windows. As in so many large regional houses, the entrance doorway is in marked contrast to the elaboration of window detail, having a simple wood lintel. The rear elevation is less formally treated, with wood lintels and frames to all windows save to parlour and stair. Attics, lit from the gables and from the central dormer, do not appear to have been partitioned, and have probably been little utilized for living space, there being no indications of ceiling or plastering. Thatch is the roofing here, as originally on all houses so far described in this chapter. The house has been extended in the 18th century, and this later work is considered in Chapter X.

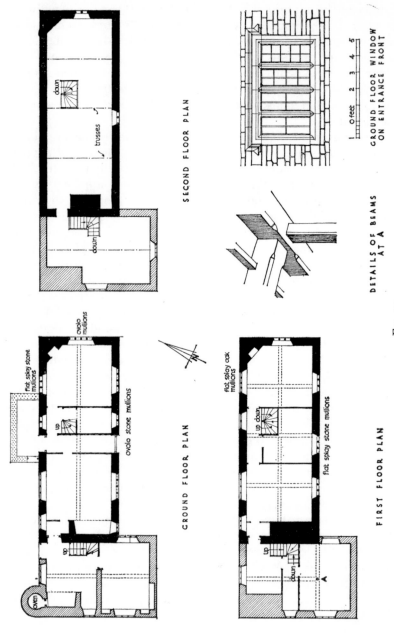

SECOND FLOOR PLAN

down

trusses

down

GROUND FLOOR WINDOW
ON ENTRANCE FRONT

0 feet 1 2 3 4 5

DETAILS OF BEAMS
AT A

Fig. 30.

flat splay stone
mullions

ovolo
mullions

ovolo stone mullions

up

oven

GROUND FLOOR PLAN

flat splay oak
mullions

up down

flat splay stone mullions

up

down

A

FIRST FLOOR PLAN

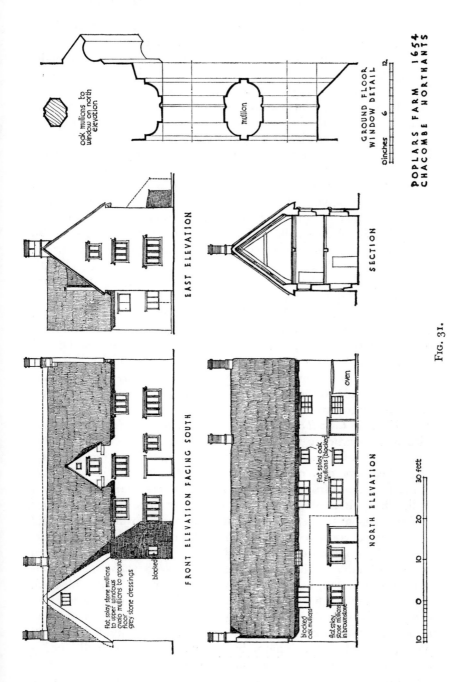

oak mullions to window on north elevation

mullion

GROUND FLOOR WINDOW DETAIL

0 inches   6   12

POPLARS FARM 1654
CHACOMBE NORTHANTS

EAST ELEVATION

SECTION

flat splay stone mullions to upper windows
ovolo mullions to ground floor
grey stone dressings

blocked

FRONT ELEVATION FACING SOUTH

oven

flat splay oak mullions blocked

blocked oak mullions

flat splay stone mullions in brownstone

NORTH ELEVATION

10   0   10   20   30 feet

FIG. 31.

The Poplars Farm retains the through-passage entrance, and is an early example of the two-unit house with central doorway, to become the most usual form at the end of the century, although the through-passage is by then abandoned in more limited plans. A number of dwellings, nevertheless, still at the end of the century and later retain the gable entrance, their plans corresponding to the hall and parlour elements of the full three-room plan already seen before 1646 at McGreals Farm. The interesting house at *Bloxham*, shown in Fig. 32, is of this type, of small dimensions (under 14-feet span) but with stone dressings to windows on both long elevations, and a fine stone doorway on the gable, now concealed by a later kitchen. The two rooms are here separated by a stone partition, the stair being against this wall in the corner of the hall, and both rooms have fireplaces on the end walls. A first floor and attics are provided above, with the principal floor beams spanning across the building. Dressed stone-work is of unusual interest, the door having a four-centred arch with moulded jambs, and lozenge-shaped stops to the label, this feature being repeated to terminate the labels of the first-floor windows facing the road, which have ovolo mullions, flat-splayed internally (Pl. 20*c*). This is the only example of decorative stops to window label-moulds recorded within the region. The house has been known as the Old Chapel, and the first floor may have fulfilled a special function to justify this elaboration of the fenestration. Considerable alterations have been made to the house in extending the accommodation, and dividing it into two cottages.

A house in *Council Street, Deddington* (Fig. 33), also has associations with a non-domestic function, being reputed to have contained a school-room over an 18th-century extension. The original house, which bears the date of 1655, is however of orthodox two-unit plan, similarly entered from the gable, with fireplaces again on each end wall. The stair is placed between the two rooms, in a rectangular projection from the rear of the building, having a well-formed, solid newel with decorative capping. There is a cellar under the parlour, reached by a separate stair from the hall. A small pantry has been introduced later at the side of these steps, with walls of stud-and-panel construction, lit by a window in the front wall, now blocked. The advantage of the central stair in providing more private access to bedrooms is well illustrated in this house. The first floor is divided into three chambers, as is usual with this plan, divided by stud partitions, and each is separately approached from a small landing at the head of the stair. Masonry details, although more limited, are also interesting, with ovolo windows in the brown stone to the

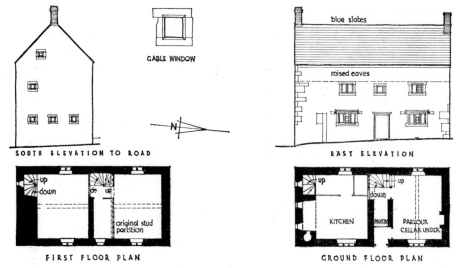

GABLE WINDOW

blue slates

raised eaves

SOUTH ELEVATION TO ROAD

N

EAST ELEVATION

up
down
dn up

original stud
partition

KITCHEN
PANTRY
PARLOUR
CELLAR UNDER.

FIRST FLOOR PLAN

GROUND FLOOR PLAN

PEAR TREE COTTAGE
MIDDLETON CHENEY NORTHANTS

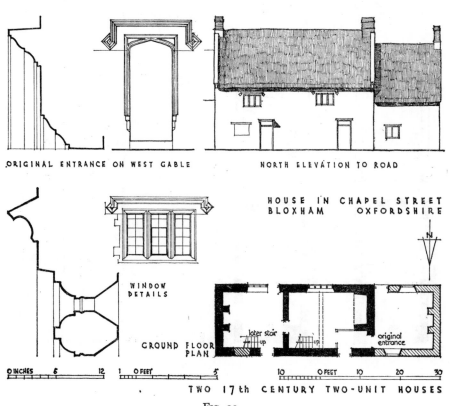

ORIGINAL ENTRANCE ON WEST GABLE

NORTH ELEVATION TO ROAD

HOUSE IN CHAPEL STREET
BLOXHAM OXFORDSHIRE

N

WINDOW
DETAILS

GROUND FLOOR
PLAN

later stair
up
up

original
entrance

0 INCHES 6 12   1 0 FEET 5   10 0 FEET 10 20 30

TWO 17th CENTURY TWO-UNIT HOUSES

FIG. 32.

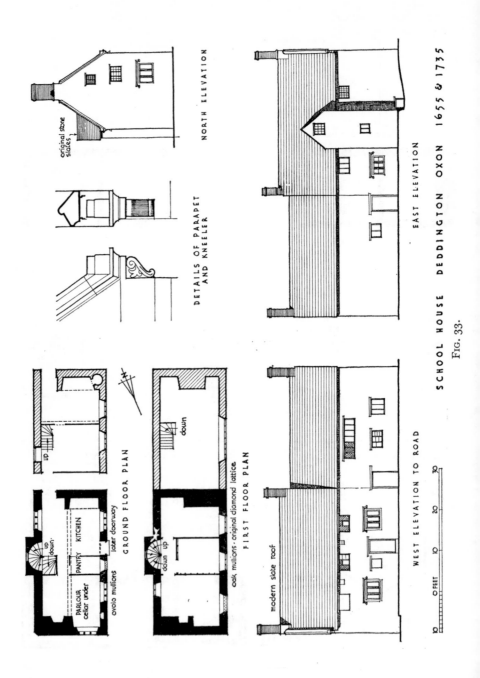

NORTH ELEVATION

original stone slates

DETAILS OF PARAPET AND KNEELER

EAST ELEVATION

GROUND FLOOR PLAN

later doorway

KITCHEN

PANTRY

PARLOUR
cellar under

up down

ovolo mullions

FIRST FLOOR PLAN

down

up down

oak mullions · original diamond lattice

WEST ELEVATION TO ROAD

modern slate roof

10   0 FEET   10   20   30

SCHOOL HOUSE   DEDDINGTON   OXON   1655 & 1735

FIG. 33.

ground-floor windows only, and a gable parapet at the upper end of unusually elaborate section, with fine kneelers of a character paralleled in only one other instance, also in Deddington. The first-floor windows, with oak mullions, retain original glass in diamond lattices. In 1735 the house was extended, and the new door made in the entrance front, these alterations being noted on page 214.

This type of plan is widely used during the second half of the century, being recorded as late as 1685 at Great Bourton, at a time when the central entrance was being more generally adopted. *Manor Farm, Great Bourton*, bears the date 1685 on the gable, which faces the street, this arrangement perhaps accounting for the retention of the end entrance. The square-headed doorway is of unusual ostentation, with a heavy, moulded architrave and a stone pedimented canopy. A rectangular projection between hall and parlour contains a spacious and well-formed newel stair, leading from the cellar to the attics, and there may also have been a pantry adjacent, as there is a window on the wall opposite to the stair. Details are of high architectural quality, with mullioned windows, parapet gables and moulded plinth, on all elevations (Fig. 63).

The gable entrance had limitations from both planning and design aspects, the parlour and bedrooms only being accessible from the entrance by passing through the hall. Placing the doorway in the centre of one elevation corrected this deficiency of plan, giving additional privacy, and at the same time assisted in providing a more formal and symmetrical elevation, in keeping with classical taste. The doorway provided a central focus, and the fireplaces at the ends of the house helped to maintain the symmetry of the plan. For these reasons, this type of plan is generally adopted after 1680, with important exceptions as already noted, whilst the gable entrance is still found in humbler dwellings throughout the 18th century. The typical plan is seen at *Little Bourton* (Fig. 60), where the central door—as so often, lacking dressed stonework—opens into the kitchen opposite to the stair, which again projects from the rear wall of the house. There is now a through-entrance passage, the doors not being opposite, but it is unlikely that this is an original feature. Both fireplaces are placed on end walls, and the front elevation, with stone-mullioned windows of flat-splay section, attains an approximate symmetry. Later additions at the rear of the house have necessitated the use of a second stair at the side of the kitchen fireplace. This may have been introduced at the time of the alterations, but the provision of two stairs even in small two-unit houses is not uncommon.

Pear Tree Cottage, Middleton Cheney (Fig. 32), probably a little

K

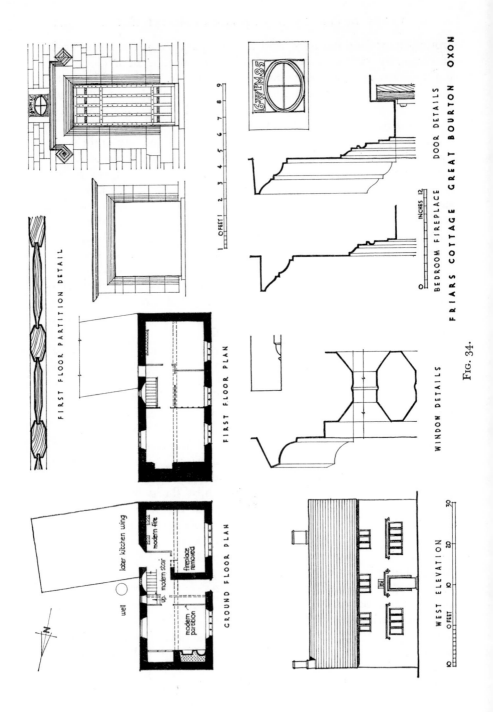

FIRST FLOOR PARTITION DETAIL

FIRST FLOOR PLAN

GROUND FLOOR PLAN

well

later kitchen wing

modern fire

fireplace removed

up. modern stair

modern partition

N

BEDROOM FIREPLACE

DOOR DETAILS

WINDOW DETAILS

WEST ELEVATION

FRIARS COTTAGE GREAT BOURTON OXON

FIG. 34.

0 FEET 1 2 3 4 5 6 7 8 9

0 INCHES 12

0 FEET 10 20 30

later in date at the end of the century, appears always to have had two stairs, although as the house is now sub-divided into two cottages this must also remain in doubt. The building lies at right angles to the road, with its entrance between hall and parlour, opening into a small vestibule at the side of a central pantry, contained by stone walls and borrowing light from the vestibule. The principal stair is on the rear wall behind the pantry, whilst on the first floor there is a narrow chamber over this central room. The hall or kitchen is the largest element, with a wide fireplace on the roadside gable, where there are three small windows, to the ground floor, a little over a foot square, with splayed stone surrounds. Two of these open into the back of the fireplace, which has an oven in one reveal; the third lights a small stair, with similar stair-windows above to first and second floors. There is a small modern fireplace in the parlour, also on the end wall, which may have replaced an original hearth. As at Little Bourton, the original thatch has been replaced by a modern slate roof, the walls raised at the eaves and the rear gable partly rebuilt in brick.

The two units of the three central-entrance houses so far considered represent the kitchen and parlour elements of the three-unit plan, omitting the hall, whilst the gable-entrance houses on the other hand represent the hall and parlour of the full three-unit arrangement, here omitting the separate kitchen, its functions being combined with the hall. All six houses share the common late-17th-century feature of both fireplaces being on the end gable walls. The two-unit plan with central entrance is, however, also found at this time with the parlour fireplace on the inner cross-wall, adjacent to the entrance, which now usually abandons the through-passage arrangement. This plan is illustrated in a second house in Middleton Cheney, not far from the last house to be described. This building, a small yeoman dwelling of the usual two-and-a-half storeys, is reputed to have been built in 1668, from graffiti on the kitchen fireplace bressumer, and this date would agree with the form of plan. Now known as *Springfield House, Middleton Cheney* (Fig. 19), it is entered from the east front into a small central bay between two rooms of similar size —kitchen and parlour—the parlour fireplace backing onto this bay. The stair is to the right of the entrance, on the front wall, by the door to the parlour, and a small pantry occupies the rear part of the centre bay, formerly defined by a stud partition. Although the cross-walls are here of stone, first-floor beams span across the building in characteristic late-17th-century manner. There are flat-splay stone-mullioned windows on the parlour gable and entrance front, having oak vertical bars for securing the leads instead of the more usual iron bars. Here, as in so many similar houses, the service accommodation has been later extended.

Great Bourton, Oxfordshire, has already provided one important example of a late two-unit house, having gable entrance: two other fine dwellings of similar size and architectural quality have been recorded in the village, with central entrances and fireplaces arranged as at Springfield House. Both dwellings in their present form introduce a new feature, perhaps derived from the lowland plans to be considered in Chapter VII, having rear entrances opening onto the side of the parlour fireplace, but in both cases these may have been introduced later. *Friar's Cottage* lies parallel with the road, opposite to Manor Farm, and bears the same date, 1685 (Fig. 34). The building has been considerably altered and provided with a new roof, but has the usual two rooms with the entrance in the centre either directly into the kitchen or into a passage, with the stair opposite on the rear of the house. The hall fireplace has been rebuilt recently on the rear wall, but it probably originally backed onto the entrance passage, for the spine-beam to the hall has been lengthened showing that the stack has been removed from that location. The stone dressings on the entrance front are of considerable elaboration, with a five-light flat-splay mullioned window to the hall and a fine doorway with rectangular head, a heavily moulded architrave and label with the diamond-shaped stops. As at Deddington, the three bedrooms are separately entered from a small landing at the head of the stair, and there is an interesting oak post-and-panel partition at the top of the stairs, with the more usual plastered stud partitions in less conspicuous positions dividing the chambers. The bedroom over the kitchen appears to have been the principal chamber, with a fine and large stone fireplace.

Spittal's Farm is probably of similar date to the other two houses in Great Bourton, and is of similar plan to the last building, with entrance, stair and fireplace in the same relationship, while here also there are good stone dressings to windows and door, and to the bedroom fireplace over the parlour or hall. The present stair is modern, the original probably being placed opposite to the hall fireplace, which here also occupies the earlier position against the entrance passage. The latter is separated from the kitchen by an early stud partition, but whether there was originally a rear entrance to the passage is uncertain, the modern stair being in this position, and the external masonry revealing no clear indications (Fig. 35).

In considering the final stage of the three-unit plan, illustrated by The Mount, Hornton, the re-introduction of the service-room at

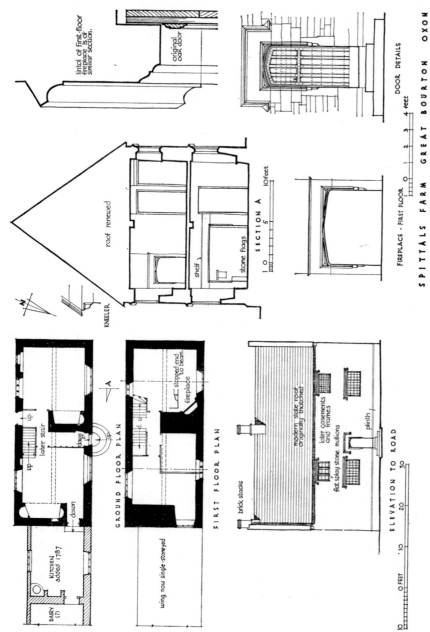

limit of first-floor fireplace is of similar section.

original oak door

roof renewed

KNEELER

shelf

stone flags

SECTION A

0   5   10 feet

DOOR DETAILS

FIREPLACE · FIRST FLOOR

0   1   2   3   4 feet

up

later stair

up

up

door

down

KITCHEN added 1797

DAIRY (?)

GROUND FLOOR PLAN

stopped end to beam.

fireplace

up

FIRST FLOOR PLAN

wing now single-storeyed

brick stacks

modern slate roof originally thatched

later casements and frames

flat splay stone mullions

plinth

ELEVATION TO ROAD

0 FEET   10   20   30

SPITTALS FARM GREAT BOURTON OXON

FIG. 35.

the lower end was noted. Similarly, the final stage of development of the two-unit house shows a return of the service end, producing a new form of three-unit plan, which points to the increase in kitchen accommodation subsequently developing during the 18th century. In addition to this service-room, the inclusion of a small cellar, and—as in the houses at Middleton Cheney and Chacombe—a small central pantry, illustrates the increased need for storage occasioned by improved social and living standards. It is noteworthy that the pantry follows by some years the introduction of the bread-oven to the region.

A house at *Milcombe, Oxfordshire* (Fig. 39), dating from not earlier than the last years of the 17th century, follows the plan-type already seen in the two dwellings at Middleton Cheney, having a central entrance, on the north front, into a small stair hall at the back of which is a small room possibly used as a pantry or even as a small parlour. Like Pear Tree Cottage, the building is placed end-on to the road, the main block being two-and-a-half storeys in height, thatched, with gable parapet. Adjoining the kitchen end is a bay of one-and-a-half storeys, similarly roofed but without a parapet, containing a large service-room entered from the north front and with a separate stair to an attic bedroom over. The reduction in height and significance of the lower end has been already noted at Hornton, and occurs in other dwellings of this date. A small basement is provided, lit from the south front, and appears to be limited to the central bay under the pantry, a most unusual arrangement. As both stairs are modern replacements, it is not now possible to gain access to the basement. The architectural character further reveals the late date of the house, two-light mullioned windows without labels being used for all windows except those on the north entrance front to the parlour and principal chamber over. These, like the three entrance doorways, have broad stone lintels and have wooden frames, originally with metal casements. There is a strong suggestion from the irregular character of the work, that the mullioned windows incorporate re-used material. In most cases having ovolo mullions, the kitchen window to the north has hollow section jambs awkwardly meeting the ovolo mullion; the south window of the parlour has a flat-splay mullion; and the dormer window of the service block makes use of ovolo mullions for its jambs. It seems probable that all openings are of one build, and the conjunction of details, in association with this late arrangement of plan, may indicate a date even later than the 17th century.

Apart from a number of single-unit houses, considered in a later chapter, one further plan-type of the later 17th century merits consideration. A small number of houses, all large and important dwellings, have been recorded which follow 'T'- or 'L'-shaped plans. In these, kitchen and hall usually form the main block whilst the parlour lies at right angles to the hall. Lodge Farm, Hook Norton, dated 1646, College Farm, South Newington, 1659; and a number of larger houses, vicarages and manors, such as Banbury Vicarage, 1649; Hook Norton Manor, 1656; The Rookery, Adderbury East, 1656; and Northend Manor, 1664, all have complex plans. Plans of 'U' and 'L' formation have already been noted in Chapter IV, occurring in houses of greater social significance built c. 1600. The larger manor-houses, of which a number were built after 1646, similarly develop complex arrangements to provide the additional and larger rooms appropriate to their social importance, and do not represent an alternative system to the regional plan, but merely an extension of its accommodation. From the 15th to the 17th centuries, the 'L' or 'T' plan is an important regional variant in certain parts of Lowland England, including South-West Suffolk and Essex, where it follows the medieval disposition described earlier, having the hall at right angles to the service wing. An alternative form, in which the kitchen is in the projecting wing, occurs in Leicestershire, as in the yeoman house at Wigston Magna, shown in Fig. 38.

Houses of this type are exceptional within the Banbury Region, and do not represent a common regional variant. In a number of the yeoman houses built in this way which have been noted, the 'L' plans have developed as the result of two stages of building, although the similarity of architectural detail often suggests that little time has elapsed between the two periods. This appears to be the case at a large house called *The Gables* (Fig. 62), standing to the south-west of the church at Middleton Cheney, where a late three-unit plan, similar to those described above, is combined with an additional parlour in a right-angle wing added at the upper end of the house, the detailing of the two parts being identical. The three-room block is set at right angles to the road, with through-passage entrance, flanked by light partitions, the fireplace being at the upper end of the hall. There is also a hearth in the parlour, but the third room, which is nearest to the road, has no fireplace, and is simply a service-room, having a separate stair, the principal stair being originally at the side of the hall fireplace. At right angles to the parlour is a wing containing a second through-passage entrance with a stair, and a parlour beyond, with cellar under. There are some slight indications of a change of build on the masonry of the rear elevation, but there is no change in detail, a chamfered plinth being continuous on the road frontage, and windows throughout being of the late hollow-chamfer section; thus it is probable that the building of the wing was almost continuous with that of the main block, probably *c.* 1690. The house may have been extended as resources became available, or it is possible that the additional apartment, with its own stair and entrance, was built as a separate residence for a member of the same family, arrangements of this nature having been recorded in Monmouthshire.[1]

An alternative arrangement in another building of more than one period is seen at *Northend Manor, Warwickshire* (Fig. 60), as rebuilt in 1664, where the kitchen and parlour are at right angles to the hall, a form which bears some relation to the medieval hall and service plan considered in Chapter III. There is little doubt, however, that the incorporation of an existing medieval hall determined the process of 17th-century improvement in this instance.[2]

Apart from such infrequent examples, six instances have been recorded of large yeoman houses built originally to an 'L' plan which appear to present certain fundamental differences to the regional pattern, arranging the normal three rooms of the yeoman plan in a different manner, uninfluenced by any site considerations. *Lodge Farm, Hook Norton*, built in 1646, is the most complete illustration of this uncommon form, and is unusual also because of its isolated location, over two miles from any village. Presumably it was built in connection with an early enclosure for sheep-farming in the south-west of the region, where also other examples are found, such as College Farm, South Newington. Lodge Farm is basically a three-unit house in which hall and service-room, separated conventionally by a through entrance, are in a gabled wing with the parlour placed behind the hall to produce the 'L' plan, its roof being of similar height to that of the main block which it intersects (Fig. 36; Pl. 10*b*).

There are now two entrances, one on the south front which faces the road, leading into the unusually small service-room with a corresponding doorway on the rear wall, whilst the second entrance is on the west gable of the hall, adjacent to the parlour wing. It is possible that this doorway was added at the time when other improvements were being made in the 18th century and later. As a result of these

---

[1] Op. cit., Vol. II, p. 75. The authors note the close association of kin-groups, whereby two or more houses of land-owning folk are found in the same complex, adjoining each other. The house already described in Little Bourton adjoins a second 17th-century dwelling in what appears to be the same yard, and may be an example of this relationship. See also Chapter XIII.

[2] The historical development of this house is described in Chapter X.

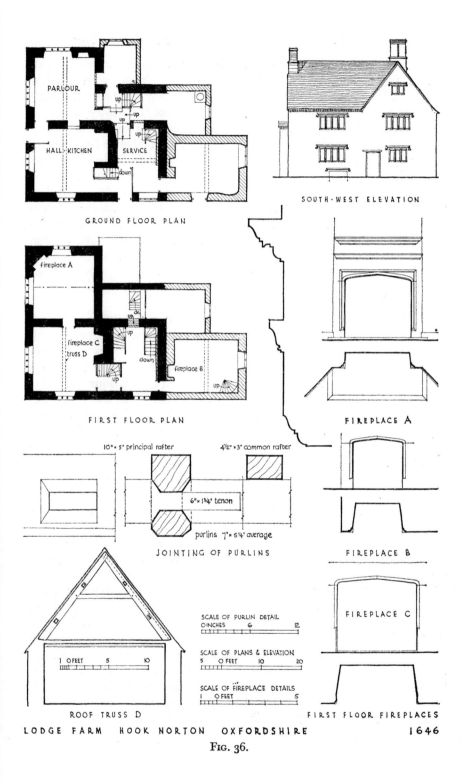

PARLOUR

HALL·KITCHEN   SERVICE

up
up
up
up
down

GROUND FLOOR PLAN

SOUTH·WEST ELEVATION

fireplace A

fireplace C
truss D

on
up
up
down

fireplace B

up
up

FIRST FLOOR PLAN

FIREPLACE A

10"× 5" principal rafter   4½"×3" common rafter

6"× 1¾" tenon

purlins 7"× 5¼" average

JOINTING OF PURLINS

FIREPLACE B

SCALE OF PURLIN DETAIL
0 INCHES   6   12

SCALE OF PLANS & ELEVATION
5   0 FEET   10   20

SCALE OF FIREPLACE DETAILS
1   0 FEET   5

FIREPLACE C

1 0 FEET   5   10

ROOF TRUSS D

FIRST FLOOR FIREPLACES

LODGE FARM   HOOK NORTON   OXFORDSHIRE   1646

FIG. 36.

alterations, there are now three stair positions in the original building. The principal stair, which gives access only as far as the first floor, is in a lean-to bay of one-and-a-half-storey height in the angle of the house, approached by the rear door from the service, and now also accessible from the parlour, and although such an arrangement is very unusual, it may well be original. The original stair from first to second floors is more conventionally located at the side of the hall fireplace, adjacent to the south entrance door. There is no evidence of there having been a stair at this point from ground to first floor, but this cannot be satisfactorily determined as this compartment was sealed at ground-floor level. The stair to the basement, which under-lies the parlour and possibly the hall also, may also be concealed at this point, there being now no access to the cellar. An additional stair has been later introduced into the service-room, from ground floor rising against the end gable, but changing its position on the first floor to rise behind the hall stack.

Apart from its fireplaces and stone-mullioned windows, there is little of quality in the masonry details, the entrance doors having simple wood lintels. Stone mullions are of flat-splay section, and windows have label-moulds. There are good fireplaces with arched heads and moulded jambs in the chambers over hall and parlour, the latter set across a corner. The building has been extended by a later bay beyond the service end, to provide a new kitchen with fireplace and separate stair, and in the chamber over this new wing there is a third fireplace of similar character, which has probably been removed here from the parlour where there is a later surround. In addition to this extension, probably of 18th-century date, there have been more recent lean-to additions on the rear of the house of rather poor character.

The roof structure provides yet another unusual feature, the arrangement of the purlins showing the intrusion of south-eastern carpentry practice (Pl. 7c). The trusses are of collar and tie-beam type, with straight principal rafters, lacking any ridge. Purlins of 10-inch by 5-inch chamfered section, butt against the principals which have chamfered housings cut on either side to give additional support to a tenon cut on the end of one purlin and taken through the principal to support the adjoining member. Only one other instance of a roof of south-eastern type has so far been described, at Shutford Manor, but the elaborate jointing at Lodge Farm shows some advance in technical knowledge. The original part of the house, including the lean-to roof over the stair, is finished with stone slates, but indications of the masonry having been raised at eaves and gables suggests that this may have replaced thatch. The extended wing is roofed with blue slates. Chimney stalks, separately expressed, were originally of ashlar stone, but with the exception of part of the original material remaining over the hall fireplace, all stalks have been renewed in brick.

The form of this very interesting and attractive building represents a step towards the two-room-deep plan. Such examples are rare exceptions at the end of the 17th century to the usual one-room-deep regional forms, which continue to be the basic type even in the following century, when it will nevertheless be seen that by subsequent extension a large number of regional houses arrive at the 'L' formation.

The Rectory at *Steeple Aston, Oxfordshire*, on the southern fringe of the region is now destroyed, but an early 19th-century drawing suggests that it may have been of 'L'-shaped formation. A full description of the house is given in a Terrier of 1683.[1] Although it is not possible to determine the plan with any accuracy from this account, it is of interest in naming the parts of a house at the end of the century and giving their internal finish. The building is described as:

A dwelling house consisting of the Rooms following, viz., One parlour wainscotted with oake and haueing a board floor with a chamber over it, and Cockloft over that, Two other lowe roomes adjoyneing with Chambers and cockloft over them, One kitchen with a corneloft over it with two corne Gardners therein; the roofes of the roomes foregoeing are covered with thatch save that the gutters thereof are slatted. The floors of the low room aforegoing are earthen except that the kitchen is stoned. Item: two low roomes, one being a dish-house and the other a mealehouse, with chamber and cockloft over them haueing the roofe slatted.

There is a further list of out-buildings which include 'One Dove house slatted', and 'A gate-house with a roome over it thatched'. The boarded parlour floor suggests a cellar under, while the drawing of the house shows a two-storey bay window at the upper end of the house, contributing to make the parlour a fine apartment.

In none of the houses included in the survey was any provision found for an internal privy. As late as the first quarter of the 19th century, George Herbert recalls vividly the problems of sanitation in Banbury before the introduction of water closets:[2]

Most of the cottages and many of the best houses had a large vault as large as a small living-room, and this was used for years without being emptied. Others of the more respectable class would have a box about

[1] C. C. Brookes, *History of Steeple Aston and Middle Aston*, 1929, p. 160.
[2] George Herbert, *Shoemaker's Window*, p. 106.

three or four foot long and about eighteen inches deep. This would be used until full.

The 'vaults' were emptied 'by taking up the floor of the room'.

Thatch continues to be the predominant roofing material, and all the houses described above were probably originally roofed in this way, although renewed in course of time in slate or tile. Only the owners of the largest dwellings, including many of the 'L'-plans noted above, could afford to import stone slates. Steeple Aston, lying nearer to the slate quarries, shows wider use of this material, and it appears likely that the Rectory had originally all been roofed with stone slates, later repaired and partly replaced by thatch.

The symmetrical road elevations of the later two-unit houses lead to the more formal and sophisticated façades of the larger houses built after 1700, and the practice of combining label-moulds as string courses, as already noted, precedes the 18th-century ashlar courses on such houses as the Dolphin Inn, Wiggington, built in 1727 (Fig. 53). Gable fenestration, of which a particularly fine example is to be seen at Kings Sutton Farm, (Pl. 24c), was a short-lived feature. The general adoption of gable fireplaces made the placing of windows more difficult, and although flues are sometimes contrived to wind between windows to the chimney, an asymmetrical disposition of windows did not please classical taste. Furthermore, the developments in the use and production of furniture in the 17th century could not have been turned to account in rooms with large windows on three sides, and a fireplace on the other, and there is increasingly a concentration of windows on one principal elevation, formally and often elaborately treated, with a reduced number of openings on the other lateral elevation, whilst the gables once more become blank walls.

CHAPTER VII

LOWLAND PLAN TYPES IN THE 17TH CENTURY

THE through-passage plan with axially disposed fireplaces can be regarded as characteristic of the regional yeoman house in the first part of the 17th century; its antecedents within the region have been established and its subsequent development after 1646 traced up to the end of the century. Within the Banbury Region two further plan-types have been distinguished. Both forms derive from differing traditions of building in the lowland areas of the south and east of England, and each appears most widely within certain areas, particularly in the north of the region.

Reference was made in Chapter V to the type of plan in which the fireplace is arranged on a long side-wall of the hall, rather than axially on a cross-wall or gable. The plan of an early 16th-century house at Wigston Magna in Leicestershire, drawn by W. G. Hoskins from documentary evidence,[1] is reproduced in the comparative plans in Fig. 13, and illustrates a timber-framed structure with hall fireplace on the rear long wall. This disposition is commonly regarded by historians as characteristic of the 'lowland' manorial plan, although it would appear to be common to manor-houses in all areas. Within the region it occurs in the greater houses, and also in a number of dwellings of yeoman class located in the north-western villages, particularly in that part of the region which lies in Warwickshire, a fact which suggests that this type of plan relates to lowland practice in the neighbouring Felden area, where indeed it has been noticed in many buildings, although these are generally of timber construction. Warmington Manor, Warwickshire (Fig. 16), built in *c.* 1603, is important among the examples in the Banbury Region, where the plan as a whole is of the usual through-passage type, but having the hall fireplace on the long side-wall. After the Civil War, Castle End, Deddington (1646); Northend Manor Farm (Fig. 45) (1654); Northend Manor, 1664; Mansion House Farm, Mollington; Laurel Farm, Shotteswell (Fig. 38), and other dwellings in this area combine a single lateral fireplace in the hall or parlour with other hearths axially disposed.

The Garden House, Mollington (Fig. 37), is one of the most interesting

[1] W. H. Hoskins, *The Midland Peasant*, p. 149.

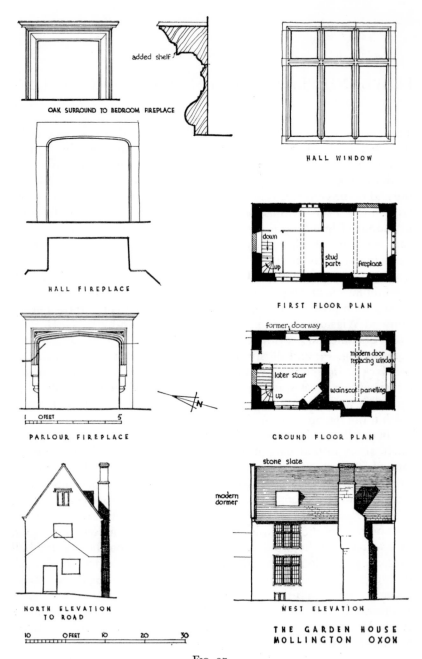

OAK SURROUND TO BEDROOM FIREPLACE

added shelf

HALL WINDOW

HALL FIREPLACE

FIRST FLOOR PLAN

down
up
stud partn
fireplace

PARLOUR FIREPLACE

0 FEET 5

N

GROUND FLOOR PLAN

former doorway
modern door replacing window
later stair
up
wainscot panelling

NORTH ELEVATION TO ROAD

10 0 FEET 10 20 30

WEST ELEVATION

stone slate
modern dormer

THE GARDEN HOUSE
MOLLINGTON OXON

FIG. 37.

examples of a two-unit house with lateral fireplaces, of architectural distinction unusual in a building of this size. Later alterations have obscured the position of the original stair and entrance, but for the rest the house has been little changed. The two units were used as hall and parlour, in the manner of the later 17th-century houses of similar scope already described, and the original entrance would be, no doubt, from the gable into the hall. The house is sited at right angles to the road. The hall, over a basement cellar which is not now accessible, has a large angle-fireplace against the inner wall, having a cambered stone head, simply chamfered; the room is lit by an unusually large window of six lights with stone mullions and transoms of flat-splay section, lacking label-moulds, a similar window lighting the chamber above. Such windows are rare in houses below manorial class, only one other example of a transomed window in stone having been recorded, at Middle Tysoe, where it is of the later four-light form dating from the end of the 17th century. A recent stair is provided in the south-west corner against the gable, of more generous proportions than the original newel stair which may well have been in this position. Beyond the hall is the parlour, a larger room with a wide but extensively restored fireplace on the side wall, with four-centred arch and moulded jambs. All the walls are completely panelled, the work being similar in character to that at Warkworth Farm, where it is dated 1658; a similar date would accord with the architectural character of this house. First floor and attics are provided above, the stone dividing wall on the ground floor terminating at first-floor level, and a stud partition separating the first-floor chambers. The quality of this small building suggests that it may have been of a social class superior to that of the farm-house, perhaps bearing some direct relationship to the adjacent manor-house, now a large Victorian structure but based on the nucleus of a 17th-century two-unit dwelling. A barn nearby is dated 1599.

The lateral fireplace is an exceptional feature within the region, and cannot be regarded as characteristic of the minor domestic architecture. There is, however, a second plan-type, also associated with lowland practice, which appears in larger numbers. Although the majority of examples are concentrated in the north and east, including those parts of Northamptonshire included in the region, buildings of this plan occur in all parts of the area. The fundamental feature of this house type is the omission of the through-passage and the placing of the single entrance on a long wall of the building opening onto the side of the hall fireplace, which occupies the usual axial position at one end of the hall. From this it is a simple development to the plan which places two fireplaces back to back, with the entrance similarly placed, opening onto a small vestibule at the side of the combined breast. This plan-type is combined with the other lowland feature of the lateral fireplace in a small number of houses, as at *Laurel Farm, Shotteswell* (Fig. 38), where two of the fireplaces are built back to back, with the third hearth on the rear wall of the kitchen.

Consideration of houses of this type can be divided to give separate regard to these two developments, the single hearth and the double, having the entrance similarly placed. The single fireplace may reasonably be presumed to be the earlier form, developed before the provision of a second fireplace became general; although earlier instances do occur, from 1625, dated buildings within the region indicate that the double stack is not widely adopted until after 1640. Precedents for this plan can be found elsewhere in Britain in both upland and lowland regions, and a selected number of comparative plans are shown in Fig. 38. Houses with the entrance opposite to a single hearth have been recorded in Wales, a noted example being *Abernodwydd, Llangadfan, Montgomeryshire*, now re-erected in the Welsh Folk Museum at St. Fagans.[1] The house is a timber-framed structure dating from the 16th century, originally of three-room plan divided by stud partitions, and of single-storey height with open hearth, the exact position of which is not known. The original entrance was presumably in its present position. In the 17th century a fireplace with stone rear wall, framed jambs and a wattled timber hood was introduced at one end of the hall, opposite to the door, while at the same time a floor was inserted with a ladder on the other side of the hearth. This plan corresponds with that of a single-stack house of this type within the region. The majority of such examples, however, including the back-to-back fireplace, occur in the lowland eastern counties, including Nottinghamshire, Lincolnshire and Leicestershire, where examples have been recorded by Dr. T. L. Marsden.[2] The house illustrated at *North Leverton, Nottinghamshire*, dates from shortly after 1600, and is a timber-framed building of three-unit plan, one-and-a-half storeys high, with a large double stack in brick between the kitchen and the hall, the entrance being on the back of the

[1] The building is described by Mr. M. F. H. Lloyd in the *Montgomeryshire Collections*, Vol. XLIV, 1935–6, pp. 84–5, and by Dr. Iorwerth Peate in *The Welsh House*, 1944, pp. 52–3. A further account of the house, with particular note of its removal to St. Fagans is included in the *Montgomeryshire Collections*, Vol. LIII, Part I, the author being again Dr. Peate.

[2] T. L. Marsden, 'Minor Domestic Architecture in the Lower Trent Valley', Manchester University Thesis, 1952.

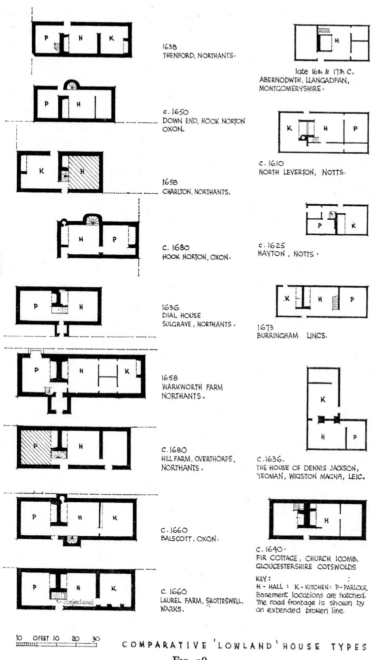

1638
THENFORD, NORTHANTS.

c. 1650
DOWN END, HOOK NORTON
OXON.

1658
CHARLTON, NORTHANTS.

c. 1680
HOOK NORTON, OXON.

1636
DIAL HOUSE
SULGRAVE, NORTHANTS.

1658
WARKWORTH FARM
NORTHANTS.

c. 1680
HILL FARM. OVERTHORPE,
NORTHANTS.

c. 1660
BALSCOTT, OXON.

c. 1660
LAUREL FARM, SHOTTESWELL,
WARKS.

late 16th & 17th C.
ABERNODWTH, LLANGADFAN,
MONTGOMERYSHIRE.

c. 1610
NORTH LEVERTON, NOTTS.

c. 1625
HAYTON, NOTTS.

1673
BURRINGHAM LINCS.

c. 1636.
THE HOUSE OF DENNIS JACKSON,
YEOMAN, WIGSTON MAGNA, LEIC.

c. 1640.
FIR COTTAGE, CHURCH ICOMB,
GLOUCESTERSHIRE COTSWOLDS

KEY:
H – HALL : K – KITCHEN : P – PARLOUR.
Basement locations are hatched.
The road frontage is shown by
an extended broken line.

10 OFEET 10 20 30

COMPARATIVE 'LOWLAND' HOUSE TYPES

FIG. 38.

L

house against the stack, and the stair on the far side of the hall fire-place. The walls of this house have subsequently been rebuilt in brick with an added outshut. The single-hearth plan is also recorded in the same region, generally in conjunction with two-room plans, as at *Hayton, Notts.*, comprising a kitchen or hall with fireplace and a parlour; the entrance is again on the back of the house opening against the side of the stack. A later example is drawn from *Burring-ham, Lincolnshire,* dated 1673, a three-unit type with double stack, the entrance here being from the street, and the stair more spaciously planned between hall and parlour. These three plans are reproduced from surveys by Dr. Marsden. An example of a lateral hearth has already been given from Leicestershire, and W. G. Hoskins illus-trates, again from documentary evidence, a further development of the early 17th century, in the house of Dennis Jackson, Yeoman, at *Wigston Magna.*[1] This is once more a timber-framed structure com-prising hall, parlour and kitchen, the latter in a wing at the back of the house with its fireplace backing onto that in the hall. The usual relationship of the entrance is not preserved in this 'L'-shaped plan, although there is again no entrance passage.

A number of reasons can be proposed for the position of the en-trance in this plan-type, and also for this arrangement of the fire-places. The through-passage in the upland plan within the region is primarily associated with dwellings placed with their frontages parallel to the street, the passage providing an access both to the street and to the yard behind: all the houses noted in Chapter V are so situated, and examples of three-unit upland plans disposed at right angles to the road are extremely infrequent.[2] With the lowland plan, lacking the through-passage, there is a difference in disposition in that by far the majority of such houses are either placed parallel to the road, but with their entrances on the rear elevation, or sited at right angles to the road, the entrance then being on the side-wall facing the yard. The rear entrance has already been noted in the Nottinghamshire examples, and within the Banbury Region, of all the houses built in the 17th century to this plan, less than 10 per cent are entered from the street—all being of later date—whilst the greater majority are equally divided between those placed in line with the roadway but entered from the back, and those placed at right angles to the road.

The lowland-type house is therefore associated with a different site

---

[1] Op. cit., p. 187.
[2] The underlying reasons for the siting of houses within the village pattern are considered in Chapter XIII.

lay out to the through-passage houses, seeking more privacy for the entrance on the rear of the house or on a side-wall. The disposition of a house with its gable to the road, at one side of its yard, would clearly reduce the utility of a through-entrance passage. The position of the entrance, moreover, gives a more advanced plan in the formation of the small vestibule at the side of the stack, with doors opening to rooms on either side, the stair being later brought into this small entrance hall to add further privacy and convenience. There is also a structural advantage in this arrangement in relation to the light, timber structures in which this form originated, the stack usually being built of brick or stone and quite independent of the wall structure, gaining increased stability from the combination of two hearths and reducing fire risk.

The use of this plan therefore relates to a lowland timber tradition, but is retained as a more advanced form of planning within certain areas of the region, where it is often associated with the more prosperous dwellings in the latter half of the 17th century; ultimately it passes to a Georgian plan-type, after 1700. One significant variation is noted between plans of this type within the region and those precedents cited from lowland areas, concerning the use of the rooms on each side of the entrance. The buildings noted above generally show the double stack combining fireplaces to the hall and kitchen, with a parlour at the other end of the house, so retaining the position of fireplace and entrance at the lower end of the hall, as in the upland plan. Only at Abernodwydd and Hayton is it suggested that the other room adjacent to the entrance vestibule was a parlour, and not a kitchen or service-room. This, however, appears to be the case in the majority of buildings of this plan recorded within the region, a measure of doubt as to the original use of rooms remaining in a number of earlier instances. Such an arrangement places the entrance and hearth at the upper end of the hall, and represents a fundamental departure from other plan-types so far considered. It is possible that this disposition is a later improvement on the form noted in Nottinghamshire.

The plan which disposes the entrance against the side of a single fireplace, to the hall, the adjoining room having no hearth or else a fireplace on the gable, is more strongly represented than the double stack. Reference to dated buildings shows this form to be somewhat earlier, although examples continue to be found throughout the 17th century. The rear or side entrance is a feature of most of these houses. The earliest dated houses of this type are Manor Farm, Barford St. John, dated 1606; the Three Conies Inn, Thorpe Mandeville, 1622;

and a small two-unit house at Hanwell built in 1625; but all these have been extensively altered. *Manor Farm* is the most informative of these, a large two-unit dwelling within the small village of Barford St. John (Fig. 39; Pl. 4*a*). The house now comprises two large rooms, presumably parlour and kitchen or hall. The parlour is in this case presumably the large room with small fireplace at the south-west end of the building, at the lower end of the sloping site. Two entrances are provided, the original doorway appearing to be that on the north-east entrance front, placed opposite the side of the parlour chimney-breast, and on the same front is a well-formed newel-stair projecting beyond the face of the building within a tall, gabled stair-tower, opening into the kitchen or hall. The second entrance is into the kitchen from the south-west front, the latter distinguished by a simple plinth.

The architectural details are not altogether in agreement with the early date of this house, but the name of the building—also given as the Manor House, or Moat Farm—suggests a social status above that of the yeoman houses to which it is nevertheless related in size, and this may account for some advance in detail. Walls average 2 feet 3 inches in thickness, usually an indication of early-17th-century or earlier build, but the floor-beams span across the building in a manner found only in larger houses of this date. Windows vary in detail, probably indicating some alteration. Many of the first-floor windows, particularly on the north-east front, have wood lintels and frames, with flat-splay oak mullions, whilst there is a window to the parlour on the north-east front with oak mullions of ovolo section. The stair tower has stone-mullioned windows, as also the parlour gable and the south-west front windows to hall and parlour, but these appear to be of later character, having mullions of flat-splay section, more slender and taller than are usually found before 1646. It is possible that these stone-mullioned windows, including the stair-tower itself, may be additions of the second half of the century. The house has been extended by a wing projecting from the kitchen, providing additional kitchen and service accommodation, and there is a further lean-to bay against the north-west gable, into which is built a re-used window of 13th-century character, having two pointed lights with central column, under a semi-circular label-mould. The house, including the stair turret, is roofed with stone slates, with gable copings and ashlar stacks.

An early example of three-unit plan of this type is at *Thenford*, in a house bearing a datestone of 1638 (Fig. 56). The building lies at right angles to the road, and is in ruinous condition, only the lower

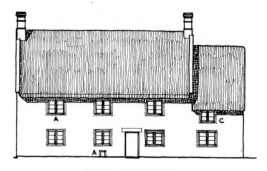

SOUTH ELEVATION

WEST ELEVATION

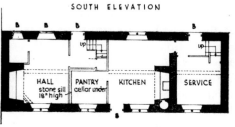

GROUND
FLOOR
PLAN

HALL
stone sill
18" high

PANTRY
cellar under

KITCHEN

SERVICE

NOTE reuse of stone mullions
A · flat splay mullions
B · ashlar lintels - wood frames
C · jambs, head & sill formed
with ovolo mullions.
Ovolo mullions to all other
windows on N. & S. fronts

HOUSE AT MILCOMBE
OXFORDSHIRE

DATE STONE ON
SOUTH GABLE
(not to scale)

later dormers
not shown.

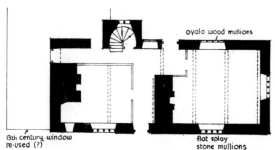

WEST ELEVATION

GROUND FLOOR PLAN

ovolo wood mullions

MANOR FARM
BARFORD ST JOHN
OXFORDSHIRE

10   O FEET   10   20

13th century window
re-used (?)

flat splay
stone mullions

FIG. 39.

courses of masonry now remaining, but it can be seen that it was of three rooms, with a second fireplace in the room farthest from the entrance, presumably the kitchen, and the stair presumably being in the parlour at the back of the hall fireplace. An early photograph shows the house to have been of one-and-a-half storeys, with wood lintels to all openings, and a steeply-pitched, thatched roof. There are some indications that the third apartment, the kitchen, may have been added at a later date. The building is of mean dimensions, the internal span being under 13 feet.

Examples of this plan-type become less frequent after 1640, giving way to the back-to-back fireplace, but are still to be found in smaller dwellings throughout the century. Of these a characteristic example is a small house at *Down End, Hook Norton* (*c.* 1650). This is a building of little larger size than the ruined house at Thenford, spanning 13 feet 6 inches internally, with a single hearth to the hall, the entrance being again on the rear elevation against the stack (Fig. 40). Stone dressings to windows survive on the rear elevation, and there are indications that the gable also had stone-mullioned windows (one label has survived later alterations), whilst the stair, opening from the hall on the rear of the house, adjacent to the entrance, is contained in a large projecting turret of semi-circular plan. An inner room is divided from the hall by a stud partition, now renewed, but it is again not clear whether this or the room to the right of the entrance is to be regarded as the original, upper end of the house. A second fireplace has been added more recently, backing onto the hall fireplace in the room which now serves as the parlour. The house is of two storeys, with thatched roof, and has been turned into two cottages, with the introduction of a second doorway and stair.

A number of small two-unit houses, related to this plan-type, have been recorded. A house at *Charlton*, dated 1658, has a central entrance against the hall stack, with a second fireplace to the kitchen on the gable wall, which is presented to the road. The cellar is here unusually planned under the hall, unless this apartment can be regarded as the parlour, in which case the plan would still present an anomaly, as the entrance would be against the side of the parlour fire. A house recently demolished at *Hook Norton* (Fig. 41) illustrated the two-unit plan more common in the second half of the 17th century, the two rooms being hall and parlour, with both fireplaces on the gables, and the entrance against the hall stack. The stair, in a fine circular turret, so characteristic of Hook Norton, was placed between hall and parlour, and there were fine, late, mullioned windows on the entrance front. The house was of very late, 17th-century

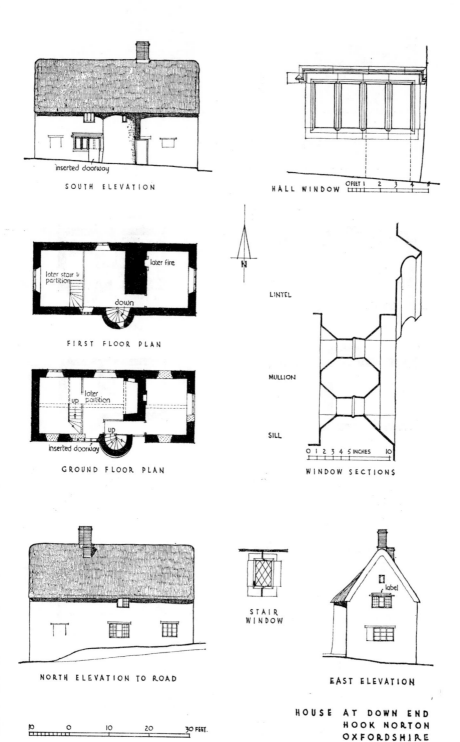

SOUTH ELEVATION

HALL WINDOW

inserted doorway

later fire

later stair & partition

down

FIRST FLOOR PLAN

later partition

up

up

inserted doorway

GROUND FLOOR PLAN

N

LINTEL

MULLION

SILL

0 1 2 3 4 5 INCHES 10

WINDOW SECTIONS

NORTH ELEVATION TO ROAD

STAIR WINDOW

label

EAST ELEVATION

HOUSE AT DOWN END
HOOK NORTON
OXFORDSHIRE

10   0   10   20   30 FEET.

Fig. 40.

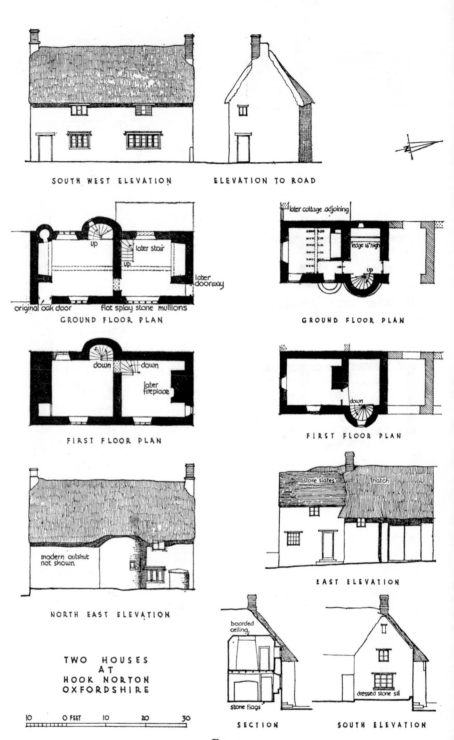

SOUTH WEST ELEVATION   ELEVATION TO ROAD

GROUND FLOOR PLAN

up
later stair
up
later doorway
original oak door   flat splay stone mullions

GROUND FLOOR PLAN

later cottage adjoining
ledge 16"high
up

FIRST FLOOR PLAN

down   down
later fireplace

FIRST FLOOR PLAN

down

NORTH EAST ELEVATION

modern outshut not shown

EAST ELEVATION

stone slates   thatch

TWO HOUSES
AT
HOOK NORTON
OXFORDSHIRE

SECTION

boarded ceiling
stone flags

SOUTH ELEVATION

dressed stone sill

10   O FEET   10   20   30

FIG. 41.

date, and although it is possible to reconcile its form with the lowland plan so far proposed, by regarding the second room as the kitchen, instead of the parlour, such a licence cannot really be justified.
There is a projecting oven against the hall fireplace, and the inner
room has more the character of a parlour. It may well be that by the
end of the century there was some fusion of the two traditions, and
that this and similar houses retain the disposition of rooms and fireplaces of the upland plan, whilst adopting the lateral entrance
characteristic of this lowland tradition. This house at Hook Norton,
of two storeys with thatched roof, was sited at right angles to the
street. Single-cell plans with entrances similarly placed in relation to
the hall fireplace have also been recorded, but are separately considered in Chapter VIII.

The back-to-back fireplace also makes its appearance within the
first half of the 17th century, early examples being recorded at
Alkerton (1625), Sulgrave (1636) and Charlton (1637). The *Old
Rectory at Alkerton, Oxfordshire* (Fig. 78; Pl. 1*b*), is a particularly fine
example of regional architecture, built in 1625 for one of the region's
most distinguished figures, Thomas Lydyat, rector of Alkerton and
a scholar and writer greatly respected in his day.[1] Born at Alkerton in
1572, the son of the Lord of the Manor, he became a Scholar at
Winchester and later a Fellow of New College, Oxford, where he
studied astronomy, mathematics, languages and divinity. He subsequently became 'Chronologer and Cosmographer' to James I's
eldest son, Prince Henry, until the latter's death, when he accepted
the vacant living of Alkerton in 1612, remaining there until his death
in 1646. While he was at Alkerton, Lydyat wrote over 600 sermons
and many books, but incurred debts partly through subsidizing
the publication of his own works, his financial difficulties bringing
him for a time to a debtor's prison in Oxford. The impact of
the Civil War was felt at Alkerton as everywhere in the Banbury
Region, and Lydyat suffered at the hands of the Parliamentary
forces, his home being pillaged on four occasions, whilst he himself,
for denying money to the soldiers and defending his books and papers,
was twice carried from his rectory and 'infamously used' by the
soldiers. The difficulties of Thomas Lydyat's scholarly life are com-
memorated by Dr. Johnson in *The Vanity of Human Wishes*.

The building of the rectory is recorded in the parish register of
Alkerton in an entry made by John Poynton, who was rector from
1663 to *c.* 1710.[2]

[1] Beesley, op. cit., pp. 386–7.
[2] Parish Register of Alkerton (Bodley, MS. DD. Par. Alkerton, p. ii).

The foundation of ye parsonage house at Alkerton was laid by Thomas Lydiat on Monday ye 2nd May 1625 and the house was built up and covered with slat and glazed ye same summer. June 1692. I slatted me half of ye parsonage house and ye chancel and new lathed it—it had 2000 of slatts—cost £1-10. besides carriage-charges in all £8 3s 9d not reckoning throughout. (sd) John Poynton. The charge of slatting ye last part of ye house 1669 £7. 4. 10 besides dyet. The particulars are amongst my Acquittances.

Subsequent alterations have done little to obscure the form of the original building, which comprises two large ground-floor rooms, each being approximately 17 feet square, separated by the central double fireplace. At a later date, probably early in the 18th century, a two-storeyed kitchen wing was added at right angles to the original hall-kitchen. The Rectory is entered on the north side by a fine moulded doorway with cambered arch and lozenge-shaped stops to the label-mould, retaining its original oak door. The fine standard of decoration is maintained throughout the house, with moulded spine-beam in the parlour, and good fireplaces. That in the parlour has moulded jambs and a Tudor arch, with the date of 1625 contained in the spandrels. The other ground-floor room originally fulfilled the functions of the kitchen, having a large fireplace with arched stone head, simply chamfered, and an unusually well-formed bread-oven over 4 feet 2 inches in diameter (Pl. 16d). A third fireplace, similar in detail to that in the parlour, is provided in the principal bedroom over the parlour. The stair was formerly on the north wall, adjacent to the entrance doorway and approached from the parlour, and still survives from first-floor level, being lit by a series of three single-light windows with splayed jambs, corresponding to the flat-splay stone-mullioned windows on north, south and west gable walls. The roof retains its 'slats' and has ashlar stone stacks and gable parapets. There has been an external entrance on the south wall, opening into the parlour adjacent to the fireplace wall, and it is believed locally that this represents the position of the original entrance doorway, removed to the north wall at the time of the Plague. Such an arrangement would be very unusual, whereas the present position of the entrance, in relation to both fireplace and stair position, accords with the regional pattern.[1] Although the north door has a camber arch, whilst all fireplaces have Tudor arches, mouldings are similar and there is no indication of the doorway having been altered. It seems more probable that the blocked south doorway was introduced at a later date and subsequently found to be an undesirable innovation.

[1] This factor is considered in Chapter XIII.

The second dated house of this type is *Dial House, Sulgrave, North-amptonshire*, a building of equally fine architectural quality, lying parallel to the road from which it is entered through a single-storey porch—an unusual feature (Fig. 42). Sulgrave lies to the north-east, on the outer fringe of the region, and Dial House, in common with most other dwellings in the village, is built in grey limestone, with dressings of the marlstone. The original two units may have served as hall and kitchen, but with the building of an additional kitchen bay in *c.* 1650, the earlier room adjoining the hall became a parlour. The present stair at the side of the fireplace by the entrance door is a renewal, probably in the original position. The form of the parlour fireplace can only be surmised in the plan in Fig. 42, as it has been completely walled up. In the chamber above, there is a fine fireplace in the north-west corner against the gable, with a four-centred arched stone head. The provision in upper rooms of a separate angle fireplace against the gable, rather than adjoining the central stack, appears to be characteristic of this plan-type. The new wing is entirely built of grey stone, including the ovolo window mullions and dressings, whilst the porch shares with the earlier two units the brownstone dressings and hollow-chamfered mouldings. Roof principals rise from the walls at eaves level, with a ridge set squarely in the fork, the single collar being halved instead of mortised to the principals, and the rafters rough poles, only partly squared, with a roofing of thatch. Trusses divide the original two units into irregular bays averaging 8 feet, with half trusses against each side of the stack, taken up only to purlin level. The similarity of the roof structure of the later kitchen bay suggests that this development followed very soon after the completion of the first part of the house, probably as more resources became available.

There is a house at *Charlton*, dated 1637, of similar two-unit plan with central stack and later stair in a square projection at the back, the entrance being from the street front, whilst there is a cellar under the parlour, the earliest dated within the region. The building has however been extensively altered in the later 17th and 18th centuries.

With the resumption of building activity in 1646, this plan-type was adopted for many large and important yeoman dwellings, and in all cases the double stack lies between hall and parlour. One of the finest and largest examples is *Warkworth Farm* (Fig. 43), in the small hamlet of Warkworth, Northamptonshire, now reduced to three or four dwellings with a fine church standing alone in the field, unapproached by any road. The house is of four-unit plan—a rare

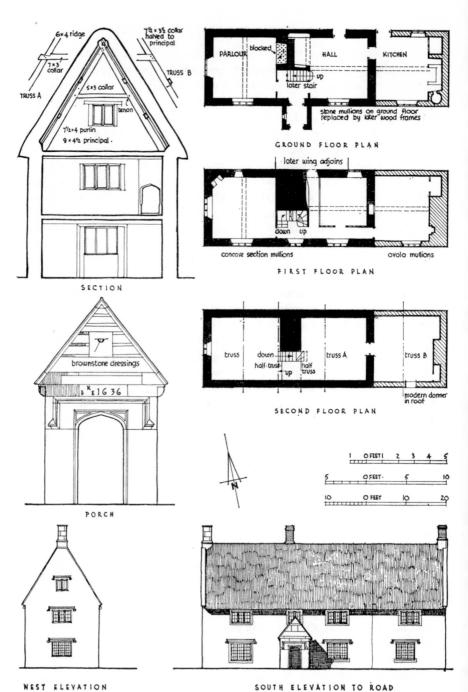

SECTION

6×4 ridge

7×3 collar

TRUSS A

7½ × 3½ collar halved to principal

TRUSS B

5×3 collar

tenon

7½×4 purlin

9 × 4½ principal.

PORCH

brownstone dressings

K E 1636

WEST ELEVATION

GROUND FLOOR PLAN

PARLOUR   blocked   HALL   KITCHEN

up

later stair

stone mullions on ground floor replaced by later wood frames

FIRST FLOOR PLAN

later wing adjoins

down   up

concave section mullions   ovolo mullions

SECOND FLOOR PLAN

truss   down   half-truss   truss A   truss B

half-truss   up   half truss

modern dormer in roof

N

1   0 FEET 1   2   3   4   5

5   0 FEET   5   10

10   0 FEET   10   20

SOUTH ELEVATION TO ROAD

DIAL HOUSE   SULGRAVE   NORTHANTS

FIG. 42.

instance of this type—lying alongside the road, with its yard and farm buildings at the back, the entrance being from the rear elevation. A three-storey porch, possessing a plinth and a four-centred stone arch, simply chamfered, seems to be an addition, as it is the only part of the building so enriched. An original studded door survives in the inner doorway, secured by a draw-bar sliding within the wall, and the entrance opens to a small vestibule, with doors to the parlour on one side and to the hall on the other. There was originally a newel-stair to the left of the door, partly contained within the thickness of the wall, but the present stair, a straight flight probably dating from the late 19th-century alterations to the house, is at the lower end of the hall, considerably reducing the original area of this room. A second stair, serving as the principal, is perhaps to be assumed between the kitchen and the hall, at the back of the pantry, as the stair adjacent to the parlour appears to have been too unassuming for a dwelling of this size, and may have only provided private access to the chamber at the upper end of the house. There is, indeed, a stair from first floor to the attics in the position suggested, between hall and kitchen. Beyond the hall, the building is divided longitudinally to provide a pantry and a buttery, the principal stair possibly being in this bay, as already noted, with the kitchen beyond, having a large fireplace on the gable wall, with a secondary door to the yard, perhaps introduced later. All internal walls are now renewed in brick, but were presumably originally stud partitions. There are four chambers on the first floor, with fireplaces to those over parlour and hall, sub-divided by stud partitions, with an attic over, lit only from the gables. There is no doubt that the room to the left of the entrance is the original parlour, as it has a large rectangular bay-window, rising through two storeys. The bay may have terminated in a gable as do other regional examples, but the renovation of the roof has removed this feature (Pl. 24*b*). The fireplace wall is faced with panelling of Jacobean character, which bears the date 1658 and the initials W^{S}S; there is no doubt that the whole of the room was originally so panelled, for further panels survive in the bay-window. A second date has been recorded, on a stone removed from an adjacent farm-building, now demolished, of 1639, with the same initials. The later date is probably correct for this house, with its gable fenestration, bay window, parapet kneelers, and the pantry introduced between hall and kitchen, all features which appear in the second half of the century. Tie-beam roof trusses divide the roof into bays which average 12 feet, the ends of the beams appearing on the rear wall of the house; the original roof covering, reputed to have been of stone

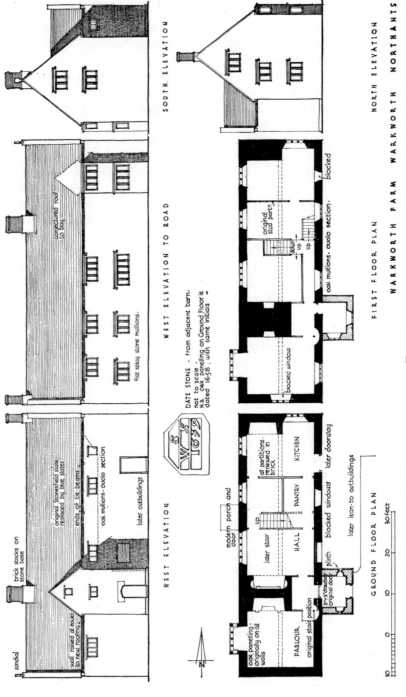

SOUTH ELEVATION

NORTH ELEVATION

WEST ELEVATION TO ROAD

WEST ELEVATION

brick stacks on stone base

original Stonesfield slate replaced by blue slates

ends of tie beams

oak mullions- ovolo section

later outbuildings

wall raised at eaves to new roofing.

sundial

conjectured roof to bay

flat splay stone mullions.

DATE STONE - from adjacent barn.
not to scale.
N.B. oak paneling on Ground Floor is dated 1658, with same initials

FIRST FLOOR PLAN

original stud partn.

oak mullions- ovolo section.

blocked

blocked window

up.
up.

GROUND FLOOR PLAN

modern porch and door

all partitions renewed in brick

later stair

PARLOUR.
oak paneling- originally on all walls
original stair position

original stair position

HALL

PANTRY

KITCHEN

blocked windows

later doorway

3'x3'double door plinth

original door

later lean-to outbuildings

0   10   20   30 feet

N

WARKWORTH FARM   WARKWORTH   NORTHANTS

FIG. 43.

slates, has been replaced by blue slate. Apart from openings on the rear elevation, all windows have stone dressings, the mullions being of flat-splay section, with a five-light opening to the hall. Both gables have large stone-mullioned windows to the principal rooms, but the rear elevation, of which only the first-floor windows remain unblocked by later additions, has wood lintels to the openings, with oak mullions of ovolo section. The present doorway on the road front is entirely modern, an alteration made by the present occupant of the farm.

This form of plan, with minor variations, is found in a number of large yeoman houses in this north-east corner of the region, all dating from *c.* 1675 to 1690, and all incorporating elaborate window-dressings, usually in grey limestone. *Hill Farm, Overthorpe* (Fig. 44), is of three-unit plan, the entrance on the rear of the house being against a double stack combining fireplaces to parlour and hall, with a cellar in the usual place under the parlour. The third room lacks a hearth, and is presumably a service-room, in which there is a second external doorway to the farmyard at the back. There are many indications of more advanced planning and design under classical influence in this house, including the arrangement of the entrance vestibule, in which the stair is placed opposite to the door. The rear elevation (the principal front) is elaborately and symmetrically treated, with a central dormer over the door and a continuous label-mould to the lower windows. To maintain a symmetrical façade to the two principal rooms, the service bay is reduced in height, but is provided with elaborate gable fenestration (Pl. 24*d*). The windows have ovolo mullions, generally of two wide lights, with a label-mould of classical profile, and with the addition of a moulding in the reveal (Fig. 74). All dressed stonework is in grey limestone, contrasting with the brown marlstone of the walls. Only the entrance doorway, placed just off centre, lacks elaboration, having a simple wood lintel, but a wood canopy has been added in the 18th century to provide a needed emphasis.

Farley's Farm, Lower Middleton Cheney has many similar features, including the elaborate gable fenestration at the upper end of the house, which here faces the road. The window dressings are again of grey stone, and have ovolo mullions and moulded reveals. Label-moulds are omitted on the lateral walls, but flat labels without the dropped ends appear on the gable (Pl. 20*d*). In both these houses, at Overthorpe and Lower Middleton Cheney, the entrance and double stack lie between what were originally the hall and parlour. Both houses were originally thatched, and have chimney stacks on the

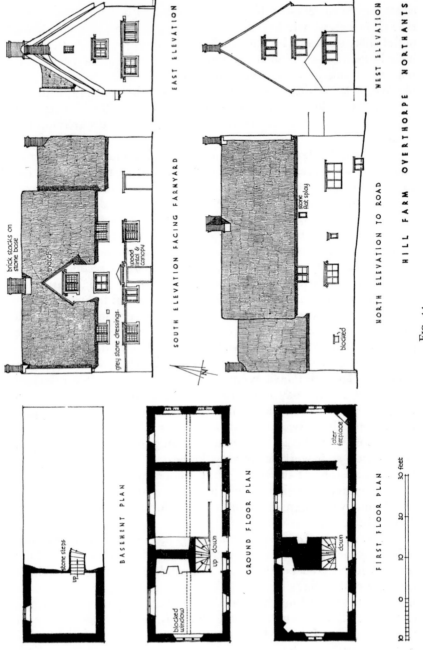

BASEMENT PLAN

stone steps

up

GROUND FLOOR PLAN

up down

up down

blocked window

FIRST FLOOR PLAN

later fireplace

down

0 10 20 30 feet

brick stacks on stone base

hatch

wood brick canopy

grey stone dressings.

SOUTH ELEVATION FACING FARMYARD

EAST ELEVATION

stone flat splay

blocked

NORTH ELEVATION TO ROAD

WEST ELEVATION

HILL FARM OVERTHORPE NORTHANTS

N

FIG. 44.

gables which relate to later bedroom fireplaces. At *Balscott* (Fig. 38), is a large yeoman house of similar plan, the stair here being contained in a square projection from the back of the hall, at the side of the entrance. A square oven, opening from the hall fireplace, projects from the street front. The house has been extended by a wing at right angles to the original service, and a lateral fireplace has been added in this room. *Laurel Farm, Shotteswell,* combining the double-stack to hall and parlour, with a lateral fireplace in the kitchen, has already been noted, and as with all these plans, the entrance is from the rear of the house. In all cases there seems little doubt that the entrance lies between hall and parlour, and therefore that the hall fireplace is at the upper end of the hall. This disposition accords with the later developments of the regional lowland plan, whereby the hall fireplace is transferred from a position backing on the through-passage to one at the upper end of the hall; this has been already noted in connection with such plans as Williamscot Home Farm (Fig. 26).

Northend Manor Farm (Fig. 45), a large house dated 1654, provides a more elaborate example of this disposition of rooms in a plan which combines a double stack with a third lateral hearth, with here the addition of a second entrance on the road frontage. The building presents a symmetrical façade, having a central hall flanked by projecting gabled wings on either side, the front entrance opening into the centre of the hall. Hall and parlour fireplaces are arranged behind each other in a common stack, both having elaborate stone dressings; the parlour occupies only the front part of the wing, with a small pantry at the rear. The kitchen is in the wing at the other end of the hall, which has been extended at the back to provide a dairy with chambers over. This extension shows a clear change of build without any alteration of the design, and the parts are so interdependent that it is probable that the work was continuous. The cellar in this case lies under the kitchen, the fireplace to the kitchen being on the rear wall against the dairy. A second entrance, protected by a porch, is provided on the rear elevation at the lower end of the hall, and the principal stair is adjacent to this doorway, with a second stair in the extended wing. The house is of full two-storey height, with attics over, lit from the gables, and the roof is of red tiles (widely used in the Warwickshire sector of the region) presumably replacing thatch. On all elevations there are stone dressings to windows, with flat-splay mullions, and a plinth is continuous around the house; gable parapets are provided, with the rare addition of ball finials. The provision of a doorway on the road frontage, in addition

M

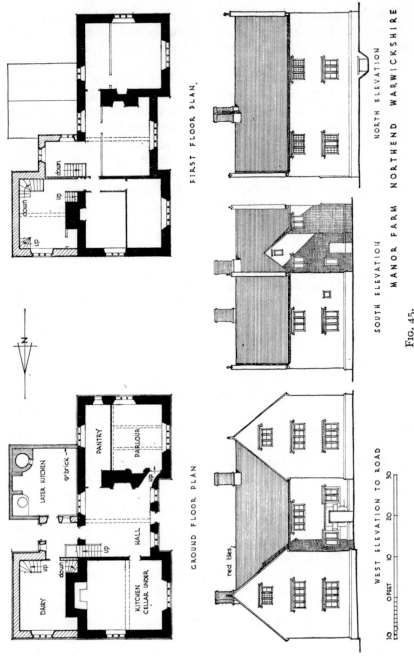

FIRST FLOOR PLAN.

GROUND FLOOR PLAN

LATER KITCHEN

9" BRICK

PANTRY

PARLOUR

UP

DAIRY

UP

down

UP

KITCHEN
CELLAR UNDER

HALL

N

up

down

down

UP

NORTH ELEVATION

SOUTH ELEVATION

WEST ELEVATION TO ROAD

red tiles

10   0 FEET   10   20   30

MANOR FARM   NORTHEND   WARWICKSHIRE

FIG. 45.

to the more usual rear entrance, can be attributed to classical influence in this unusually large and fine yeoman dwelling, and anticipates the central front entrance opening into a stair hall which
appears from the end of the 17th century.

The arrangement of the double stack in houses of this type
shows some variation, the two flues being usually arranged longitudinally rather than side by side across the ridge, although both forms
are to be found. The Old Rectory at Alkerton (Fig. 78) has elaborate
ashlar stone chimneys to the double stack between hall and parlour.
The three chimney stacks—the third being that of the bedroom fireplace—with moulded stone cappings, are placed diagonally over the
stone base, a feature of Renaissance influence which is commonly
found in the neighbouring Cotswolds, but which is not characteristic
of the Banbury Region.

The distribution map (Fig. 83) which shows the disposition of all
dated houses within the region before 1800, distinguishes those buildings which are of the 'lowland' plan-type. The marked prevalence of
this house-type in the north and east of the region is supported by the
number of undated instances recorded in these areas, while examples
also occur at Alkerton and Hook Norton and other villages in the
south-west, where the practice is continued in many Cotswold
houses.[1] In the City of Oxford, the double-stack is a characteristic
feature of many early timber-framed houses from the 16th century,
and of later 17th-century stone houses, the majority of which are
sited at right angles to the street; only in the less-crowded suburbs is
the plan arranged parallel with the street. Many such examples have
been recorded by Mr. W. A. Pantin,[2] in no case possessing a passage
entrance, and all with either back-to-back hearths or else fireplaces
on the side-walls. The through-passage appears to be essentially a
rural expedient, and its validity in a restricted site with narrow
frontage is immediately reduced. The form of the double stack has
obvious advantages in relation to timber-framed buildings because of
its increased stability and safety against fire, and its use within the
region may be due, at least to some extent, to the earlier timber-
framed tradition. Although this plan-type can account for the
majority of houses planned at right angles to the road within the
region, particularly at the end of the 17th century when space for
further building would be more restricted with the needs of larger

[1] A number of plans with the central double stack are illustrated in *Old
Cottages, Farmhouses, Etc., in the Cotswold District*, by W. G. Davie and E. G.
Dawber, 1905, pp. 12–16.
[2] W. A. Pantin, 'The Development of Domestic Architecture in Oxford', *The
Antiquaries Journal*, Vol. XXVII, July–October 1947, p. 120.

village populations who would be unwilling to encroach on the open fields, it is clear that this is not the only reason for the adoption of this form, as many of the larger houses still were disposed parallel to the street. The single entrance against the breast, from the rear of the house, has clearly been adopted for many larger dwellings for its superior planning advantages, in privacy and convenience, the through-passage plan from the end of the 17th century being generally relegated to poorer and less-sophisticated dwellings. Throughout the region, in all villages, the upland-type plans outnumber those with the single entrance, but consideration of dated buildings in the 17th century shows that the proportion of lowland-type plans is as high as 40 per cent. This disproportionately large percentage suggests that it is generally the larger and more prosperous dwellings—these being the buildings which are normally dated—which have followed the lowland plan.

The addition of a central entrance on the street front, as at North-end in 1654 and Charlton in 1658, becomes general in examples of this plan-type after 1700, the entrance being frequently into the hall at the opposite end of the room to the hearth. In the 18th century the lowland house continues to find expression as an alternative to the later developments of the upland plan in which fireplaces are placed on opposite gables; in these later dwellings of more formal layout and design, the plans approximate to those of national Georgian architecture.

CHAPTER VIII

SINGLE-CELL HOUSES BEFORE 1700

IN almost every village in the region, examples have been recorded of dwellings, originally free-standing, of single-unit plan, dating from the middle of the 16th century to the 19th century. The numbers increase after 1700, and whilst many if not most of the later dwellings may safely be described as cottages, there are some prior to this date which are much too elaborate to allow of such a classification. They are manifestly of fairly high social status, incorporating stone-mullioned windows and other masonry dressings, and differ from the average yeoman dwellings of their day in little but the peculiarities of their arrangement. It is not too easy to explain the purport of these dwellings, of which the masonry enrichment is in some instances more elaborate than that of the larger three-unit houses of the period. To regard them merely as reduced versions of the normal plan, for farmers of modest substance, does not seem satisfactory to meet the case, and two other solutions invite consideration. The possibility cannot be excluded that these houses represent a mode of living in which a vertical arrangement of the accommodation is retained from the tower house of earlier times, in preference to the horizontal extension that had come into popular favour. Alternatively, these dwellings may have been planned to fulfil a different function as the homes of men of special calling, not associated with the land.

The arrangement of the principal domestic apartments one above the other within a tower is a medieval form of living which besides affording some degree of protection—according to the rigour of the defensive measures taken—has the merit too of supporting prestige. Particularly for the latter advantage, tower houses were almost the universal form of living in Scotland into the 17th century, whilst in the border country, in the meaner form of peles, the defensive purpose remained a reality until the 16th century. The traditions died hard, and their fading left a train of features which appear inconsequent against the settled conditions of later times. There are, for example, in the tall, sometimes embattled, porches of Westmorland's statesman (yeoman) dwellings of the 17th century, faint echoes of the tower-dwellings of former days.[1]

[1] R. W. Brunskill, 'Traditional Domestic Architecture in the Eden Valley', Manchester University Thesis, 1952, p. 50.

The remote origins of vertical living lie with the powerful donjon towers of the early castles of the 11th century, but the truly domestic version is the manor-house, a rural residence but protected defensively in sufficient degree. In this type of dwelling, as already noted, there was an important but numerically diminishing class, almost invariably in stone, in which the principal accommodation was on the first floor. Such was Boothby Pagnell, Lincolnshire, built at the end of the 12th century, a noted example of the first-floor hall over vaulted cellars, entered at the first floor. In the neighbourhood of Banbury, Cottisford Manor provides the only instance of this type, which had similar arrangements of early 14th-century date. These are instances in which the accommodation is tending towards lateral living; but there are many other manor-houses in which the tower motif remains dominant, despite the reduced or almost non-existent need, well beyond the medieval period. In these buildings the prestige motif is the dominant reason behind the retention of the tower.

There are no instances amongst the great houses of the region of the true tower-house. *Castle House, Deddington, Oxfordshire,* the rectorial manor-house, which lies to the north of the church, largely dates from the 17th century, but incorporates within its plan an unusual tower-like structure, of medieval origin, extensively altered in the later rebuilding (Pl. 9*a*). The lower two storeys of the tower, having walls over 3 feet in thickness, are of 13th-century date, but their original function is obscure, although it seems probable that there was a chapel on the first floor. Rainwater heads bear the date and initials 1654 TAM, and at that time or a little earlier, the 13th-century block was largely rebuilt, being raised in height to three storeys over a semi-basement, refaced and refenestrated, whilst any adjoining buildings were replaced by a new wing on the south side containing hall and parlour with chambers over, a fine stair with turned balusters being added in a projection on the west side of the tower, to produce a complex, double-depth plan. Windows have flat-splay stone mullions, and the stone walling approximates to ashlar, the stone being well squared and coursed, making decorative use of alternate bands of the grey limestone and brown ironstone which are both obtainable in this eastern fringe of the region.

One of the two brick towers survives which terminated the wings of Hanwell Castle, a great house built around three sides of an open court, marking one of the first uses of brick in Oxfordshire at the end of the 15th century.[1] These towers, of characteristic Tudor design,

---

[1] Tattershall Castle, Lincolnshire, probably the most important brick tower-house, dates from 1440.

were however supplementary to the normal living apartments of the house.

In the lower scale of the minor domestic architecture, a number of houses have been recorded which appear particularly to represent this anomaly of fine architectural quality in a building of very small dimensions. The problem of differentiation between yeoman houses and later cottages is no light one, as the plan types persist in the cottage developments until the beginning of the 19th century. There is, moreover, the perpetuation of architectural details in dwellings of lower class, with the archaistic use of stone mullions noted in humble dwellings until the middle of the 18th century. Poorer quality of workmanship and materials, reduced ceiling heights and floor areas, are distinguishing features; yet since these may also be features of the meaner yeoman houses of the previous century it is unavoidable that the social identity of some 18th-century examples must remain in doubt. The undoubted 17th-century single-cell houses are generally of a full two-storey height, usually with attics over, contained in the roof, as compared with the one-and-a-half-storey height of the later cottages. A cellar is added in the Bakery, Lower Middleton Cheney, half below ground level, and there is also a basement in a single-unit house at Shotteswell, the only two examples recorded with this feature. Almost all houses are now adjoined by later extensions which add the further problem of determining whether the single-cell structure in fact ever existed alone as such, and in a number of cases this point will be debated. The alternate rebuilding of upper and lower ends of a house has left many wings which at first sight appear to be independent units.[1]

The plans of these single-unit buildings show considerable variation, and follow a pattern of evolution which corresponds to that already outlined for larger 17th-century houses. There is a division into the same two classes as have already been noted in the previous chapters, i.e. (a) houses with gable entrances—related to the through-passage plan—and (b) those entered from the lateral wall against the side of the chimney breast. The types are illustrated in Fig. 46. Of the ten houses to be considered, six fall within the first group—to be further sub-divided according to the relative positions of door and hearth—and four follow the 'lowland' plan which, it has been suggested, developed in the region particularly in the latter half of the 17th century, as an alternative to the later developments of the

[1] Chinners Farms, Chacombe (Fig. 7), is a good illustration of this successive rebuilding of different parts of the house, which has left the two-and-a-half storeyed parlour wing with the appearance of a self-contained dwelling in contrast to the adjoining medieval hall (p. 37; Pl. 4b).

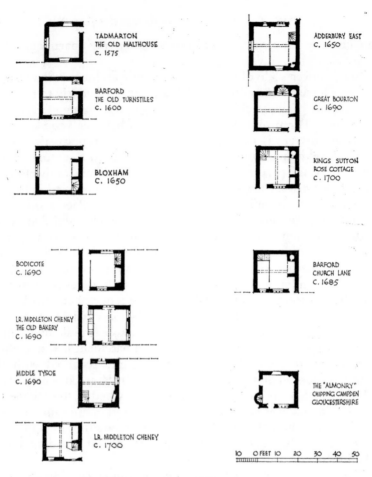

TADMARTON
THE OLD MALTHOUSE
c. 1575

BARFORD
THE OLD TURNSTILES
c. 1600

BLOXHAM
c. 1650

ADDERBURY EAST
c. 1650

GREAT BOURTON
c. 1690

KINGS SUTTON
ROSE COTTAGE
c. 1700

BODICOTE
c. 1690

LR. MIDDLETON CHENEY
THE OLD BAKERY
c. 1690

MIDDLE TYSOE
c. 1690

LR. MIDDLETON CHENEY
c. 1700

BARFORD
CHURCH LANE
c. 1685

THE "ALMONRY"
CHIPPING CAMPDEN
GLOUCESTERSHIRE

10   O FEET 10   20   30   40   50

NOTE : All plans are shown with ridge line horizontal.
The road frontage is shown by an extended broken line.

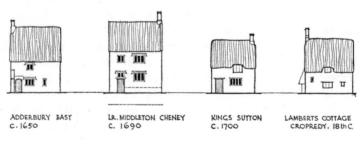

ADDERBURY EAST
c. 1650

LR. MIDDLETON CHENEY
c. 1690

KINGS SUTTON
c. 1700

LAMBERTS COTTAGE
CROPREDY. 18th C.

COMPARATIVE PLANS OF SINGLE UNIT HOUSES

FIG. 46.

passage plan. Within these two groups, the houses can be considered in an approximate chronological sequence.

The Old Malthouse, Tadmarton, has already been noted (Fig. 61) as containing in its northern bay certain structural features which can be attributed to the second half of the 16th century, and this building relates the single-cell house type to the antecedents of the main regional building period. Subsequent alterations of the late 17th century, and more recent modernization in 1954, have left little of the original plan save the thicker 30-inch walls of a single cell, divided by a centrally placed truss and horizontally by a first-floor spanning from a central spine-beam. The original entrance was probably in the gable, and now links the two periods of building. Of a fireplace or stair in this bay there is no evidence. The assumption that the dwelling was a single-bay hall open to the roof with open hearth is not supported by any obvious smoke marking of the truss, and although this possibility cannot be excluded, it is more probable that later alterations have removed both stair and fire, if indeed the bay ever enjoyed a separate existence.

The Old Turnstiles, Barford (Fig. 47; Pl. 11*b*), is probably the next oldest in date, the original single-unit plan with gable entrance between stair and fireplace having been developed by the addition of an elaborate unit comprising through-passage and hall, with unusually fine details of porch and bay window, dated 1653. The earlier part of the house is of two-and-a-half-storey height, and does not lack architectural refinement, the windows having stone mullions of concave section, worked in brown stone in contrast to the grey limestone dressings of the 1653 build.[1] This form of mullion, related to the medieval sections, is rarely found within the region and suggests a date at the end of the 16th or early in the 17th century. The stair has been altered on several occasions before the present stairway was introduced, but it is probable that the original position was to the right of the entrance, in which location it would relate to the existing stair from first floor to attics which starts immediately over. The oven in the angle of the fireplace would not accord with this early date, but this appears to have been introduced later, as the bressumer spans to the outer wall. It may date from the conversion of the original hall to kitchen status with the additions of 1653. The ground floor is a spacious and lofty apartment, measuring 17 by 14 by 8 feet high to the underside of the joists spanning from spine-beam to the lateral walls. This building well illustrates the problem of asserting an original existence as a single cell, for the later wing itself might well

[1] The subsequent development of this house is considered in Chapter X.

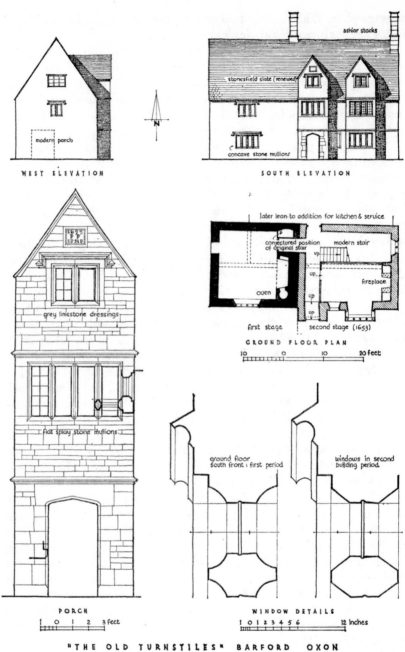

WEST ELEVATION

modern porch

SOUTH ELEVATION

ashlar stacks

stonesfield slate (renewed)

concave stone mullions

1675
ꟼ ꟼ
1759

grey limestone dressings

flat splay stone mullions

PORCH

1 0 1 2 3 feet

later lean-to addition for kitchen & service

conjectured position of original stair

modern stair

up

up

up

up

fireplace

oven

first stage

second stage (1653)

GROUND FLOOR PLAN

10 0 10 20 feet

ground floor south front : first period

windows in second building period.

WINDOW DETAILS

1 0 1 2 3 4 5 6 12 inches

"THE OLD TURNSTILES" BARFORD OXON

FIG. 47.

appear to constitute a complete single unit, containing the entrance with cross-passage and separate stair and fireplace, especially if the earlier bay had itself been later rebuilt, as has frequently happened.

Two other plan arrangements which combine the entrance, fireplace and stair on the same gable in single-cell buildings have been recorded in a number of houses. The first arrangement can be studied at *Bloxham* (Fig. 46), in a small house of two-and-a-half-storey height, with flat-splay stone-mullioned windows to the three floors on the south gable, overlooking a small green. The house has been much altered, and is now adjoined by a more recent range of buildings, but originally it comprised a single ground-floor room, now entered by a modern doorway in the front gable, with fireplace and stair and probably the original entrance on the north gable wall. Originally thatched, the roof is now finished with red tiles.

The alternative combination of entrance stair and fireplace on the same gable is to be found in a small house at *Lower Middleton Cheney* (Fig. 48). Dating from the very end of the 17th century or the early years of the 18th, this house lacks the architectural enrichment of the buildings previously described and is more closely related to 18th-century cottage developments. Its plan is of interest as confirming those characteristics of later development in the sequence noted in the previous chapters. The ground-floor room measures internally only 15 feet by 13 feet—nevertheless larger than those of the 18th-century cottages, which are as little as 12 feet by 10 feet—and the entrance is on the gable, with the stair rising immediately adjacent to it on the same side as the wide fireplace, forming a small lobby. Of two-and-a-half-storey height, the principal beam spans across the structure on the line of the roof truss above, the latter of characteristic 17th-century type, with well-finished timbers. There is a fireplace in the bedroom, on the opposite gable to the hall fire, which may well be a later addition. The windows have wood lintels and frames with iron casements, and the roof is thatched, the workmanship throughout being of a quality that merits its inclusion as being in a category higher than that of the cottage. A lean-to bay has been added to the gable opposite to the entrance, the poor quality of its workmanship and materials indicating a date in the 19th century, when the building had clearly sunk to a meaner social status.

The above houses share the common characteristic of having the entrance door on the gable wall, against which both stair and fireplace are also disposed in varying relationships, the ground-floor apartment corresponding to the hall of the full three-unit 'upland' plan. Within this group of houses entered from the gable or cross-passage,

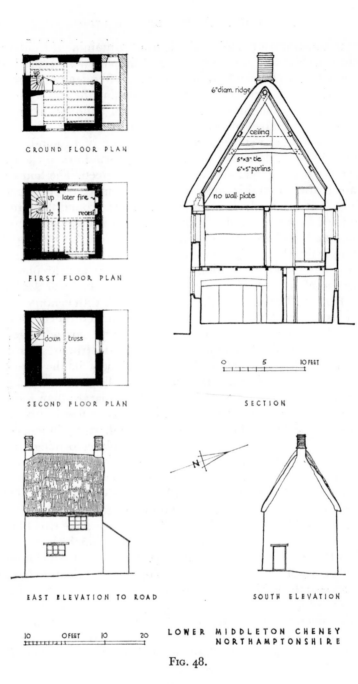

GROUND FLOOR PLAN

FIRST FLOOR PLAN

SECOND FLOOR PLAN

6"diam. ridge

ceiling

5"×3" tie
6"×5" purlins

no wall-plate

0   5   10 FEET

SECTION

EAST ELEVATION TO ROAD

SOUTH ELEVATION

10   OFEET   10   20

LOWER MIDDLETON CHENEY
NORTHAMPTONSHIRE

FIG. 48.

there remain a number of buildings which differ in that the entrance door and fireplace are on opposite walls, and in all but one instance, the through-passage is incorporated in the plan. This arrangement may be related to the hall element of the later 17th-century three-unit plan, in which the hall fireplace no longer backs onto the cross passage, but is taken to the upper end of the room, and these houses typologically represent a subsequent form to those already described.

This type of house has been studied in Farm Place, Bodicote, and at Wardington; it is, however, best illustrated in a yeoman house in Northamptonshire which is at the same time one of the most significant instances of single-cell structure recorded in the region, which does invite considerations of vertical planning. *The Bakery, Lower Middleton Cheney* (Fig. 49), lying opposite to the house already noted in this village, comprises a single-unit house with through-passage built within the latter half of the 17th century, with a kitchen added against the passage in the 18th century. The through-passage is almost in the nature of an entrance hall, being of unusual width—5 feet 6 inches—with the doors not opposite to each other, and containing a stair of unusual size and convenience. This is the earliest framed stair recorded in a small house within the region, having an open well; although of rough, almost vernacular, character, it has good flat balusters and square newels with moulded capping. Rising opposite to the door, the first three steps lead to a landing which gives access to the raised ground-floor room, with a 'dog-gate' at this level. The ground-floor apartment is of good size, spanning 15 feet 6 inches by 16 feet 6 inches long, well lit by flat-splay stone-mullioned windows on three walls, and having a small fireplace set in the centre of the gable, flanked by windows. The raising of the ground floor accommodates the basement cellar below, also approached from the through-passage, and lit by mullioned windows on the gable and rear elevation. The stair is lit by large windows at intermediate landing levels, and leads to first floor and attic, the latter originally lit from the gable but now having 18th-century dormers additionally. The floor-beams are constructed in the manner noted as typical of the end of the 17th century, with the principal beam spanning across the structure. This circumstance, together with the commodiousness of the stair, suggest a date near 1690. The addition of the basement, only partly below the ground, makes this house the most tower-like structure yet noted; in all, three-and-a-half storeys in height.

By comparison, the later kitchen is of poor construction, with large gable fireplace and wood lintels to window openings. The lack

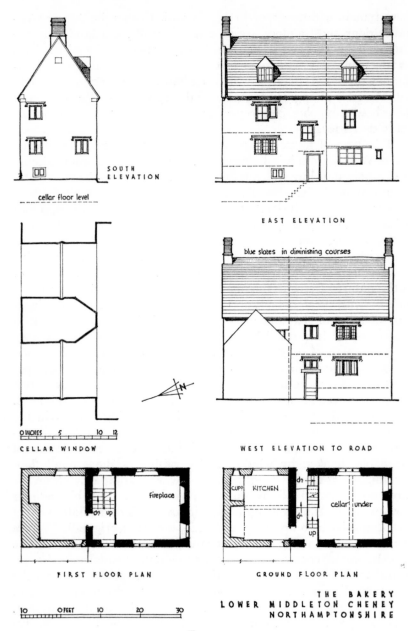

SOUTH ELEVATION

cellar floor level

CELLAR WINDOW

0 INCHES 5 10 12

EAST ELEVATION

blue slates in diminishing courses

WEST ELEVATION TO ROAD

N

FIRST FLOOR PLAN

Fireplace

dn up

GROUND FLOOR PLAN

CUPD KITCHEN

dn

cellar under

up

10 0 FEET 10 20 30

THE BAKERY
LOWER MIDDLETON CHENEY
NORTHAMPTONSHIRE

Fig. 49.

of a similar 'cottage' fireplace in the original portion may suggest that this unit was always amplified by further accommodation, but this is by no means conclusive, as examples have also been recorded of larger dwellings having only small hearths, and the refinement of the fireplace may reflect the particular use of the building or the social standing of the owner, as will be considered later. The house as it now exists represents a characteristic, late two-unit plan. Full consideration has been given to the possibility that the 18th-century kitchen may have replaced an earlier wing, maybe of timber, to which in *c.* 1690 the parlour had been added in a succession of alternate modernizations, but there are circumstances opposing such an interpretation. The joint between the two periods of work shows large quoin stones on the 17th-century portion, and the doorway linking the two units is roughly formed, and supports the theory that it has been inserted in the original external gable.

A parallel is found between this most interesting house and a tall single unit of two-and-a-half storeys at *Middle Tysoe* (Fig. 50) which, on three elevations, has windows with stone mullions and transoms of the late, concave section, for which a date *c.* 1690 has been proposed. The entrance doorway from the road front is enriched by stone architrave and label, and the fireplace, set at an angle within the room, is of considerable size and dignity with heavy bolection-moulded stone surround. From comparative evidence in the region, these details would agree with a date at the end of the 17th century. Only two houses in the area, apart from manor-houses, have been recorded with stone-transomed windows, and the other—the Garden House, Mollington, previously described (Fig. 37)—is also distinguished by its elaborate stone fireplaces. This single unit is adjoined on the north side by further building of poorer character and indeterminate date, the whole now forming one house in which the more elaborate unit is relegated to use as a shop and store. There are no windows on the gable which now separates the two stages of building, but this would not be surprising if the unit stood alone, as the entrance is on this side, and presumably the stair also. There are new doorways on the rear wall and also on the gable leading to the rest of the house, but the difference in character supports the belief that they have been introduced later, in which case the most probable position for the stair would be in this corner. It has not been possible to investigate fully the upper chambers of this building, or the adjoining structure, and some doubt must attach to the original plan. The noteworthy character of the stone dressings, and the fine nature of the masonry walling all contribute to the appearance of a

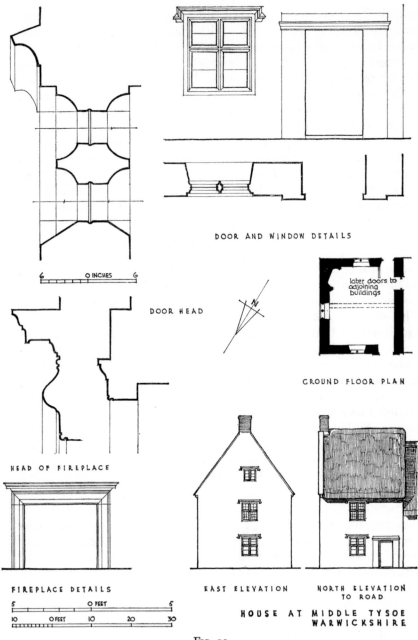

O INCHES

DOOR AND WINDOW DETAILS

DOOR HEAD

later doors to
adjoining
buildings

GROUND FLOOR PLAN

N

HEAD OF FIREPLACE

FIREPLACE DETAILS

5 O FEET 5

10 O FEET 10 20 30

EAST ELEVATION

NORTH ELEVATION
TO ROAD

HOUSE AT MIDDLE TYSOE
WARWICKSHIRE

FIG. 50.

separate, tower-like structure, in marked contrast to the poorer work which adjoins.

The remaining houses differ from the previous examples in having entrances on the lateral wall, in three cases opening onto the side of the chimney breast, and the plan of Middle Tysoe lies between these two groups. The single-cell house at *Adderbury East* is one of the most important examples (Fig. 51), distinguished by fine masonry details, including flat-splay stone mullions on the entrance and gable fronts, adjacent to the road, with a four-centred arched stone doorway (Pl. 11*c*). The scarcity of stone dressings to doorways within the region has already been noted. The stair opens immediately opposite to the entrance and ascends at the side of the fireplace, which is provided with a small oven in the opposite reveal. Here again the building is of two-and-a-half-storey height, with three tiers of windows in the gable, and in area this is the largest of all these houses, measuring internally 19 feet by 17 feet 6 inches to the fireplace. The space is now divided into two almost equal areas on both floors, but it seems improbable that the ground floor was originally partitioned, because of the long and narrow room shapes so created, and the arrangement of the fenestration. There are, nevertheless, two windows on the entrance front, one being a small opening of a single light, which might suggest some internal division. The partition has been plastered and papered, and gives no clue to its own date. This house is also adjoined by later cottages, but there is no suggestion here of it ever having been part of a more comprehensive house plan.

The sub-division of this plan finds a parallel in a small dwelling in *Church Lane, Barford St. John,* which is clearly of two-room plan, and therefore not strictly admissible in this section. The building, nevertheless, forms a single structural unit of high architectural quality and is of the same class and type of house as those already described. The house, standing near the church, measures internally 17 feet by 15 feet to the fireplace, and is of the usual two-storey height with attic over. The entrance is in the road frontage by a doorway with a richly moulded architrave in stone, opening against the side of the chimney breast. The small dimensions of the house appear to have left too little room for a comfortable stair on the fireplace wall, and it is therefore placed on the opposite gable, against a separate room screened off to form a cellar or parlour. Stone-mullioned windows are provided to the windows of both the ground and first floor, with label-moulds to the lower openings, the attic being lit from the gable. The provision of the separate ground-floor cellar or parlour, the more convenient stair, the late label-mould to the cellar window,

N

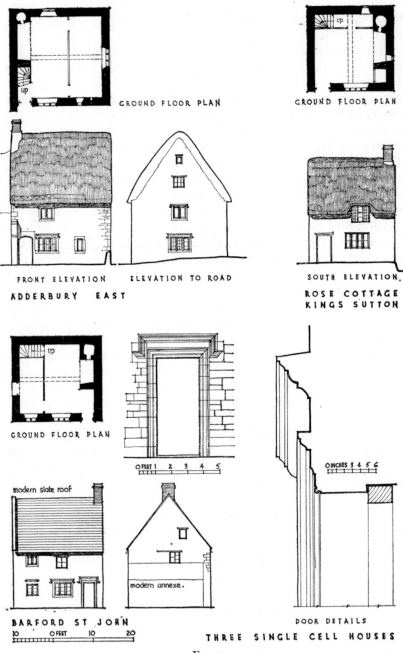

GROUND FLOOR PLAN

GROUND FLOOR PLAN

FRONT ELEVATION   ELEVATION TO ROAD

ADDERBURY EAST

SOUTH ELEVATION.

ROSE COTTAGE
KINGS SUTTON

GROUND FLOOR PLAN

O FEET 1 2 3 4 5

O INCHES 3 4 5 6

modern slate roof

modern annexe.

BARFORD ST JOHN

10   O FEET   10   20

DOOR DETAILS

THREE SINGLE CELL HOUSES

FIG. 51.

and the mouldings of the door indicate a date between 1680 and 1690 for this building (Fig. 51).

The remaining two houses may be of lower social order, dating from the last years of the 17th century, or shortly after 1700, and can be regarded as the homes of small farmers. Both include flat-splay stone-mullioned windows to the single ground-floor room, but are otherwise of less elaborate character.

Boddington's Cottage, Great Bourton (Fig. 52) is the larger and earlier of the two, and merits the title of house rather than cottage. Standing apart from other houses in the village, the building is again of two-and-a-half-storey height, with a particularly steeply-pitched thatched roof—almost 60 degrees. The entrance, having a wood lintel, is from the lateral wall, against the side of the chimney-breast. The spacious newel-stair is on the opposite wall, contained in a thatched projection, which also includes the large bread-oven. Only the hall-window on the entrance front has any pretension, being of four lights with stone mullions and label-mould with dropped ends. The windows to the two bedrooms above have wood lintels and frames, as also have the openings on the rear elevation, and on the gable lighting the attic.

Still later, perhaps dating from the beginning of the 18th century, the final example, *Rose Cottage, Kings Sutton* (Fig. 51), lies with its gable end to the road. The fireplace is on this wall, flanked by an oven with a small glazed opening from the back of the hearth. The entrance is on the side wall, at the opposite end of the room to the hearth, and the stair is contained in the corner opposite the door. A small pantry is now screened off at the side of the stair by a partition which is not original. The ground-floor window on the entrance front is the only evidence of dressed stonework, with flat-splay stone mullions without a label-mould, a form which persists throughout the first half of the 18th century for humbler dwellings. There is only one upper floor, contained partly within the roof space, the thatch being swept up over the window, and the building is therefore lower in height than any previously considered. The upper floor is supported on a transverse beam in the manner which becomes general after 1700.

Analysis of the features of these dwellings presents a number of important considerations. It is an ill chance that there are no dated examples in this group, and the attribution of date must depend on the evidence of structure, plan-type and detail, by comparison with dated dwellings already noted of two- and three-unit plan. Only in the Old Malthouse at Tadmarton is the roof structure of pre-17th-century date; the construction of all other roofs gives no indication of

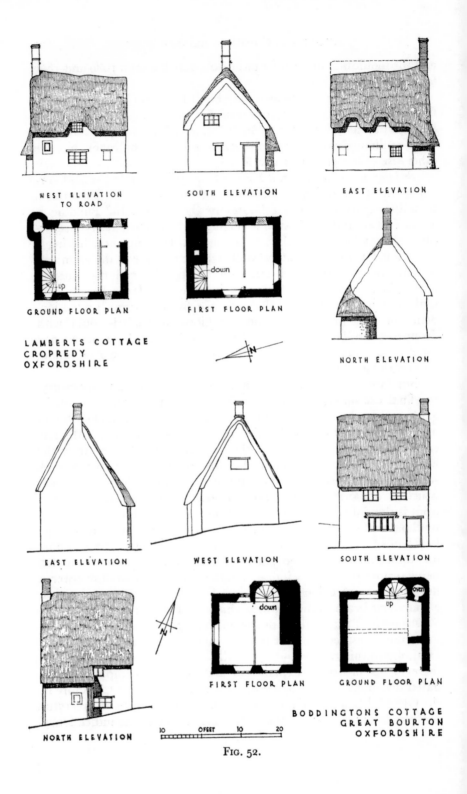

WEST ELEVATION
TO ROAD

SOUTH ELEVATION

EAST ELEVATION

GROUND FLOOR PLAN

FIRST FLOOR PLAN

up

down

NORTH ELEVATION

LAMBERTS COTTAGE
CROPREDY
OXFORDSHIRE

N

EAST ELEVATION

WEST ELEVATION

SOUTH ELEVATION

NORTH ELEVATION

N

FIRST FLOOR PLAN

down

GROUND FLOOR PLAN

up

oven

BODDINGTONS COTTAGE
GREAT BOURTON
OXFORDSHIRE

10   OFEET   10   20

FIG. 52.

dating within the 17th century. The upper-floor construction is of more assistance in dating, the earlier dwellings possessing the central spine-beam support, whilst the later examples, including Kings Sutton and the two houses at Lower Middleton Cheney, have the main transverse beam, which has already been noted as a development of the later 17th century, widely adopted after 1700.

Further evidence is provided by the nature of the architectural details. Window mullions of the early cavetto-section have been recorded at the Old Turnstiles, and the later more slender hollow-section mullions at Middle Tysoe, where the windows have transoms. The latter hollow-section type has been shown to be limited to the period 1690 to 1700, and the transomed window also falls largely within this period. The majority of houses, as in all classes of 17th-century dwelling in the region, have the flat-splay mullions, which afford no evidence of date within this period, but the omission of the label to the ground-floor windows at Kings Sutton places this building near the turn of the century. Fireplace and door details at both Middle Tysoe and Barford St. John assist in dating these houses to the last ten years of the 17th century. The presence of an oven in most cases indicates a date after 1650, whilst the large external projection of the oven, as at Great Bourton, is rarely found before 1690.

Valuable as these indications of date undoubtedly are, the plan is the best guide to chronological sequence. Of the three categories of plan considered—(1) gable entrance on the fireplace wall; (2) gable or through-passage on the wall opposite the fireplace; (3) entrance from lateral wall, against the chimney breast—the latter two arrangements correspond to those developments described in Chapters VI and VII respectively, and are to some degree alternative and contemporary in the latter half of the 17th century.

The removal of the stair from the fireplace wall generally occurs near 1700, to provide a more commodious stairway in an unrestricted corner. The separation of a cellar or pantry also becomes more common towards the end of the century, corresponding with developments in the larger buildings, whilst the basement cellar of the house at Lower Middleton Cheney probably puts the house after 1650—other features already noted indicating a date nearer 1690.

The size of the house offers little guide to date; the clear area of the ground-floor room varies from 19 feet by 18 feet to 15 feet by 13 feet, no two houses being identical, and this factor is more likely to relate to the prosperity or personal inclinations of the householder. The first house described at Lower Middleton Cheney is probably the latest of these dwellings and is also the smallest in area.

These houses share no common orientation, but in the majority of cases are similarly situated, lying parallel to the street. The three buildings considered last are the exceptions, the houses at Adderbury and Kings Sutton being gable end to the road, whilst that at Great Bourton is isolated at the end of a narrow track.

There remains the explanation of these single-cell dwellings—one almost unique in the region for the richness of its window details—within the social pattern of the area. In no case is there evidence of a first-floor hall, or its later equivalent, the houses all appearing to function as normal abbreviations of the full three-unit plan. Second fireplaces are provided in the upper room at Bloxham, Barford St. John and the Bakery, Lower Middleton Cheney. It is possible to envisage the latter instance as having a first-floor parlour, an attic chamber, and a service-room combined with cellar partly below ground level, the tower tradition perhaps being retained to give ostentation and difference to a building of different social status than the three- and two-unit farm-houses.

This introduces the second possibility that some at least of these houses—the larger and finer examples—were built for members of the village community who, not being engaged wholly or even partly in agrarian pursuits, did not require the large service-rooms and extra accommodation of the yeoman house, including the large open fireplace, omitted at Lower Middleton Cheney and Middle Tysoe. At Warmington Church there is an interesting single-cell annexe of two storeys adjoining the chancel, which is recorded as the dwelling of a chantry priest of the 16th century. The unit measures internally 18 feet by 13 feet with small fireplaces on both floors, the ground floor also serving as a chapel.

The *priest's house at Little Dassett* in Burton Dassett parish, Warwickshire, already noted in Chapter III, provides a comparable example. A chapel of ease was here provided for Little Dassett and Northend, and is of late-13th-century date, measuring 36 feet by 17 feet with a west window of two lights with cinque-foil heads within a two-centred arch, now destroyed. In 1632, Lady Wotton, the widow of Edward, Lord Wotton, who was living at Northend Manor House nearby, restored the chapel, by then fallen into disuse, and added at its east end a dwelling for a recusant priest, the new work being inscribed on the south-west corner with the date 1632 and the initial W. The priest's dwelling consisted of a single apartment at ground floor level, measuring 27 feet by 20 feet, entered on the south side, with three-light stone-mullioned windows on both side walls, one of which has subsequently been made into a doorway. The walls are built in squared coursed rubble, with large quoins, in contrast to the small irregular rubble walling of the earlier chapel. Above the hall, a chamber was provided partly within the roof, which has trusses of collar-and-tie-beam type with curved queen struts, the principals crossing at the apex to receive the ridge. Lady Wotton left Northend at the outbreak of the Civil War, during which the chapel was badly damaged by Parliamentary forces at the time of the battle of Edge Hill. Subsequently the structure degenerated into a cattle shed, known as 'Chapel Hovel', the dividing wall between chapel and house being removed and the west end totally destroyed, whilst the thatch has, regrettably, been replaced by corrugated iron.

The similarity in size and architectural quality with these two dwellings suggests that such houses as those at Middle Tysoe and Barford St. John might also have had ecclesiastical associations, the particular situation of the latter dwelling, opposite the church, inviting such a solution. There are other members of the community, including schoolmasters and craftsmen, to whom such small dwellings might also be attributed.[1] In this respect, comparison is also invited with a small house in an adjoining region. The 'Almonry' at Chipping Campden, Gloucestershire (Fig. 46), formed part of the buildings of the great house built by Sir Baptist Hicks in 1613, the greater part of which was destroyed during the Civil Wars to prevent it falling into the hands of the Parliamentarians.[2] The house, which lodged one of the household officials, is of single-unit plan, measuring approximately 14 feet by 16 feet internally, and as befits the richer Cotswold architecture, is even more finely finished. The entrance is by a four-centred arched stone doorway, and all windows are stone-mullioned, the ground-floor label-mould forming a continuous string course around the building. There is a fine, stone newel-stair, projecting from the gable near the entrance, and angle fireplaces are provided on the two principal floors, there being an attic in the roof. The tall, ashlar stone stacks, placed diagonally over each end of the gable, are features common to the Cotswolds, but which are not found around Banbury.

There remains only the third consideration that these dwellings were simply reduced versions of the larger plan built for less prosperous

[1] In Monmouthshire, the authors examined a number of houses which at first sight appeared to be of one-room plan, and concluded that with one exception they were surviving units of larger houses. Llanddewi Court, in Llanddewi Vach parish, is quoted as a probable independent unit, although adjoining another house, and it is suggested that it may have been a 'dower' house (op. cit., pp. 59 and 76).

[2] Davie and Dawber, *Old Cottages, Farmhouses, Etc., in the Cotswold District*, p. 65.

farmers or cottagers. Later dwellings, such as the first house described at Lower Middleton Cheney, and those at Great Bourton
and Kings Sutton, may fall into this class, but this does not account
for the unusually fine architectural quality of the remaining dwellings, which rank with the more elaborate yeoman houses of the 17th
century, as distinct from the less exotic class earlier defined. The
single fireplace has already been stated as not being an indication of
cottage status.[1] It is probable that the homes of the labourers at the
end of the 17th century were yet of primitive construction, presumably perpetuating the use of timber framing in frail structures,
until they were renewed in stone later in the 18th century. The less
significant and later houses noted above as of lower social class are
related to an increasing number of single-unit houses built after
1700, similar in plan, but of increasingly poor architectural quality
as they are built progressively lower in the domestic scale, until this
plan-type becomes the true cottage of the later 18th century, to be
considered in the following chapter.

[1] Fox and Raglan, in Monmouthshire, also refute the suggestion that houses
with a single fireplace in the hearth tax returns of 1685 were necessarily cottages
(op. cit., Vol. III, p. 121.)

CHAPTER IX

THE DECLINE OF THE REGIONAL STYLE
1700–1800

THE minor domestic architecture of the Banbury Region during the 18th century presents the picture of a declining regional tradition, perpetuated in the building of smaller dwellings of lower social class, with little evidence of the continuing evolution of late Renaissance domestic architecture as expressed in the houses of yeoman class with which this study has so far been concerned. The two major factors which extended the regional character of the 17th century throughout this later period are physical and economic. The regional materials of brownstone, thatch and stone slate continue in almost exclusive use until the latter years of the century. Stone slates have a rather wider distribution than before 1700, becoming general for all larger houses until the latter half of the century, when blue slate is introduced in the Banbury Region, together with brick. The latter materials, however, did not spread to outer parts of the region until the latter part of the 19th century,[1] where meantime the continued use of the traditional native materials assisted in the perpetuation of traditional and regional forms of minor domestic architecture. Even in the rebuilding in the 17th and 18th centuries of such great houses and manors as Astrop House, Farnborough Hall, Thenford Priory and Thorpe Mandeville, the local stone continues to be exclusively used, retaining that almost vernacular air which the soft native material imparts to the most sophisticated façade.

The second factor influencing architectural development is social, with a change in the principal building type from the larger houses of prosperous farmers to a smaller class of dwelling. Declining prices in wool and grain were ending the prosperity of the region by 1700, and although the Banbury area did not share the depression of parts of the Cotswolds, rural building was considerably curtailed. The development of industry in Banbury and the neighbouring villages continued to provide occupation for an increasing class of

[1] The Census returns of 1841 for Oxfordshire show that there were in the rural areas of the county still 33 thatchers as against 83 slaters and no tilers, with 846 masons compared with 190 bricklayers. These figures take no account of regional distribution, which greatly increases the proportion of thatchers and masons working in the northern half of the county.

craftsmen and tradesmen, and it is in these larger centres that building is concentrated. Generally smaller in size and poorer in architectural quality, showing little improvement in plan or convenience
from the end of the 17th century, and often retaining until mid-18th
century such traditional features as stone-mullioned windows, these
smaller houses show little of the classical distinction of their larger
neighbours. Many are of one-and-a-half storeys, the majority of two,
and many dwellings of this class, built for small-holders, craftsmen
and labourers, merit the title of cottage rather than house. In the
larger villages these small homes assume a little more significance,
and their symmetrical two-storey façades with central door flanked
by a tall window each side show some of the influence of the larger
houses of the period.

At the upper end of the scale is a small number of large farm-
houses, the successors of the 17th-century yeoman houses, in which
the further development of this house-type in the 18th century can be
studied. Revealing some classical pretension in elevation, and incorporating new forms of windows and wider stairs, there is however
little development in plan, even the largest farm-houses remaining
one room in depth, with the disposition of the three, or more frequently, two ground-floor rooms unchanged from mid-17th century.
The final process of 17th-century planning noted in the previous
chapter, of creating a more compact 'L'-shaped plan in the larger
yeoman houses, proceeds no further, and the single-span plan is
adopted for almost all houses below manorial rank until the end of
the century. There is also little increase in the height of the house,
two rooms with attics over continuing to be general for even the
largest dwellings, although there is some increase in the heights of the
rooms.

The 'L'-shaped plan, however, frequently occurs in the 18th
century in the extension of earlier dwellings, many of which were
improved by the addition of further rooms and the alteration of
windows, or even complete façades, to bring them into line with the
new trends in national architecture.[1]

The reduction in social status of the majority of 18th-century
buildings—apart from the few larger houses, and extensions to
others—creates problems of assessment. Separate consideration has
now to be given to two classes of house, within the general classification of minor domestic architecture, whereas up to 1700 it has been
possible to regard all surviving dwellings as of one broad class, with
merely minor variations in size or character. The further evolution of

[1] Such improvements are separately considered in Chapter X.

the yeoman house can now only be followed in the comparatively few
larger houses, the emphasis changing to a lower order of building
which perpetuates features of the regional house of the 17th century,
ultimately handing them down further to the cottages. Presumably
many of these smaller dwellings replaced more perishable structures
in timber of 17th-century or earlier date. The poorer character of so
much of the building is accompanied by a lack of architectural enrichment around openings, together with a reduction in the use of
date-stones—only thirty-two recorded in the region as compared with
seventy prior to 1700. Dating therefore presents a new problem, in
which it is first important to assess the social status of a dwelling,
generally by its size, condition and character, before its date can be
proposed. Apart from being generally similar in size, there is little in
external appearance to differentiate a two-unit small house or cottage
of the later 18th century from many smaller farm-houses built before
1700, in so many of which the stone mullions have been replaced by
wood lintels and frames. Internally, minor variations in roof and
floor structure and in the finish of the work can generally be distinguished. The occasional addition of an 18th-century date-stone to
an earlier building has increased the difficulty of dating in a number
of cases.

In addition to the classification of buildings by their social character as already noted, it now becomes necessary further to subdivide
the yeoman houses according to their architectural quality, distinguishing firstly a formal or sophisticated class, the homes of the lesser
gentry and more prosperous farmers, which incorporate the characteristics of national architecture of the period to some degree; and
secondly a class retaining the vernacular complexion—buildings of
similar size and function, but of cruder, more archaic form which
shows resolute resistance to new developments, and retain quasi-
medieval characteristics until the latter part of the 18th century.

The first buildings to be noted are the larger farm-houses of three
and two units in which can be traced the ultimate expression of the
regional yeoman plan. Both three- and two-unit types can be further
sub-divided into the formal and vernacular classes noted above. All
alike show little improvement in planning, but the more important
and sophisticated dwellings become progressively distinguished externally by their ordered façades and tall windows, until c. 1730 using
wood-framed windows with central mullions and transom, having
metal casements and small, square panes of glass set in lead cames.
The development of the larger yeoman house cannot be traced beyond mid-18th century; building from 1750 onwards was largely

restricted to a few greater mansions, beyond the scope of this work, together with the smaller cottages, apart from the extensions and improvements to earlier dwellings, and the rebuilding of barns and farm buildings which seems to have been carried on more widely in this century than domestic work.

The perpetuation of earlier domestic forms, gradually giving way to a simple, vernacular Georgian, can be studied in the smaller vernacular buildings of two- and one-unit plans, which simply consolidate the planning developments already noted on a rougher and smaller scale, with little development in structure or detail.

In the first group to be considered, of the more important yeoman houses of three-unit plan, the medieval tradition is still dominant in the first years of the 18th century, as is seen in a farm-house at *Avon Dassett*, dated 1702 (Fig. 54). The plan here is related to the 'lowland' type described in Chapter VII, of three units with the fireplaces to hall and adjoining room back to back, with a third fire in the remaining apartment. It would appear that the adjoining fireplaces in this instance are to kitchen and hall, and not to parlour and hall, as more commonly occurs in the 17th century. The house, which was extensively altered in the late 19th century, is entered from the street into the hall by an original doorway with stone canopy over, with a further entrance on the rear elevation against the centre stack. The latter entrance, although in the appropriate position for this plan, appears to be a modern replacement, having a stone camber-arch. The original stair was probably by the side of the hall fireplace, the present more spacious staircase having been introduced at the parlour end. The windows are still all stone-mullioned, of flat-splay section, but all lack label-moulds, and the roof—now tiled —has gable parapets with kneelers and a moulded stone eaves-course, the earliest to be recorded (Pl. 21f). All bedrooms have fireplaces, and the chimney stacks are of ashlar, but it is not possible to determine the extent to which these features are due to later rebuilding.

The Red Lion Inn at Fenny Compton, dated 1710, also has been a three-unit house of similar plan, but the arrangements cannot be readily distinguished in consequence of extensive later alterations. These two houses are among the last of their class—the large house— to bear the traditional complexion, for the next dated example of the three-unit house—*the Dolphin Inn at Wigginton* (Fig. 53) dated 1727— confirms a change in architectural character which had been pending since the end of the 17th century, principally due to the abandonment of stone-mullioned windows in these larger houses, except to light basements. Instead, tall wood-framed transomed windows are employed, first recorded in an extended wing at Cropredy Old Manor House in 1694 (Pl. 15b), and continuing to be used in all larger dwellings until at least 1728, this being the last actual date recorded for the type. The use of such windows is confined to the formal class of building, and is accompanied by a more ordered treatment of the principal elevation, in a balanced or symmetrical disposition of windows and doorway, with the addition of more finely dressed stonework, string courses and plinths, usually with stone flat-arches to the openings.

The Dolphin Inn (Fig. 53) has fortunately been preserved with little alteration or restoration and reveals a number of developments. It seems probable from the unusual construction and extent of the basement that the building has always been an inn, but in plan and character there is no variation from contemporary yeoman houses, and the Dolphin is of particular interest in providing a firm dating point. Of three-unit plan, the entrance is from the road front to one end of the hall; this appears to be, as at Avon Dassett, the upper end of the house, adjacent to the parlour, the kitchen with a large fire-place and oven being at the end farthest from the entrance. Such an arrangement may result from the particular function of the building as an inn. There was originally no fireplace in the hall, although one has been added in brick, with a flue which contrives to ascend on the rear face of the structure. A straight-flight stair is taken off the hall at the lower end, ascending to the attics, whilst below there winds the stair to the cellars, approached from the kitchen. An original rear entrance also opens from the kitchen, now into a lean-to annexe of 19th-century build which has served as a brewhouse. The cellars, as might be expected, are unusually spacious, forming two apartments under kitchen and hall, with a cambered, stone barrel vault, a feature rarely found even in the largest houses until the 19th century. The cellar under the hall has a wood-joist floor over; this does not suggest a change of build, but may have been so constructed to provide a wood board floor to the hall itself. The two ground-floor partitions are both stone walls, and the first-floor joists span between these supports and lateral beams which divide each room, the ceilings being now flush-plastered except in the kitchen. Room heights here show no increase over work of the 17th century, being 8 feet 3 inches and 7 feet 8 inches to ground and first floors respectively, with attics over. Only the one bedroom over the parlour has a fireplace, at an angle in the corner. It is possible that there was a second stair by the side of the kitchen fireplace, but, if so, this has been removed and built up as a cupboard on both floors.

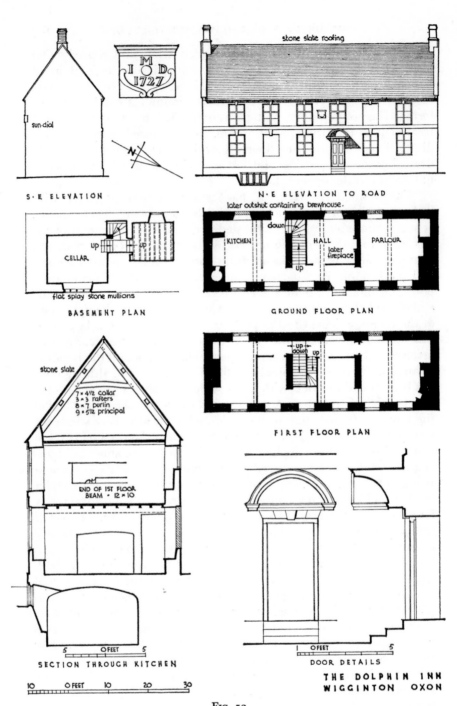

S·E ELEVATION

sun·dial

I M D 1727

N·E ELEVATION TO ROAD

stone slate roofing

later outshut containing brewhouse.

KITCHEN   down   HALL   PARLOUR
CELLAR   UP   UP   later fireplace
UP

flat splay stone mullions

BASEMENT PLAN

GROUND FLOOR PLAN

up
down   up

FIRST FLOOR PLAN

stone slate

7 × 4½ collar
3 × 3 rafters
8 × 7 purlin
9 × 5½ principal

END OF 1ST FLOOR
BEAM = 12 × 10

5   O FEET   5

SECTION THROUGH KITCHEN

10   O FEET   10   20   30

DOOR DETAILS

1   O FEET   5

THE DOLPHIN INN
WIGGINTON OXON

FIG. 53.

The cross-walls are both taken up to support purlins, with principals dividing each bay to reduce the centres of supports to approximately 8 feet. In the roof structure can be seen the evidence of the more up-to-date constructional practice of the 18th century, based on the south-eastern tradition of building. The purlins are deeply housed into the principals to bring the common rafters into almost the same plane as the principal rafters, the latter being crossed and pegged at the apex without any seating for a ridge. There is, however, a ridge, a slip of wood averaging 3 inches by 1 inch thick, not secured to the principals and serving only to unite the heads of the rafters.

Externally the house presents an ordered elevation to the road, the front being built in a smoothly dressed and evenly coursed stone with fine joints, that approaches ashlar, with a flat, projecting string forming a sill to the upper windows. The windows are tall in proportion, having the transomed wood frames already noted, the openings headed by flat, stone arches of which the keystones are large and projecting. The transomed lights have been replaced at the parlour end by large metal casements of light section with horizontal astragals. There is a shallow plinth, also confined to the road elevation, in which is set a four-light window to the cellar, having grey stone, flat-splay mullions. The front and rear doors also have flat stone arches, with a fine, arched stone canopy to give further distinction to the principal elevation, together with an elaborately carved date-stone in the centre of the façade. A number of windows have been blocked, no doubt as a result of the severe window taxes of the later 18th century. Of particular note are the wrought-iron casement fasteners, which are elaborately cut and perforated, some depicting animals, testifying to the skill of the local smith (Pl. 22a). Such features occur commonly in the Cotswolds but are extremely rare around Banbury. The rear elevation and gables are of inferior masonry and finish, the windows, some with wood lintels, being set in a coursed rubble stonework. There is a good stone sundial set on the southern angle, in a position similar to that at another inn, the Red Lion, Fenny Compton, noted above.

The Dolphin Inn has been described fully as it is representative of a number of other large houses of similar date. The largest of these is *Manor Farm, Claydon* (Pl. 12c), in many features resembling the former house, with a formal main elevation to the road, bearing string-course, stone lintels and four-light, transomed windows; as a more important structure than the Inn, it may be a little earlier in date. Despite the sophistication of the architectural character, the three-unit plan here shows no variation from the through-passage arrangement of the mid-17th century, the hall fireplace backing onto the entrance passage, although there is some increase in the size and height of rooms on both floors, all of which have fireplaces. The house is set well back from the road, and has been extended at the lower end by a service annexe of 19th-century date, built in brick with hipped roof. The roof of the house was probably originally stone-slated, now replaced by blue slates, with a stone eaves cornice, gable parapets and ashlar stone stacks.

Not all three-unit houses of the first half of the 18th century have the architectural distinction of the preceding examples, a number having been recorded which, although of similar size, show little advance on poorer 17th-century work, and fall into a second classification as informal, archaic structures. There is such a house at *Chacombe*, dated on the gable 1739, of similar cross-passage plan to that at Claydon; here the stair is in the parlour, adjacent to the fireplace. The house is of two-storey height, with the first-floor windows taken into the roof, the thatch being swept up over them, and the attics above are of mean proportion. Casement windows are employed, with iron opening lights and horizontal astragals, and apart from the date-stone, there is no ashlar stonework in the building, or any attempt at classical pretension. The house is placed at right angles to the road, a less usual disposition after 1700.

The latest date for a large three-unit house is 1757, the instance being in *Fenny Compton*; like the last house, this dwelling is also of simple vernacular character, with thatched roof, rubble walling, and small casement windows. The plan follows that of the later three-unit houses recorded before 1700, with the hall fireplace at the upper end of the room, away from the cross-passage.[1]

Inviting parallel consideration with the two classes of three-unit plans of the first half of the 18th century so far described are a number of large two-room houses, which can similarly be divided into formal and archaic classes. The former are similarly distinguished by the use of the transomed window of four-lights, with the entrance and stair centrally placed, and fireplaces on the gables, following the development of the yeoman house as it stood at the end of the 17th century. Fine houses of this type are to be seen in Chacombe and Hook Norton (Pl. 13*b*, 12*a*), both having the entrance centrally placed in a balanced elevation of five bays, with good dressed stonework and tall windows. The house in *Silver Street, Chacombe*, has flat, stone-voussoired lintels continued as a string course to each floor, with gable parapets, and stone stacks serving fireplaces in all rooms. The

---

[1] The plan corresponds to that of Home Farm, Williamscot, 1699 (Fig. 26).

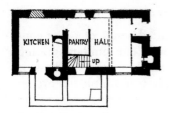

CHURCH ENSTONE
OXFORDSHIRE

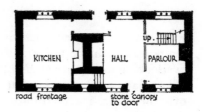

AVON DASSETT 1702
WARWICKSHIRE

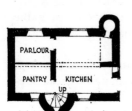

HOMESTEAD COTTAGE
ALKERTON   1710
OXFORDSHIRE

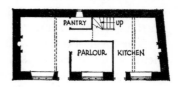

HOUSE TO NORTH OF CHURCH
MIDDLETON CHENEY NORTHAMPTONSHIRE

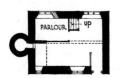

SHOTTESWELL
WARWICKSHIRE

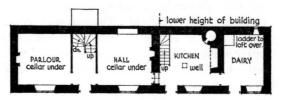

THE OLD RECTORY
THENFORD NORTHAMPTONSHIRE

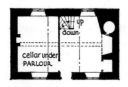

CHURCH ENSTONE
OXFORDSHIRE

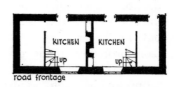

COTTAGE PAIR KINGS SUTTON
NORTHAMPTONSHIRE

HOUSE AND COTTAGE PLANS
OF THE
EIGHTEENTH CENTURY

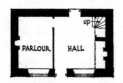

ADDERBURY EAST
OXFORDSHIRE

o

FIG. 54.

windows are tall casements, with square, leaded panes, of a type contemporary with the tall, transomed windows. The similar building overlooking the square at *Hook Norton,* now used by Barclays Bank, is of less elaborate but rather later character, having simple flat arches over the square-leaded transomed windows. The arrangement of the stair here perpetuates the tradition of the projecting stair turret so characteristic of 17th-century houses in Hook Norton, being contained in a rectangular, gabled projection, centrally placed at the rear of the house. Chimney stacks are of brick, and there are no gable parapets to the stone-slated roof, which has original dormer windows on the entrance front.

The form of these two houses can be related to the final development of the 'upland' plan type within the region, with gable fireplaces, but a few houses of similar class reveal the 'lowland' feature of a centrally placed double stack, serving hall and parlour. *Cliftons Farm, Great Tew, Oxfordshire,* dated 1728 in an elliptical panel over the entrance, but representing more than one period of building, is an attractive instance of this type of plan, in a building of good architectural quality (Pl. 12*d*). The entrance, centrally placed on the road front, opens to a small vestibule at the side of the double fireplace. As at Hook Norton, the stair is on the rear of the house, in a large rectangular bay beyond the central stack, entered from the principal room. Windows, more limited in number than in the previous examples, are transomed, with small, rectangular leads, and all openings have voussoired flat arches with stressed keystones. The roof is stone-slated, with gable parapets having ball finials, and the central chimney-stack has twin ashlar stalks with moulded cappings. On either side of the house is a single-storey extension, the smaller stone-slated wing at the lower end acting as a service-room. This may be an original bay, but the larger wing at the upper end, having a thatched roof, is more probably an added kitchen. In a number of houses of three or four units, the kitchen and other rooms at the lower end are similarly suppressed in height, as already noted at the end of the 17th century, to avoid interruption of the symmetry of the principal apartments. *Thenford Old Rectory* (Fig. 54) dating from *c.* 1800, has secondary accommodation of this nature, of the same build but lower height, providing servant's bedrooms in the first-floor attics.

The fourth group of houses to be considered is the informal or archaic class of two-unit dwellings, which includes by far the majority of the smaller 18th-century houses in the region, showing little advance on 17th-century work in plan or detail. The gable position for the fireplaces is generally adopted and usually there is some

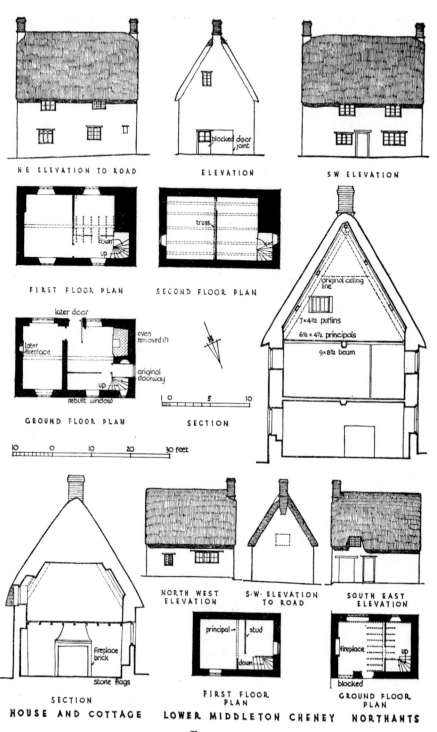

NE ELEVATION TO ROAD

ELEVATION

SW ELEVATION

blocked door joint

FIRST FLOOR PLAN

down
up

SECOND FLOOR PLAN

truss

GROUND FLOOR PLAN

later door

oven removed (?)

later fireplace

original doorway

up

rebuilt window

SECTION

original ceiling line

7 × 4½ purlins

6½ × 4½ principals

9 × 8½ beam

1 O   5   10

10   O   10   20   30 feet

SECTION

HOUSE AND COTTAGE

fireplace brick

stone flags

NORTH WEST ELEVATION

S·W· ELEVATION TO ROAD

SOUTH EAST ELEVATION

FIRST FLOOR PLAN

principal   stud

down

GROUND FLOOR PLAN

fireplace

up

blocked

LOWER MIDDLETON CHENEY   NORTHANTS

FIG. 55.

provision for storage in a pantry or basement cellar. *Homestead Cottage, Alkerton* (Fig. 54), dated 1716, has none of the refinement of the houses of the more sophisticated class already considered, and is more closely related to the preceding century than to its larger contemporaries. It was probably built as the home of one of the smaller farmers who had sufficient pride in his new home, however simple, to have his initials and the date somewhat crudely inscribed in the stone lintel over the door. Of two-unit plan, and one-and-a-half storeys in height, the house is entered on the gable by the side of the only fireplace, there being a large projecting bread-oven in the other reveal. The stair is a spacious newel, projecting as a semi-circular turret between hall and parlour. There is no basement cellar, but the inner room is sub-divided to provide a pantry at the side of the parlour. The masonry is of irregularly coursed rubble, the roof thatched with the usual clipped verges, and there are later brick stalks on the original stone vent. There are small casement windows with heavy stone lintels to the openings (Pl. 18*d*).

The spaciousness of the stair in so humble a house is surpassed in a house of similarly small dimensions recently demolished in *Hook Norton* (Fig. 41; Pl. 14*c*). This house, of two-unit plan, similarly had a single fireplace, in the hall, but here it was centrally placed, with the entrance onto the side of the breast. The stair was contained in a large projecting turret occupying the whole of the side of the second room, which appeared to have been sub-divided as at Alkerton. The general character of the workmanship was of a low order, but it seems that the building originally was roofed with stone slates, which even in Hook Norton, nearer to the Stonesfield and Cotswold slate quarries, are rarely used for the humbler dwellings. This house probably dates from the first years of the 18th century.

Stairs projecting from the outer walls are infrequent after 1700, and in the traditional type of house are normally cramped in a corner or by the side of the principal fireplace. The entrance from the gable is still to be found in many houses of the first half of the 18th century, with stairway on one side of the door, the chimney-breast on the other, as may be seen in two houses of very similar size and plan, at *Thenford* (Fig. 56) and at *Lower Middleton Cheney* (Fig. 55), larger and better-finished structures than those at Alkerton or Hook Norton. At Thenford, the inner room is again sub-divided into parlour and pantry, and the windows are of the four-light transomed type with wood lintels. Both houses are thatched, and the walls are built in a coarse rubble.

A number of these smaller houses retain stone-mullioned windows,

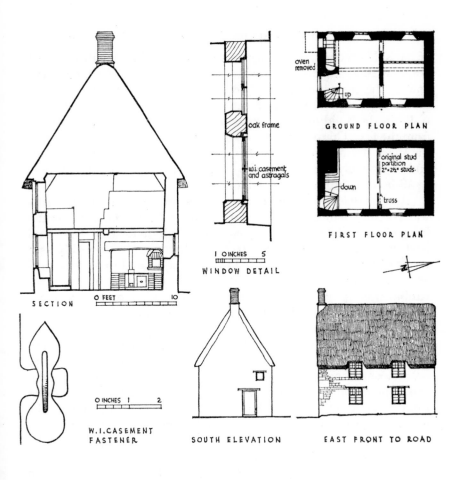

GROUND FLOOR PLAN

oven removed

up

FIRST FLOOR PLAN

original stud partition 2"×2½" studs.

down

truss

oak frame

w.i. casement and astragals

1 0 INCHES 5

WINDOW DETAIL

0 FEET 10

SECTION

0 INCHES 1 2

W.I. CASEMENT FASTENER

SOUTH ELEVATION

EAST FRONT TO ROAD

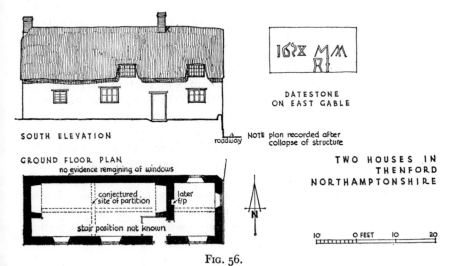

SOUTH ELEVATION

roadway

GROUND FLOOR PLAN
no evidence remaining of windows

conjectured site of partition

later f/p

stair position not known

16?8 MM RI

DATESTONE
ON EAST GABLE

NOTE plan recorded after
collapse of structure

TWO HOUSES IN
THENFORD
NORTHAMPTONSHIRE

10 0 FEET 10 20

FIG. 56.

of flat-splay section, as at *Shotteswell* (Fig. 54), in a small thatched house with a single gable fireplace, from the back of which opens one of the most prominent ovens recorded, its size and position suggesting a date in mid-18th century. The stair is here placed centrally in the building, with the entrance on the lateral wall farthest from the fire. This is virtually a single-unit plan in which a portion of the space has been closed off by a stud partition to form a parlour, and is probably the cottage of a labourer, many of whom had some small-holding of their own to farm.

An equally diminutive two-cell house of one-and-a-half storeys was recently demolished at *Lower Middleton Cheney* (Fig. 55), dating from *c.* 1800. The two apartments were sub-divided by light stud partitions, and the small fireplace had brick jambs—possibly as a result of later alteration, as the brickwork appeared to be quite separate from the stone walling. With wood lintels, casement windows, rubble walling and thatch, stud partitions and a narrow winding stair, there was little other than the scale to distinguish such a building from poorer work of the 17th century.

In the majority of the smaller 18th-century houses, the gable entrance gives way to a centrally placed door either on the street front, or, almost as frequently, on the rear elevation. The central front entrance predominates in the larger villages, in quite small dated houses from 1700 to 1793 (both these dates being in Shenington). The houses, of two-storey height and small dimensions—averaging 28 feet by 16 feet overall—are sub-divided into two principal rooms by stud partitions, whilst the staircase is invariably in one corner of the building, usually by the side of the fireplace. There is some variation in character, some buildings having stone-voussoired lintels, occasionally with transomed four-light windows, but the majority have timber lintels and frames with iron opening lights. The house at *Adderbury East* (Fig. 54) is a humbler version of this type, whilst the *Mary Knoll Cottage, Gaydon*, is illustrated (Pl. 12*b*) as a rather more pretentious example of the same size and plan, built in 1714. Built in the area of mixed building stone in the north-west, the walling is of grey stone with marlstone quoins and other dressings.

Two houses recorded at *Church Enstone* (Fig. 54) of similar size and social type, reveal the change in planning in the first half of the 18th century, no doubt influenced by the larger houses of formal character already described. The earlier is entered from the gable by the side of the fireplace with the stair and a pantry placed between the hall and an inner room or kitchen, also with a large fireplace. Projecting ovens are provided to both hearths, and floor-beams span across the building. The second house is more formal in layout, with the entrance placed centrally in a balanced façade, opening into the hall where there is a large hearth with oven. The parlour has a smaller fireplace, perhaps added later. Here the stair is in the hall, opposite to the entrance, with flights to the attics and to the cellar under the parlour. Both houses are of two-and-a-half storeys, thatched, with wood lintels and casement windows.

A small thatched cottage north of the church at *Middleton Cheney, Northamptonshire,* demolished in 1954 (Fig. 54), represents a still later version of the two-unit plan, following the arrangements already noted at Milcombe (Fig. 39) and in the first house at Enstone. Of poor, late 18th-century workmanship, further indications of its late date were provided in the small fireplaces on the gable walls, instead of the earlier broad hearths, and in the lateral floor beams. Doors were provided on the symmetrical street front to both rooms, which were separated by a bay containing a small third room—probably used for service or as a small parlour—with the stair on the back of the house.

It remains to consider a number of single-cell cottage plans which occur with increasing frequency after 1700. Usually of one-and-a-half storeys, of small dimensions and poor construction, lacking dressed stonework, with thatched roofs and small casement windows, these dwellings present a number of variations in the placing of the stair, corresponding to those already formulated in Chapter VIII, but appearing to be without chronological significance after 1700. *Lambert's Cottage, Cropredy* (Fig. 52), illustrates the plan most widely encountered, having a single room on the ground floor, measuring internally 16 feet 6 inches by 15 feet 6 inches, with a stair at the side of the fireplace and the entrance on the opposite gable. A large bread-oven projects from the reveal of the fireplace; more frequently in these houses the oven now opens from the back of the hearth. This is one of the largest instances of this type recorded, the majority being of very mean dimensions. The single-cell cottage at *Milcombe* (Fig. 57) measures only 12 feet 6 inches by 10 feet 6 inches internally, the entrance here being by the side of the fire, with the stair on the opposite wall. This is clearly a true cottage, dating from not earlier than the end of the 18th century and forming the nucleus for a terrace of cottages of equally mean dimensions and character which are probably little later in date. All have the 'cottage fireplace', bread-oven and winding stair, to provide a humble miniature of the regional house-type.

The true cottage of the landless labourer is, in the Banbury

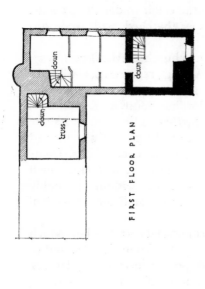

FIRST FLOOR PLAN

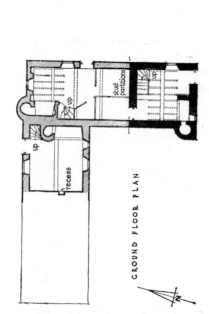

GROUND FLOOR PLAN

NORTH ELEVATION

EAST ELEVATION

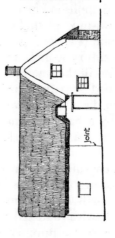

SECTION   SOUTH ELEVATION TO ROAD

COTTAGE TERRACE AT
MILCOMBE OXFORDSHIRE

FIG. 57.

Region, a feature of the 19th century, and scarcely comes within the scope of this study. Most of the cottages date from the period after the Parliamentary enclosures of the late 18th century, which here, as elsewhere, seriously reduced the status of many small-holders. It is, however, in these small dwellings that the last faint traces of regional character are preserved. There was a reversion to the stone-mullioned window in many of the cottage pairs which were built by large land-owners on their estates at the end of the 18th and early in the 19th centuries. That at *Radway* (Fig. 58; Pl. 14*b*) serves as an instance of the more conscious expression of the regional tradition associated with revivalist building, but there were many more genuine small buildings in which the vernacular tradition was preserved throughout the 19th century.

It is possible that the Radway cottages with their consciously traditional character, may be due to the influence of the architect Sanderson Millar (1717–80), an amateur of some distinction whose ventures in the romantic Gothic manner found their first expression within the region. Millar was born at Radway Grange in 1717, his father having bought the house five years earlier, and he spent much of his life there, altering and developing the Grange. His works at Edge Hill represent Millar's first venture in Gothic and provide a rare intrusion of 'fashionable' architecture into the regional pattern. The thatched cottage (Pl. 14*a*) known as Egge Cottage, was built in 1744 and designed to appear from the road as a romantic ruin. In 1747, work was started on the adjacent tower, or castle, and this was completed in 1750 as a landmark overlooking the site of the battlefield of Edge Hill.

At Great Tew, the ordered buildings and landscaping, with formal cottage gardens, clipped box-hedges and well-grouped trees, and the consciously preserved regional character of the architecture, may be attributed to the influence of another distinguished figure, John Claudius Loudon, the agriculturalist and landscape architect. The Great Tew estate, enclosed as early as 1614, was acquired by a Colonel Stratton, who invited Loudon to take over the management of part of his estate. Loudon took up residence at Tew Lodge, and although only there from 1809 to 1811, he applied his principles to the reorganization of the property and these appear to have been carried on by Matthew Boulton, the subsequent holder of the estate. In the carefully preserved regional style of the houses can be seen the influence of Loudon's own published cottage designs.[1]

The 18th century is the aftermath of the period of major building

[1] Christopher Hussey, 'Great Tew' (*Country Life*, 22nd July 1949).

activity, and its contribution to the regional tradition is small. The structural system, with few variations, continued to be that of the preceding century. There is some improvement in the character of the masonry, a better dressed and squared stone with finer joints being more widely used, even for quite small dwellings, by the end of the century, as at Shotteswell (Pl. 13c), whilst the coursed rubble of the façades of the larger houses occasionally attains the character of ashlar work. The more modern roof structure of the Dolphin Inn, with its indication of a broader, national, stamp, does not represent a general development, occurring only in a few barns and houses, and in the great majority of roofs there is no change from the 17th century. Already before 1700, as noted previously, the trend in upper-floor construction was to abandon the spine-beam in favour of transverse beams, and this now becomes general practice, although exceptions continue to occur. Partitions are invariably of light stud construction, with thin, stone, internal walls in the larger houses. Thatch continues as the dominant material, although the distribution of stone slates is wider than in the previous century, and slates are used on smaller dwellings which earlier would only have merited thatch.

Plan development is divided now between two classes of house, of sophisticated or vernacular character, the three-unit plan appearing rarely and usually with some elaboration of the principal elevation. The large two-unit house-type, which was most common at the end of the preceding century, continues to predominate, assisting as it did in providing a symmetrical façade about the centrally placed doorway. The 'lowland' plan with double stack is recorded solely in a few large houses, fireplaces generally being on one or both gables in houses of all sizes. The centrally placed entrance, between kitchen and parlour, which became general in yeoman plans before 1700, extends even to small houses, but the gable entrance and the projecting stair-turret may still appear in the first half of the century, particularly in the smaller and more remote hamlets.

The provision of a pantry noted in some yeoman houses at the end of the 17th century now becomes more general in smaller homes, usually contrived by dividing the parlour by a longitudinal, stud partition. Alternatively, basement cellars may serve the larger houses, where they provide the only storage space. Apart from additions to earlier dwellings, there is little development in depth beyond the single width plan before 1800. A few dwellings have been noted on the western fringe of the region possessing original outshut extensions on the rear, normally serving as a pantry, service or dairy, as in the small house at *Radway, Warwickshire*, illustrated in Fig. 58. This

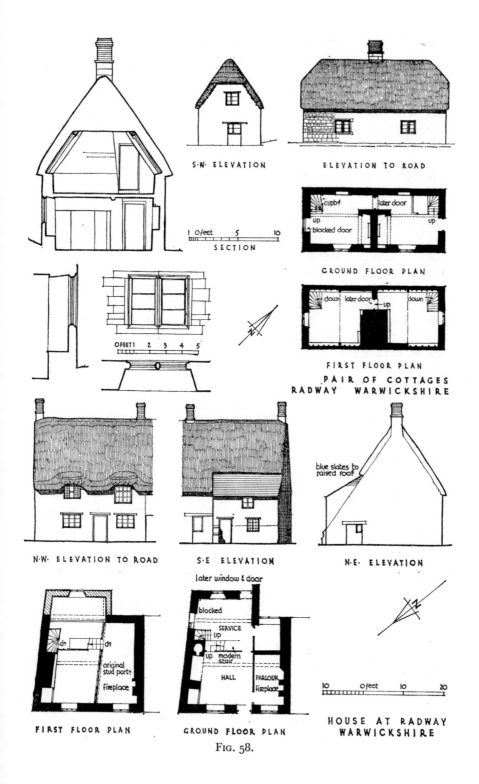

S·W· ELEVATION

ELEVATION TO ROAD

1 0 feet 5 10
SECTION

GROUND FLOOR PLAN

cupb^d   later door
up   up
blocked door

FIRST FLOOR PLAN
down   later door   down
up

PAIR OF COTTAGES
RADWAY WARWICKSHIRE

0 FEET 1 2 3 4 5

N·W· ELEVATION TO ROAD

S·E ELEVATION

N·E· ELEVATION

blue slates to
raised roof

FIRST FLOOR PLAN

dn   dn
original
stud part?
fireplace

GROUND FLOOR PLAN

later window & door
blocked
SERVICE
up
up   modern
     stair
HALL   PARLOUR
        fireplace

10   0 feet   10   20

HOUSE AT RADWAY
WARWICKSHIRE

FIG. 58.

arrangement is not typical of the region and is related to practice in the lowland plain of Warwickshire.

The full, double-depth plan is represented by rare instances in the larger villages, usually in the second half of the 18th century. *Grove Farm, Warmington, Warwickshire* (Fig. 13a), provides an unusual example of a large yeoman house of early 18th-century date in which this more advanced form of plan is adopted. Dating from *c.* 1700, and showing evidence of later building, the house is built in ashlar stone, with stone, moulded windows in the basement and transomed wood frames to the upper floors. The entrance front is symmetrically disposed, with a wood canopy over the central entrance, and the tiled roof is hipped. Internally, there are back-to-back fireplaces in two large stacks, moulded ceiling beams and a fine open-well staircase with turned balusters at the rear of the long, central entrance hall.

A similar plan, two rooms deep with pantry and kitchen beyond hall and parlour, disposed astride a centrally placed entrance and stair hall, appears before 1800 in smaller dwellings of Georgian character having sash windows and flat-pitched slate roofs, as in a house dated 1778 at *Fenny Compton, Warwickshire* (Fig. 12e). After 1800, similar houses of Georgian stereotype become more frequent, a third floor being added in larger instances.

It is in the early part of the 18th century that the larger houses go through the final phase of regional development, before giving way completely to characteristics of a national, universal, complexion. The phase is that characterized by the two-light transomed window, the precursor of the Georgian sash,[1] but still accompanied by such traditional features as parapeted gables with kneelers. This phase ends *c.* 1740, and thereafter it is unnecessary to follow developments of houses of the class since they are outside the scope of this investigation, the only trace of regional character which they retain being imparted by the brown stone walls. They were, in any case, few in number, and due, no doubt, to such prosperity as was brought by the enclosures to the larger landlords. In the more rural areas, the lesser houses alike diminished in numbers, but these smaller dwellings and the cottages for long maintained the final expression of the regional style.

---

[1] The two-light transomed window was frequently replaced soon after the advent of the Georgian sash, and consequently is now rather rare to find. Cf. Nathaniel Lloyd, *A History of the English House*, p. 337.

CHAPTER X

THE PROCESS OF IMPROVEMENT
1600–1800

CONSIDERATION has so far been limited to the evolution of the vernacular house within the region as expressed in new buildings, from the later middle ages until 1800, and the examples chosen for study have been primarily those which clearly incorporate new developments of plan and structure current in the region at the time they were built. The decline in prosperity, and hence in building activity, from the end of the 17th century resulted in a corresponding decline in the replacement of buildings by newer structures, and the farming community in the villages around Banbury had often to content themselves with endeavouring to improve and extend their older homes to bring them into line with the new architectural trends. This process of alteration and addition is a commonplace of architectural development, but the economic history of this area has made it here a factor of regional significance. The principal period for alteration, as opposed to building anew, is from the end of the 17th century to the beginning of the 19th, after which there is a period, static both architecturally as well as economically, which has been invaluable in preserving the region in so unspoilt a state until the spate of modernization which has only since 1945 seriously affected the area. Many buildings have survived from the 17th century with no other alteration than the replacement of such short-lived items as glass and thatch, but the majority of dwellings built within the main period of building activity, from _c._ 1600 to 1700, show some subsequent work of the 18th century.[1] The many forms of domestic improvement concern aspects of planning, structure and detail, usually all three together at the same time. It has been shown that the 17th century saw the replacement of almost all the medieval timber houses by stone structures, and all new dwellings were built with stone walls, apart from the cottages, which did not attain permanent form until after

---

[1] Warden Woodward, visiting the estates of New College in North Oxfordshire at the end of the 17th century, continually records such alterations and improvements in such notes as 'To Widow Huckins, 2 Elmes to rebuild the west part of her dwelling house and make it equal with the other' (_Progress Notes of Warden Woodward round the Oxfordshire Estates of New College, 1659–1675_, Oxford Record Society, 1945, p. 45).

1700. The few medieval buildings which survived this general re-building were manor-houses or first-rate vernacular structures, where stone construction was earlier adopted, and all have undergone extensive modernization in later centuries. Only such larger and more permanent stone-built medieval structures survived in sufficiently sound condition to permit of improvement rather than replacement. In the case of the majority of smaller homes, built of timber and no doubt somewhat decayed by 1600, it was necessary to demolish them completely and to replace them by new stone structures, probably rebuilding on or near the same site.[1] The great houses of the region have all undergone extensive rebuilding, and lower down the scale it is the stone-built manor-houses such as Swalcliffe and Cottisford, and such fine houses as Leadenporch House, which were still structurally sound, and planned on a sufficiently spacious scale to make them acceptable and amenable for improvement in the succeeding period. It is unlikely that sentiment or tradition was behind the retention of a house for improvement, rather than building anew—too many fine houses within the region have totally disappeared to make way for their more up-to-date successors.

The three dwellings mentioned above were brought into conformity with 17th-century requirements by drastic alteration involving plan, structure and detail. At Swalcliffe the single-storey hall was sub-divided in height and length and a fireplace introduced against the screens passage, whilst a new kitchen wing was added. Leadenporch House was similarly amended by the introduction of a first floor and fireplace, with the addition of a new parlour with cellar under, to produce a characteristic regional plan, with the introduction of new fenestration. Cottisford, already of two storeys, with the hall on the first floor, also received the addition of a parlour wing, and the ground-floor apartments now became the principal rooms, with bedrooms over, in accordance with late 16th-century usage. All three houses underwent major structural renovation—only Leadenporch House retaining its original roof structure—whilst there was similarly extensive modernization in detail of fireplaces, stairs and above all of windows, with further amendment of these features in the 18th century.

In Chapters III and IV a number of houses were considered and

---

[1] Some earlier structures may have been permitted to survive for a while in baser use as farm dwellings before finally perishing. Many fine 17th-century dwellings similarly underwent this social decline, to finish as cottages or farm buildings to the newer houses which replaced them. The ancient manor-house of the Greviles at Drayton was turned into a poor-house in the 18th century before finally being demolished.

classified as of mid-16th-century date, in particular the fine houses at Balscott and at Bloxham, which all survived subsequent rebuilding in the 17th and 18th centuries. These few houses survived for similar reasons to the earlier medieval structures; being built finely in stone in advance of the main regional building period, they were still sound and appropriate for improvement in the later period. The evolution of the two houses at Balscott, from the 16th to the 18th centuries, epitomizes architectural development within the region and their subsequent history will be considered as a sequel to this chapter.

Blue Gates and the nearby 16th-century house in Sycamore Terrace, Bloxham, also underwent the introduction of upper floors, stairs and dormer windows, with further amendments to the former building in the 18th century, when the street entrance was closed by a new oven, the original stone doorway then being rebuilt on the rear elevation.

Chinners Farm, Chacombe, and the two houses in Kings Sutton appear to have survived for somewhat different reasons, their structure and finish being of poorer quality that would not merit retention if the owner were able to build anew. The history of Chinners Farm (Fig. 7) has already been investigated, and the most probable conclusion to be drawn is that the building, a large hall-house of the mid-16th century, survived until the middle of the 17th century in its original form because its owners were then less prosperous than their neighbours. Even when an attempt was made in 1657 to bring the house into line with current standards, the added parlour wing, lacking dressed stonework to doors and windows, and with a date-stone of which the carving is singularly crude, compares unfavourably with many of its 17th-century neighbours, including the fine house now called Poplars Farm, built three years earlier less than 50 yards away.

A similar sequence of building can be studied at *Hempton, Oxfordshire*, in a house belonging to College Farm, sometimes known as *Parish's Farmhouse* (Fig. 59). The nucleus is again a 16th-century dwelling, here of one-and-a-half storey height with upper crucks supporting a thatched roof. In the second half of the 17th century the house was improved by the addition of a fine parlour wing of two tall storeys with attic over, built in squared rubble with masonry detailing of unusual distinction. As at Chacombe, the new block may have replaced the lower end of an original two-unit house, the older part of the structure now serving as the kitchen. The house is entered by a new doorway on the road front of the same build as the parlour, with ovolo-moulded stone lintel, opening into a passage which separates the two periods of building. The stair at the rear of the passage is

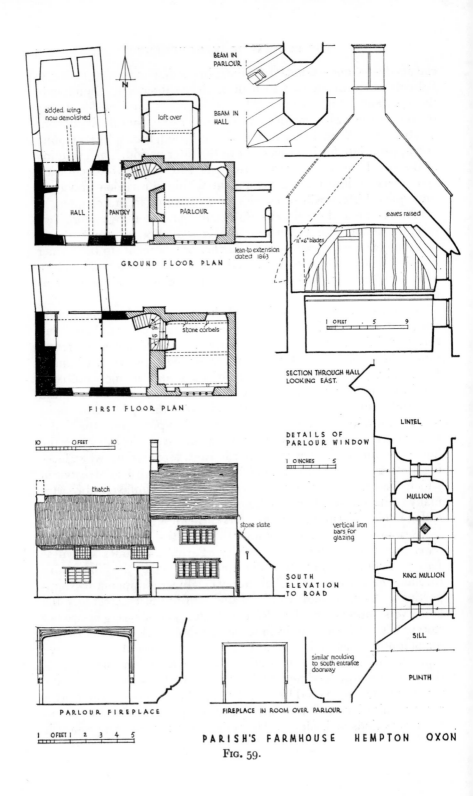

BEAM IN PARLOUR

BEAM IN HALL

added wing now demolished

loft over

HALL   PANTRY   PARLOUR

lean-to extension dated 1863

GROUND FLOOR PLAN

eaves raised

11"×6' blades

0 FEET   5   9

SECTION THROUGH HALL LOOKING EAST.

dn   up   stone corbels

FIRST FLOOR PLAN

DETAILS OF PARLOUR WINDOW

1   0 INCHES   5

10   0 FEET   10

thatch

stone slate

LINTEL

MULLION

vertical iron bars for glazing

KING MULLION

SOUTH ELEVATION TO ROAD

SILL

PLINTH

PARLOUR FIREPLACE

FIREPLACE IN ROOM OVER PARLOUR.

similar moulding to south entrance doorway

1   0 FEET 1   2   3   4   5

PARISH'S FARMHOUSE   HEMPTON   OXON
FIG. 59.

crudely constructed and probably served the original house. Adjacent to the passage, light stud partitions enclose a small service-room, and the final plan approximates to the late 17th-century pattern which has been illustrated at Milcombe and Middleton Cheney.

The new parlour wing has ovolo-moulded mullioned windows on the principal front, the six-light, ground-floor window providing the only instance of a king mullion recorded in a house below manorial level, although these are commonly found in the true Cotswolds. The road frontage is further distinguished by a plinth, whilst the tall stack has twin ashlar stalks with moulded capping. As in other late-17th-century houses, the eaves level is raised well above the first-floor windows, and the roof is stone-slated, without parapets. Internally there are good moulded fireplaces on both floors, and the chamfered spine-beam has unusual enriched stops. Unusual features at this date are the inclusion of longitudinal wall-beams, supported on corbels from the side walls, together with the thicker walls, averaging 2 feet 3 inches. A stone lean-to extension with stone-slated roof adjoins the parlour, and is accessible only from outside; it bears the date 1868 over a small window. There had been a further extension in a wing projecting to the rear of the kitchen, but this had been taken down before the building was recorded.

A third instance of the addition of a tall parlour block is provided by a house on School Green, Wardington, whilst the possibility has been recognized that the tall single-unit at Middle Tysoe, already described in Chapter VIII (Fig. 50), may also bear such a relationship to its adjoining humbler structure.

Northend Manor House, Warwickshire, provides a more complex illustration of 17th-century improvement (Fig. 60). In the first half of the century, the house was the residence of the widow of Edward, Lord Wotton. Already noted as the builder of the nearby priest's house, Lady Wotton left Northend at the outbreak of the Civil War, during which her chapel was seriously damaged by the Puritans, and it seems probable that the Manor House also suffered. After the war, the estate came into the possession of Sir Richard Temple, who in 1664 restored the building for the use of his former steward, Barak Tustian.[1] The two principal periods of building can be recognized, although recent modernization, which included the erection of the south wing, has considerably obscured the earlier work. The hall, elevated over a basement cellar, only partly below ground, is the earliest

---

[1] E. C. Westacott, 'Some Account of the Parish of Burton Dassett, Warwickshire, from Nov. 1660 to Jan. 1665' (Account book of Sir Richard Temple), *Transactions of the Birmingham Archaeological Society*, Vol. LX, 1936.

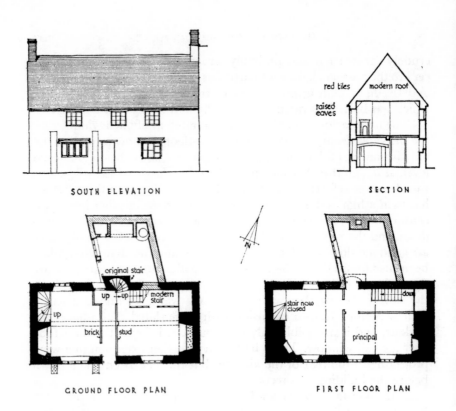

SOUTH ELEVATION

SECTION

red tiles modern roof

raised
eaves

original stair

up up modern
stair

up

brick stud

stair now
closed

principal

dow

GROUND FLOOR PLAN

FIRST FLOOR PLAN

N

HOUSE AT LITTLE BOURTON
OXFORDSHIRE

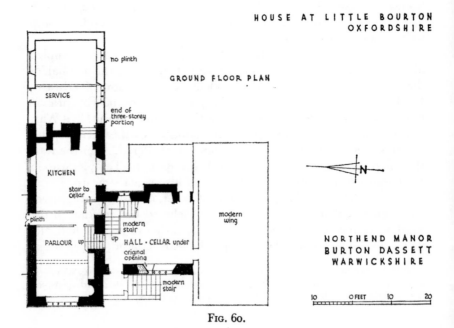

GROUND FLOOR PLAN

no plinth

SERVICE

end of
three-storey
portion

KITCHEN

stair to
cellar

modern
wing

plinth

modern
stair

PARLOUR up up HALL · CELLAR under

original
opening

modern
stair

N

NORTHEND MANOR
BURTON DASSETT
WARWICKSHIRE

10   0 FEET   10   20

FIG. 60.

part of the building, not later in date than the 16th century, and has walls of 2 feet 6 inches in thickness with a moulded plinth on front and rear walls. The fireplace on the rear wall may represent an original feature, now largely modernized, and a former opening can be distinguished on the entrance front, obscured by a modern window. It is not clear whether the hall was originally of more than single-storey height, the present first floor perhaps belonging to the 1664 improvements, which included the erection of a north wing, at right angles to the former hall, containing two ground-floor rooms, hall and parlour, separated by an entrance passage entered from the north front. This wing is a full three storeys in height, to align with the height of the hall block, a third room of lower height being added still later to provide a service-room or outer kitchen at the rear of the wing.

Such amendment of earlier structures is common to all places and building types, and it is the scarcity of such examples before 1600 that is noteworthy in the Banbury Region. The process of improvement and addition within this area generally commences with structures dating from the 17th century, but it is still usually those houses of greater social importance and finer architectural character which are subjected to amendment. The primary purpose of these alterations is to make the building accord with the new standards and practices of living as embodied in new houses, as well as to restore the structure, but progressively more attention is paid even in the smaller houses to the dictates of fashion, and to conformity with the new classical principles of design, which reached the sphere of minor domestic architecture in the 18th century.

In the great majority of cases, planning improvement is achieved simply by the addition of extra rooms, occasionally thereby changing the functions of existing apartments, but save in the larger houses it rarely involved the structural alteration of the existing building. Such extensions are generally to provide kitchens and other service-rooms, including pantries and dairies, and only in a few larger houses are new parlours or living-rooms added. The process develops in the period of renewed building activity which followed the end of the Civil War, and was accelerated in the 18th century.

Early single-bay plans particularly invited extension, as is seen in houses at Tadmarton and Barford, the original forms of which are described in Chapter VIII. The Old Malthouse, Tadmarton (Fig. 61), was developed into the mid-17th-century yeoman plan by the addition to the original hall of two further rooms to serve as a new hall and parlour, with the stair at the upper end of the hall and a cellar under the parlour. The later 17th-century work, inaccurately set out, aligns

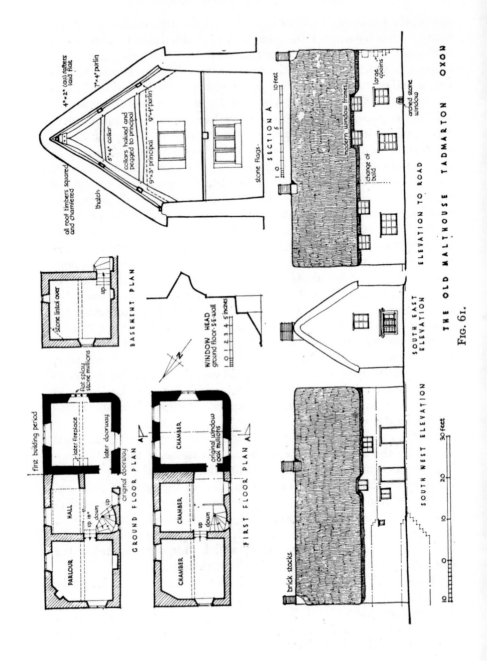

all roof timbers squared and chamfered

thatch

4"×2" (all) rafters laid flat

7"×4" purlin

5"×4" collar

9"×4" purlin

collars halved and pegged to principal

9"×3" principal

stone flags.

SECTION A

0 5 10 feet

BASEMENT PLAN

stone lintel over

up

WINDOW HEAD
ground floor-S E wall

1 0 1 2 3 4 5 inches

first building period

later fireplace

later doorway

original doorway

flat splay stone mullions

up 18"

up down

HALL

PARLOUR

GROUND FLOOR PLAN

A

CHAMBER

original window
oak mullions

up down

CHAMBER

CHAMBER

FIRST FLOOR PLAN A

large quoins

arched stone window

modern window frames

change of build

ELEVATION TO ROAD

SOUTH EAST ELEVATION

THE OLD MALTHOUSE TADMARTON OXON

FIG. 61.

SOUTH WEST ELEVATION

brick stocks.

10 0 10 20 30 feet

with the original bay, the entrance to which it presumably blocked. Instead of providing an internal through-passage between new and old work, the new entrance was placed on the rear of the building, against the chimney-breast of the hall, to produce in the completed scheme a plan of the type which has been associated with lowland practice.

In similar additions, where the original gable entrance was blocked, it was more usual to provide a through-passage, but at Tadmarton this would have involved the construction of an additional stone cross-wall, and the solution adopted is the more economical. The through-passage entrance was provided at the Old Turnstiles, Barford St. Michael (Fig. 47), where in 1653 a new parlour was added to the original hall. The new work is of high architectural quality, and includes a three-storey porch and bay window.

Dial House, Sulgrave (Fig. 42), on the north-eastern fringe of the region, a two-unit house built in grey limestone, dated 1636, was extended in mid-17th century by the addition of a kitchen, with fireplace and oven, again in line with the older structure, and producing a plan of the 'lowland' type, of which a number of examples have been recorded in this neighbourhood. There is here a change in the section of the stone window mullions between the two periods of building, ovolo mullions in grey stone being used in the new work, contrasting with the earlier hollow-moulded brown stone dressings. In this building, as in the house previously described at Barford, no alteration of the original stair position was involved.

In a number of houses of 17th-century date it would appear from the almost identical character of masonry and enrichment in two portions of a house, with only a straight joint between, suggesting two periods of building, that they were amended in an almost continuous succession of building. This continuous development probably occurred at Northend Manor Farm, dated 1654 (Fig. 45), where the service wing has been extended on the rear of the house to provide a pantry or dairy, with chamber and attic over, served by a separate stair to the wing. A change in the coursing of the masonry indicates two periods, but the character of the work is identical throughout the house. In addition, the cellar below the kitchen, and the attics over all the house are now approached from the new wing, involving some amendment to the original stair, or to that originally intended. It is probable from the close integration of these parts that the additional rooms were added very soon after the original work, or even as a direct continuation, modifying the original plan.

The Gables, Middleton Cheney, of 'L'-shaped plan (Fig. 62),

also has indications of two closely consecutive building periods without variation in the character of the architecture. Here a new bay was added to the upper end of a three-unit house, itself of late-17th-century date, to provide a new parlour with cellar under. Included in the new wing are a through-passage entry and an improved stairway. Windows throughout the house are stone-mullioned, of the long hollow section which appears *c.* 1690, and the plan of the original structure, as described on p. 133, accords with this date.[1]

In the first two dwellings described above, at Tadmarton and Barford, the earlier work was reduced in status by the additions to become the lower end of the new house, as also happened at Chinners Farm, Chacombe. Similarly at the Gables, Middleton Cheney, the provision of the new parlour changed the functions of the earlier three rooms, which became respectively the hall, adjacent to the new work, the kitchen, and a service-room without fireplace. Additions to the smaller houses were, however, as mentioned earlier, more often designed to improve the service and kitchen accommodation, without changing the functions of the existing rooms; it is in the larger houses only that additional accommodation is sometimes added to improve the upper end of the house.

In the 18th century this process of improvement was greatly accelerated, particularly in the larger farm-houses, where in almost every case kitchens were added to rectify the omission of the lower end in so many fine two-unit houses of the latter half of the 17th century. A number of one-unit houses were similarly enlarged at this time, including the Old Bakery, Lower Middleton Cheney (Fig. 48), where a kitchen with a large fireplace was added adjacent to the original entrance. The character of the 18th-century work is markedly inferior to that of the original house, with wood lintels to openings and other clear indications that the new portion was intended as the lower end of the house.

Two-unit houses could be enlarged in two ways, by extensions in length or by a wing projecting from the rear of the building, restrictions of the frontage of the croft or the desire for more compactness of plan influencing the decision. The majority show the offset wing, particularly those houses which lay at right angles to the road, or were closely confined by other early dwellings. An early 18th-century example of linear extension is seen at McGreal's Farm, Milton (Fig. 21), a fine and large example of the two-unit plan of *c.* 1640, in which there were gable fireplaces, the entrance and stair also on the gable,

---

[1] The possibility that this building represents two adjoining and related houses is considered in Chapter XIII.

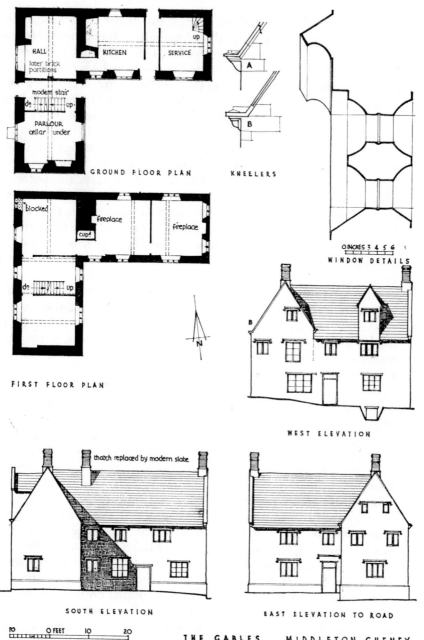

HALL
later brick partitions

KITCHEN

SERVICE

up

modern stair

dn up

PARLOUR
cellar under

GROUND FLOOR PLAN

KNEELERS

A

B

blocked

fireplace

cup⁴

fireplace

dn up

FIRST FLOOR PLAN

N

0 INCHES 3 4 5 6

WINDOW DETAILS

B

WEST ELEVATION

thatch replaced by modern slate

SOUTH ELEVATION

EAST ELEVATION TO ROAD

10   0 FEET   10   20

THE GABLES   MIDDLETON CHENEY
FIG. 62.

and a cellar under the parlour. The extension was to provide a kitchen at the lower end of the hall, and included a through-passage entrance. Within the kitchen, two steps lower than the hall, is the usual
broad hearth with an oven built into the reveal and a further shallow
oven projecting on the gable from the back of the fire. A chamber and
attic are provided over the kitchen, the former with a good fireplace
with a chamfered oak lintel. The second-floor joists span from a transverse beam instead of from spine-beams as elsewhere in the building.
There are rubble stone-voussoired lintels over the openings, a feature
of many buildings of the first half of the 18th century. Little variation
is to be noted between the wood-framed windows of the two portions
of the house, and it is clear that new frames were introduced throughout in the 18th century, replacing mullion windows in the earlier
build, which still survive in the cellar. The original stair also suffices
to serve the kitchen bay, but forks from the first floor to approach the
attics separately, an arrangement adopted in a number of similar
cases.

Extensions of this nature are the most widely recorded within the
region after 1700, differences arising particularly in relation to the
entrances. The George and Dragon Inn at Chacombe (Pl. 20b), a
late-17th-century two-unit house of similar plan, with gable entrance to the hall and late, stone, ovolo-mullioned windows without
labels on the opposite gable, has similarly been extended by a kitchen
at the lower end, of two-and-a-half storeys, more roughly built with
wood lintels, and dated 1734. Instead of allowing a through-passage
to give access to the original entrance, a new doorway was formed
opening onto the side of the hall fireplace, the four-centred arched
stone head of the original doorway being removed and crudely reset
over the new opening, again producing an arrangement in accordance with the lowland plan-type noted earlier.

Spittals Farm, Great Bourton (Fig. 35), dating from c. 1680, like-
wise received the addition of a kitchen, dated 1787, here of single
storey only. As the stair and door were centrally placed in the original house, they were not in any way affected by the added bay, in
which is provided a broad, kitchen fireplace with brick jambs. School
House, in Council Lane, Deddington (Fig. 33), is of particular
interest because both periods of work are dated on the face of the
house. The original building of 1655 is a fine house of two units,
two-and-a-half storeys high, with elaborate stone dressings, a fine
projecting stair, and gable fireplaces and entrance. This was extended in length in 1735 by a further two units of two storeys, a through-
passage being allowed between the new and old work. On the ground

floor the new work provides a service-room and kitchen, but above is an unusually large chamber extending over the whole of the wing, lit by a long window of seven lights, with wood lintel and frame. It is claimed locally that the chamber was originally a school-room, but the name of the house is modern, and no record has been found to support the statement: it is possible that the room originally served as a workshop for weavers or other workers. Despite the new through-passage, giving access to the original entrance, a new entrance was made in the centre of the street façade to accord with 18th-century planning practice, and the later date-stone of 1735 appears above the door.

The buildings so far described illustrate the variants practised in the 18th century on the general method of extension by adding to the length of the original plan. The more generally adopted principle of extension is by a wing projected from one face of the house, the angle of projection being rarely a precise right angle. In those houses sited at right angles to the road, this arrangement is invariably adopted.

Manor Farm, Great Bourton (Fig. 63), dated 1685, is one of the many two-unit houses of this period which in architectural quality are superior to the larger, three-unit dwellings. Sited with its entrance gable to the road, from which it is set well back, the house was enlarged by a new wing at right angles to the original hall. The extension is of two-and-a-half-storey height, providing a kitchen and pantry on the ground floor. The windows of the new wing are of the four-light, transomed type in timber, which, as has been seen, indicates a date in the first quarter of the 18th century. A separate stair is provided, communicating with both parts of the house, lit by a tall stair-window through two storeys, in the same bay as the pantry. Beyond this is the new kitchen, with wide fireplace, and above that a bedroom in which is a fine fireplace with bolection-moulded stone surround. The original entrance is undisturbed, but there is now an additional entrance from the gable of the new wing which is probably of more recent date.

Alkerton Old Rectory, built in 1625 (Fig. 78); Friar's Cottage, Great Bourton, lying opposite to the house described above, and like it, dated 1685 (Fig. 34); and a house at Little Bourton (Fig. 60) are all two-unit 17th-century houses of similar size and character, with centrally planned entrance and stairs. Friar's Cottage lies parallel with the road; Alkerton Rectory is sited near the church, above the roadway, with its lower end gable against a small lane; and at Little Bourton, the house stands in a close adjoining a 17th-century dwelling which limits linear extension. All buildings have an 18th-century

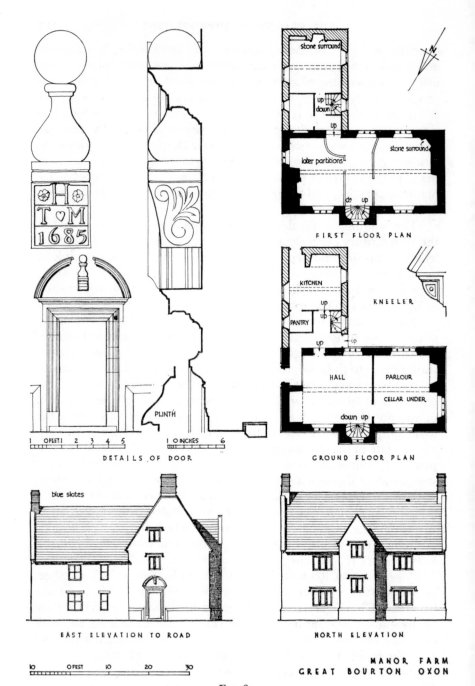

DETAILS OF DOOR

PLINTH

FIRST FLOOR PLAN

stone surround

up
down

up

later partitions

stone surround

dn up

GROUND FLOOR PLAN

KITCHEN

KNEELER

PANTRY

up
up

up

up

HALL

PARLOUR

CELLAR UNDER

down up

EAST ELEVATION TO ROAD

blue slates

NORTH ELEVATION

MANOR FARM
GREAT BOURTON OXON

FIG. 63.

extension in the shape of a two-storey wing projecting at an angle from the original hall-kitchen, providing a new kitchen with fireplace on the ground floor and chamber over. The new wings at Great Bourton and Little Bourton are so acutely angled as to result more probably from site limitations than from incorrect setting out. At Little Bourton, alone, the added wing involved re-siting the stair in a position at the side of the hall fireplace; it has been subsequently removed once more to a location nearer to the original position.

A more complex addition to an exceptionally fine two-unit house, extending the plan in length as well as at right angles, is seen at Poplars Farm, Chacombe (Figs. 30, 31), which as originally built in 1652 afforded an early instance of a plan more generally adopted later in the 17th century, with gable fireplaces, and central entrance flanked by stairs and pantry. The new wing provides two rooms on the ground floor, that adjoining the original hall being a kitchen with wide fireplace and a large semi-circular oven, projecting beyond the outer wall. The second room projects forward from the kitchen, in advance of the front of the house, and was used as a dairy or additional service-room. There are bedrooms and attics over the whole new wing, to which a separate stair gives access.

Alterations to three-unit houses are generally similarly planned, at right angles to the original building. Beech Tree House, in Lower Middleton Cheney (Fig. 19), has such a wing projecting obliquely from the back of the parlour, further extended by still later farm buildings. The room so provided, though large, lacks a fireplace and was probably a service-room or dairy, dating from c. 1725 when the large transomed windows replaced the earlier windows in the original house.

Titcombe's Farm, Bloxham, a fine house of c. 1650 with stone-mullioned windows and an arched stone doorway, also lies parallel to the road and is similarly extended by a wing at the rear of the house. Instead of the roofs intersecting with valleys, as is more commonly arranged, in this instance the thatch is continuous around the angle to form a hip on the entrance front.

More elaborate extensions have been made to many of the larger houses, and typical arrangements can be studied in instances at Hook Norton and Cropredy, where the improvements follow corresponding lines. A 17th-century house at Hook Norton has been extended by a pair of structural bays which project forward from the road elevation, and show a front double-gable, a rare feature in the region (Pl. 15a). This is dated 1707 on a lead rainwater head into which the internal gutter drains. The new work is planned on a more spacious scale than the original house, with tall rooms on three floors, lit by fine, four-light transomed windows in wood, with small rectangular panes of glass. These newer and more commodious apartments became the principal living-rooms, with the 17th-century house reduced in importance as the service and kitchen elements.

This replacement of the principal rooms is paralleled by contemporary developments at the Old Manor House, Cropredy (Pl. 15b). The original 17th-century house, containing an unusual six-light window, having no king mullion, was extended in length by a new parlour or hall, dated 1693, with stair and entrance. In 1715, a further wing was added at right angles to provide an additional living-room, the original building here also being reduced to the status of a service wing, eventually falling into disuse. Loftier rooms, with flush-plastered ceilings and mullioned-and-transomed windows again distinguish the 18th-century work, whilst new windows were at the same time introduced into the upper storey of the original house.

Only one other system of extension is sufficiently important to merit notice. In this method, extension is contrived by the use of rear outshuts, only eight cases being recorded, all on the western fringe of the region. This system is more common in Warwickshire and generally in western England, but is not characteristic of the Banbury Region. The major instance is that of the Mansion House Farm, Mollington (Fig. 64), a large house of considerable architectural distinction, which again underwent extensive modernization in the 19th century. The major amendment of the original plan dates from the later 18th century, and takes the form of an added outshut on the rear of the house to provide two rooms, a pantry and dairy, in all 12 feet wide by 32 feet long, with a loft over. The roof of the house is extended over the outshut at a slightly flatter pitch, covered with blue slates, whilst the gable parapet is also continued along the outshut, finishing with the kneeler removed from the gable itself. The original house is now roofed with red tiles, which occur quite commonly in this neighbourhood, probably having been introduced from Warwickshire in the 19th century to replace thatch.

In addition to the more extensive developments which have been so far described, there are many smaller improvements which have been repeatedly noted in the course of this investigation, in particular, the addition of such features as bedroom fireplaces and bread-ovens to improve the standards of comfort and convenience. These are simple practical improvements, but there remain for consideration a number of alterations which although improving the efficiency of the house probably rise as much from the desire to conform

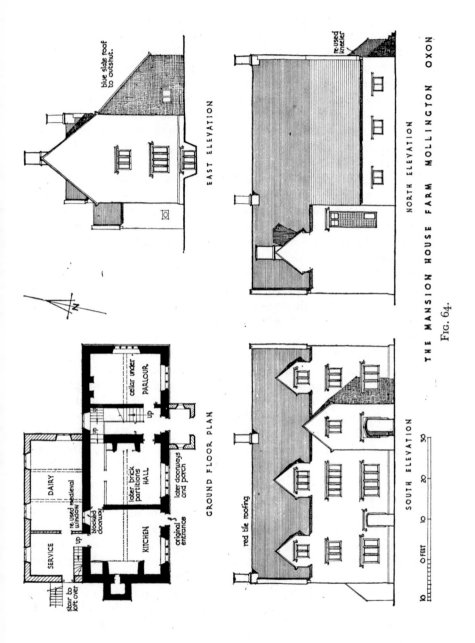

blue slate roof
to outshut.

EAST ELEVATION

re-used kneeler

NORTH ELEVATION

stair to
loft over

SERVICE

DAIRY

re-used medieval
window

blocked
doorway

KITCHEN

original
entrance

up

later brick
partitions

HALL

later doorways
and porch

up

cellar under
PARLOUR

GROUND FLOOR PLAN

N

red tile roofing

SOUTH ELEVATION

10 OFEET 10 20 30

THE MANSION HOUSE FARM MOLLINGTON OXON

FIG. 64.

with current architectural fashion as to produce practical advantages. Only such large houses as Horley Manor could completely remodel their front elevations to provide a Georgian façade to a 17th-century house, which reveals itself on the rear elevation. For minor domestic building it sufficed to reorganize elevations largely by altering windows and doors. This occasionally involved considerable structural alteration, as in the two 16th-century houses at Balscott, and also Sunnyside Cottage, Swerford, where the walls of the houses, originally of one-and-a-half storeys in height, were raised to allow for the insertion of taller 18th-century windows, the upper-floor ceiling height being lifted under an altogether new roof finished in blue slate. It is probable that the decayed condition of many roofs at this time made reconstruction a practical necessity, and advantage was taken of the occasion. The planning alterations already noted were, moreover, in almost every case accompanied by further subsidiary alterations to the original building, in particular the replacement of mullioned windows by larger openings with wood lintels, or occasionally with flat stone arches; timber-framed casements were used for the windows in smaller dwellings, and transomed wood frames and, later, sliding sashes for larger houses.

Lexton House in Lower Middleton Cheney (Pl. 18b), is a large yeoman house built in 1691 which was completely modernized at the same time as it was extended late in the 18th century. A two-and-a-half-storey projecting wing was added at the back of the parlour, providing kitchens and pantries with bedrooms over, and at the same time the front of the earlier building was rebuilt with evenly spaced Georgian sash windows to both floors, whilst internally the character was completely changed to that of the late 18th century, with plastered ceilings, shuttered windows, new stair and fireplaces and alterations of doors and architraves.

Many such improvements were made to the smaller houses, even though no major extension or alteration might be attempted; in particular the alteration of windows and glazing was widespread from the end of the 17th century. Diamond-shaped panes of glass were replaced by rectangular panes in mullioned windows, and later, the mullions and stone dressings were themselves frequently removed to provide larger openings with timber lintels, equipped with wood frames, whether casement or sash. The original label-mould or sill occasionally survives as the only evidence of earlier mullioned windows.

The extent to which improvement was carried out in the 18th century is very considerable in the Banbury Region. Over 150 buildings built before 1700 have been recorded which show the later additions of one or more rooms, and almost every house has some minor characteristic of 18th-century work, particularly in the renovation of the windows. The decline in the building of new farm-houses within the region after 1700 is clearly compensated by this process of improvement and modernization of existing buildings.

The improvements noted above can be briefly summarized under the three headings proposed earlier. Plan development takes the form of extension in length or at right angles—the latter arrangement probably preferred as resulting in more compact planning—to provide in most cases a two-storey kitchen wing with bedrooms over. Less commonly, and in larger dwellings only, new living-rooms were added, the original house as a whole becoming the inferior quarters. Very rarely does improvement involve the demolition of any part of the existing house, except in the minor degree requisite for the modernization of windows, doors, chimneys, etc. Structural alterations were therefore small, the most important being the raising of the height of walls to provide loftier rooms with tall windows, necessitating the construction of a new roof. At the end of the century this could be achieved by the provision of a flatter-pitched structure making use of the newly-introduced blue slates. Dormers then were more easy to construct and could be wholly contained within the roof. Finally, superficial and minor alterations were most widespread in all classes of building earlier than c. 1700, in the larger buildings for the purpose of amending the façade to accord with the current architectural style, but more commonly limited to a less ambitious replacement of windows, doors, stairs, chimneys and similar features.

In conclusion, two important houses may be noted in which the whole process of improvement is summarized, from medieval times to the 18th century, the work of the successive periods being clearly evident. The architectural history of *Priory Farm, Balscott* (Figs. 8, 9; Pl. 3a), is typical of the progressive modernization of a house of some social significance from the 14th to the 18th centuries, incorporating most of the improvements noted above. The original state of this building has been described in Chapter III, and whilst there must remain some doubt, the existing evidence supports the theory that this was a hall-house built by Wroxton Priory in the 14th century, as a large and fine hall with open hearth, either standing alone or with contemporary service-rooms. The hall was extended c. 1500 by a new service bay, separated by a through-passage from the hall, the Perpendicular doorway being introduced at this time. The subsequent history of the house can be established with more certainty. It has been suggested (Chapter III) that with the dissolution of Wroxton Priory in 1537, Priory Farm fell into disrepair and required major rebuilding in the 17th century. This took the form of improving the original hall, the north wall being completely rebuilt to the then usual thickness of 1 foot 10 inches—the medieval walls are all of heavier construction—and the roof structure altered accordingly. The hall itself was subdivided by a stud partition to provide a separate parlour, whilst the first floor and fireplace may well be attributed to this period, and new mullioned windows were provided in the north wall, the great medieval window being blocked. At the same time, the stair was added in the north-west angle of the service bay, the upper floor there probably also being improved by raising the walls and inserting new windows.

In the 18th century, the early form of the sash windows suggesting a date c. 1750, it became the turn of the former service end to be modernized, a new first floor being introduced with a ground-floor ceiling height of almost 9 feet, the new floor spanning from a transverse beam, in accordance with current practice, and the ceiling flush-plastered. At the same time, the front and rear walls in this bay were raised, and a new roof provided to give added height to the new bedrooms over, with large sliding sash windows in tall openings with flat stone arches to both floors on the south front, and a new canopied doorway at this end of the through-passage. The former service-room, partitioned from the stair passage, now becomes the principal apartment, or parlour, having a fine bolection-moulded fireplace, a similar fireplace being provided in the principal bedroom over. The plan was therefore reversed, the 17th-century parlour becoming the service-room, and the hall fulfilling the functions of kitchen.

It is apparent from the way in which the work has been left, that it was intended also to raise the roof over the original hall, to align with the other, and to extend the fenestration of the south elevation to provide a balanced Georgian façade, with the earlier character retained on the north face. The latter was clearly regarded as the rear of the house, the corridor on both floors being on this side. Priory Farm is unusually sited, set back from a narrow road from which it is almost screened by farm buildings. It is more than possible that the present course of the road is of recent date.

The history of this most interesting house finds a close counterpart in the neighbouring Grange Farm (Fig. 10), a late-medieval house already described, and similarly modernized in the 18th century.

Castle End, Deddington (Fig. 65; Pl. 9*b*), provides the final illustration of the alternation of building and of status of upper and

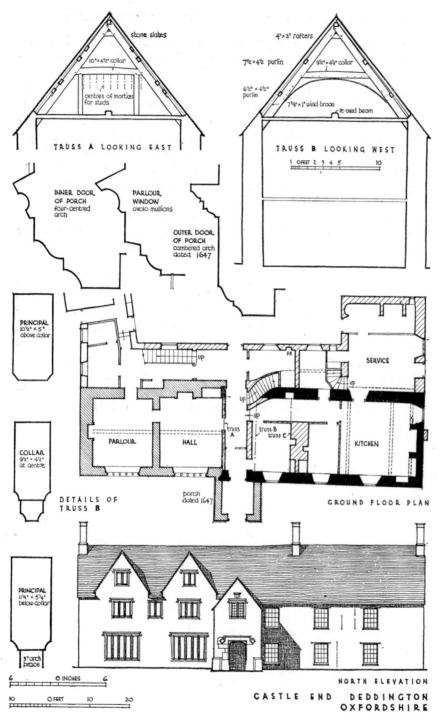

stone slates

10"×4½" collar

centres of mortices
for studs

TRUSS A LOOKING EAST

INNER DOOR
OF PORCH
four-centred
arch

PARLOUR
WINDOW
ovolo mullions

OUTER DOOR
OF PORCH
cambered arch
dated 1647

4"×3" rofters

7½×4½ purlin   9½"×4½" collar

6½" × 4½"
purlin

7¾"×1" wind brace   re-used beam

TRUSS B LOOKING WEST

1 OFEET 2 3 4 5   10

PRINCIPAL
10¾" × 5"
above collar

COLLAR
9½"×4½"
at centre

DETAILS OF
TRUSS B

PRINCIPAL
11¾" × 5¼"
below collar

3" arch
brace

PARLOUR   HALL

truss
A

truss·B
truss C

SERVICE

FR

up

up

up

up

KITCHEN

porch
dated 1647

GROUND FLOOR PLAN

6   O INCHES   6

10   O FEET   10   20

NORTH ELEVATION

CASTLE END   DEDDINGTON
OXFORDSHIRE

FIG. 65.

lower ends of a dwelling during the course of successive improvement. As already noted, the west wing incorporates an early-16th-
century hall, entered by the existing doorway, presumably to a
through-passage. In 1646, at the conclusion of the Civil Wars in
which Deddington was seriously involved, the house was rebuilt, the
new work presumably replacing the original service bay. A fine hall
and parlour were provided, unusually large and lofty rooms with
ovolo-mullioned windows of exceptional height, the hall having a
fireplace on the rear long wall, with gable fireplace to the new parlour. Chambers were provided on the first and second floors, the latter lit by large dormers.

In the 18th century, probably after 1750, there was further rebuilding, this time of the medieval hall, to provide new dining- and
service-rooms and kitchen, with sliding-sash windows on two floors.
At the same time, or later in the 18th century, the plan was increased in depth by the addition of a lean-to extension on the south
side, containing a new staircase and hall, with further service-rooms
at the west end, whilst wings were projected from each end of the
house on the rear to extend the service accommodation. The stair has
a tall window with round-arched head and tracery of late Georgian
character, and the lean-to roof is finished with blue slates, the main
building being stone-slated. Throughout the three periods of building, the original entrance doorway was retained, being improved in
1646 by the addition of the two-storey porch which bears the date-
stone.

CHAPTER XI

REGIONAL BUILDING PRACTICES

THE chronological examination of regional building has been primarily concerned with the evolution of planning, and it has been left
until the concluding chapters to examine collectively the structural
development of these smaller houses, the architectural quality of their
elements in stone, timber, brick, iron and lead, and finally, the overall
pattern of settlement within the village. It is these, no less than the
planning, that have produced the individual character of vernacular
architecture in the Banbury Region. The nature of the local building
stone has characterized the survey area and has produced a single
primary walling material, the marlstone, used from the 16th to the
present century for almost all minor domestic building, with a still
longer period of use in larger building types, so contributing to a
continuous history which even at its end maintained something of the
medieval tradition. The scarcity of surviving timber structures which
here, as throughout England, ante-dated the use of stone, has already
been noted, examples being found only in the Cherwell valley, in
Banbury—where they belong to an urban sequence with which this
study is not concerned—and in Kings Sutton. The influence of this
early timber tradition, has, however, been felt throughout the subsequent building periods, and the evolution of timber roof structure
presents a clear and continuous pattern; this is shown graphically in
Figs. 66 and 67. The division of England into two major areas of
different basic tradition, as defined by Sir Cyril Fox,[1] separates the
highland zone of the north-west from the lowland south-east, and
this division appears to find architectural expression in fundamental
differences in timber structure between the northern cruck forms and
the more sophisticated box-framed structures of the south-east. With
rare exceptions, all the structural evidence indicates conformity with
the northern upland tradition within the region, although not wholly
without some influence of south-eastern practice. This allegiance is
characterized by the use of a 'framed' form of roof, with clearly
defined principal members or blades supporting purlins and ridge-
beam, as distinct from the 'single' system of ridgeless continuous
trussed rafters of the south-eastern counties. The cruck frame and the

[1] Sir Cyril Fox, *The Personality of Britain*, p. 32.

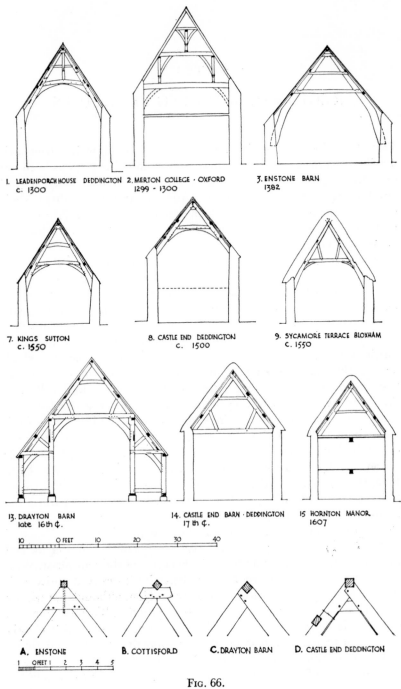

1. LEADENPORCH HOUSE DEDDINGTON
   c. 1300

2. MERTON COLLEGE · OXFORD
   1299 - 1300

3. ENSTONE BARN
   1382

7. KINGS SUTTON
   c. 1550

8. CASTLE END DEDDINGTON
   c. 1500

9. SYCAMORE TERRACE BLOXHAM
   c. 1550

13. DRAYTON BARN
    late 16th c.

14. CASTLE END BARN · DEDDINGTON
    17 th c.

15 HORNTON MANOR
   1607

10   0 FEET   10   20   30   40

A. ENSTONE

B. COTTISFORD

C. DRAYTON BARN

D. CASTLE END DEDDINGTON

1   0 FEET 1   2   3   4   5

FIG. 66.

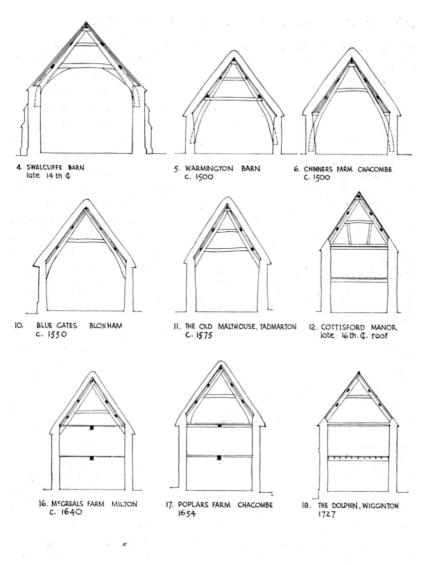

4. SWALCLIFFE BARN
late 14th ₵

5. WARMINGTON BARN
c. 1500

6. CHINNERS FARM CHACOMBE
c. 1500

10. BLUE GATES BLOXHAM
c. 1550

11. THE OLD MALTHOUSE, TADMARTON
c. 1575

12. COTTISFORD MANOR
late 16th ₵. roof

16. M^cGREALS FARM MILTON
c. 1640

17. POPLARS FARM CHACOMBE
1654

18. THE DOLPHIN, WIGGINTON
1727

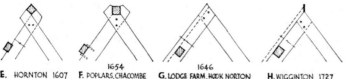

1654   1646
E. HORNTON 1607   F. POPLARS, CHACOMBE   G. LODGE FARM, HOOK NORTON   H. WIGGINTON 1727

REGIONAL TIMBER STRUCTURE · COMPARATIVE DIAGRAMS

Fig. 67.

derivative arch-braced collar truss are characteristic upland forms, as also is the true king-post of which Leadenporch House, Deddington (1, Fig. 66), provides the only, if remarkably early, domestic example, strutted in a manner reminiscent of the crown-posts, which support the collar purlin in south-eastern-type roofs. The roof of the Warden's Lodging at Merton College, Oxford, built in 1299–1300, is included for comparison (2, Fig. 66) as a complex example of this neighbouring tradition found only 20 miles from Banbury.

The main characteristics of the medieval crucks located within the region, all of pre-1550 date, have already been described in detail,[1] and need only be summarized briefly in relation to later developments within the region. The true cruck has only once been recorded, at Chacombe, with cruck spurs and a ridge supported on a saddle, and this is a late example, probably dating from c. 1500. The more general form, found in barns and minor domestic work from the 14th to the 16th centuries is the raised cruck (3, 4, 5, 7, 9, 10), a form which arises from an early recourse to stone walling, from which the cruck blades spring at an intermediate level between floor and eaves. The ridge beams in all these cases are supported on saddles mortised to the tops of the blades (A), with one or two collars below, the lower occasionally arch-braced. The roof trusses of the early house in Sycamore Terrace, Bloxham (9), and at Blue Gates (10), represent evolution within the 16th century towards the later derivative roof trusses, the principals being curved at the feet and tapered to the ridge, with one or two collars; at Sycamore Terrace there are in addition arch-braces and queen-post struts. The ridge support is different from the earlier examples, the beam being supported in the crossing of the blades, in the manner which becomes general in the 17th century. Castle End, Deddington (8), and the Old Malthouse, Tadmarton (11), illustrate alternative interim developments in the 16th century, the principals in both cases being straight tapering members, although retaining the earlier support for the ridge at Tadmarton and the arched-braced collar at Deddington.

All the types so far discussed are associated in the first place with single-storey halls, and later with those of one-and-a-half-storeys, i.e. having a first floor partly contained within the roof space. Throughout the 17th century the practice of taking the first floor into the roof became less general, and after 1700 this form persists in smaller houses only, as it resulted in some economy in the height of the stone walling. The roof of McGreal's Farm at Milton (16), a large yeoman

---

[1] Roofs 1 to 12 are fully described in relation to medieval building in Chapters II–IV.

house of unsophisticated character dating from *c.* 1640, is typical of the majority of houses of this period, and roofs of this construction persisted in a rougher form in the smaller houses and cottages of the 18th century. The relationship to the earlier raised crucks is apparent, but there is here the later form of apex whereby the ridge is seated in a squared recess in the crossing of the blades (F). The absence of a tie at the feet of the principals has resulted in signs of spreading in many of these collar roofs, and from the end of the 16th century a new roof truss is recorded in minor domestic work, which gains greater strength by a tie-beam at second-floor level, to which the principals are tenoned. This first appears in the single surviving truss at Parish's Farmhouse, Hempton (Fig. 59), where it establishes a relationship with the cruck form of construction; the cruck blades spring from a tie-beam at first-floor level to produce an 'upper cruck', the only recorded instance in a building of one-and-a-half-storey height, the roof being thatched. The raised crucks usually had only a shallow, 6-inch seating within the walls of houses, but the tie-beams are deeply embedded and frequently their ends can be seen on the external wall-face, as at Warkworth Farm (Fig. 43).

The primary reason for the adoption of the tie-beam roof was the desire to increase room heights, and to rid the upper chambers of the obstructive roof principals. With the height of larger buildings at the end of the 16th century increasing to two full storeys with attics over, the tie-beam roof provided a more appropriate and convenient structure, adopted in the first instance in the barns and manor-houses. The Buckler drawing of a barn at Drayton[1] in south Oxfordshire is of considerable interest as showing a precursor of these taller buildings, relating them to a preceding timber-framed structure probably of late-16th-century date. In this building (13) the tie-beam is supported on timber posts, thickened at the top in the manner of the box-frame structures of the lowland tradition. The principals are tenoned to the tie-beam, and the ridge-beam is laid diagonally in the fork (C), whilst queen-post struts and arch-braces are also provided. The aisled construction of this barn finds no parallels in domestic architecture in the region.

Equally of interest as the earliest domestic example of this type of roof-truss is the 16th-century structure replacing the original roof of Cottisford Manor (12), where the straight principals similarly rise from the tie-beam at eaves level, with the ridge (B) supported diagonally in a notch cut in the saddle which joins the principals at the apex (Pl. 6c). The manor-house at Hornton, 1607 (15), is an early

[1] British Museum Add. MS. 36436, f. 679.

example of the roof truss to be generally adopted in the 17th and 18th centuries for the larger dwellings, with straight tapering principals, tenoned to the tie-beam, braced by a collar, and crossed to support the ridge at the apex. The ridge is here set diagonally, as in the last two examples, but generally in the 17th century the beam is set squarely in a shaped seating in the fork. The roof of the Poplar's Farm, Chacombe, 1654 (17), reveals a last influence of the upper-cruck tradition in the curved shape of the blades springing from the tie-beam. This truss, with straight principals, was widely employed from 1600 to almost 1800, queen-post struts being frequently introduced in barns, as at Castle End, Deddington (14).

The south-eastern tradition of roof construction is represented by one recorded example before 1600, although its influence can be detected in other instances. The roof of Shutford Manor is wholly south-eastern in type, a collar-rafter roof with principal rafters against which purlins are butted and supported on tenons. Although this could not be determined, it is probable that there is no ridge-beam. The roof, of late-16th-century date, has some affinity with the regional tradition in that the principal rafters are jointed to wall-posts rising from tie-beams at second-floor level, producing a form which might be termed a jointed upper-cruck. There are also heavy, straight wind-braces. Shutford Manor is a building of greater scale and social significance than the class of regional building under consideration, and it is to be expected that the more sophisticated alien tradition would first appear in these greater houses (Pl. 7a).

Although this is the only example recorded of a roof of south-eastern type, the butt-purlin which is associated with this tradition appears in a small number of other dwellings before 1700, sometimes in association with raised cruck structures. The mid-16th-century house in Sycamore Terrace, Bloxham (Fig. 66 (9)), had butt-purlins supported on tenons taken through principals of raised cruck form, and here also it seems probable that there was no ridge. The Court House at Kings Sutton (Fig. 69), also dating from the 16th century, has straight principals tenoned to a tie-beam, with purlins similarly supported, the apex unfortunately obscured by a later ceiling. Apart from this feature, both roofs are in keeping with regional character, the latter instance having two tiers of wind-braces.

Lodge Farm, Hook Norton (Fig. 36; Pl. 7c), built in 1646, has already been noted as having unusual features in its 'L' plan and isolated location. The roof structure further emphasizes the departure from regional practice, being clearly related to south-eastern structural tradition. The straight principal rafters, rising from a tie-beam at eaves level, are halved and pegged at the apex (G), having no ridge, and the purlins butt against the principals with a joint of unusual sophistication. Additional support for the end of the purlin is gained by a bevelled housing in the principal, with the tenon of one member passing straight through to support the purlin in the next bay. At the Court House, there is a comparable joint, with shallow splayed housings in the principals, both purlins in this instance having tenons which pass through the same mortise.

After 1700, roofs of this kind become more common, probably as a result of the new treatises on building construction which appeared in the 18th century, and which are largely based on south-eastern practice. The roof of the Dolphin Inn, Wigginton (18), has straight principals without taper, with purlins deeply housed to bring the common rafters into the same plane, and there is no ridge-beam—only a small batten to link the common rafters (H). A similar roof is seen at Sunnyside Cottage, Swerford (Fig. 20), rebuilt at the end of the 18th century with a flatter pitch for the new blue slates. Such examples, which reflect the spread of south-eastern practice, are, however, few in number and these and more modern methods of roof structure find little introduction until after 1800.

The details of these roofs show some variation, and in particular the ridge supports assist in placing the structure in chronological sequence. The squared ridge seated squarely on a saddle (Fig. 66 (A)) —sometimes raised further by a triangular block—is followed by a diagonally placed beam, similarly supported on a saddle at Cottisford (B), but more usually placed in the crossing of the blades. In the 17th century the ridge-beam is normally rectangular and set squarely once more in a shaped seating in the fork, or in poorer work a rougher ridge-pole is used in the same position, and both these methods continue throughout the 18th century. There is also some variation in the support of purlins, the method most generally adopted throughout the whole period being to house them partially into the back of the principals. Two alternative methods of securing them in position have been noted in earlier structures, the purlins being pegged right through the principal on which they rest at Enstone, and supported by cleats pegged to the cruck blade as occasionally found at Blue Gates, Bloxham.

With few exceptions, the jointing of the trusses is by mortise and tenon, pegged at right angles with the pegs left to project. At the Enstone barn an earlier system is recorded of dove-tailed halving, and occasionally simple halved joints between collars and principals are found in later and poorer work, as in the Warmington barn (Fig.

16) and Dial House, Sulgrave (Fig. 42). The character of the work also shows considerable variation in accordance with the period and the status of the building. The Enstone barn, and the later barn structure at Warmington, are basically similar in their cruck frames, but the scale and finish are quite different, the rough half-round undressed crucks at Warmington contrasting with the finely dressed and paired blades at Enstone. In the earlier structures, where the roofs were exposed to view within the halls, the principal members are generally well squared and chamfered, and even in 17th- and 18th-century barns there is some finely dressed timber, with decorative stops to the chamfered beams. In general, however, with the provision of upper floors, the character of the work becomes rougher, arch-braces are omitted, and in some roofs of the late 17th and 18th century the craftsmanship is very coarse, even in such fine houses as the Dolphin Inn at Wigginton. The shortage of suitable timber undoubtedly accounts for the poorer work at this time.

In medieval work, rafters are of heavy squared section, laid flat, but from c. 1600 rough poles invariably are used even in large houses, particularly when thatch is the covering. The absence of the wall-plate has already been noted, verified from observation in houses in course of demolition, where the rafters were seen to have been built into the stonework of the wall. In later 17th-century tie-beam roofs, wall-plates are found, near the inner face of the wall, with the rafters birdsmouthed to them. Wind-braces are only occasionally found, in the roofs of larger buildings, generally under stone slates, but also provided at Chinners Farm and at Castle End barn, Deddington, both of which are thatched.

An analysis of bay spacing reveals some differences between buildings roofed with stone slates and the great majority which have thatch. Spans vary between an average of 8 feet at Leadenporch House; 8 feet 6 inches at Castle End, Deddington; 9 feet 6 inches at King's Sutton Court House, all of which are stone-slated, to 14 feet at Chinners Farm and Blue Gates, both thatched.[1] The average span is however 12 feet, and in the 17th century this figure appears to be almost always adopted for both roofing materials. The characteristic 17th-century roof, shown at (17), Fig. 67, is found with bay spacing of 12 feet at Hornton Manor (1607), and Poplars Farm, Chacombe (1654), both thatched houses, and at the same spacing at Wark-

---

[1] The average bay spacing in Monmouthshire, where roofs are of heavy stone slates, is 11 feet 9 inches. In Leicestershire examples, with thatched roofing, the bay spacing is increased to 17 feet. (Information derived from Fox and Raglan, *Monmouthshire Houses*, Vol. 1, and V. R. Webster, *Cruck-Framed Buildings of Leicestershire*.)

worth Farm (1639–58), which it is understood was originally roofed with stone slates. At the Dolphin Inn, Wigginton, in 1727, the roof is, however, again sub-divided by cross-walls and trusses into 8-feet bays, to support stone slates.

Consideration of upper-floor structures throws further light on timber construction in the region. At Cottisford, which probably represents the earliest two-storey building in north Oxfordshire, the first floor is supported on transverse beams, renewed in the 16th century, the absence of cross-partitions on the ground floor probably making this arrangement necessary.[1] Later buildings of the 16th century generally show the central spine-beam, with joists spanning on to lateral wall beams, which in certain cases indicates an inserted floor.[2] This method would, however, simplify the new practical problem of building-in the ends of small joists into the masonry, by perpetuating the timber framing of the whole floor. The wall-beams soon disappear, but the spine-beam becomes general practice from c. 1600 at first- and second-floor levels, usually being of approximately square section, averaging 11 inches each way, supported on gable, fireplace and cross-walls, or on stud partitions. These members frequently attain lengths of over 20 feet when continuous over a partition. Second floors are similarly constructed, with spine-beams usually independent of the trusses, but occasionally, as at the Poplars Farm, Chacombe, gaining support from the tie-beam to which the floor-beam is tenoned.

From the end of the 17th century, a change is noted in the arrangement of the floor-beams, the spine-beam being abandoned in favour of principal members spanning across the building. This is primarily the result of developments in planning, i.e. the practice of placing fireplaces on gable walls, and eliminating all masonry cross-walls, thus reducing the support for spine-beams at a time when the longer timbers required were in increasingly short supply. Joists are tenoned or housed into the tops of the beams and at first are laid flat, as at Kings Sutton, but from the beginning of the 17th century they become lighter in section and are invariably laid on their narrower edges.

There is very little enrichment of woodwork, beams and joists being usually chamfered with squared ends, but only occasionally is there a simple ornamental stop to the chamfer. The deeply moulded

---

[1] In the hall at Warmington Manor, dating from the 17th century, transverse beams are employed for a similar reason, the clear length being too great for a spine-beam (Fig. 16).

[2] This factor is considered in relation to particular buildings in Chapter IV.

beams to the second floor at Cottisford Manor of late-16th-century date, and those in the Court House at Kings Sutton (Fig. 69) are quite exceptional, and even the simplest variation on the plain chamfer—as at Kings Sutton, and the Old Rectory, Alkerton (Fig. 78)—is of rare occurrence outside the larger manor-houses.

Upper floors are boarded in oak or elm in random widths, planks being between 9 and 15 inches wide by $1\frac{1}{4}$ inches in thickness. No other type of floor has been recorded. Up to the end of the 17th century, and later in smaller houses, the joists appear to have been left exposed underneath, the soffit of the boarding between being sometimes daubed with clay and hair plaster. The enclosure of the joists by a ceiling on split laths is introduced in the larger and more sophisticated houses early in the 18th century.

Internal partitions in timber are of singularly simple, even rough character, and although this may result from the shortage of good timber, it gives little evidence of a mature tradition of timber walling developed before stone was generally adopted. Three types of partition have been recorded, of which by far the most common is that made of light chamfered studs, averaging 3 inches square—lighter still in 18th-century work—about 15 inches apart and tenoned to a head and sill. The covering is of a coarse hair plaster on wattles or more frequently on split laths. Such partitions occur from the end of the 16th to the 19th centuries with little change in character, later work tending to become, if anything, lighter and more crude in construction. Door posts in partitions are tenoned at head and sill, and in earlier work the timber sill is frequently continued across the opening as a threshold. A second type of partition comprising large panels of mud on wattles, averaging 6 inches in thickness, is of rarer occurrence, and has only been recorded as the infilling of trusses in the late 16th-century house at Kings Sutton, and in an indeterminate structure, now ruinous, at Upper Tysoe. Still less frequent—only one instance having been discovered—is the oak post-and-panel partition, discovered on the first floor of Friar's Cottage, Great Bourton, (Fig. 34) built in 1685, where chamfered panels between 7 and 10 inches wide and $1\frac{1}{2}$ inches thick are tongued-and-grooved to posts, also chamfered, which average $4\frac{1}{2}$ by 2 inches in size. Although this particular partition appears to be of some antiquity, its very isolation as an example invites doubts of its having been introduced from outside during a later rebuilding, particularly as original partitions of the more usual stud form are also found in this house.

The variety of timber used in roofs and floors, and particularly in partitions, in the 17th and 18th centuries, together with the increasingly poor quality of the material and workmanship, are expressive of an increasing shortage of suitable timber in the region, already noted. Oak still was widely used in the 17th century for roof principals and beams, but there was an increasing recourse to elm, whilst in later structures, including barns, the re-use of old timbers has been noted, as in the roof of the 17th-century barn at Church Farm, Bloxham, where the principals reveal housings for joists. Warden Woodward, whose visits to Oxfordshire between 1659 and 1675[1] included Adderbury, Swalcliffe and Heyford, was constantly concerned with claims for timber for the repair of buildings. The timbers most frequently mentioned are ash—generally used for plough timber—and in particular elm, both timbers being common to the limestone belt. Typical extracts are 'Peter Coles to make a partition in his house, one Ash and one Elme'. There is a reference to 'Widdow Meaker's House that wants a Topp piece (ridge), some rafters and flooring for two lofts, to be allowed 3 elmes'.

At Great Tew, the inhabitants were presented with particular problems of repair when the manor was bought by Sir Lawrence Tanfield in 1614, the commons then being enclosed. The villagers were driven to petition against him at the House of Lords, complaining that whilst 'under their leases tenants are customarily granted great timbers for repairs, they now found themselves denied their customary timber yet liable to be fined for failing to keep their houses in repair.' It is probable that rebuilding of the village in stone largely dates from this period.

The two surviving buildings in Kings Sutton[2] which alone in the region outside Banbury itself have fragments of timber-framed walling, both have stone walls to the ground floor with timber studding above, jettied over the stonework. The *Court House, Kings Sutton* (Figs. 68, 69; Pl. 3*b*), is a building of rich architectural character, dating from *c*. 1500, extended later in the 16th century and again in the 18th century. Although not strictly a domestic structure, it seems probable that it combined domestic functions with its special use as the setting for the manorial court, and in its construction and its

[1] *Progress Notes of Warden Woodward round the Oxfordshire Estates of New College, 1659–1675*, Oxford Record Society, 1945.
[2] On the 15th July 1785, Kings Sutton—still predominantly a thatched village—suffered a serious fire in which forty houses were destroyed in three hours, it being reported as follows: 'The same day another fire broke out at Kings Sutton in this County, which owing to the Dryness of the Weather spread so rapidly that it is said the greatest part of the town is burnt down' (*Northampton Mercury*, 18th July 1785). This incident may well account for the scarcity of surviving timber-framed structures.

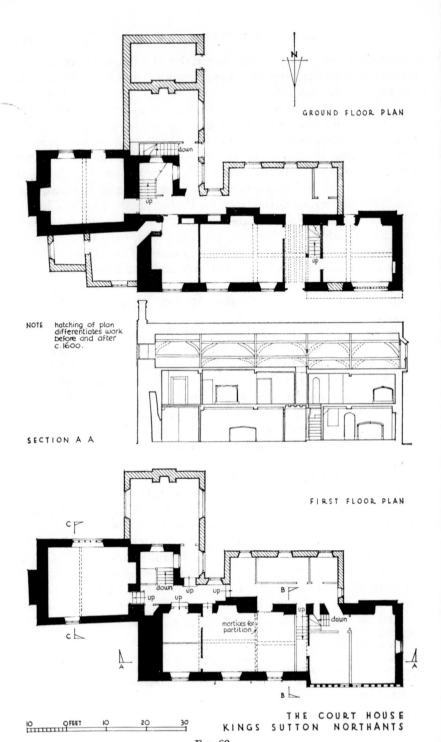

GROUND FLOOR PLAN

NOTE hatching of plan
differentiates work
before and after
c.1600.

SECTION A A

FIRST FLOOR PLAN

mortices for
partition

THE COURT HOUSE
KINGS SUTTON NORTHANTS

Fig. 68.

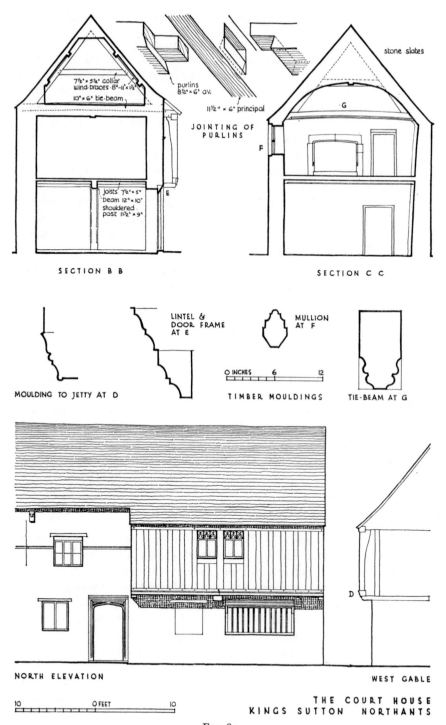

7½" × 5¾" collar
wind-braces · 8" – 11' × 1½'
10" × 6" tie-beam

purlins
8½" × 6" av.

11½" × 6" principal

JOINTING OF
PURLINS

joists 7½" × 5"
beam 12" × 10"
shouldered
post 11½" × 9"

E

stone slates

G

F

SECTION B B

SECTION C C

MOULDING TO JETTY AT D

LINTEL &
DOOR FRAME
AT E

MULLION
AT F

O INCHES   6   12

TIMBER MOULDINGS

TIE-BEAM AT G

NORTH ELEVATION

D

WEST GABLE

THE COURT HOUSE
KINGS SUTTON NORTHANTS

10   O FEET   10

FIG. 69.

238 DOMESTIC ARCHITECTURE OF THE BANBURY REGION

wealth of detail, it is of importance in the study of regional architecture. Basically the building is of three-room, cross-passage plan, the entrance passage being unusually wide, and containing a broad stair, now renewed. All three ground-floor rooms have fine fireplaces, in two instances arranged on the rear long wall. The special function of the building is expressed on the first floor, which may originally have had a separate external entrance on the rear elevation—the doorway to the eastern chamber having an unusually heavy frame and fastenings. This room is without a fireplace, and may have served as an ante-room, separated by a stud partition with two doors from the central great chamber which is enriched by heavily moulded tie-beams and a large fireplace. The western room on the first floor has the timber-framed wall, jettied over the stone wall below. It is formed of closely spaced studs, averaging 7 inches wide, the wall being in all 10 inches thick, lacking any bracing members and with shouldered angle posts. The walling includes two windows with traceried heads, and in the stone wall below there is another fine window of twelve narrow lights with deeply moulded wood lintel and mullions. The entrance door, with moulded jambs and four-centred arch is also in oak, and a moulded wood string is applied along the stonework of the north front, the timber enrichment in general revealing a higher degree of elaboration than recorded elsewhere in the region, other than in Banbury itself. At the rear of the east end of the house is a projection containing a fine stair with elaborately shaped and pierced flat balusters, and this is adjoined on the east by a two-storey block, of which the first-floor chamber is lit by a five-light window with moulded oak mullions and transom. The stair and window indicate a late-16th-century date, and these parts of the building were probably added to the original structure. A further addition of more recent date, on the south front, has created a plan of two-room depth.

The timber-framing in the other instance at Kings Sutton, a much-altered small house, is more fragmentary, only one section of walling surviving, jettied over the ground-floor stone wall. In both cases, the wall-framing is quite different from that seen beyond the west border of the region, being more closely related to southern practice. Timber walls of similar character, for first floors, are more frequently encountered in the Cotswolds, dating from the end of the 16th to the early 17th centuries, good examples surviving at Northleach and Aston Subedge.

To the west of the Banbury Region, beyond the Edge Hill escarpment, there is a marked change of circumstances. The timber-framed

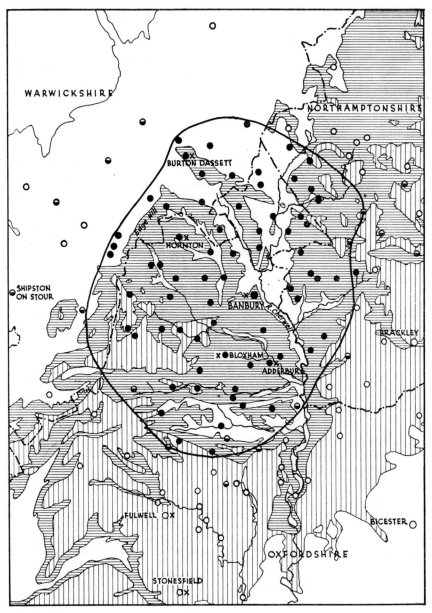

WARWICKSHIRE

NORTHAMPTONSHIRE

BURTON DASSETT

Edge Hill

HORNTON

SHIPSTON
ON STOUR

BANBURY

R. Cherwell

BRACKLEY

X●BLOXHAM

ADDERBURY

FULWELL ○X

BICESTER ○

OXFORDSHIRE

STONESFIELD
○X

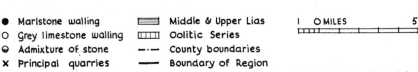

● Marlstone walling   ☰ Middle & Upper Lias | ○MILES   5

○ Grey limestone walling   ⊞ Oolitic Series

◓ Admixture of stone   —·— County boundaries

✕ Principal quarries   —— Boundary of Region

**THE BANBURY REGION
GEOLOGICAL MAP**

R

Fig. 70.

structures of Warwickshire, with later brick infilling to the panels, extend well into the 17th century. The village of Bishops Tachbrook, Warwickshire, is almost entirely made up of timbered dwellings of 17th-century date, with widely spaced vertical studs, the walls divided into square panels by cross framing. No reflection of neighbouring practice, in the shape of an admixture of timber and stone, has been recorded within the region adjacent to this boundary.

Above all, it is the building stone of north Oxfordshire that is responsible for the special architectural character of the region. It is known that a number of quarries hereabout were producing stone for use beyond their immediate neighbourhoods from the 13th century, in particular those near Edge Hill, where the best and thickest beds of the lias limestone occur, and at Bloxham. Plot mentions the quarries at Adderbury, Barford and Hornton, 'whereof the last has the best firestone in the country', and there were also quarries at the end of the 17th century near Banbury, producing a fine limestone known and exported as Banbury marble. The appalling state of the roads, to which reference has been made elsewhere, made it desirable to obtain stone as near as possible to where it was to be used, and it is clear from the variations in the material that most villages had recourse to a local quarry providing material for housing and other works. As a consequence there are considerable variations in the character of the brown marlstone walling within the region.

Wall thicknesses are remarkably consistent, being generally 2 feet 6 inches or over in medieval work, but from the end of the 16th century there was a reduction to an average of 1 foot 10 inches, a dimension which continued as the standard thickness until the 19th century or later.[1] The walls are without foundations, taken down at most to 2 or 3 feet below the ground, sometimes bedded on larger stones. Where the rock is close to the surface the walls frequently

---

[1] An indenture of 1516, noted by L. F. Salzmann in *Building in England down to 1540*, p. 510, records the building of a house in Holywell, Oxford, by two masons 'according to a plate drawonne for the same, first the walls to be made xviij foote in hyghte iiij foote beneyght the flore, and ij foote and vj inches thick above the flore; and in the walls beneight the flore to be made ij dores of stone, and chemes one of viijth foote wide in the hall, another of iiij foote wide in the parlere, and one wyndow of iiij lizghts in the sowizthe partie of the hall and another of ij lizghts on the north parte of the hall, every lizght xv ynche brode, and every wyndow iiij foot of james in hyghte; and five wyndows of ij lizghts and one wyndow of one lizght in the nether story; in the story above the flore to be made ij chamnes and ij dores of stone foe the widdrawts and vj wyndows of ij lizghts and vj wyndows of one lizght and all seided wyndows above rehersid to have luntells of tymber and the seid Richard and Thomas shall rovecaste and pargett all the stone walls with beme fillying of the same howse' etc.

appear to go little below ground level. A batter on the inner face reduces the thickness of the wall from the base to the eaves, this being particularly marked in buildings of 16th-century date and earlier. In two-storey buildings, of 17th-century date and later, there is frequently a further reduction in thickness of about 3 inches at the floor level, the upper stages of the walling often being reduced to as little as 15 inches. Gable walls, particularly before 1600, are sometimes of increased thickness, presumably to allow for their extra height: walls carried below ground to cellars are also normally thickened by at least 6 inches on the inner face. Writing in 1841, Beesley notes that 'a considerable number of ancient stone houses which have been taken down of late years, would seem, from the fact of coins of Elizabeth's reign having been found in the walls and chimneys, to have been erected before the period of the great Fire (of Banbury) in 1628', adding that these houses 'were chiefly built of the ferruginous limestone of the district, the walls inclining a little outward at the top, the roofs of a steep pitch and slated'.[1]

There is considerable variation in the stonework, both in the size, shape, and the colour of the material, as well as in its working and weathering properties. The differences appear to depend primarily on the quality of the local quarry, for they vary as a whole between one village and another. A better class of stonework is notable on the larger and more sophisticated class of dwellings; the type of walling appears, however, to have no chronological significance. The most frequently recorded class of walling is a small, roughly squared rubble laid in irregular courses of unequal depth with uneven joints, typical work of this nature being shown on Pl. 24. Within this general description, there are nevertheless some differences between different areas, the stone at Hook Norton, for instance, apparently being more fissile, as the walling there is built in narrower courses of long, thin stones (Pl. 23b). In all, the range of wallings is wide, from a small random rubble of unshaped stones, roughly coursed with thick joints, to a good squared block-in-course stonework of larger units, smoothly dressed on the face and laid in regular but unequal courses with fine joints (Pl. 2c). The latter type is generally found in better-class work throughout the period, approximating in many buildings to ashlar (Pl. 13a); it is used more widely in the 18th century for all classes of work. In the majority of buildings after 1600 there is some increase in the size of quoin stones which are occasionally of considerable size, face-bedded and averaging 18 inches deep on the face, with a thickness shown on the return of only 4 inches.

[1] Beesley, op. cit., p. 277.

Such larger quoins are found in conjunction with both rubble and more finely worked stone. The variation in size of stones sometimes is used for decorative effect, with courses of small flat stones alternating with larger squared blocks. There is, moreover, frequently a difference in character of the stonework in different elevations, particularly after 1700, the principal elevations being of superior finish, with the semi-ashlar already described.

On the south and east of the Banbury Region there is a broad belt in which the marlstone is admixed with the grey oolitic 'Cotswold' limestone; this area extends into Gloucestershire, south Oxfordshire, Buckingham and Northamptonshire (Fig. 70). The two stones, both available from the same local quarry in many areas, have been used together in a number of ways, with some lack of decision as to which stone was of superior quality and hence to be used for dressings. Both the grey limestone and the marlstone—the latter presumably imported from better beds of the material—are used alternatively for dressings to windows, doors and quoins, and gable parapets, to contrast with the other, serving as the general walling material. The most interesting admixture is the use of the two stones in alternative courses, giving an attractive horizontal striped effect found on both northern and southern boundaries; instances occur at Culworth in Northamptonshire where the greystone is the basic walling material, and at Hook Norton in the south-west of the region, a predominantly brownstone village. Castle House, Deddington (Pl. 9a) illustrates this decorative banding of the masonry. The use of marlstone for dressings occurs most commonly in Northamptonshire, as at Culworth, Sulgrave and Aynho, but examples also occur on the Warwickshire border, at Gaydon (Pl. 12b). Along the eastern boundary, notably in Deddington and Chacombe (Pl. 24a), grey limestone is used for dressings on larger houses, including the rather rare ovolo-mullioned windows: it is possible that these derive from a common source. A similar admixture, whereby worked stone dressings and spires are in this finer white stone, is found in the majority of the churches in the region.[1]

The jointing material is generally an earth mortar, showing a proportion of lime in better-class work and in certain regions. Beesley describes the late-15th-century brick house at Hanwell as 'being cemented with a mixture of Southam lime and powdered granite'.[2]

---

[1] Stone from the important quarries at Taynton, in the Oxfordshire Cotswolds, was used in the churches of north Oxfordshire. Repeated purchases for Adderbury church chancel are recorded between 1408 and 1419 (T. F. Hobson, *Adderbury 'Rectoria'*, Oxfordshire Record Society, Vol. viii).

[2] Op. cit., p. 191.

In 1676, Robert Plot[1] provides interesting information about jointing and plastering in the region, referring to a

whitish earth, which corruptly, I suppose from the colour is called Which-earth; mixed with straw, they use it for side-walls and ceilings, and with horse-dung make it into mortar for laying of stone; it seems a natural mixture of lime and sand, found at Thame, Waterperry and Adwell and slakes in water (like Gypsum) without any heat.

The villages mentioned are in the lowlands of south-east Oxfordshire, but Plot proceeds to refer to practices within the Banbury Region.

At Milton, near Adderbury, Great Tew and Stunsfield, I met also with another sort of spungy chalk, which though it will not slake like the former; yet at Milton and Adderbury used for pointing, seems to bind the stones of their walls very well; and theirs at Great Tew being somewhat finer, serves as well to white their rooms within (as I saw at Swerford) as to point walls without.

Throughout the region walls are plastered internally, with a coarse and sandy lime plaster of rough and uneven finish.

Ground floors are invariably flagged, with large flat stones averaging 2 inches in thickness, of random sizes, laid directly on the earth, no patterning being observed; no doubt in many cases flags have been later added as an improvement on original earth floors. The hard, blue lias stone, found at Hornton and perhaps elsewhere in the region, is generally used for this purpose, the brownstone not being sufficiently durable. In no case has an earth floor been recorded, even the humblest dwellings now having floors of brick or tiles, probably laid over the original compacted earth. At Taynton, Plot mentions that 'within a spit of the surface they dig a sort of earth they call Lam, of a whitish earth inclining to yellow; which mix'd with sand and some other earth, makes the best earth floors for ground-rooms and barns'. It is very probable that within the region earth flooring was the original finish for many of the smaller houses of the 17th and 18th centuries.

With the general adoption of stone walling in the 16th century, cross-walls too were at first of stone, either taken up to the roof to support roof-beams, or finishing at a truss at first-floor level. In a number of cases the through-passage is flanked by stone walls on either side, carried up to the roof to leave a narrow, 4-foot wide chamber on the first floor, as at Cromwell Cottage, Hornton (Fig. 18). At Blue Gates, Bloxham, the stone partition between hall and parlour finishes at first-floor level, and is continued on the first floor as a stud partition infilling the truss. The number of stone cross-walls

[1] Op. cit., p. 66.

decreases in the 17th century, and with the removal of the fire-places to the gables, *c.* 1675, the interior of the house is generally sub-divided only by timber partitions, with the consequent change in the upper-floor structure already noted.

The third primary material, brick, plays a negligible part in the traditional domestic architecture of the region. There are two 'great' houses within the region built of brick; Hanwell Castle, built in 1495, marking the first use of the material in the region, and Compton Wynyates in the Warwickshire plain below Edge Hill, dating from 1520, windows and other architectural features continuing to be in stone. The latter house shows affinity to the practices of the lowland plain of Warwickshire, where brick is widely used in the 17th century. The manor-house of Wormleighton, Warwickshire, built about 1512 by John Spencer, was also of Tudor brick—the north wing remaining—but the native stone was again used for the extensions to the house in 1613. These early introductions of brick into the region were exceptional and without influence even on the architecture of other great houses and manors, wherein the native material continued to be used throughout the 18th century. In 1604, bricks were being made at Woodstock to the south of the region—near to Stonesfield, from whence slates were being imported—at a cost of 10*d.* per hundred, but there is no evidence that any of these bricks reached the region. It is not until the beginning of the 19th century that there is any notable recourse to brickwork, and then only in Banbury itself and in the fringe areas north and west of the town. By 1852 there were as many as ten brickmakers in Banbury, but still the use of the material was largely confined to the town and its immediate locality. Even now the principal evidence of brick within the region is in the chimney-stacks raised on the original stone smoke vents. The ready availability of the native stone provided no in-ducement for the introduction of brick, whilst the taxes on brick at the end of the 18th century would provide a further deterrent, and stone continued to be the dominating material for all classes of dwellings until the present century.

Thatch is the primary roofing material of the Banbury Region, with a limited use of small grey limestone slates. Of buildings which retain their original roofing, over 80 per cent are thatched, and it is probable that, as the greater number of earlier dwellings now re-roofed with blue slate or tile were originally thatched, the proportion was originally greater. Stone slates are not obtainable within the region, but have probably been introduced from both north and south, the principal quarries being at Collyweston in Northamptonshire, and Stonesfield, just south of the region in Oxfordshire, the slates from the two places being generally similar in character. The slate occurs in fissile strata at the base of the oolitic system, and is split by a process of frosting. At both quarries the beds are very thin and restricted and probably had little value until this method of working was discovered. Robert Plot[1] describes how they are 'dug first in thick cakes about Michaelmas time, or before, to lye all the winter and receive the frosts, which make it cleave in the spring following into thinner plates, which otherwise it would not do so kindly.' Both the Collyweston and Stonesfield quarries have a long history,[2] the former quarry providing material in 1375 for the castle at Rockingham.[3]

The Stonesfield beds are a very localized deposit limited to a small area centred on the village and extending for about three miles east and north, and the slates were obtained therefrom by mining. The finished products vary in size from 5 to 22 inches in length, and from $\frac{3}{4}$ to $1\frac{1}{2}$ inches in thickness: they are laid in diminishing courses from eaves to ridge—each slate hung by two oak pegs onto battens—and are finished at the ridge with a cut stone member. Collyweston slates are similar in appearance, but tend to be a little larger in size. Valleys, which occur rarely in the region, are swept, and the eaves, uplifted by the 'cussome', a slate bedded to the wall top, projects about 6 inches. Slated roofs are in the majority of cases finished by raking parapets, but where there is no such finish, the slating projects about $1\frac{1}{2}$ inches. Unfrosted slates, known as 'presents', are obtained from coarser fissile beds of limestone in the Cotswolds and at Fulwell, near Enstone, and were also used within the region.[4]

The distribution of stone slating within the region is shown in Fig. 71. Almost every great house and manor is now finished with this material. For the smaller houses there is a more restricted distribution, slates being provided on all classes of building on the

[1] Op. cit.

[2] W. J. Arkell notes that 'the Stonesfield slate mines are generally assumed to be at least medieval, but the absence of early references to them raises considerable doubt as to whether the discovery of the process of splitting the "green" rock by frost, which is the raison d'être of the Stonesfield mines, was made before the end of the 16th century. Once that discovery was made Stonesfield became the paramount source of slates, but before that other naturally fissile rocks would have been used for preference and slates would have come mainly from the Cotswolds beyond Stow and locally from the Forest Marble and Taynton stone' (*Oxford Stone*, p. 131).

[3] L. F. Salzmann, *Building in England down to 1540*, p. 232.

[4] The slating practice within the region appears to be identical with that of the Cotswolds in method and nomenclature, where Stonesfield slates as well as more locally obtained 'presents' are used. A full description of practice in this region is given by Nathaniel Lloyd in *Building Craftsmanship*.

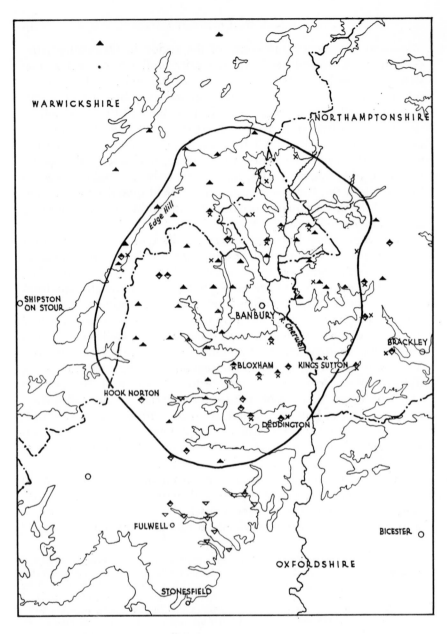

▲   Thatch   }   The symbol indicates that
▽   Stone slate   }   over 10% of village buildings
✕   Blue slate   }   are roofed with the material.
—— Boundary of Region   —·—
The 400 ft contour is shown

THE BANBURY REGION
DISTRIBUTION OF ROOFING MATERIALS

Fig. 71.

southern fringe, nearer to Stonesfield, and also being more wide-spread in the north-east and along the eastern fringe where transport was presumably more convenient along the valley from either Northamptonshire or the Oxfordshire quarries. In the central and western parts of the region, thatch is almost exclusively used, even for such large houses as Hornton Manor. Within the fringe area of mixed building stone on the east, there is an almost equal division between stone slates and thatch. As the proportion of grey limestone increases, on all fringes of the region, the use of stone slates shows a similar increase, and Church Enstone, a predominantly greystone village, is almost wholly slated, presumably using the 'presents' from the neighbouring Fulwell quarries.

In Banbury, the danger of fire which caused such destruction in 1628 and again in 1643 would cause thatch to lose popularity at an early date; it is only on the fringe of the town that thatched roofs are now to be seen. Fire almost destroyed the neighbouring villages of Kings Sutton in 1785, and Warkworth in 1811, and there must have been many such disasters in the smaller villages.

Thatch is nevertheless the dominant roofing material in the greater part of the region. The thatch is of wheat straw, laid across the common rafters, and secured with withies, usually showing lines of stitching along the ridge in a series of parallel lines forming a broad saddle to the roof. There are further continuous lines of stitching along the eaves and up the edges of the roof, following the verges, with an overhang of from 12 to 15 inches at the eaves, rising slightly over the windows. Where there is no gable parapet, the raking edge of the gable is left saw-toothed, with bundles of thatch placed in the angles of these courses with the butt outwards at the line of the gable face, and held in position by daubs of clay or by large stones. The thatch itself is carried to the edge of the gable and secured with withies to this verge course of straw. It is possible that there was originally a curtain of thatch hung over the gable verges, tied at the lower edge with continuous stitches of withies, but this feature has only been noted in a few renovated roofs, and may be a foreign importation, comparable to the more decorative reed thatch now also appearing in this area. The finish of the thatch at the apex of the gable with a small bonnet hip, which has been occasionally noted, may also be foreign to the region. Plot also has something to say on the subject of thatching at the end of the 17th century, without defining any specific region of the county:

The uppermost turf is not unfrequently used by Thatchers and laid on Mud-walls, and the top of houses, in the place and manner of those we call Ridge tiles; not that it is so good as thatching (though some say it better resists the wind) but because in some places wood is so scarce, that they cannot get spraies to fasten on Thatch; or else the people so poor that they care not to buy them.[1]

The use of turf, to which the thatch can be secured, has been noted in the thatching of the large oven projections of the 18th century, where the turf is laid on the top of the stonework.

For both slates and thatch similar roof pitches were employed, ranging between 50 and 58 degrees, with an average of 54 degrees. As is to be expected in this region, within the sphere of the upland cruck tradition, gable roofs are general until the end of the 18th century. From about that time the larger and more sophisticated Georgian-style houses are built with characteristic shallow-pitched hipped roofs, covered with blue slates. Barns are also found with hipped roofs over their entrance porches dating from this period, with thatch or stone-slate coverings. The cottage pair at Radway (Pl. 14*b*), with half-hips in a thatched roof, probably dates from *c.* 1800, and a number of similar cases of this period have been recorded.

The introduction of the true slates[2] on roofs of lower pitch or replacing earlier roof coverings occurs at the end of the 18th century. The earliest dated example of a roof, of approximately 35 degrees, built for the thin new slates is at Fenney Compton, in a two-unit house of Georgian character dated 1778 (Pl. 12*e*). The opening of the Oxford Canal in 1769 provided communication with the rest of the country, and no doubt accelerated the introduction of new materials, including brick and slate. The use of all these, however, as earlier indicated, was largely limited to the immediate neighbourhood of Banbury and the north of the region until the latter part of the 19th century.

In his recollections of Banbury from the first quarter of the 19th century, George Herbert notes that

'nearly all the houses were of a similar style and never alike or in line with each other. They were all built but one storey from the ground with the exception of a garret over. They were nearly all of stone and covered with the old stone slates. They were called Stonesfield slates and came from somewhere in the neighbourhood of that name. These quarries have long since been worked out. I do not remember any place being covered in with blue slates (perhaps they were not known then) and I can only remember one house more than one storey from the ground and that is in

[1] Op. cit., p. 64.
[2] The local stone slates are not geologically classed as a true slate, but are a fissile stone, splitting only along their bedding planes.

the Market Place and same as when I first knew it. This is now occupied by Mr. Thomkins the draper. (Understand when I say one storey perhaps I ought to say two, that is one storey from the shop).[1]

Roof drainage appears to have been unknown in vernacular building until the second half of the 17th century. There are lead rainwater heads dated 1654, with the initials T.A.M., at Castle House, Deddington, and at Wardington Manor, the more elaborately-fashioned lead rainwater heads are dated 1665, these being houses of importance. In yeoman houses, similar details first occur in conjunction with twin-gable roofs, such as occasionally have been noted in larger dwellings at this time. At Hook Norton, in an added wing with double gables (Pl. 15a), there is a lead internal gutter opening to a rainwater head of the same material, bearing the date 1709. Such examples are, however, very rare and can not be regarded as being characteristic of minor domestic building.

Throughout the period (to 1800) constructional practice within the region gives evidence of the strong traditional influences underlying the work, which—based on the two native materials of marlstone and thatch—shows resistance to the introduction of new materials and new ideas, and thereby kept alive the regional tradition of building. Conservatism is the keynote, the medieval character never being entirely lost, as is seen even more clearly in the architectural features and details of minor domestic building, to be considered in the following chapter.

[1] George Herbert, *Shoemaker's Window*, p. 68.

CHAPTER XII

ARCHITECTURAL FEATURES OF THE REGIONAL STYLE

IT has been established that the vernacular 'regional style', expressed in stone, was in full flower from *c.* 1575 to 1700. Whilst so little now remains of the medieval antecedents, their influence survived strongly, and little is to be seen of the alien classical Renaissance forms fashionable in the great houses of the country in the 17th century. Even in the 18th century, when for economic reasons building activity was much reduced, the medieval complexion was tenuously retained in the lesser dwellings until medieval architecture returned to popular favour with the Gothic Revival. Such is true not only of the Banbury Region but of all that area from Gloucestershire to Rutland which, architecturally, is often included in the general 'Cotswold' classification. The strongly persisting medieval tradition has been explained in adjacent regions on the evidence of professional pedigrees which have been traced for Oxford masons and carpenters.[1] These reveal that the craftsmen of the later 16th and early 17th centuries were trained by men who had worked in the last phase of the medieval period, at the beginning of the 16th century, and does much to account for the endurance of sub-medieval features even into the 18th century.

Fundamentally medieval, the regional style nevertheless evolves characteristically, in architectural detail as in plan and structure, the Renaissance influences being absorbed almost imperceptibly into the traditional style, eventually producing modifications of a hybrid character. This stylistic development is of particular value in providing data for establishing the history of the buildings. All buildings bearing authentic date-stones which have been recorded within the region are listed in Appendix I; they provide invaluable criteria for determining the rate of chronological advance, but the evidence they afford is not by any means as conclusive as might at first appear. Each house is an individual expression of architectural practice, maybe advanced in certain particulars and belated or retrograde in others. Thus each affords only a rough clue to the stage of develop-

[1] P. S. Spokes and E. M. Jope, 'The Priory, Marcham, Berkshire', *Berkshire Archaeological Journal*, Vol. LVII, 1959.

ment of particular items; and in the subsequent assessment of any undated building, an average must be struck from the indications of the building as a whole and from its individual features. The relative time lag between the introduction of new characteristics into the larger houses and their adoption in the smaller dwellings has also to be considered, particularly as the use of date-stones within the region is largely confined to the more important dwellings.

It is not only in urban Queen Anne architecture that houses had regal fronts and plebeian backs. The enrichment of the main façade, whether it be the road entrance front, the rear entrance front or gable end towards the road, is a distinctive feature of the regional style from first to last. In particular, the elaboration of the gable fenestration between the years 1650 and 1675 is more noteworthy in this region than in the Cotswolds or Northamptonshire. In the majority of all the 17th-century dwellings recorded there was a decorative emphasis laid upon a single chosen façade, or perhaps upon two adjoining façades, the emphasis taking a variety of forms. No clear principle could be determined in the selection of the façade to be elaborated, although in the main it was that which could be seen from the road. To judge by the fact that houses of manorial class usually are treated uniformly on all elevations, the discrimination in the case of the lesser dwellings indicates a desire to economize on the less significant fronts.

The variation of material in the fringe areas of mixed practice beyond the regional boundaries has already been noted, whereby the principal front may even be in a stone of different type and colour to the rest of the house. Reference has also been made to the practice within the region of varying the character of stonework, with a more carefully dressed and coursed material on the principal elevation often contrasting with coarser rubble on the other walls, a discrimination which is resorted to more frequently after 1700. In architectural details a number of other variations may be noted. Most common is the limitation of dressed stonework in windows and doors to the principal elevation or elevations, the gables not infrequently being treated in the same way as the main front, with wood lintels and frames on the inferior walls. This practice is carried to a further stage whereby the more elaborate and less common mullions of ovolo section are sometimes limited to one elevation only, or to the ground-floor windows, or even to one particular window, usually that of the parlour.

The distinction becomes more pronounced between 1650 and 1700, and in the sense that it indicates a growing aesthetic consciousness can be associated with Renaissance influence, but even the earlier yeoman houses of the 16th century show some discrimination. Blue Gates, Bloxham, and Grange Farm, Balscott, both differentiate between elaborate doors on the front elevation and simpler details on the rear. These are among the very few houses, apart from the manors, in which both entrances to the through-passage have stone dressings; in the 17th century, when stone door surrounds were relatively few, they were always placed on the principal front. Dial House, Sulgrave, built in 1636 (Fig. 42) has dressed stonework limited to the road elevation and gable, including a fine porch. The extension of 1653 at the Old Turnstiles, Barford (Fig. 47), has added some of the richest architectural features within the region—more appropriate to the Cotswolds which lie so near—including a three-storey porch and bay, all confined to the entrance elevation. Poplars Farm, Chacombe, built in 1654, shows minute discrimination between window types, used in the following manner: stone-mullioned windows in grey limestone on front elevation and gable, where the mullions of the ground-floor windows alone are of ovolo section, the rest of flat splay; mullioned windows in brown stone of flat splay section on the rear elevation to parlour and stair only; oak mullions elsewhere on the back of the house (Fig. 31; Pl. 20f, 24a).

All these dwellings, and the majority of 17th-century houses, stress the elevation to the road, even when the entrance is from the back, as is the case in the majority of 'lowland' plans. Warkworth Farm, 1639–58, is of this plan-type, but the stone dressings, which include a fine two-storey stone-mullioned bay, are still limited to the road front and gables, the windows having wood lintels and ovolo mullions on the rear, entrance, front—later distinguished by the addition of a three-storey porch (Fig. 43; Pl. 24b). In contrast, Hill Farm at Overthorpe, built c. 1680 to the lowland plan, places the emphasis on the rear, entrance, elevation, together with the gable at the service end (Figs. 44, 74; Pl. 24d).

Even in the dwellings of poorer architectural character which do not provide dressed stonework at all, there is occasional differentiation between sections of wood mullions, as in the 1657 wing of Chinners Farm, Chacombe (Pl. 4b), where ovolo mullions occur only on the front elevation, there being flat splays elsewhere. At the opposite end of the scale, the same respect for this more pretentious mullion section in stone is seen at the Manor House, Lower Boddington, in 1660 (Pl. 8d), where it is found only in the parlour window, flat splays appearing on all other openings. These variations occur so frequently as to exclude the possibility of the work being of two periods.

Until 1640, the character of the elevations is entirely medieval, with little sense of conscious order in the arrangement of the fenestration, but thereafter in the 17th century the importance attached to the principal elevation is attended by an increasing care for symmetry and formality. The influence of such great houses as Kirby Hall in Northamptonshire, with its ordered façade, and square-headed windows with mullions and transoms of ovolo section, dating from 1570, has already been noted, but was not to make itself felt in minor domestic work around Banbury until after 1640. Before this date, informal elevations clearly indicate the internal planning, the only sense of deliberate order being in the placing of windows one above the other in the larger dwellings, the number of lights reducing in each storey from ground floor to attics.

With the resumption of building after the Civil Wars, the classical influence produces some effect, at first in such large houses as Manor Farm, Northend (1654) (Fig. 45), where the entrance is brought to the centre of the hall to obtain symmetry, the labels being joined as a string course in the central bay. A continuous label-mould around the building occurs at Chacombe House Lodge, of the same date, whilst a third house also built in this year, Poplars Farm, Chacombe, shows a central dormer on the façade. A little later, c. 1680, Hill Farm, Overthorpe (Fig. 44), acquires a symmetrical effect on the rear elevation of a three-unit plan by virtue of the depressed height of the service bay, and the siting of a dormer centrally between hall and parlour bays, with a continuous label to the upstanding portion of the house (Fig. 74). The entrance doorways of the latter three houses all lack stone dressings, and have simple wood lintels. Developments in plan in the second half of the 17th century contribute to this elevational formality, with the preference for the two-unit plan, having entrance and stair placed centrally, and fireplaces on the gable walls. Friar's Cottage, Great Bourton (1685), illustrates the resulting façade (Fig. 34).

The expression of the upper storey in the more important of the two-and-a-half-storey dwellings of the 17th and 18th centuries is generally limited to gable windows and infrequent dormers, as at Hornton Manor; these increase in number and size in later and larger houses to produce a series of gablets, such as are seen in the Manor House, Kings Sutton, Northants, of mid-17th-century date (Pl. 8b). Dormer windows are not, however, characteristic of the region, as they are of the Cotswolds, the full dormer with parapeted gable being confined to the larger and more important yeoman dwellings, and in all cases lighting a third storey, never the first floor as in Gloucestershire. First-floor windows partly taken into the roof space do occur in a number of early 17th-century houses, and in later cottages, but they are achieved simply by raising the walling around the window and sweeping the thatch over, as in Sycamore Terrace, Bloxham (Pl. 23a). Shutford Manor House, dating from the end of the 16th century, is a rare example of a dwelling with three tiers of mullioned windows, those to ground and first floors being transomed (Figs. 14, 15). The only example of a yeoman house before 1700 with a third row of small mullioned windows is one recorded at Shening-ton. Apart from a few, 18th-century dwellings of urban character in the larger villages, three-storey façades do not occur in the minor domestic architecture of the region until after 1800.

The emphasis placed on the gable has already been noted as a characteristic of the regional architecture; gable fenestration in-creasingly expresses classical orderliness after 1650. Earlier dwellings, including those before 1600, are usually without windows on the end walls, and later in the 17th century gables again lack windows as fireplaces come to be located at their centres. When the house is sited at right angles to the road, the end elevation naturally invites particular attention, but even when houses are not so arranged, the end walls are usually fully fenestrated. The most usual arrangement is a series of windows diminishing in the number of lights in each tier, centrally placed where there is no stack, or placed to one side of the fireplace. Earlier gables, as at Lower Boddington (Pl. 18a), are more usually asymmetrical in the disposition of windows, but the desire for symmetry later produced such arrangements as at Hill Farm (Pl. 24d), and The Gables (Fig. 62), with linking label-moulds. The flues of fireplaces placed on such walls have to wind tortuously between the openings to reach the apex of the gable. The end walls of the George and Dragon, Chacombe (Pl. 20b), and Farley's Farm, Lower Middleton Cheney (Pl. 20d), are arrange-ments of c. 1680, the former without label-moulds at all, the second house having flat labels without dropped ends. The disposition of a series of single lights as at Pear Tree Cottage, Middleton Cheney (Fig. 32), the lower opening being a fire window, occurs at the end of the 17th century when gable fenestration was losing popularity.

The date-stone, frequently protected by a small label-mould, is sometimes placed on the gable wall, sometimes on the principal elevation, often over the entrance (Pl. 21a, b). Occasionally, other decorative features are introduced, a small oval window, sometimes unglazed, beneath a label, appearing high in the gable in several late-17th-century houses. In no less than eight buildings a twin lancet window has been recorded, usually in the gable, unglazed or blocked; despite its medieval appearance this is almost certainly a feature of 17th-century craftsmanship included for purely decorative purposes (Pl. 21*d*).

The window, together with its frame and glazing, in the course of its evolution never entirely loses its medieval characteristics. Stone-mullioned windows contribute forcefully to the character of the regional style, being found in association with the earliest yeoman houses in the region, and continuing in use in smaller homes until the middle of the 18th century, virtually to the point when the period of revivals saw their re-introduction in manorial cottages, the 'cottage orné' and in 19th-century lodges and mansions. Very many houses have had their windows rebuilt in later periods to provide better lighting, but the sections of the mullions that remain, the profiles of the reveal and label above, all provide useful data for determining the date of a house: they do not however provide as clear a pattern as has been established in the Cotswolds or Monmouthshire, which are included for comparison in the schedule in Fig. 73.[1]

A number of medieval windows have been recorded, including the 13th–14th-century examples at Cottisford and Swalcliffe Manors, and that dating from *c.* 1325 at Leadenporch House, together with a number of more fragmentary remains introduced into later dwellings. The medieval windows recorded in the two houses described at Balscott are more closely related to later regional forms, with their square heads and mullions of concave section. After 1500, three principal types of stone mullion appear—the hollow or cavetto mould, the flat splay, and the ovolo section—together with a small number of derivative variations; all are illustrated in Fig. 72.

The first of these, the cavetto or hollow-section mullion, is most closely related to the medieval prototype, and appears rarely, under twenty houses possessing such windows being recorded. In only four cases—the earlier part of the Old Turnstiles, Barford; Williamscot Manor, reputed to date from 1574; Shutford Manor and Dial House, Sulgrave, 1636—do the buildings clearly belong to the first half of the regional building period, i.e. before 1640. The Cotswold region, with its longer history of building in stone, is considerably richer in examples of this mullion section, and G. L. Worsley,[2] from the study of dated examples, has determined the period of use to

---

[1] The comparative data in Fig. 73 is derived with permission from G. L. Worsley, 'Traditional Domestic Architecture in the Cotswold Region', Manchester University Thesis, 1956; and from *Monmouthshire Houses*, op. cit.

[2] Op. cit., p. 58.

s

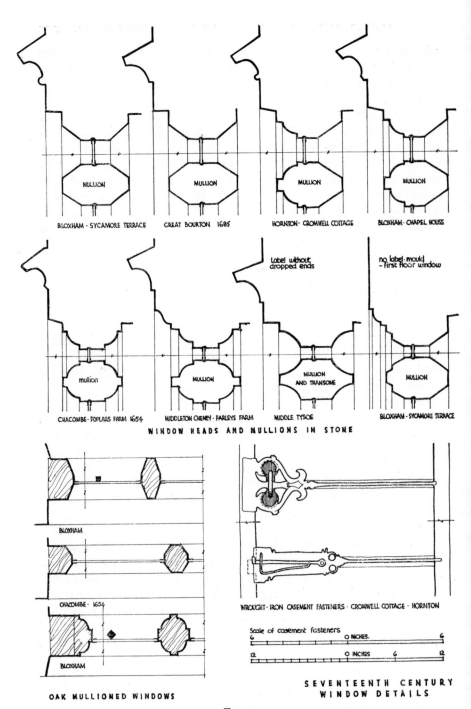

BLOXHAM · SYCAMORE TERRACE   GREAT BOURTON. 1685   HORNTON· CROMWELL COTTAGE   BLOXHAM · CHAPEL HOUSE

Label without dropped ends

no label·mould – first floor window

CHACOMBE· POPLARS FARM 1654   MIDDLETON CHENEY · FARLEYS FARM   MIDDLE TYSOE   BLOXHAM · SYCAMORE TERRACE

WINDOW HEADS AND MULLIONS IN STONE

BLOXHAM

CHACOMBE · 1654

BLOXHAM

WROUGHT· IRON CASEMENT FASTENERS · CROMWELL COTTAGE · HORNTON

Scale of casement fasteners

6   0 INCHES.   6

12   0 INCHES   6   12

OAK MULLIONED WINDOWS

**SEVENTEENTH CENTURY
WINDOW DETAILS**

Fig. 72.

have been *c.* 1575 to 1618. In the earlier Cotswold examples the hollow section is associated with pointed-arched heads to the lights, as at Temple Guiting Manor, Gloucestershire, but the incidence of this earlier form has only been noted in two buildings around Banbury. These are Hanwell Castle, of late-15th-century date, and a house in Banbury, Nos. 2 and 3, the Market Place; in both instances, mullions are of cavetto section, with four-centred arched heads to the lights and recessed spandrels. It is not clear whether the infrequency of these earlier forms in the Banbury Region, as compared with the Cotswolds, is due to the later commencement of the stone building period for minor domestic work, or because of the poorer quality of the marlstone and of craftsmanship. Only ten dated buildings have, however, been found in the Banbury Region of the period up to 1620, the same period affording many more instances in the Cotswolds.

In the Cotswolds, some resurgence of the cavetto mould in a narrower section with long mullions is noted at the end of the 17th century, from 1669 to 1700. This appears to have its counterpart within the Banbury Region, for the majority of hollow-moulded mullions are of this second period, being found in association with late-17th-century plans, as in the Gables, and other houses in Middleton Cheney, or again in the Old Shop, Middle Tysoe, where the section is associated with transomed windows.

The second mullion section, the flat splay, is ubiquitous, with dated examples from *c.* 1574 at Williamscot Manor, to 1719 at South Newington, and was undoubtedly used much later to cellars and in the smaller houses and cottages. This form occurs in most of the houses in the region which still retain their stone dressings.[1] The poorer properties of the marlstone in working and weathering are probably responsible for this general acceptance of the simpler profile within the region.

The classical ovolo section is the third type in order of date. Like the cavetto mullion, and unlike the splay, it is limited in use and in period. It has been suggested (Chapter V) that the building of Warmington Manor in *c.* 1603 marks the introduction of stone ovolo mullions into the region, in a house of high architectural quality, in which the stone dressings bear a profusion of mason marks, the only instance of these noted in the region (Fig. 75). The first dated instance is in a great house, Wroxton Abbey, built in 1615, where hollow mullions are used contemporaneously in the cellars. In vernacular building there is no dated example before 1647, when ovolo

[1] Of the total number of houses which have been recorded with stone window dressings, over 90 per cent had window mullions of this flat splay section.

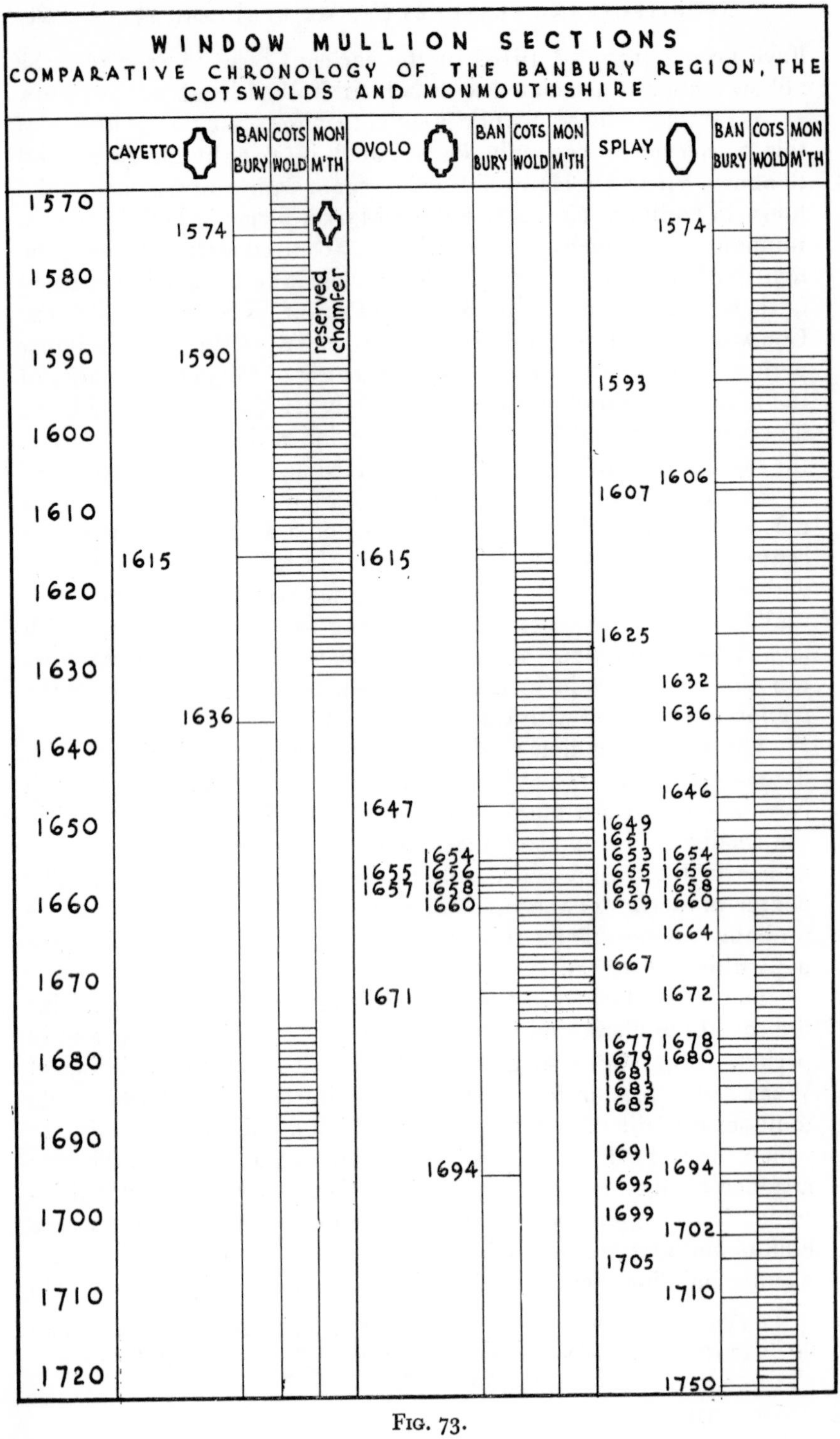

WINDOW MULLION SECTIONS
COMPARATIVE CHRONOLOGY OF THE BANBURY REGION, THE COTSWOLDS AND MONMOUTHSHIRE

	CAVETTO	BAN BURY	COTS WOLD	MON M'TH	OVOLO	BAN BURY	COTS WOLD	MON M'TH	SPLAY	BAN BURY	COTS WOLD	MON M'TH
1570												
	1574			reserved chamfer					1574			
1580												
1590	1590								1593			
1600												
1610									1607	1606		
1615	1615				1615							
1620												
1630									1625			
	1636								1632 / 1636			
1640												
1650					1647				1646 / 1649 / 1651 / 1653 / 1655 / 1657 / 1659	1654 / 1656 / 1658 / 1660		
1660					1655 1656 / 1657 1658 / 1660							
									1664 / 1667			
1670					1671				1672			
1680									1677 / 1679 / 1681 / 1683 / 1685	1678 / 1680		
1690									1691 / 1695	1694		
					1694				1699	1702		
1700									1705			
1710									1710			
1720									1750			

Fig. 73.

mullions, in unusually fine and lofty windows, appear at Castle End, Deddington, a yeoman house of exceptional scale (Pl. 9*b*). In the period of renewed building activity following the Civil Wars this type was used in many of the larger yeoman dwellings, with dated examples occurring up to 1660, after which only one more is noted, at Milton in 1694. Altogether only seven dated examples have been discovered, and the use of this more elaborate detail is far less frequently encountered in undated houses than that of the flat splay.[1] Ovolo mullions occur mainly in the larger yeoman and manorial dwellings, the window dressings being frequently of grey limestone, particularly in the north and eastern parts of the region, as at Middleton Cheney, Chacombe, Overthorpe, and Deddington, adjacent to the grey stone areas of Northamptonshire, where their use is more general. It is interesting to note that at Dial House, Sulgrave (Fig. 42), a house built in the oolitic limestone, the hollow mullions in the earlier part of the house are in a dark brown stone, whilst the later ovolo mullions are in the same grey stone as the walling. It would appear that the marlstone was less suited for working these more complex profiles, for it was less frequently used for this purpose.

Mullions have been occasionally found of ovolo section on the external face with an internal flat splay,[2] as at Cromwell Cottage, Hornton, *c.* 1615, executed in the brown stone. A number of other less common sections occur, and are illustrated in Fig. 72. Mullions of all sections are grooved to receive the glazing lattices, with opening wrought-iron casements, usually occupying only part of the height of the light.

Windows are generally of two, three or four lights, with five-light openings occurring infrequently, usually in larger houses. The 'king' mullion, a more common feature of Cotswold architecture, is exceptional around Banbury, being generally limited to the larger manor-houses, only one example having been found in a house of yeoman class—at Parish's Farm, Hempton, where the window is of six lights with ovolo mullions (Fig. 59). At Warmington Manor, *c.* 1603, the two six-light windows on the south front, to hall and parlour, have 'king' mullions of similar section, but more elaborately treated internally as decorative piers to support the inner lintel. A second manorial example is illustrated at Shutford Manor, the gable

[1] In all, approximately fifty buildings with ovolo mullions have been recorded in the region.

[2] The 'Priory', Marcham, Berkshire, dating from *c.* 1570 to 1590, has mullions of comparable section in windows with arched heads to the lights. The mullions are of ovolo-section on the outer face, with recessed splays—the reserved chamfer—internally (op. cit.).

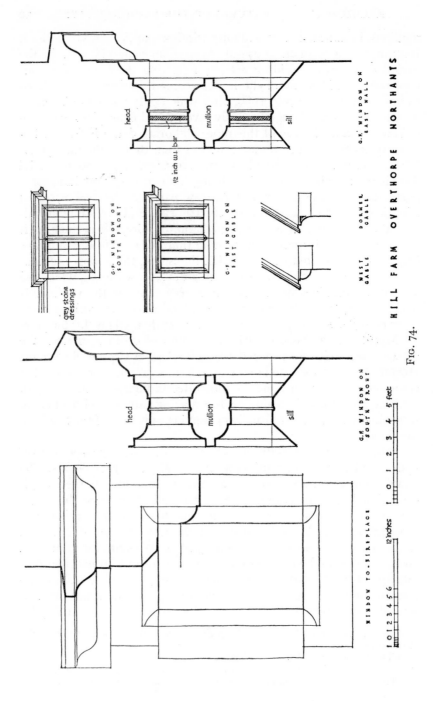

head

mullion

sill

G.F. WINDOW ON
EAST WALL

½ inch w.i. bar

G.F. WINDOW ON
SOUTH FRONT

grey stone
dressings

G.F. WINDOW ON
EAST GABLE

WEST
GABLE

DORMER
GABLE

head

mullion

sill

G.F. WINDOW ON
SOUTH FRONT

1 0 1 2 3 4 5 feet

WINDOW TO FIREPLACE

12 inches

1 0 1 2 3 4 5 6

HILL FARM OVERTHORPE NORTHANTS

FIG. 74.

windows having 'king' mullions and transoms of cavetto section. The average mullion height is 3 feet 6 inches, but towards the end of the century the average increases to 4 feet, and windows take on a vertical form: the ovolo mullions of Castle End, Deddington, already noted, are 5 feet 4 inches in height. Occasionally, towards the end of the century, the spacing of the mullions is increased above the usual 18-inch centres; it measures almost two feet at Overthorpe (Fig. 74) with full classical profiles.

Transomed windows in stone are equally rare in the region.[1] The surviving window of early-14th-century date at Leadenporch House, Deddington, with heavy, flat-splay mullion and transom (Pl. 2b), is the earliest example, followed by the hall window of c.1500 at Grange Farm, Balscott (Pl. 2d). Transomed windows in stone occur at Shutford Manor, at the end of the 16th century, at Wroxton Abbey in 1615, at Castle House, Deddington, dated 1654, and at the large house called the 'Rookery', Adderbury East, in 1656. Apart from such great houses and manors, only two examples have been recorded within the region, both dating from the late 17th century, by which time this feature had descended to the lesser yeoman's houses to light the more lofty rooms introduced at the end of the century. The Garden House, Mollington (Fig. 37), has three-light transomed windows, with flat-splay mullions and without label-moulds, to the first and second floors, whilst the Old Shop, Middle Tysoe (Fig. 50), includes two-light transomed windows with mullions of the late cavetto section with label-moulds. Both these dwellings have earlier been noted as being of unusual architectural distinction for their size.[2] There is a fine, five-light transomed window with oak mullions and transom in the Court House at Kings Sutton (Pl. 20e), the section being an enriched cavetto externally and a flat splay on the inner face, its date being c. 1575: it provides the only instance of such a window in wood of this date, although transomed wood frames become widespread at the end of the 17th century.

The variations in the mullion section find a counterpart in the profile of the label-mould with dropped ends which is generally employed until the end of the 17th century, the moulding showing some variation. Priory Farm, Balscott, in its Perpendicular doorway

[1] In Oxfordshire, south of the regional boundary, a number of early domestic transomed windows have been noted, at Tackley's Inn, Oxford, c. 1310; Ham Court, Bampton, c. 1320; and Hill House, Burford, c. 1370 (E. T. Long, *Minor Domestic Architecture in Oxfordshire*, Oxford Architectural Society, Vol. 84, 1938, pp. 45–55).

[2] Transomed windows in stone occur more frequently in the Cotswolds, as at Donnington, 1699, and at Bourton-on-the-Water, 1698.

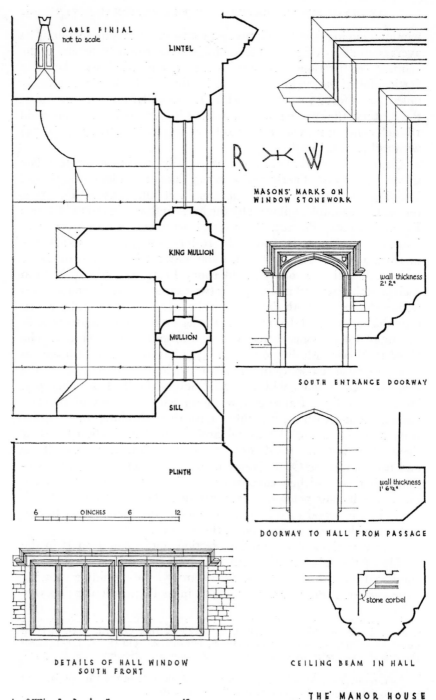

GABLE FINIAL
not to scale

LINTEL

KING MULLION

MULLION

SILL

PLINTH

6   0 INCHES   6   12

MASONS' MARKS ON
WINDOW STONEWORK

R >|< W

wall thickness
2' 2"

SOUTH ENTRANCE DOORWAY

wall thickness
1' 6½"

DOORWAY TO HALL FROM PASSAGE

stone corbel

CEILING BEAM IN HALL

DETAILS OF HALL WINDOW
SOUTH FRONT

1   0 FEET 1   2   3   4   5   10

THE MANOR HOUSE
WARMINGTON   WARWICKSHIRE

FIG. 75.

(Fig. 8) provides a rich medieval example which closely relates to the derivative form over the principal door at Blue Gates, Bloxham. Other examples of this profile are few, the simpler form shown at B (Fig. 72) being used throughout the century in the greater majority of buildings, with only minor variations. Warmington Manor presents an isolated instance of an ovolo-moulded label of early-17th-century date, whilst the classical cyma moulding is almost equally rare, always found in conjunction with ovolo mullions in larger houses of the latter half of the 17th century, occasionally with an additional cyma mould introduced in the reveal, as at Hill Farm, Overthorpe (Fig. 74). The moulding of labels to entrance doors is commonly more decorative and advanced than that of windows. The ends of the window labels normally are dropped in a short return, the only example of an enriched window-stop being on a house in Chapel Street, Bloxham. Here the lozenge terminations, more generally reserved for door surrounds, occur additionally in the first-floor windows (Pl. 20c). The dropped end is omitted altogether at the end of the 17th century, as at Farley's Farm, Lower Middleton Cheney, c. 1680, where only the gable windows have flat labels, without returned ends (Pl. 20d); the windows on the lateral wall lack labels altogether. Eventually, label-moulds tend to disappear entirely. Before 1640 it seems that upper windows were often considered to be adequately shielded by the overhang of the thatch, and by 1680 the omission of the label extends to the lower windows also. The fine series of windows on the gable of the George and Dragon, Chacombe (Pl. 20b), is completely devoid of label-moulds. In the first decade of the 18th century, windows of better-class dwellings are similarly without the label, as seen in the house described at Avon Dassett, dated 1702, although in smaller dwellings their use continues a little longer.

The attempt to resolve classical and medieval forms in windows of this type occasionally produces some unusual vernacular results, as in the window illustrated at Home Farm, Middle Aston (Pl. 22c).

In all these rectangular-headed windows, the stone head and mullions are set on the outer face of the wall, leaving a deep internal reveal, with one or two timber lintels supporting the inner half of the wall. In the poorer stone dwellings, the proportion of which increases as time passes, oak-framed windows with external timber lintels appear quite early in the history of the vernacular style, and with increasing frequency, they are found on the inferior façades of the better-class houses where elsewhere the windows are fully dressed with stone mullions.

The external timber lintels are occasionally chamfered, the chamfers rarely having moulded stops, but are more commonly of simple squared section, extending beyond the opening from 6 to 9 inches for a seating. Sometimes in late 17th–18th-century work a moulding is introduced below the lintel, to meet the head of the frame, as at Williamscot Home Farm (Fig. 26). Mullions are alternatively of ovolo or flat-splay section, averaging 5 inches deep by $2\frac{1}{2}$ to 4 inches in width, sometimes grooved for glazing. A more elaborate section occurs in the 16th-century Court House at Kings Sutton. Comparatively few original frames now exist, in consequence of later replacement, and for this reason it is difficult to date the introduction of the square section mullion, rebated to receive the glass and the opening casement. The earliest of known date belong to the end of the 17th century, and the type becomes general after 1700.[1] The transomed-window phase already noted in connection with stone windows has its counterpart in the use of the two-light transomed wood frames. Instances of this form occur between 1693 at the Old Manor House, Cropredy, and 1727 at the Dolphin Inn, Wigginton. It is noteworthy that the periods are virtually coincident for stone and wood, a circumstance which is a useful guide to the dating of wooden windows in general. These dates are for the larger class of yeoman dwellings; in the lesser houses, two- or three-light transomed wooden windows occur later, as is shown by a smaller house at Bodicote, dated 1740, with windows of this nature. The frames are set almost flush with the external wall face, in openings which may have either wood or flat stone-voussoired lintels, according to the character of the work, with glazing in square panes set in lead, and with iron opening casements. A simple form of small transomed window, in a modest house of about 1725 at Thenford, is illustrated in Fig. 56. So far as can be determined owing to the scarcity of examples, the wood two-light transomed window gave way to the vertical sliding sash window somewhere before mid-18th century. The earliest dated examples of a sash does not occur until 1766, the instance being at Hook Norton, in a small house in the square.[2]

In the 18th century, at first in better-class work, but later in quite small dwellings, the use of stone flat arches or lintels to open-

---

[1] In Monmouthshire, the flat rebated frame is introduced c. 1680, the authors noting that at that time 'window frames designed for glazing were a normal product of the craftsmen in the market towns catering for our farmer class' (op. cit., Vol. III, p. 97).

[2] The sliding sash first appeared in the Home Counties at the end of the 17th century. The first sash window used in Oxfordshire is reputed to be at Sibford Gower, dating from 1728 (*Dictionary of Architecture Publications Society*).

ings becomes common practice, varying in treatment according to the character of the masonry walling. The rubble flat arch is found in dated buildings from 1700 to 1763, a voussoired arch in ashlar being used in larger houses over the same period. The three-piece stone lintel in ashlar, with the keystone frequently emphasized, occurs less often over the same period, the only two dated examples being 1714 and 1727. The single flat stone lintel appears to be characteristic of 19th-century work within the region, although large single stones, roughly shaped, are occasionally used to bridge window openings in quite small houses, as at Homestead Cottage, Alkerton, in 1716 (Pl. 18d), and ashlar lintels have been noted in a house of c. 1700 at Milcombe. Projecting sills do not appear in the 18th-century work around Banbury, except in the form of a projecting string coinciding with the base of the windows, as is seen in certain of the formal façades of large houses of the early 18th century, including the Dolphin Inn, Wigginton.

Bay windows of any period are exceptional features. In the 17th century, stone-mullioned bays of rectangular plan occasionally have been noted in the more important yeoman dwellings, of three storeys with gable at Kings Sutton Manor, Northants, and the Old Turnstiles, Barford, 1653, whilst two-storey versions are equally infrequent, with good examples at Warkworth Farm, 1639–58 (Pl. 24b), and Banbury Vicarage, 1649, the latter having a horizontal castellated parapet. A stone-mullioned bay with the sides splayed on plan—a form occurring more commonly in both the Cotswolds and Northamptonshire—is seen only at Hook Norton Manor House, dated 1656 (Pl. 8c). In the 18th century, single-storey bays were sometimes built, usually at the parlour end of a house, sometimes added to earlier dwellings. They are of square or half-hexagonal plan, roofed with stone slates or with lead-covered flats, and have wood window-frames with iron casements. A good example is illustrated at Williamscot Home Farm (Pl. 22d). The curved Regency bay is also to be seen in houses in Bloxham, Deddington and Swerford (Pl. 15c). All windows appear to have been glazed from the commencement of the regional stone period in the 16th century, and no unglazed windows or early shuttered windows have been discovered.[1] Diamond-shaped panes of thin, greenish glass, set in lead cames, are the earliest type of glazing in the region of which singularly few examples survive. The house dated 1655 in Council Lane, Deddington (Fig.

[1] The glasshouse at Henley on Thames was renowned for its glass manufacture at the end of the 17th century, when glass was also being manufactured in other parts of Oxfordshire (Plot, op. cit.).

33), has original diamond lattices in the upper windows; by this time the rectangular panes of glass in lead also were being used, and are to be seen in houses throughout the 18th century. In both cases the glazed lattice is secured by strips of lead to iron bars of square section, at first set vertically in both stone- and wood-mullioned windows. There is one bar to each light, except that in the wider lights at the end of the century two may be used. The hinged casements, usually occupying only part of a light in height, have flat, iron frames with light cross-bars, to which a smaller lattice is secured. In wood frames, from the end of the 17th century, the iron bars are usually set horizontally, two or more to each light, with the square lattices secured in the same manner as before, whilst casements become taller, fitting in the rebate of the frame. Renaissance influence is seen in the decorative leadwork at Williamscot Home Farm (Pl. 22d). The introduction of sliding sashes and later of wood casements brought into use wood astragals, with glazing in rectangular panes which became increasingly large as glass manufacture was improved.

There is little evidence of craftsmanship in wrought iron, window fastenings being of simple contrivance as appear at Cromwell Cottage, Hornton, representing the 17th century and at Thenford Cottage representing the 18th (Figs. 56, 72). The workmanship seen at the Dolphin Inn, Wigginton, in 1727, where animals are depicted in the perforated handle plates of the casements, is an attractive and quite exceptional feature (Pl. 22a), although to the south-west such elaboration occurs quite frequently in Cotswold houses. Door hinges and fittings are direct and simple, and only one decorative iron fireback has been found; this is at Lower Boddington Manor, and bears the date 1660.

The number of houses with stone dressings to window openings which also have moulded stone doorways is singularly small, the entrances even to large and important yeoman houses generally having a simple wood lintel. It seems probable that mullioned windows of stock size and pattern were being fabricated in the 17th century at certain of the more important quarries in and near the region, and were available to builders throughout the area. The difference between the stone of window dressings and that of the walling—even if of similar brown colour—indicates that the dressed stone has come from a different source to that of the walling. In many cases, the tooling between the mullions and head or sill is inaccurate and unfinished, supporting this theory, there being generally no skilled mason to finish the stone on site. The grey limestone ovolo mullions which have already been noted in a number of fine large houses dating

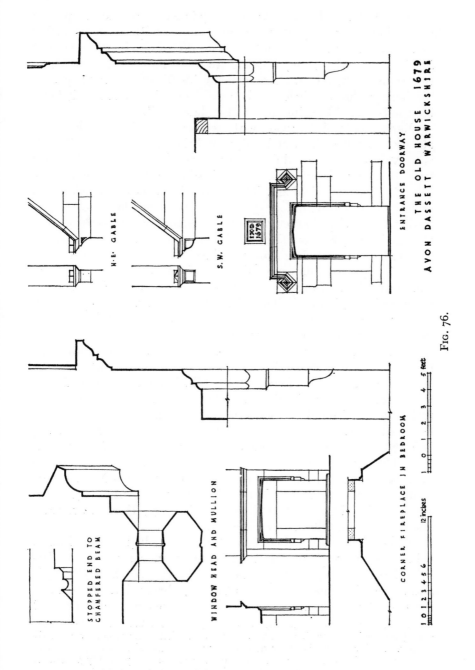

STOPPED END TO
CHAMFERED BEAM

WINDOW HEAD AND MULLION

CORNER FIREPLACE IN BEDROOM

N·E· GABLE

S.W. GABLE

ENTRANCE DOORWAY

THE OLD HOUSE 1679
AVON DASSETT WARWICKSHIRE

12 inches

0 1 2 3 4 5 feet

FIG. 76.

from the latter half of the 17th century in the north-eastern part of the region, are very probably from a common quarry, presumably in Northamptonshire.[1] Moulded stone doorways, in the relatively few instances where they appear, are more individual features, no two examples within the region being identical; clearly they were specially produced only for the best class of work, some actually bearing the householders' initials and the date motif.

Early medieval doorways with two-centred pointed arches have already been described at Leadenporch House (Pl. 2b) and Swalcliffe Manor (Pl. 2a), and there are other early examples which have been re-used in later dwellings, as in the house lying behind the Joiner's Arms at Bloxham. The more characteristic four-centred arched head set within a rectangular label-mould, finds a late medieval prototype in the fine Perpendicular doorways at Priory and Grange Farms, Balscott (Pl. 2d). The door of Blue Gates (Fig. 12) with foliated spandrels is closely related to these earlier examples, and this type continues until the second half of the 17th century, with little change save in the character of the mouldings. A later version of 1649 is seen in The Vicarage, Banbury. Door-heads with four-centred arches vary from a single flat stone, simply chamfered, to more elaborately moulded versions with flat labels and recessed spandrels, that illustrated at Avon Dassett (Fig. 76) being the type most widely encountered. This building, built in 1679, provides the last dated example of a four-centred arch. The lozenge-shaped stop, first noted in the medieval door at Balscott, occurs throughout the region in dated buildings between 1610, the date of a doorway with rectangular head in a wall to the churchyard at Bloxham (Fig. 22), and 1685, the time of erecting Friar's Cottage, Great Bourton (Pl. 23d). The latter doorway, also with rectangular head, has an elaborate classical profile to the label and jamb. The cambered arch occurs contemporaneously in the first half of the 17th century, good examples being illustrated at Cromwell Cottage, Hornton, c. 1615, and at Alkerton Old Rectory, dated 1625.

Square-headed openings have little chronological significance, being used throughout the 17th century; an early form of flat-shouldered lintel appears at Sycamore Terrace, Bloxham (Pl. 23a), and in the rebuilding of Northend Chapel, where it is dated 1632. At the end of the century some rectangular openings show classical

---

[1] L. F. Salzman notes the case of William Johnson of Barrington, freemason, supplying for Hampton Court five windows of 'iij fote jame of oon lyghte redy made and delyvered at Barenton quarry' at 5s. each, and also eighty lights 'redy made' at 4s. 6d. each. Such commercial prefabrication was probably general at quarries in the 17th century (*Building in England down to 1540*, p. 123).

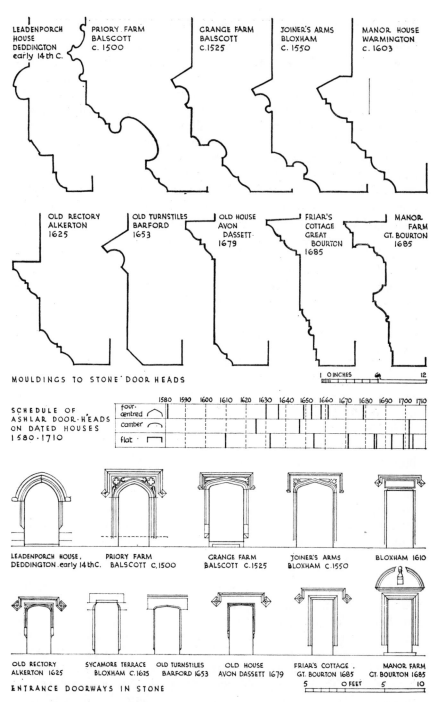

LEADENPORCH HOUSE DEDDINGTON early 14th C.

PRIORY FARM BALSCOTT C. 1500

GRANGE FARM BALSCOTT C.1525

JOINER'S ARMS BLOXHAM C. 1550

MANOR HOUSE WARMINGTON C. 1603

OLD RECTORY ALKERTON 1625

OLD TURNSTILES BARFORD 1653

OLD HOUSE AVON DASSETT 1679

FRIAR'S COTTAGE GREAT BOURTON 1685

MANOR FARM GT. BOURTON 1685

MOULDINGS TO STONE DOOR HEADS

1 0 INCHES   12

SCHEDULE OF ASHLAR DOOR-HEADS ON DATED HOUSES 1580-1710

	1580	1590	1600	1610	1620	1630	1640	1650	1660	1670	1680	1690	1700	1710
four-centred														
camber														
flat														

LEADENPORCH HOUSE, DEDDINGTON. early 14thC.

PRIORY FARM BALSCOTT C.1500

GRANGE FARM BALSCOTT C.1525

JOINER'S ARMS BLOXHAM C.1550

BLOXHAM 1610

OLD RECTORY ALKERTON 1625

SYCAMORE TERRACE BLOXHAM C.1625

OLD TURNSTILES BARFORD 1653

OLD HOUSE AVON DASSETT 1679

FRIAR'S COTTAGE. GT. BOURTON 1685

MANOR FARM GT. BOURTON 1685

ENTRANCE DOORWAYS IN STONE

5   O FEET   5   10

COMPARATIVE DETAILS OF ENTRANCE DOORWAYS IN STONE

FIG. 77.

influence in the form of the architrave, as for instance at Middle Tysoe (Fig. 50), Barford St. John (Fig. 51), the Roebuck Inn, Drayton, and elsewhere, whilst a more elaborate scheme, with broken pediment over occurs at Manor Farm, Great Bourton, in 1685 (Fig. 63). The door of a house in Lower Tysoe dated 1671—now a shop—combines a similar broken pediment and moulded architrave with the traditional lozenge-shaped stops, embellished with carved human faces. Doorways to 18th-century dwellings are generally of simpler character, only occasionally having canopies of wood or stone. A flat stone canopy is to be seen at Avon Dassett, dated 1702, and a more elaborate curved example is illustrated at Wigginton in Fig. 53. Another fine canopy in wood was added to Williamscot Home Farm in the mid-18th century (Fig. 26).

Porches are not characteristic features of the regional architecture. There are single-storey examples at Dial House, Sulgrave, of 1636, and at Shutford Manor, the latter showing an unusual combination of medieval and classical detail, with a four-centred arched opening placed within an enclosing classical entablature in the framework of the single-storeyed gable, crowned by a ball finial (Fig. 15). More frequently, porches are of two storeys, including examples at Castle End, Deddington, of 1647, Banbury Vicarage of 1649 and the Rookery, Adderbury East, dated 1656, with small powder closets over the entrance. Three-storey versions are rare, instances being noted at Warkworth Farm (1658), and the Old Turnstiles, Barford, added in 1653.

No significance attaches to internal doorways in the regional houses; almost all have square heads with wooden lintels.

A number of original entrance doors survive, as at Great Bourton and Avon Dassett, consisting of vertical planks backed by horizontal boards, with battens covering the joints on the door face, finished by iron studs and strap hinges. A heavy ash or oak draw bar, averaging 4 inches square, sliding within the thickness of the wall was occasionally used, and can be seen at Grange Farm, Balscott, Warkworth Farm and elsewhere.

The gables of stone-slated roofs normally are finished by raking parapets, save in the fringe areas where this form of roofing occurs in smaller and architecturally poorer dwellings. Parapets are also provided on the gables of the more important thatched structures, occasionally at the upper end of the house only. The stone parapet-coping is almost always of flat-topped section, and projects $1\frac{1}{2}$ inches beyond the face of the gable, with the projecting soffit splayed or moulded. Decorative kneelers of a great variety of designs become general from early in the 17th century, and the parapet coping is tied into the gable by bonding stones at intervals. Typical examples of copings and kneelers recorded within the region are illustrated in Pl. 21. The saddle-back coping at Deddington (Fig. 33), dated 1655, is found only in one other house below manorial status, a larger dwelling in the same village. At the apex of the gable, where there is no stack, and also above the kneeler, there is usually a seating for a finial, but it is very rarely, and only in large houses of manorial type, that such features are found. There is a sundial standing on the gable at Warkworth Farm, ball finials at Manor Farm, Northend, obelisks at the Rookery, Adderbury, and small pinnacles at Warmington Manor (Fig. 75), but such ornaments are infrequent. It would seem unlikely that all finials should so completely disappear from the smaller dwellings, despite their exposed position, and it is more probable that these were never provided in the greater number of instances. Where there is a gable chimney-stack, the parapet coping is either continued to an apex on the face of the stack, or returned horizontally across its base (Pl. 18).

Chimney-stacks present a very different appearance to those of the Cotswolds, the stone stalks so characteristic of the region rarely being found around Banbury save in the largest yeoman houses and manors, particularly in the south-west, nearest to the Cotswolds. They are then square in plan, constructed of flat stone slabs, with a moulded capping, the flues usually expressed separately even when two or more are based on the same stack. The diagonally placed stalks, characteristic of Jacobean work, can be seen at the Old Rectory, Alkerton—three flues grouped over a central stack—but this is an isolated example related to the practice in the neighbouring Cotswolds. In the majority of small houses of the region, throughout the period under consideration, the stone chimney, diminishing in size by a series of internal steps, rises to a smoke vent surmounted by a heavy stone capping a few inches above the roof covering. In all cases these stone bases are now surmounted by later brick stalks, usually 1 foot 10½ inches square, which were presumably added from the end of the 18th century when brick began to enter the region.[1]

The fireplace is the most important internal feature of the regional house. Its position and general arrangement have been considered in

[1] The danger of fire was ever present with thatched roofs, and the extended stacks must have added some protection. Their introduction may have been encouraged by the spread of fire insurance within the region, as shown by the large number of houses which bear insurance plates. The Sun Insurance, whose plates appear most widely, numbered their fire marks between 1710 and 1807, reaching three-quarters of a million by the latter date.

T

earlier chapters, and it is not necessary to speak here of these factors. The usual form of ground-floor fireplace from the 16th to the 18th centuries is the broad open hearth (Pl. 17*b*), usually 3 feet deep and up to 12 feet wide, normally spanned by a timber bressumer of oak or elm at about 5 feet height, the latter chamfered and cambered, with the chamfer sometimes returned down the stone jambs. Above the hearth opens the tapering stone flue rising though the upper floors to the smoke vent, always at the apex of the roof. In the reveals are cut shallow seats of square or semi-circular plan, together with small recesses to contain minor objects—even to provide an elbow rest. Occasionally, small cupboards are provided for storing and drying foodstuffs. A hinged iron trivet is seen in a number of cases, which supported cooking vessels over the open wood fire. There are one or two instances of fire windows opening onto the side of the ingle, or even at the back of the fire, as at Pear Tree Cottage, Middleton Cheney (Fig. 32). These appear always to have been glazed, and are not simply 'smoke-holes' for additional ventilation. From 1646 there is usually found in one or more of the fireplaces of a household a bread oven opening from one reveal, at first of circular plan, contained within the thickness of the walls and jamb, but later increased in size and height, to project far beyond the walls. The fine oven adjoining the hall fireplace at the Old Rectory, Alkerton (1625) (Fig. 78), is one of the earliest recorded in the region, and is 4 feet 2 inches in diameter, well shaped and finished with a shallow saucer dome in dressed stones, contained entirely within the jamb of the hearth. The size of these oven projections increases through the 18th century, the projection at first being of semi-circular plan; later on they are more often rectangular and open off the back of the fire instead of the reveal, presumably to leave room for ingle seats. Externally such projections are either thatched or stone-slated, according to the roofing of the house (Pl. 16). The opening from the hearth is usually about 2 feet by 18 inches in size, with a removable or hinged iron door, and the base of the oven is flat, many being later re-surfaced with bricks.[1] Later in the 18th century, ovens are occasionally built quite apart from fireplaces, with separate stone hearths before their openings and a separate flue over. An oven of this type was added at Blue Gates, Bloxham.

Stone heads to fireplaces occur in many of the houses of more refined architectural quality, always coinciding with stone dressings to the exteriors of entrance doorways, to which they normally

---

[1] Plot mentions Taynton stone as making the best hearths for ovens, set edgeways.

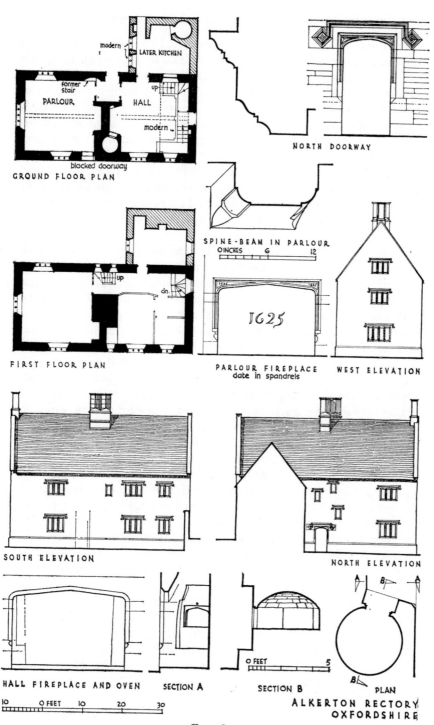

modern

LATER KITCHEN

former stair

PARLOUR   HALL

up

modern

blocked doorway

GROUND FLOOR PLAN

NORTH DOORWAY

FIRST FLOOR PLAN

up

dn.

SPINE-BEAM IN PARLOUR

0 INCHES   6   12

1625

PARLOUR FIREPLACE
date in spandrels

WEST ELEVATION

SOUTH ELEVATION

NORTH ELEVATION

HALL FIREPLACE AND OVEN   SECTION A   SECTION B   PLAN

B   A

B

0 FEET   5

ALKERTON RECTORY
OXFORDSHIRE

10   0 FEET   10   20   30

FIG. 78.

correspond in detail. The only late-medieval fireplaces occur in large houses, including Cottisford, Swalcliffe Manor House (Pl. 17a), and Hanwell Castle, all of late 16th-century date. Seventeenth-century fireplaces generally are similar in form, apart from the profiles of mouldings. It is usually the smaller hearths, in parlours and bedrooms, which have stone dressings, but at Cromwell Cottage, Hornton, there is a fine opening of early-17th-century date in the kitchen, with cambered stone arch spanning 7 feet, corresponding in the details of mouldings and label with the principal doorway. At the end of the century flat-headed openings with bolection moulds occur at Manor Farm, Great Bourton, 1685, and there is a comparable example in oak to a bedroom fireplace at the Garden House, Mollington (Fig. 37).

The elaboration of the fireplace is in marked contrast to the lack of pretension in the stair throughout the 17th century in these smaller buildings. Usually concealed behind doors, even in large yeoman houses, until 1700 and later in the smaller homes and cottages of the 18th century, the stair is of timber, winding irregularly around a newel with treads supported on bearers built into the masonry and mortised to the newel. There is some improvement in size and convenience as the 17th century progresses, although little in design, the stair at first being contained within the building, then taken shallowly into the thickness of the wall, and by mid-17th century projecting beyond the outer wall face in a semi-circular or, later, a square projection (Pl. 18c, d). No less than eight of these stair turrets were found in Hook Norton alone. Good stairs, with well-shaped newels, contained in projecting bays are seen in Council Lane, Deddington (Fig. 33), and at Manor Farm, Great Bourton (1685) (Fig. 63), ascending from the cellar to the attics. When projections rise to the level of the roof they are covered in the same way as the rest of the building, rounded projections being generally associated with thatched dwellings, probably because of the problems associated with roofing such forms in slate. Stone newel stairs are very rare, apart from those to basement cellars, the only example noted being at Cromwell Cottage, Hornton, where the lower nine steps are in stone. The elaboration of this stair and of other masonry details of this house, and of other dwellings in the same village, is no doubt due to the proximity to the important quarries here. In larger dwellings, stair projections of considerable height and dimension have been noted, as at Castle House, Deddington, and Shutford Manor, the latter rising through four floors around a built-up central newel, with solid baulk steps in oak, 5 feet wide.

These more elaborate forms of stair which occur in larger 17th-century manor-houses are rarely found in contemporary yeoman dwellings. The broad stair of *c*. 1690 in the Old Bakery, Lower Middleton Cheney, framed in straight flights around an open well, with shaped newels and flat balusters, is an exception for a house of its class, but is still of vernacular character. A more finely executed stair, of early-17th-century character, exists in the Old House, Avon Dassett (1679), with flat-shaped and pierced balusters, re-sited at the time of the 19th-century alterations; this is so much out of character with vernacular work that it almost certainly represents an introduction from a larger building. On the first-floor landing, above the well-shaped and broad newel-stair at Springfield House, Middleton Cheney (Pl. 19*b*), is a balustrade of similar character with flat balusters. The newel has a simple decorative capping, and the nosings are moulded, presenting an unusual degree of elaboration in such a building. The fine stairs of Warmington Manor and the Court House, Kings Sutton, are of similar character but larger in scale. A number of larger stairs with turned balusters occur at the end of the 17th century, but these are limited to the most important yeoman dwellings, as at The Mount, Hornton (Pl. 19*d*), and Williamscot Home Farm, with dog-gate at its foot. In the 18th century, more significance is given to the stair in the larger, sophisticated class of dwellings, and a fine open-well stair with elaborately turned balusters and decorative newel posts survives at Grove Farm, Warmington. Such stairs are all, however, exceptions to the simple, unpretentious newel-stairs which characterize the regional period of building.

Few exceptions have been recorded in the region to the usual plastered wall finish. Wall panelling is confined to the manor-houses and a few larger yeoman dwellings, including the parlour at Warkworth Farm, where there is a good overmantel dated 1658 (Fig. 79). Some similar work exists at the Garden House, Mollington. The detail does not, however, compare with the craftsmanship of such panelled rooms as in the ground floor of Prestcote Manor House, Cropredy, dated 1718. Fragments of wall painting, probably of 16th-century date, have been discovered in the attic of a much-altered small house at Clifton, just beyond the south-eastern boundary of the region, but this is a solitary instance.

The seeming similarity noted between the vernacular architecture of the Banbury Region and of the neighbouring Cotswolds, despite the obvious difference in the colour and character of the building stone, has led popular opinion to merge their identities, and since the 19th century the modifications which have been made to certain of

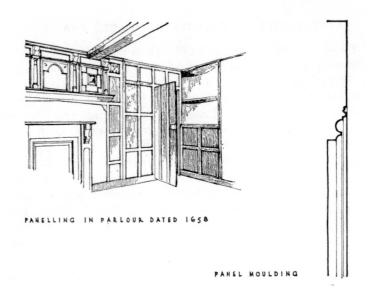

PANELLING IN PARLOUR DATED 1658

PANEL MOULDING

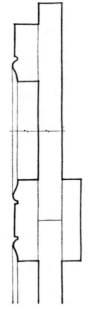

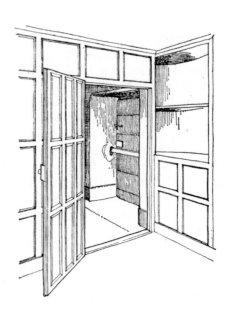

SECTION OF DOOR   ENTRANCE DOORWAY FROM THE PARLOUR

WARKWORTH FARM
WORKWORTH
NORTHAMPTONSHIRE

0 INCHES   6   12

FIG. 79.

the houses of the region have resulted in the introduction of many features which might be appropriate to the Cotswold zone but which are alien to the local tradition. There are in fact subtle differences at very many points; yet in the face of the details described above, it cannot be denied that architecturally the Banbury Region is markedly inferior not only to the Cotswolds but also to the neighbouring areas of Northamptonshire. Three clear conclusions can be derived from this study of detail within the region. Firstly, the shorter period of regional building activity in stone as compared with the Cotswolds is indicated by the virtual absence of 16th-century enrichment, whilst at the other end of the period there is a similar lack of the richer decorative quality of doors and façades found in Gloucestershire in the 18th century. Secondly, the poorer quality of the building stone, apart perhaps from that quarried in particular centres such as Hornton, as compared with the oolitic limestone, is seen in the simpler character of windows, the relatively few stone door-heads, and the absence of dormer windows, stone chimney-stacks and finials in all but the larger houses. There is moreover comparatively little evidence of any tradition of craftsmanship in iron or wood. These facts point to the third conclusion that the area around Banbury was less prosperous than the neighbouring regions of Northamptonshire and Gloucestershire; whilst sharing the economic vicissitudes of the Cotswolds, it did so with something of the subservience of a poor relation.

The larger manor-houses and great houses are properly beyond the scope of this work, but it is interesting to note that apart from scale, it is generally they which attain a quality more consistent with that associated with domestic architecture in general in the Cotswolds, with the use of stone slates, stone chimney stacks, dormer windows, bays and porches, together with dressed-stone doorheads and fireplaces and gable finials. All these are features which in the Cotswolds are common even to the smaller yeoman houses. It is also significant that within the Banbury Region, the finest quality in yeoman houses of the 17th century occurs in those areas on the north-east and south-west best placed to profit by the richer traditions of craftsmanship of their more-favoured neighbours.

CHAPTER XIII

THE REGIONAL PATTERN OF DEVELOPMENT

THE development of regional domestic architecture is closely related to the pattern of rural settlement, which in England falls generally into a two-fold classification. This includes firstly nucleated settlements, in which the homes of the peasantry are closely grouped into villages and hamlets, and secondly, dispersed settlements, where the community is wholly scattered over the countryside, with smaller nuclei around the churches and manors. These two forms, and their many variants, are closely related to the geographical, geological and economic background of the region, as well as to its political evolution. The nucleated settlement is common to the Midlands as a whole, and its form is particularly characterized in the rich cluster of large villages around Banbury, each growing up near to the sources of water at the head of small streams cut into the limestone.

It has been shown that in general the nucleated village is a settlement of ancient origin.[1] Such settlements are clearly related to soil fertility and water supply, and villages of similar character to those around Banbury, large, nucleated and closely spaced, can be found on land of similarly high fertility in such regions as Huntingdonshire, south Cambridgeshire, parts of Somerset and along the northern edge of Salisbury Plain.[2] The majority of villages around Banbury are known to be of pre-Conquest origin, and their names are recorded in Domesday.[3] Of their early foundations, the earliest evidence is provided by the churches, the first structures to attain architectural permanence, making use of the local stone with some importation of freestone.[4] Norman work can be seen in many of these structures, although most have been extensively rebuilt in the 14th century.[5]

[1] F. W. Maitland, *Domesday Book and Beyond,* 1897.

[2] F. W. Ledgar, *The Pattern, Structure and Character of Building Settlement in Rural England, 1550–1850,* Manchester University Thesis, p. 32.

[3] Adderbury is a typical instance of a pre-Conquest settlement, its name deriving from the Saxon Eadburgebyrig, the borough of Edburg. At Domesday it formed with Bloxham a Royal Manor (Alexander, *Oxfordshire Place Names*).

[4] In addition to imported freestone, local stone for Adderbury church was obtained from a quarry in the rectory garden, filled in when the building of the chancel was completed in 1418 (L. F. Salzmann, op. cit., p. 120).

[5] Hornton, Barford St. Michael and South Newington churches have retained the most extensive evidence of Norman work.

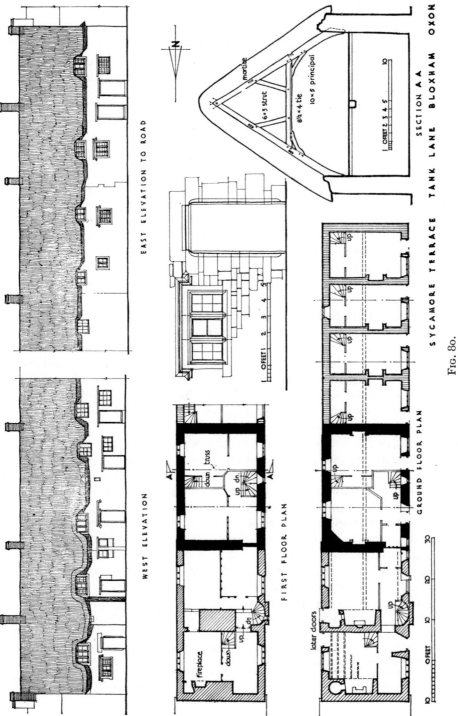

EAST ELEVATION TO ROAD

WEST ELEVATION

SECTION A A

mortice

6×3 strut

8½×4 tie

10×5 principal

O FEET 1 2 3 4 5

FIRST FLOOR PLAN

down truss

down

up dn

up

fireplace

GROUND FLOOR PLAN

up

up

up

up

later doors

up

O FEET 10 20 30

O FEET 1 2 3 4 5

SYCAMORE TERRACE · TANK LANE · BLOXHAM · OXON

Fig. 80.

Usually placed at the highest point of the village[1]—as is well seen at Warmington and Mollington, where the churches stand on eminences —they were usually closely adjoined by the manor-house, the next building in importance and in permanence. This relationship is still preserved in many of the villages including Kings Sutton (Pl. 1a), Deddington and Shutford.

Isolated farmsteads are occasionally to be found in the south-west of the region, of 17th-century date or earlier, as at Lodge Farm, Hook Norton, dated 1646. These rare instances are occasionally protected in their relative isolation by a moat, a number of such sites having been recorded, including Manor Farm, Barford St. Michael, Priory Farm, Clattercote, Prestcote Manor, Cropredy and possibly Castle End, Deddington. All are dwellings of manorial or equivalent status, to which the moated enclosure adds pretension. Considerations of security must, however, have been important even in the 18th century, when the notorious Culworth gang terrorized the region for nearly twenty years before finally being apprehended in 1787.

The architectural history of the region is one of the progressive conversion of timber-framed structures into stone, the whole process taking well over four centuries to descend from the manor-houses (13th–14th centuries) to the cottage (18th century). The timber-framed progenitors have largely been assumed, for apart from those few surviving structures noted in the 'lowland' part of the region, there is elsewhere nothing but the rare instance of a skeletal frame, now encased in stone walls. In the upland parts of the region, rough stone rubble walling might always have played an important part in the humbler structures, but if so, there is nothing surviving as evidence of this fact, nor is there the least indication of the use of any alternative building material, such as cohesive earth, which is known to have been used in south Oxfordshire.

The manor-houses were of course the first domestic structures to appear in stone, the earliest native examples having been noted at Cottisford and Swalcliffe, of 13th–14th-century date, whilst Leaden-porch House, Deddington (c. 1325) is a rare surviving structure below manorial rank, representing the beginnings of vernacular building before 1500. Apart from this, local history of domestic architecture begins with the 16th century. Yet still by 1600, there were

[1] The location of the church at the highest point of the village, and the dependence on wells and pumps for water supply, have been named as characteristics of hill villages; both features are common to the region (D. Sylvester, 'The Hill Villages of England and Wales', *Geog. Journal*, Vol. CX, 1947).

remarkably few stone vernacular buildings in the region. It was the century following, the 17th, that saw a spate of new building to house increasing populations, and whatever buildings had existed in timber prior to that period were almost comprehensively swept away, and substituted in stone on or near their former sites. The completeness with which the presumed timber buildings have disappeared, leaving scarcely a trace, warrants the assumption that they were of a poor quality, for in so many other parts of the country, old timber frameworks were quite frequently retained as the nuclei of new buildings. In the 17th century, the frail booths and hovels of the lowest social class do not come into the story at all as a class; their conversion into stone was not to begin until the next century.

The houses of the farming community grew up within the villages, along the village street, in back lanes and in cul-de-sacs which ran out into the open fields beyond. The sites were long and narrow, and the earliest houses—to judge by those few that have survived of pre-17th-century date—were invariably built parallel to the street, sometimes with a garden in front of the house.[1] The dwelling, particularly with the development of the long through-passage plan, would often extend across the whole width of the site, apart from a cartway at one end, and the passage itself provided access from the street to the yard. No consideration of orientation was given to these dwellings before 1600, the houses being disposed to follow the line of the street.

Behind the house lay the farmyard, flanked by farm buildings which are later linked with the house, the barn being generally at the back of the yard, usually lying parallel to the house. The croft or enclosed pasture, and an orchard would presumably complete the holding, and the strip would stretch out to the great fields which surrounded the village until the time of the 18th-century enclosures. Frail timber outhouses or hovels would be provided to house stores and implements, these being converted into more permanent form by the end of the 18th century. Farm buildings before 1700 seldom lie in line with the house, the long low ranges of buildings combining house and farm under a continuous roof being a characteristic of farms on open sites in such areas as Westmorland and the Pennines,

[1] The tradition of the cottage garden is well founded in history, and both flower and herb gardens appear to have been common in the 17th century. A record has been preserved of the flowers in bloom in the garden of 'Goodwife Cantrey', a Northamptonshire yeoman's wife in 1658. Amongst the plants listed are larkspur, sweet william, spiderwort, lupins in four colours—'the great blew, the little blue, the yellow and the white', scabious, marigolds, London pride and hollyhocks. Such practical additions as double fennel flower, camomile and white lilies, used for medicinal purposes, are also included (Northants. MSS. FH. 2452, quoted in Campbell, op. cit., p. 241).

where settlement is dispersed.[1] Information on the extent of the ancillary accommodation of the farm is available from documentary sources. A lease of 1562 for a messuage, tenement and lands in 'Stepheaston, otherwise Stepleaston [Steeple Aston] lately occupied by Robert Person and late of the Monastery of Bysseter' (Bicester Priory) includes a 'Wollhouse, Shepehouse, cowehouse, garden' in the property leased for twenty-one years to Ysabel Parsons, widow, and William Parsons, husbandman. A second wool-house is noted in Steeple Aston on a property formerly belonging to Cold Norton Priory in 1581, when 'John Harwardin lets to Henrye Bostock, merchant of the Staple, the woll-house new buylded by Henrye Bostock in the second year of Edward VI on a parcel of ground graunted and set-forth by lease . . . '[2]

Other buildings listed in these early inventories include the brewhouse and dairy.[3] Apart from the arrangement described at Shutford Manor, no outer kitchens, of the type recorded in Monmouthshire, and also noted by Hoskins in Wiltshire,[4] have been noted before the 18th century, when kitchens related to farm buildings adjacent to the house commonly occur, presumably serving the labourers who lived and slept in lofts over the farm buildings. Such a kitchen in the yard of Hornton Manor is illustrated in Pl. 16c.

By the beginning of the 17th century the village population was increasing rapidly, and together with the rebuilding in stone of earlier dwellings, new houses had to be provided for the increased size of the community. The new dwellings were all accommodated within the limits of the old village—land was too valuable to allow dwellings to encroach on the open fields, and sites could not be 'assarted from the waste' as in Monmouthshire.[5] Whilst older dwellings were rebuilt on their original sites, new houses had to be contrived in any open spaces within the village, encroaching on the green or the street itself, and producing a more compact grouping, with some houses now being planned at right angles to the road. The narrow sites would perhaps leave inadequate frontage for new three-unit houses, sometimes occasioning the new dwelling to be built with

[1] This form is also related to the highland 'long house' tradition (R. W. Brunskill, op. cit., pp. 137–9).
[2] Brasenose College S. A. Deeds, Nos. 13 and 15, quoted in C. C. Brookes, *History of Steeple Aston and Middle Aston*, p. 279.
[3] William Harrison noted that yeomen and gentlemen usually brewed sufficient for home consumption (*Description of England*, Vol. II, pp. 156–9).
[4] Surveys taken in Wiltshire in 1631–2 are noted by Hoskins as evidence that detached kitchens existed in the early 17th century in southern England (*The Midland Peasant*, p. 287).
[5] Op. cit., Vol. II, p. 69.

its gable to the road, a disposition which also gave greater privacy. It is probable that this arrangement was adopted because of site restrictions, which had similarly caused houses to be arranged in this way in the medieval towns. The association of the right-angle siting with the introduction of the 'lowland' type plan, having a single doorway, has been considered in Chapter VII.

A characteristic late-17th-century disposition and agglomeration of building is to be seen in the house called *The Glen, Hornton* (Fig. 81; Pl. 11*a*), and its neighbouring dwelling, a complex group of thatched structures which presents many interesting features. The deeds indicate that for much of its history, The Glen was a smithy, and this fact may account for its arrangement. Formerly of 'L' plan, the house comprises a hall or kitchen, at present entered from the road by a doorway in the gable, with a parlour at the rear, whilst adjoining the hall on the road frontage is a large room, reputed to be the smithy. This was probably of single-storey height, with a wide doorway to the road, but it has been raised and adapted in the 18th century to provide rooms on both floors with sash windows. A small dairy has been added on the opposite side of the hall, its lean-to roof extending the slope of the thatched roof of the hall block. There are large fireplaces in hall and parlour, and in the chamber over the hall, a good newel-stair enclosed behind doors, and original windows with flat-splayed stone mullions. Beyond the smithy is a through cart-way, also floored in the 18th century, with the insertion of a larger and later sliding-sash window to the first-floor chamber. This formerly appertained to a separate dwelling at the lower extremity of the range of building, a small two-unit house of similar date and character, placed end-on to the road, but very unusually arranged in that the long walls are gabled, giving a roof of exceptional length of slope towards the road.

The density of planning has led in a number of cases to so close a relationship of buildings—frequently adjoining, and sharing a common yard—as to suggest a kinship between the two dwellings. Proffits House, Hornton, appears to combine two periods of building within the 17th century, placing two houses in line, of three and one unit, sharing a common entrance passage onto which the fireplaces back on both sides. Approximately 20 feet distant behind the Joiner's Arms in Bloxham lies a second dwelling, of late 17th-century date, with the through-passages almost in line in the two houses. The Joiner's Arms has been described in Chapter IV, to illustrate the regional house of mid-16th-century date, and the second dwelling provides an interesting comparison, being equally characteristic of its respective stage of development in plan and structure (Fig. 82). A

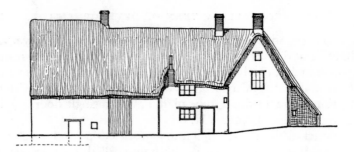

EAST ELEVATION

SOUTH ELEVATION

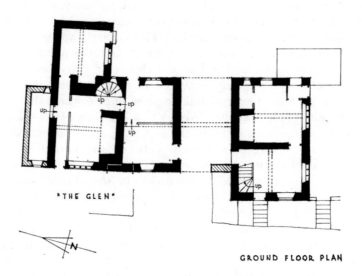

"THE GLEN"

N

GROUND FLOOR PLAN

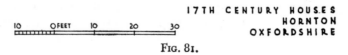

10   0 FEET   10   20   30

17TH CENTURY HOUSES
HORNTON
OXFORDSHIRE

FIG. 81.

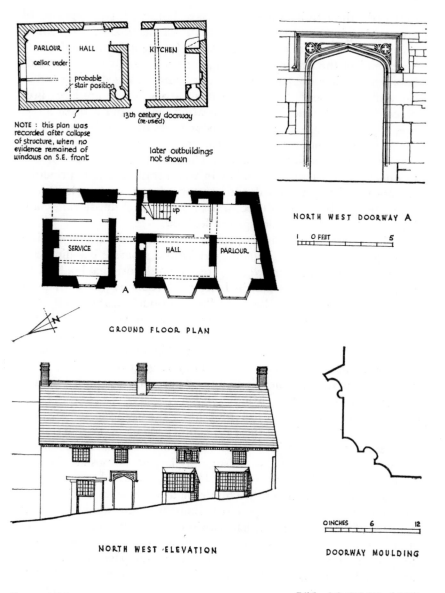

PARLOUR   HALL   KITCHEN

cellar under

probable
stair position

NOTE : this plan was
recorded after collapse
of structure, when no
evidence remained of
windows on S.E. front

13th century doorway
(re-used)

later outbuildings
not shown

SERVICE   up   HALL   PARLOUR

A

N

GROUND FLOOR PLAN

NORTH WEST DOORWAY A

1   0 FEET   5

NORTH WEST ELEVATION

DOORWAY MOULDING

0 INCHES   6   12

10   0 FEET   10   · 20   30

THE JOINERS ARMS
BLOXHAM OXFORDSHIRE

FIG. 82.

thatched, three-unit, through-passage house of two storeys, of greater height but smaller area than its neighbour, its plan is reversed in relation to the Joiner's Arms, having its 'upper end' at the lower end of the site in order to include a cellar at lower ground-floor level, below the parlour, the stair being arranged at this end of the building to serve from basement to attics. There are large fireplaces in kitchen and hall, incorporating ovens, and a small angle fireplace in the parlour, whilst the floor-beam over the kitchen spans across the building in contrast to the earlier form of the spine-beam adopted in the 16th-century house. The later house has wood lintels to openings and metal casements in wood frames; for its principal entrance, a finely moulded 13th-century doorway of ecclesiastical character has been introduced, one of several such medieval details incorporated in later buildings in Bloxham.

The relationship of family groups which such siting suggests is a practice widespread in England and Wales, separate dwellings for members of the same family being erected on the original holding. In addition, Hoskins notes that in Leicestershire many 'an old man or old woman had "his Parlour" or "her Parlour" in the house, and here they rested in quiet among a few possessions while the rest of the ancestral house was given up to a son and his wife and the clamour of another infant generation'. The 'house within a house' is also defined in Monmouthshire, and in the Banbury Region provides an alternative explanation for the self-contained parlour wings added to such dwellings as The Gables, Middleton Cheney (Fig. 62).

The hearth tax returns of 1665 have already been noted; they enable the composition of the 17th-century village to be determined with some accuracy.[1] The small village of Williamscot submitted eleven returns, and the two, presumably largest, houses are those of William Taylor, Yeoman, with six hearths, and another with three hearths. Of the remainder, five houses had two hearths and four had only one. In a larger village, Great Bourton, there were thirty-four returns, of which seventeen had two fireplaces, fifteen had one and fourteen had three, whilst one large house had as many as thirteen fireplaces. Among those dwellings exempted for poverty, a number are to be found with two hearths. It is clear that one-hearth houses were by no means all cottages, but often were the homes of smaller husbandmen, tradesmen and craftsmen, and it has also been shown that fine workmanship does not depend on the size of the house, as in many of the dwellings described in Chapter VIII.[2] Apart from the

---

[1] M. B. Weinstock, *Hearth Tax Returns for Oxfordshire*, 1665, op. cit.
[2] This conclusion is also reached with regard to building in Monmouthshire

yeomen, husbandmen and cottagers, engaged primarily in farming pursuits, the larger communities at this time would include the homes of many tradesmen and craftsmen, the smith, the carpenter and the wheelwright, the miller, the baker and the innkeeper. All would combine their craft or trade with the working of a small-holding, and little variation is likely in the form of their dwellings from the usual farm-house types. Many inns[1] have been preserved in the region but there is less evidence of such other important buildings of the village as the windmills and watermills[2] and the court-houses.[3]

The Account Book of Sir Richard Temple, Lord of the Manor of Burton Dassett, Warwickshire, has revealed a valuable picture of the pattern of parochial society within the region from 1660 to 1665.[4] Farmers, of greater and lesser importance, are named, together with many other members of the community including Thomas Basse, blacksmith, who made ironwork for doors as well as horse-shoes; John Basse, mason; William Whithead, carpenter, who earned a daily wage from 1s. to 1s. 2d., and also served in the Militia; the millwright, the miller, the farrier, the carrier; these and many others occupied the regional houses in the villages around Banbury. To their dwellings, and the manor-houses were occasionally added in the 17th and 18th centuries fine houses built by rich merchants. The Rookery, Adderbury West, a house of unusually fine architectural quality, with two-storeyed porch, dated 1656, is such a house, reputed to have been built by a member of the banking family of Montague.

The spate of new building declined at the end of the 17th century, and after 1700 buildings were more frequently altered than rebuilt, as a declining economy restricted the incentive and the wherewithal for entirely new building. The decline in the number of larger farm-houses being built in the 18th century was accompanied

---

(op. cit., Vol. II, p. 45). Hoskins cites the case of a Wiltshire farmer of a fifty-four-acre farm who occupied a house of one room in 1631–2 with loft over, the barn and hay house each being larger than the dwelling. A neighbour, on the other hand, farming under forty acres, had a dwelling house of five ground-floor rooms, each one lofted over (*Surveys of the Manor of Philip, first Earl of Pembroke and Montgomery, 1631–2*, Wiltshire Archaeological and Natural History Society, 1953, quoted in Hoskins, op. cit., p. 289).

[1] In Shotteswell, the Flying Horse Inn dates from the 17th century, and is of courtyard plan.

[2] A wooden post-mill, reputed to be of 16th-century date, survived at Burton Dassett until destroyed by fire in 1946. There are also a number of water mills in the valley bottoms, mostly of later date but presumably replacing earlier buildings.

[3] The Court House at Kings Sutton has been described and a second court house remains at Bloxham.

[4] E. C. Westacott, *Some Account of the Parish of Burton Dassett, Warwickshire,* Trans. Birmingham Archaeological Society, Vol. LX, 1936.

U

by a relative increase in the building of the smaller dwellings, as the cottage of the labourer at last found permanent form, frequently reproducing the characteristics of the earlier yeoman houses.[1] Dated structures after 1700 are evenly distributed throughout the region, as shown in the distribution map (Fig. 83), but these are generally the better class of dwelling, and the greater part of the 18th-century small-house building is to be seen in the larger settlements, in particular those near Banbury, whose industrial activities and prosperity they shared to some degree. At the end of the century the enclosure of the common fields by Parliamentary decree, to promote greater efficiency and production, was followed by the growth of large landed estates and an extension of tenant farming, with consequent hardship among the lesser members of the farming community.

An account of Deddington in 1795 reveals something of the impact of these inclosures on the community, Deddington itself not being inclosed until 1808:[2]

The high Rates, in this parish (Deddington) are ascribed to the common-field, of which the land principally consists; whereas the neighbouring parishes have been inclosed many years, and many small farms in them have been consolidated; so that many small farmers, with little capitals, have been obliged, either to turn labourers, or to precure small farms in Deddington, or other parishes, that possess common field. Besides this, the neighbouring parishes are, many of them, possessed by a few individuals, who are cautious in permitting newcomers to obtain a settlement.

The general opinion here, is that canals are a great injury to the Poor, by enabling farmers to send their corn abroad. . . . A boat laden with flour was lately seized by the populace, but was restored, on the miller's promising to sell it at a reduced price.

The same account includes a description of Deddington:

This parish contains, by estimation, 4000 acres. The number of houses that pay the window-tax is 102; the number exempted near 300. The inhabitants . . . are mostly employed in agriculture. There are ten inns, or ale-houses in the parish; the number, a few years ago, was 21. . . . The principal articles of cultivation are wheat, barley and beans. There are about 45 acres of common in the parish.

Many fine manors and yeoman houses of the 17th century and earlier declined socially from this time and ended their days by being

[1] 'Simple plans, common among well-to-do members of the community in medieval times tend to survive in the post-medieval dwellings of the crofter or landless labourer' (Fox and Raglan, op. cit.).
[2] F. M. Eden, *The State of the Poor*, 1797, pp. 589, 591.

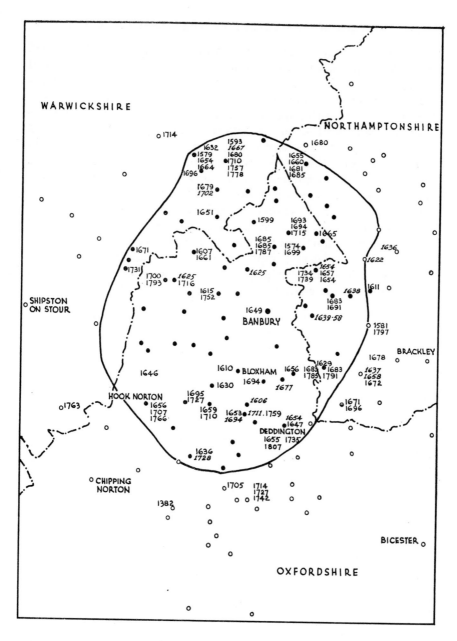

Dates in italics indicate 'lowland' plan houses - *1657*

● Predominantly Marlstone villages.

— Boundary of Region

-·- County boundaries.

I 0 MILES   5

THE BANBURY REGION
DISTRIBUTION OF DATED BUILDINGS
Fig. 83.

subdivided into single-cell cottages, whilst the village streets changed their appearance with the building of cottage terraces at the end of the century, infilling between earlier detached dwellings. Sycamore Terrace, Bloxham (Fig. 80), which has already been noted as giving evidence of 16th and 17th-century building, is also an illustration of this final phase in the pattern of development. The two original houses have each been sub-divided as cottages and extended in a terrace of small single-unit dwellings, providing homes for weavers. By virtue of the continued use of marlstone and thatch the whole block preserves a singularly uniform and homogeneous character despite the extension of its building period for over 250 years.

In cottage building such as made up this terrace, the regional tradition was maintained throughout the 19th century, and despite recent depredations and improvements, the Banbury Region today preserves in its compact villages, its brownstone walls and thatched roofs, much of the character of the regional style of its prime.

DATED STRUCTURES

DATE	LOCATION	Class	2-unit	3-unit	4- & complex	cellar	'upland'	'lowland'	storeys	concave	flat splay	ovolo	casement	transomed	sash	wood	stone	4-centred	flat	thatch	stone slate	blue slate
			PLAN						**Ht.**	**Mullions**			**Wood Windows**			**Lintels**		**Door Heads**		**Roof**		
1382	Church Enstone Tithe Barn																					
1579	Northend	SH	*				*		2											*		
1581	Farthinghoe Abbey Lodge	LH			*		*		2½				*			*		*			*	
1593	Fenny Compton	LH			*				2½	*											*	
1599	Mollington Date-stone on barn at Manor House																					
1606	Barford St. John Manor Farm	SH	*					*	2½	*			*								*	
1607	Hornton Manor House	LH		*			*		2½	*											*	
1610	Bloxham Doorway in churchyard																		*			
1611	Marston St. Lawrence Manor House	LH							2½													
1615	Wroxton Abbey	GH			*	*			3	*		*									*	
1622	Thorpe Mandeville Three Conies Inn	SH		*				*	2½				*			*					*	
1624	Adderbury West	SH							2												*	
1625	Alkerton Old Rectory	SH	*					*	2½	*								c			*	
1625	Hanwell	SH	*					*	2				*			*					*	
1629	Kings Sutton	LH																				
1630	Milcombe Reused doorway																	*				
1632	Little Dassett Priest's House	SH							1½	*										*	*	
1636	Great Tew	SH	*						2	*											*	
1636	Sulgrave Dial House	SH	*					*	2½	*						*				*		
1637	Charlton	SH	*			*		*	2½							*				*		
1638	Thenford	SH		*				*	2				*			*				*		
1639	Warkworth Date on barn at Warkworth Farm																					
1646	Hook Norton Lodge Farm	SH			*	*	*		2½	*											*	

DATE	LOCATION	Class	2-unit	3-unit	4- & complex	cellar	'upland'	'lowland'	storeys	concave	flat splay	ovolo	casement	transomed	sash	wood	stone	4-centred	flat	thatch	stone slate	blue slate
1647	DEDDINGTON Castle End	SH		*			*		$2\frac{1}{2}$			*						c			*	
1649	BANBURY Vicarage	LH		*			*		$2\frac{1}{2}$	*								*			*	
1651	WARMINGTON	SH	*				*		$2\frac{1}{2}$	*											*	
1653	BARFORD ST. MICHAEL Addition to The Old Turnstiles	SH					*		$2\frac{1}{2}$	*								*			*	
1654	CHACOMBE Poplars Farm	SH	*				*		$2\frac{1}{2}$	*	*		*			*					*	
1654	CHACOMBE Chacombe House Lodge	SH		*				*	$2\frac{1}{2}$	*			*			*					*	
1654	NORTHEND Manor Farm	SH		*		*		*	$2\frac{1}{2}$	*										*		
1654	DEDDINGTON Castle House	LH			*	*		*	$2\frac{1}{2}$	*											*	
1655	LOWER BODDINGTON	SH		*			*		$2\frac{1}{2}$	*											*	
1655	DEDDINGTON School House	SH	*			*	*		$2\frac{1}{2}$		*		*			*					*	
1656	ADDERBURY EAST The Rookery	LH		*		*			$2\frac{1}{2}$	*	*										*	
1656	HOOK NORTON Manor House	LH		*		*			$2\frac{1}{2}$	*											*	
1657	CHACOMBE Chinners Farm added Parlour	SH							$2\frac{1}{2}$		*					*					*	
1658	CHARLTON	SH	*			*		*	$2\frac{1}{2}$	*											*	
1658	WARKWORTH Warkworth Farm	SH		*				*	$2\frac{1}{2}$	*			*			*		*			*	
1659	S. NEWINGTON College Farm	SH		*					$2\frac{1}{2}$	*											*	
1660	LOWER BODDINGTON Manor House	LH		*				*	$2\frac{1}{2}$	*	*											
1661	HORNTON	SH																*				
1664	NORTHEND Manor House	LH			*	*			$2\frac{1}{2}$	*											*	
1665	WARDINGTON Manor House	LH			*								*								*	
1667	FENNY COMPTON extended in 1680	SH	*			*		*	$2\frac{1}{2}$	*											*	
1671	LOWER TYSOE	SH	*						$2\frac{1}{2}$											*	*	
1671	AYNHO Old Grammar School											*										
1672	CHARLTON Walnut Tree Farm	SH				*			$2\frac{1}{2}$	*											*	
1677	ADDERBURY WEST	SH	*			*		*	$2\frac{1}{2}$	*											*	
1678	HINTON IN THE HEDGES Rectory	LH		*		*	*		$2\frac{1}{2}$	*											*	
1679	AVON DASSETT The Old House	SH		*			*		$2\frac{1}{2}$	*								*				

DATE	LOCATION	Class	PLAN						Ht.	Mullions			Wood Windows			Lintels		Door Heads		Roof		
			2-unit	3-unit	4- & complex	cellar	'upland'	'lowland'	storeys	concave	flat splay	ovolo	casement	transomed	sash	wood	stone	4-centred	flat	thatch	stone slate	blue slate
1680	FENNY COMPTON Two-unit extension to house built 1667	SH							2½	*											*	
1681	LOWER BODDINGTON	SH		*			*		2½	*											*	
1683	KINGS SUTTON	SH		*			*		2½				*			*					*	
1683	KINGS SUTTON Kings Sutton Farm	SH							2½	*												
1683	LOWER MIDDLETON CHENEY Middleton Farm	SH							2½	*												
1685	GREAT BOURTON Friars Cottage	SH	*				*		2½	*									*	*		
1685	GREAT BOURTON Manor Farm	SH	*			*	*		2½	*									*	*		
1685	LOWER BODDINGTON Old House Farm	SH			*				2½	*										*		
1691	LOWER MIDDLETON CHENEY Lexton House	SH		*		*	*		2½	*												
1693	CROPREDY Old Manor House extensions	LH							2½					*		*			*	*		
1694	CROPREDY	SH		*			*		2½				*			*				*		
1694	MILTON	SH	*			*			2½	*	*									*		
1694	BARFORD	SH		*					2½				*				*			*		
1695	WIGGINTON	SH	*				*		2½	*			*			*				*		
1696	BURTON DASSETT Vicarage	SH																				
1696	AYNHO	SH	*										*									
1699	WILLIAMSCOT Home Farm House	SH		*		*	*		2½	*			*			*				*		
1700	SHENINGTON	SH	*						2½				*				*			*		
1702	AVON DASSETT	SH		*				*	2½	*									*	*		
1705	SANDFORD ST. MARTIN (transomed windows)	LH			*				2½	*				*					*		*	
1707	HOOK NORTON	LH			*				2½					*			*				*	
1710	FENNY COMPTON Red Lion Inn	SH		*					2½													
1710	S. NEWINGTON Newton House	SH	*			*	*		2½	*			*			*					*	
1711	BARFORD ST. MICHAEL	SH	*					*	2½				*			*				*		
1714	GAYDON Mary Knoll Cottage	SH	*				*		2½				*			*				*		
1714	MIDDLE BARTON	SH	*				*		2					*			*			*		
1715	CROPREDY Old Manor House extensions	LH							2½					*		*						
1716	ALKERTON Homestead Cottage	SH	*				*		2				*				*		*	*		
1721	SHENINGTON Mizpah Cottage rebuilt in 1793	SH																				

DATE	LOCATION	Class	2-unit	3-unit	4+ & complex	cellar	'upland'	'lowland'	storeys	concave	flat splay	ovolo	casement	transomed	sash	wood	stone	4-centred	flat	thatch	stone slate	blue slate
1727	Wigginton Dolphin Inn	SH		*		*	*		2½	*			*					*		*	*	
1727	Middle Barton	SH	*						2				*					*	*		*	
1728	Great Tew	SH	*					*	2½				*					*			*	
1731	Upper Tysoe Date-stone reused	SH																				
1734	Chacombe George & Dragon Inn added kitchen	SH																				
1735	Deddington School House added wing	SH							2				*			*						
1739	Chacombe	SH		*			*		2½				*			*					*	
1742	Middle Barton	SH	*						2					*			*	*			*	
1750	Barford St. Michael Glebe Cottage	SH	*						2½	*											*	
1752	Wroxton Post Office	SH	*						2				*					*	*		*	
1757	Fenny Compton	SH		*			*		2½				*			*					*	
1763	Long Compton	SH	*						2⅔				*				*				*	
1766	Hook Norton	SH	*						2½						*		*	*	*			
1778	Fenny Compton	SH	*						2						*		*	*				*
1785	Kings Sutton Reused date-stone																					
1785	Kings Sutton	SH	*						2½				*			*					*	
1787	Great Bourton Spittals Farm added kitchen								1				*			*						
1791	Kings Sutton	Cot	*						1½				*			*					*	
1793	Shenington Mizpah Cottage rebuilt after fire	SH	*						2½				*			*					*	
1797	Farthinghoe Added kitchen	SH							2				*			*						*
1807	Deddington Cottage terrace	Cot							2				*			*					*	

Note: Classification is by social class;

    GH—Great house

    LH—Manor-houses and mansions

    SH—All smaller dwellings other than cottages

    Cot—Cottages

      c—Cambered arch

POPULATION OF THE DISTRICT COMPRISED WITHIN THE BANBURY POOR LAW UNION, JUNE 7TH, 1841

THE district comprised within the Banbury Poor Law Union represents the greater part of the Banbury Region, and provides the only known political definition of the area. The population figures are here included as an indication of the relative sizes of the settlements at the end of the survey period.

1. *Northern Division of Banbury Hundred, Oxfordshire*

	Persons
BANBURY borough	3,736
The Gaol there	10
Neithorpe, Calthorp, Wickham, Hardwick, and Easington—Township in the Parish of Banbury	2,850
CLATTERCOT—Extraparochial	15
CROPREDY—Parish	547
Great Bourton and Little Bourton—Township in the Parish of Cropredy	593
Claydon—Chapelry in the Parish of Cropredy	337
Prescot—Township in the Parish of Cropredy	19
Wardington with Williamscot—Chapelry; and Coton—Hamlet; in the Parish of Cropredy	865
SWALCLIFFE—Parish	338
Epwell—Chapelry in the Parish of Swalcliffe	316
Shutford East—Chapelry in the Parish of Swalcliffe	31
Shutford West—Township in the Parish of Swalcliffe	418

2. *Bloxham Hundred, Oxfordshire*

ADDERBURY EAST—Parish	1,050
Adderbury West—Township in the Parish of Adderbury East	442
Barford St. John—Chapelry in the Parish of Adderbury East	126
Bodicot—Chapelry in the Parish of Adderbury East	729
Milton—Township in the Parish of Adderbury East	168
ALKERTON—Parish	190
BLOXHAM—Parish	1,319
Milcombe—Chapelry in the Parish of Bloxham	224
BROUGHTON—Parish	181
North Newington—Township in the Parish of Broughton	448

CROPREDY, part of, namely:
That portion of Mollington Chapelry which is in the County of
Oxford 283
DRAYTON—Parish 206
HANWELL—Parish 297
HORLEY, with:
Associated Parishes 425
HORNTON 592
SWALCLIFFE, part of, namely:
Sibford Ferris, Townships, forming together 287
Sibford Gower, the District of Sibford 534
TADMARTON—Parish 404
WIGGINTON—Parish 369
WROXTON—Parish, with:
Balscott—Chapelry in the Parish of Wroxton 819

3. *Part of Wootton Hundred, Oxfordshire*

BARFORD ST. MICHAEL—Parish 370
SOUTH NEWINGTON—Parish 434

4. *Part of Chadlington Hundred, Oxfordshire*

HOOK NORTON—Parish 1,422
The Lunatic Asylum there 103

5. *Part of Sutton Hundred, Northamptonshire*

CHACOMBE—Parish 488
MIDDLETON CHENEY—Parish 1,410
WARKWORTH—Parish; together with:
Grimsbury, Hamlets in the Parish of Nethercot, Banbury 655

6. *Part of Wardon Hundred, Northamptonshire*

ASTON-LE-WALLS—Parish 160
Appletree—Township in the Parish of Aston-le-Walls 92
BODDINGTON, LOWER—Parish 324
Boddington, Upper—Township in the Parish of Lower
Boddington 351
CHIPPING WARDON—Parish 545

7. *Part of the Burton Dassett Division of Kineton Hundred,
Warwickshire*

AVON DASSETT—Parish 287
FARNBOROUGH—Parish 367
CROPREDY, part of, namely:
That portion of Mollington Chapelry which is in the County of
Warwick 102

TOTALS

Houses —Inhabited		5,935
	Uninhabited	265
	Building	36
Persons—Males		14,214
	Females	14,317
	Total	28,531

BIBLIOGRAPHY

SOCIAL HISTORY—GENERAL

Beresford, M., *The Lost Villages of England*. 1954.
Campbell, M., *The English Yeoman*. 1957.
Fox, Sir Cyril, *The Personality of Britain*. 1943.
Fussell, G. E., *The English Rural Labourer*. 1949.
Hoskins, W. G., *The Rebuilding of Rural England, 1570–1640*. Past & Present, No. 4, 1953.
   The Midland Peasant. 1957.
Martin, E. W. *The Secret People*. 1954.

VERNACULAR ARCHITECTURE—GENERAL

Addy, S. O., *The Evolution of the English House*. 1933.
Allmark, K., 'Post-Medieval Timber-Framed Houses in England'. Manchester University Thesis, 1955.
Atkinson, T. D., *Local Style in English Architecture*. 1948.
Batsford, H., and Fry, C., *The English Cottage*. 1938.
Crossley, F. H., *Timber Building in England*. 1951.
Innocent, C. F., *Development of English Building Construction*. 1916.
Lloyd, N., *History of the English House*. 1931.
Parker, J. H., and Turner, H., *Domestic Architecture in England, 1851–9*.
Salzmann, L. F., *Building in England down to 1540*.
Seebohm, M. E., *The Evolution of the English Farm*. 1927.
Walton, J., 'The Development of Cruck Framework'. *Antiquity*, Dec. 1948.
   'Hog-Back Tombstones and the Anglo-Danish House'. *Antiquity*, June 1954.
Wood, M., *13th Century Domestic Architecture in England*. 1950.

VERNACULAR ARCHITECTURE—REGIONAL STUDIES

Barley, M. W., *The English Farmhouse and Cottage*. 1961.
Broadbent, A., and Minoprio, A., *Minor Architecture of Gloucestershire*. 1931.
Brunskill, R. W., 'Traditional Domestic Architecture in the Eden Valley'. Manchester University Thesis, 1952.
Davie, W. G., and Dawber, E. C., *Old Cottages, Farmhouses, Etc., in the Cotswold District*. 1905.
Fox, Sir Cyril, and Lord Raglan, *Monmouthshire Houses*. 1951.
Long, E. T., 'Medieval Domestic Architecture in Oxfordshire. *Oxfordshire Archaeological Society Reports*, Nos. 84, 85—1938–9.
Marsden, T. L., 'Traditional Domestic Architecture in the Lower Trent Valley'. Manchester University Thesis, 1952.
O'Neil, B. H. St. J., *Some Seventeenth Century Houses in Great Yarmouth*. 1953.
Pantin, W. A., 'The Development of Domestic Architecture in Oxford'. *The Antiquaries Journal*, Vol. XXVII, 1947.
Peate, I. O., *The Welsh House*. 1944.
Spokes, P. S., and Jope, E. M., 'The "Priory", Marcham, Berkshire'. *The Berkshire Archaeological Journal*, Vol. LVII, 1959.

Walton, J. H., 'Cruck-Framed Buildings of Yorkshire. *Trans. Yorkshire Archaeological Society*, Vol. XXXVII, 1948.

Webster, V. R., 'Cruck-Framed Buildings of Leicestershire'. *Trans. Leicestershire Archaeological Society*, 1954.

Worsley, G. L., 'Traditional Domestic Architecture in the Cotswold Region'. Manchester University Thesis, 1956.

THE BANBURY REGION—GEOLOGY

Arkell, W. J., *Oxford Stone*. 1947.

British Regional Geology, *London and Thames Valley*.

Howe, J. A., *The Geology of Building Stones*. 1910.

Hull, E., *Memoirs of the Geological Survey*. 1859.

Victoria County Histories for Oxfordshire, Northamptonshire and Warwickshire.

THE BANBURY REGION—CONTEMPORARY ACCOUNTS

Dugdale, W., *History of Warwickshire*. 1730.

Eden, Sir F. M., *The State of the Poor*. 1797.

Herbert, George (Ed. Cheney, C. S.), *Shoemaker's Window*. 1948.

Hobson, T. F., *Adderbury 'Rectoria'*. Oxford Record Society, 1940.

Lewis, Richard, *General View of the Agriculture of the County of Oxford*. 1794.

Morton, J., *Natural History of Northamptonshire*. 1712.

Norden, John, *A History of Northamptonshire in the Year 1610*.

Plot, Robert, *Natural History of Oxfordshire*. 1676.

Skelton, Joseph, *The Antiquities of Oxfordshire*. 1823.

Weinstock, M. B. (Ed.), *Hearth Tax Returns for Oxfordshire, 1665*. Oxford Record Society, 1940.

Wood, Anthony à, *Life and Times*. Oxford Historical Society, Vol. XIX, 1891.

Woodward, *Progress Reports of Warden Woodward round the Oxfordshire Estates of New College, Oxford, 1659–1675*. Oxford Record Society, 1945.

Young, Arthur, *View of the Agriculture of Oxfordshire*.

THE BANBURY REGION—LOCAL HISTORY

Alexander, H., *Place-Names of Oxfordshire*. 1912.

Beesley, Alfred, *The History of Banbury*. 1841.

Blomfield, J. C., *History of Upper and Lower Heyford*.

Dickens, M., *A History of Hook Norton*. 1928.

Gepp, H. J., *Adderbury*. 1924.

Henderson, M. S., *Three Centuries in North Oxfordshire*.

Hilton, R. H., *Social Structure of Rural Warwickshire in the Middle Ages*. Dugdale Society Occasional Papers No. 9, 1950.

Jordan, J., *Parochial History of Enstone*. 1857.

Leeds, E. T., 'Early Settlement in the Upper Thames Basin', *Geography*, Vol. 14.

Marshall, E., 'Historical and Descriptive Notes of the Parish of Deddington'. *Trans. North Oxfordshire Archaeological Society*, Vol. XIV, 1878.

Metcalf, G., *Some Account of Broughton and North Newington*. 1893.

Westacott, E. C., 'Some Account of the Parish of Burton Dassett, Warwickshire'. *Trans. Birmingham Archaeological Society*, Vol. LX, 1936.

INDEX

(a) Kings Sutton, Northamptonshire (p. 280).

(b) The Old Rectory, Alkerton, Oxfordshire. 1625 (p. 151).

PLATE I

(*a*) Swalcliffe Manor. Doors to service
rooms. 13th century (p. 25).

(*b*) The Leadenporch House,
Deddington. *c*. 1300 (p. 31).

(*c–d*) Grange Farm, Balscott. *c*. 1500 (p. 49).

PLATE 2. MEDIEVAL DETAILS

(*a*) Priory Farm, Balscott, Oxfordshire. 14th–18th centuries (pp. 42, 221).

(*b*) The Court House, Kings Sutton. *c.* 1500 (p. 235).

PLATE 3

(a) Manor Farm, Barford St. John. 1606 (p. 146).

(b) Chinners Farm, Chacombe. c. 1500 (p. 37).

PLATE 4

(*a*) Blue Gates, Bloxham, Oxfordshire. *c.* 1550 (p. 59).

(*b*) Cromwell Cottage, Hornton, Oxfordshire. *c.* 1615 (p. 84).

PLATE 5

(a) Rectorial Barn, Church Enstone.
1382 (p. 15).

(b) House at Kings Sutton. c. 1550
(p. 57).

(c) Cottisford Manor Farm. 16th-century roof (pp. 24, 64).

PLATE 6. REGIONAL TIMBER STRUCTURE

(*a*) Shutford Manor House, Oxfordshire. *c.* 1580 (p. 72).

(*b*) Priory Farm, Balscott. Hall roof.
14th century (p. 48).

(*c*) Lodge Farm, Hook Norton. 1646
(p. 136).

PLATE 7. REGIONAL TIMBER STRUCTURE

(*a*) Abbey Lodge, Farthinghoe. 1581 (p. 82).

(*b*) Kings Sutton Manor. *c.* 1650
(p. 253).

(*c*) Hook Norton Manor. 1656
(p. 265).

(*d*) Lower Boddington Manor. 1660 (p. 252).

PLATE 8. LARGE HOUSES OF THE BANBURY REGION

Copyright 'Country Life'

(*a*) Castle House, Deddington. 13th century and 1654 (p. 164).

(*b*) Castle End, Deddington. *c.* 1500, 1646 and 18th century (pp. 36, 222).

PLATE 9

(*a*) The Mount, Hornton, Oxfordshire. *c.* 1680 (p. 118).

(*b*) Lodge Farm, Hook Norton, Oxfordshire. 1646 (p. 134).

PLATE 10

(*a*) The Glen, Hornton, 17th century (p. 283).

(*b*) The Old Turnstiles, Barford St. Michael. *c.* 1600 and 1653 (p. 167).

(*c*) House at Adderbury East. *c.* 1650 (p. 175).

PLATE 11

(a) House at Hook Norton. *c.* 1710 (p. 192).

(b) Mary Knoll Cottage, Gaydon. 1714 (p. 196).

(c) Manor Farm, Claydon, Oxfordshire. *c.* 1720 (p. 189).

(d) Clifton's Farm, Great Tew. 1728 (p. 192).

(e) House at Fenny Compton. 1778 (p. 202).

PLATE 12. 18TH-CENTURY HOUSES

(*a*) Grove Farm, Warmington, Warwickshire. *c.* 1700 (p. 202).

(*b*) House in Silver Street,
Chacombe. *c.* 1710 (p. 190).

(*c*) House at Shotteswell. *c.* 1750
(p. 200).

PLATE 13. 18TH-CENTURY HOUSES

(*a*) Egge Cottage, Edge Hill, Warwickshire. 1774 (p. 199).

(*b*) Cottage Pair at Radway. *c.* 1780
(p. 199).

(*c*) Cottage at Hook Norton. *c.* 1700
(p. 194).

PLATE 14. 18TH-CENTURY COTTAGES

(*a*) House at Hook Norton. 17th century and 1707 (p. 217).

(*b*) Cropredy Old Manor House. *c.* 1650, 1693 and 1715 (p. 218).

(*c*) Sunnyside Cottage, Swerford. *c.* 1630 and 18th century (p. 90).

PLATE 15. THE PROCESS OF IMPROVEMENT

(a) Thatched oven at Charlton (p. 272).

(b) Stone-slated oven at Hook Norton (p. 272).

(c) Detached kitchen at Hornton Manor. 18th century (p. 282).

(d) Oven at Alkerton Old Rectory. 1625 (pp. 152, 272).

PLATE 16. BREAD-OVENS

(*a*) Swalcliffe Manor. Chamber Fireplace, 16th century (pp. 25, 274).

(*b*) Kitchen fireplace in house behind Joiner's Arms, Bloxham (p. 286).

(*c*) Sycamore Terrace, Bloxham. Chamber fireplace, *c.* 1625 (p. 92).

PLATE 17. FIREPLACE DETAILS

(a) House in Lower Boddington, 1655 (p. 254).

(b) Lexton House, Lower Middleton Cheney. 1691 (pp. 112, 220).

(c) House to south of Church, Bloxham. c. 1640 (p. 99).

(d) Homestead Cottage, Alkerton. 1716 (p. 194).

PLATE 18

(a) McGreal's Farmhouse, Milton.
c. 1640 (p. 93).

(b) Springfield House, Middleton
Cheney. 1668 (pp. 129, 275).

(c) Court House, Kings Sutton. late
16th century (p. 235).

(d) The Mount, Hornton. c. 1680
(p. 118).

PLATE 19   STAIR DETAILS

(a) Hall window, Warmington
Manor. c. 1603 (p. 78).

(b) George and Dragon, Chacombe.
Gable windows. c. 1690 (p. 214).

(c) House in Chapel Street, Bloxham.
c. 1655 (p. 124).

(d) Gable window, Farley's Farm,
Lr. Middleton Cheney. c. 1680 (p. 157).

(e) Court House, Kings Sutton. Oak-
framed window, late 16th century
(pp. 235, 261).

(f) Poplar's Farm, Chacombe. 1654
(pp. 121, 252).

PLATE 20. WINDOW DETAILS

(a) Cropredy Old Manor House. Datestone, 1693 (p. 218).

(b) Warkworth Farm Barn. Datestone, 1639 (p. 155).

(c) The Mount, Hornton. Stair window (p. 120).

(d) House in Shutford (p. 255).

(e) Warkworth House Barn. Kneeler, 17th century (p. 271).

(f) Avon Dassett. Kneeler, 1702 (p. 186).

PLATE 21. DECORATIVE FEATURES

(a) The Dolphin Inn, Wigginton.
1727 (p. 186).

(b) The Old Bakehouse, Bodicote.
1740 (p. 264).

(c) Home Farm, Middle Aston
(p. 263).

(d) Home Farm House, Williamscot.
1699 (p. 112).

PLATE 22. WINDOW DETAILS

(a) Sycamore Terrace, Bloxham.
c. 1625 (p. 92).

(b) The Mount, Hornton. c. 1680
(p. 118).

(c) Spittals Farm, Great Bourton.
c. 1680 (p. 130).

(d) Friar's Cottage, Great Bourton.
1685 (pp. 130, 268).

PLATE 23. DOOR DETAILS

(a) Dormer window, Poplars Farm, Chacombe. 1654 (p. 121).

(b) Bay window, Warkworth Farm, Warkworth. 1658 (p. 155).

(c) Gable fenestration, Kings Sutton Farm, Kings Sutton. 1683 (p. 138).

(d) Gable fenestration, Hill Farm, Overthorpe. c. 1680 (p. 157).

PLATE 24